POLITICAL ANALYSIS

Technique and Practice

Fourth Edition

POLITICAL ANALYSIS

Technique and Practice

Fourth Edition

Louise G. White
George Mason University

THOMSON
WADSWORTH

Australia • Canada • Mexico • Singapore • Spain • United Kingdom • United States

Publisher   Earl McPeek
Acquisitions Editor David Tatom
Project Editor   Michael E. Norris
Production Manager   Kathy Ferguson
Art Director   Vicki Whistler

ISBN: 0-15-505522-4

Library of Congress Catalog Card Number: 97-77137

Wadsworth/Thomson Learning
10 Davis Drive
Belmont CA 94002-3098
USA

For information about our products, contact us:
Thomson Learning Academic Resource Center
1-800-423-0563
http://www.wadsworth.com

For permission to use material from this text, contact us by
Web: http://www.thomsonrights.com
Fax: 1-800-730-2215
Phone: 1-800-730-2214

Printed in the United States of America
10 9 8 7 6 5 4

DEDICATION

To Evelyn, Andrew, Emily, Samuel, Haley, Sarah,
Cameron, Molly, Lillian, Louise, and Madelyn
who challenge me to ask more interesting questions.

About the Author

Louise G. White is professor of government and politics at George Mason University in Fairfax, Virginia. She teaches courses in policy analysis, research methods, political theory, and development. Her books, *Creating Opportunities for Changes* (1987) and *Implementing Policy Reforms* (1990), apply management and policy theory to developmental issues. Recent articles look at particular experiences in using analysis to promote development and at ways to improve discourse about policy alternatives.

PREFACE

This fourth edition of *Political Analysis*, like earlier editions, continues to take a practical and applied approach to research. First, it assumes that we all engage in analysis of the political world as we hear about and respond to events. It invites students to learn and practice techniques so they can better understand and explain their political world. The book, therefore, engages students directly in thinking about research by building on their natural curiosity and observations about the political arena—voter turnout, the role of the media, the influence of TV. And, as suggested by one reviewer, I have included exercises that draw on aspects of the collegiate experience—examining privatization of food services and activities to encourage communal interaction on campuses.

Second, the book emphasizes that research begins by asking clear, empirical questions and looking for supporting evidence to answer them. Thus, it stresses research design rather than the quantitative manipulation of numbers. This edition puts even more emphasis than earlier editions on sources of evidence and introduces them earlier in the book. It recognizes that we need to formulate our research questions with one eye on what we want to know and the other on the kinds of information reasonably available to us. This fourth edition reorders the first six chapters to emphasize the interaction of formulating questions, defining terms, and finding evidence. It also adds references to sources of information on the Internet that are particularly relevant to answering political questions.

Third, this book assumes that students learn best by doing. As it introduces techniques to make their observations and analysis more systematic, it provides examples of how the techniques have been applied in current research. There are practice exercises within most chapters and further exercises at the end of each chapter, many of them building on current events and data. For example, there are exercises on campaign finance, on the value of promoting democracy abroad, and on citizen action groups. The fourth edition updates these exercises and adds a significant number of new ones. A final chapter asks students to bring all of the techniques together and develop a full research design, one that would be appropriate in many of their substantive courses.

Fourth, a continuing theme is that there is no single right way to design or carry out research. Students need to consider alternative ways to state their questions and alternative ways to think about them. Therefore, the book encourages them to explore alternative perspectives and sources of evidence. It stresses the value of comparing different strategies for collecting evidence and the inevitable trade-offs in selecting alternative research designs. This theme is even more pronounced in this fourth edition, and students are repeatedly asked to compare different explanations, different theories, and different sources of evidence. In a final exercise they are asked to explore a political issue from at least two perspectives, drawing on both quantitative and qualitative data.

Fifth, the book builds connections between everyday concerns and the political science literature. Even as chapters and examples build on the natural curiosity of students to develop research questions, these are linked to research in current journals. The purpose is to engage students in thinking creatively about the political world that they experience and about the scholarly interpretations of that world that are encountered in their substantive classes. This edition draws much more heavily from major theories and current research in the political science literature than prior editions and invites students to think of their research as exercises in theory building. A new section discusses social capital theory and the work of Robert Putnam, as well as the correlates of democracy. A conscious effort has been made to draw from the breadth of the literature in political science, including American political behavior and institutions, comparative politics, international relations theory, public policy, and urban politics.

Sixth, the book emphasizes political issues, concerns, and variables. This involves more than just using political examples. Political topics and data raise some unique issues that need to be taken into account in designing and interpreting research. These are laid out in chapter 1 and are referred to throughout the book. There is an important implication in this emphasis. Whereas sociological and cultural data enable us to understand broad trends, political data often point to intentional actions and policies. Thus, there is an implicit assumption that political actors and citizens can play a role in shaping the future; their success depends partly on how clearly they understand political events and how skilled they are in formulating and finding evidence to support alternatives.

As noted earlier, the chapters in Parts One and Two have been rearranged, supplemented with more examples and theories, and substantially rewritten. Part Three, with three chapters, covers sources of information, both quantitative and qualitative. Part Four, with five chapters, deals with quantitative analysis. These include descriptive and explanatory statistics, and statistical significance. These chapters have been completely rewritten, with clearer explanations of the statistical techniques. Part Four also includes a chapter on presenting and analyzing data in tables and graphs. The final chapter brings the different elements together in a discussion of the choices that need to be made in designing research.

This fourth edition is greatly indebted to the comments from four reviewers who had previously used the book: John J. O'Rorke, Frostburg State University; Kelly D. Patterson, Brigham Young University; Hamoud Salhi, California State University—Dominguez Hills; and Jeffrey S. Walz, Wheaton College. Their comments were reassuring in affirming the basic rationale and emphasis of the book. I believe I have followed through on virtually all of their suggestions, and I am grateful for their continuing interest and insights. I would also like to once again express my appreciation to reviewers of the previous editions, including William Blomquist from Indiana University, R. Steven Daniels from University of Alabama at Birmingham, Mark Hyde from Providence College, John Bowman from Frostburg State University, Charles Grassell from West Chester University, Peter Hovde from Concordia College, Valerie Hudson from Brigham Young University, Edward J. Laurance and Slava Lubomudrov from University of Utah, Wayne Peak from Colorado State University, Jonathan Pool from University of Washington, and Bart R. Salisbury. I am also grateful to Michelle Sager for her editorial and research assistance; she has greatly enriched the examples included in the text.

I am wholly responsible for the material in this fourth edition. Nonetheless I continue to be very indebted to Robert Clark, who coauthored the first edition. His earlier work is important throughout but particularly so in chapters 1, 9 and 13. I remain deeply indebted to his practice of careful analysis and scholarship and his concern for effective communication with students.

Louise G. White

CONTENTS

CHAPTER FIVE
Types of Relationships: Associations and Causality   126

CHAPTER SIX
Exploring Relationships: Building Theories and
Causal Models   152

CHAPTER EIGHT
Collecting Data: Qualitative Data and Field Research   218

CHAPTER NINE
Collecting Data: Working with Secondary Sources   242

CHAPTER TWELVE
Determining the Significance of Our Results   345

CHAPTER THIRTEEN
Presenting and Analyzing Tabular and Graphic Data   371

CHAPTER FOURTEEN
Designing and Writing a Research Paper 393

POLITICAL ANALYSIS

Technique and Practice

Asking Empirical Questions

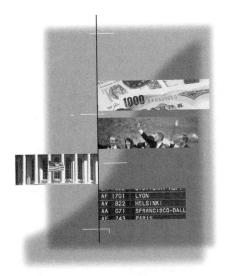

You have just opened a book on doing political analysis. The very word *analysis* may suggest that you are going to be immersed in quantitative exercises. In fact, Part One contains very little quantitative analysis. Instead, it emphasizes the importance of thinking clearly and logically about political events and of being systematic in examining ideas, opinions, and arguments. It begins by exploring the nature of political terms and the problem that they often lack clarity and hence are hard to analyze. *Power* and *apathy* are examples of terms that are used freely but whose meanings are usually not spelled out. In spite of this lack of clarity, these terms point to important dimensions of the political arena. In dealing with such ideas and terms, therefore, we have to look for ways to be more precise and clear about what we mean. Part One agrees with George Orwell that much political discourse is "slovenly" but also agrees with him that "the process is reversible."

After chapter 1 reflects on the nature of political terms and concepts, chapters 2 and 3 describe how to formulate questions that lead us to think systematically about our political world, and how to state these questions so that we can gather evidence to answer them. Sometimes the questions will build on our natural curiosity about political events and apparent trends. Sometimes the questions will be stimulated by the political science literature or even by research and theories read in other courses. The book takes a pragmatic approach to research and analysis. It invites us to select questions that seem interesting and important and then to select an appropriate way to find and analyze evidence that sheds light on our questions.

CHAPTER ONE

Politics, Analysis, and Research

"When I use a word," Humpty Dumpty said in rather a scornful tone, "it means just what I choose it to mean—neither more nor less."

"The question is," said Alice, "whether you can make words mean so many different things."

"The question is," said Humpty Dumpty, "which is to be master—that's all."

—Lewis Carroll, *Through the Looking Glass*

If a substantial part of our adult population believes in astrology and the efficacy of pyramids in promoting health, why should we expect thoughtful analysis?

—Donald Kennedy, "The Anti-Scientific Method," *Wall Street Journal,* 29 October 1987.

It is a sobering fact that the most intensely scientific century in all human history has also been a time when tens of millions of people have perished at the hands of leaders who were unwilling to alter their presumptions according to objective evidence. . . . Though science is stronger today than when Galileo knelt before the Inquisition, it remains a minority habit of mind, and its future is very much in doubt. Blind belief rules the millennial universe, dark and rangy as space itself.

—Timothy Ferris, "The Wrong Stuff," *New Yorker,* 14 April 1997.

[The English language used in politics has become] ugly and inaccurate because our thoughts are foolish, but the slovenliness of our language makes it easier to have foolish thoughts. The point is that the process is reversible.

—George Orwell, "Politics and the English Language," 1946.

3

Empirical Research and Political Discourse

The headline in the newspaper article is succinct: "U.S. Power Declining." You turn the page and notice that the article continues under a subheading: "Decline in Public Spiritedness Erodes U.S. Power." The main headline is a simple descriptive statement about changes in the power of the United States; the second suggests a reason for the changes. Statements like these are common in the arena of politics, and we tend to accept them if they fit what we already know about politics. The purpose of this book is to give you some skills for thinking about such statements and for doing research to determine whether or not they are accurate. You will learn to ask: What does the reporter mean by "power" and by "public spiritedness"? What evidence is there to support the assertions? Are there other forces at work that have a greater influence on a country's power?

Questions about the meaning of terms and about the relationship between terms and actual events are central to the research process in every field of study. They are particularly challenging for people studying politics, because the terms used to describe and explain political events and ideas are not always clearly defined. Politics may even resemble the world Alice found when she stepped through the looking glass and encountered the strange creatures who could reverse rationality and turn ideas and arguments on their heads. Too frequently, the cynicism reflected in the quotes from the *Wall Street Journal* and *New Yorker* cited at the beginning of the chapter intrudes into political discussions and distorts policy outcomes in ways that harm people and waste resources. As students of politics, however, we cannot simply shrug our shoulders and turn away from the political arena with a sense of fatalism. We need to become as well educated as we can about the language and data of politics in order to appreciate how easily they can mislead us and to learn how to use them more accurately and effectively.

political discourse
Communication of politically relevant thoughts via words.

This book is dedicated to improving your ability to understand and use political discourse. The term **political discourse** includes the many ways in which political language and information can be used, ranging from a presentation you might make in support of a particular policy to formal statements by political leaders, from letters to the editor to laws passed by Congress, from simple statistical tables in newspaper articles to complex policy analyses prepared by a government agency. The book has two goals: to help you develop *habits* of thinking systematically about politics, and to help you learn and practice *skills* for doing analysis or research. It should improve your ability to write in political language more effectively and to analyze political information and data more accurately. Exercises throughout the book provide you with opportunities to sharpen skills of gathering, arranging, and analyzing political ideas and information.

These thinking and analytic skills are important in several ways. First, they will help you to *understand* better the dynamics and problems of a society and to compare strategies for dealing with them. Why is poverty so persistent in the

United States? Would reforms in the welfare system such as workfare programs reduce the amount of poverty? Second, these skills will enable you to *critically evaluate* policy studies and political arguments. What does it mean when one candidate says we are better off now than we were four years ago, and another candidate says we are worse off? Third, these skills can be used to define politically interesting questions and *design research* that attempts to answer these questions. What kind of study would be most useful to show why large percentages of people do not vote? Fourth, they will help you look to the future and give you a basis for *designing policies* to cope with problems. For example, the skills described in this book will enable you to compare the costs and likely results of different health care policies. Fifth, these skills will enable you to *participate* more effectively in the political arena. You can think of the skills as an important political resource. The ability to analyze issues, collect relevant information, analyze the information, and present your results effectively will greatly enhance your capacity as citizen and participant in the political arena. Those with the ability to marshal and analyze information will have more opportunities to have an influence on public events.

political analysis
Process used to discover the reasons why a given political phenomenon occurs.

Systematic analysis does not require learning new languages or thought processes—quite the contrary. The fundamentals of **political analysis** are used to solve problems or make decisions in everyday life. This book helps you master these fundamentals. It explains what they are, shows how to use them to understand complex issues, and allows you to apply them in practical exercises. Most social science texts cover these same habits of thinking and skills of analysis. Political discourse, however, has certain unique characteristics that easily get in the way of good analysis. Before turning to the fundamentals of analysis, therefore, this chapter describes some of the characteristics of the language and information used in dealing with politics. These characteristics make systematic thinking even more challenging and important than would otherwise be the case.

The Language of Political Discourse

The Nature of the Political Process

politics
Process of deciding how resources will be distributed in a society.

Political discourse is challenging for people doing analysis and research because of the nature of the political process. **Politics** is the process by which a society decides what it values and how its resources should be distributed in the form of tax deductions, grants, public services, etc.[1]

Political decisions about resources are based on a great variety of activities by a similarly varied set of actors. There are officials and members of the public who carefully think through policy issues and seek to ensure that all groups receive a share of resources. There are advocates who seek to promote the interests of some group or point to a common problem in the society that is being overlooked. There are actors who avoid controversial issues but simply carry out policies in an orderly manner. There are officials and members of the public who are ardent partisans for a position and seek every opportunity to document and promote it. This variegated mosaic of actors and motives affects the nature of political discourse. Terms may be used to enlighten, persuade, or mislead. As a result, systematic and careful analysis is both more difficult and more critical than it is in other arenas. This section explores a number of problems raised by political terms in order to set the stage for later discussions of the importance of clarity and precision.

Consider an example of a political argument that is increasingly important in political campaigns, namely, the issue of assessing the health of the economy and the probability that it will continue to grow. During the 1992 presidential election, Democrats, who were challenging a Republican incumbent, repeatedly charged that the economy was in a serious decline, pointing to such factors as the deficit and the unemployment rate. Republicans, admitting that economic growth was far too low, pointed to more positive factors, such as the low inflation rate and increased manufacturing productivity. Four years later, with a Democratic incumbent in the White House, the Democrats emphasized the extent to which the deficit had been reduced, while Republicans warned that unless taxes were lowered, the tax burden would deflate the economy in the future. The interesting point is that both sides could produce evidence to back up their claims.

How can we, as participants in the democratic process, sort out these conflicting claims and analyze the issue of economic growth? How we attack the question influences the answer we get. One approach is to formulate a statement that relies on concrete terms and a specific comparison, such as: "Manufacturing productivity (output per worker) grew at a faster annual rate from 1981 to 1990 than at any time in the postwar period." To determine if the statement is correct, you would have to find some source that listed the output per worker during different years. If you turned to the annual *Economic Report of the President*, you would find information supporting that statement. This approach takes time, however. Because it is often difficult to obtain such information when you need it, you are more likely to make a statement such as: "The American economy was healthier during the 1980s than it was in prior years."

Note how different the second statement is from the first. The first statement contains specific items that can be directly observed and measured. We can actually determine if it is true or false. It is not possible, though, to observe, measure, or compare directly a term such as *economic growth* or *economic health*. The second statement itself does not tell us what the term *healthier* means. Therefore, people who agree with the statement can look for whatever evidence they can find to support it; those who disagree could probably find other information that disproves it. The authors may have in mind the facts contained in the first statement but neglect to make them explicit. Or perhaps they are thinking of more intangible ingredients of economic health, such as capacity for technological innovation. Because these are harder to define and measure, political actors may find it easier to leave them unstated. Or they may prefer the term *healthier* to other terms, because its vagueness makes it an effective tool to sway public sentiment. Because terms such as *healthy economy* are undefined and overly broad, they may mislead people, whether or not their users so intend.

A second example of an ambiguous term that can be defined in a number of ways is the government's strategy for reducing drug use. For many years officials used the term "war on drugs," suggesting an all-out attack on the enemy—those who sold drugs and those who became addicts. In his second administration President Clinton changed the rhetoric, or the way in which he talked about drugs, in important ways. The phrase "war on drugs" was rarely heard. "Instead of talking about locking up crack dealers or busting drug cartels, President Clinton emphasized goals like 'giving our children the straight facts.' Rather than portraying drug addicts as the enemy, Clinton said that 'often people who use illegal drugs are people who go to class or hold jobs or have families.'"[2] According to Kenneth Sharpe, a professor of political science at Swarthmore College, "It is the first significant step towards talking about illicit drug use as more of a public health issue than as a crime problem."[3] At the same time the administration changed its rhetoric about alcohol and tobacco and began referring to them as dangerous "gateway behaviors" to the use of drugs.

A third example of a vague term that can take on different meanings is the idea of "national defense." Political leaders often state that the defense budget is too big. Listeners may picture a specific sum of money for items clearly related to the military defense of the United States. In fact, there is considerable disagreement about which items should be counted as part of the defense budget. The U.S. budget lists under national defense most expenditures by the Defense Department, the Energy Department's atomic weapons programs, civil defense, and the Selective Service system. It does not include any of the following: veterans' benefits and services; interest on the public debt attributed to defense expenditures; or international affairs costs, even though more than half of this figure is usually for national security purposes. The budget for the Coast Guard and for research and development by the National Aeronautics and Space Administration (NASA) are included under transportation, even though one could argue they are related to our defense preparedness.

Answer the two following questions: Why would a conservative who favored spending more on defense be comfortable with the list of items that the U.S. budget lists as part of national defense? Why would a person who believed that the defense budget was generally too large be troubled by this way of defining national defense?

Terms may be left vague by groups that simply want to protect their positions. This observation is obviously true for political parties, interest groups, and lobbying organizations. It is also true of government organizations. Agencies have a natural tendency to identify with the importance of their policy mandate and to develop norms and procedures that reinforce their biases. Members of these organizations and agencies also come to feel comfortable with the procedures they have set up and are reluctant to make major changes in managing programs. As a result, administrators may discourage analysts from raising questions about ongoing activities. Similarly, government workers want to improve their professional status and present their programs most positively. As a result, they are tempted to use terms that place their performance in the best light.

Studies in the aftermath of the *Challenger* space shuttle disaster in 1986 provide some unusual evidence of the ways in which bureaucracies can misrepresent or obscure facts. Recall that the *Challenger* exploded seconds after takeoff, killing the seven astronauts on board. The studies show that NASA had adopted a number of practices that allowed officials to cover or skew actual figures about space flight missions. In order to build support for their programs, NASA officials wanted to show they were cost effective. This understandable goal led them to misrepresent figures on the cost of the shuttle and to inflate figures on the number of flights the shuttle would make. Characteristics of the NASA leadership reinforced these tendencies. Former Director William Lucas was notably intolerant of criticism, and he intentionally or not discouraged midlevel officials from reporting any information that would raise questions about the shuttle or about planned flights. In consequence, managers aware of the potential problems with the rocket joints that caused the shuttle disaster did not report the information.[4]

Often terms are not clearly defined simply because politics deals with ambiguous and complex issues. National defense, just such an issue, is one over which there is often honest disagreement. There is no guarantee, for example, that spending on defense equates with a country's ability to fight a war, since the countries that spend most on defense are not always those with the strongest military establishment. The Center for Defense Information, in fact, argues that reduced defense expenditures would make the United States stronger, not weaker, if the result was to strengthen the national economy on which the defense establishment must ultimately rest.

Terms Used in Political Discourse

tangible resources
Things of value that can be directly observed and measured.

empirical data
Data gathered directly from personal experience, experimentation, or observation.

intangible resources
Things of value that cannot be directly observed and measured.

Politics allocates two kinds of resources. **Tangible resources** can be directly observed and measured and include food, clothing, housing, weapons, money, automobiles, and space capsules. When we directly measure such resources, we acquire **empirical data,** so called because the data are derived directly from our own personal experience, experimentation, or observation. **Intangible resources,** on the other hand, usually can be observed only indirectly. They include values, such as power, freedom, nationalism, respect, dignity, equality, rights, and justice. It is more challenging to gather empirical data about these items because they can be measured only indirectly. Also, political actors often talk about them in abstract terms and fail to link them with concrete or tangible terms.

Suppose we were concerned with differences between the standards of living in Sweden and Bolivia. We could develop a statement using concrete terms, like "The infant mortality rate of Bolivia is higher than that of Sweden." The term *infant mortality rate* refers to something measurable, and therefore the statement can be proved true or false. However, a statement like "Swedes are better off than Bolivians" cannot be tested empirically. The term *better off* refers to an abstract quality, and it must be redefined in more concrete or empirical terms.

As a second example, take the assertion "Elites are more democratic than poor people." Virtually the entire sentence consists of abstract phrases for which the empirical references are unclear: *elites*, *democratic*, and *poor*. The term *elite* might refer only to wealthy people, or it could refer to people who control large organizations or hold political office. The concrete meanings given to such a term can differ greatly from one observer to another. However, if we rewrite the sentence to read "Families with incomes of more than $50,000 a year express greater support for free speech and freedom of the press than do families with an income of less than $20,000," then we have terms (*family income* and *expressions of opinion*) whose precise meanings can be examined. The solution to these ambiguities is not to stop thinking about such concepts. The terms *poverty* and *elite* are both important terms because they refer to dimensions of our political life that are significant, even though it is hard to be very precise about their meanings or to translate them into concrete terms. And as noted earlier, the lack of precision in many abstract terms means that they can be used purposefully to mislead people, to promote particular interests, or to express strong emotions. In spite of these several problems, abstract terms deal with very important issues and cannot be ignored. Rather, special care has to be taken in clarifying our discourse, in translating abstract terms into more concrete terms, and in linking them with empirical evidence. Those tasks are central to the skills described throughout this book.

Types of Abstract Symbols

Abstractions often are translated into symbols, posing a further challenge to careful analysis. As a general rule, *symbols* are signs or representations people use to communicate about things that cannot be talked about or understood easily. For example, when we think about the United States of America, we may think of such symbols as maps, flags, portraits of great leaders, photographs of heroic events (like those of the marines' raising of the flag on Iwo Jima or the moon landing), or pictures of well-known buildings. One of the major themes in the 1988 presidential campaign was the Pledge of Allegiance, which was used as a symbol of a person's patriotism.[5] Symbols that stand for tangible resources are called **concrete symbols,** because they refer to objects that can be observed and measured. In contrast, **abstract symbols** stand for intangible resources and values, which cannot be observed. People whose political world is dominated by such abstractions have a harder time testing their understanding of reality.

concrete symbols
Symbols that stand for, or in place of, things that can be directly observed and measured.

abstract symbols
Symbols that stand for, or in place of, things that cannot be directly observed or measured.

Symbols have a special appeal because they can simplify complex and ambiguous terms. Those concerned with the U.S. economy and comparisons between the economies of the United States and Japan frequently rely on such vague terms as *national character* and *cultural values* to explain reasons for differences in economic practices. The purpose often is to simplify a complex world and make it more manageable. Many of these refer to myths or stories that reassure us that we can cope with events. Murray Edelman, a political scientist, describes this process of creating metaphors and myths to deal with complexity:

The causes and remedies of the depressions, inflations, wars, and riots that threaten the world are complex, and they hinge upon the small and large decisions of vast numbers of people. Myths and metaphors permit men to live in a world in which the causes are simple and neat and the remedies are apparent. In place of a complicated empirical world, men hold to a relatively few, simple, archetypal myths, of which the conspiratorial enemy and the omnicompetent hero-savior are the central ones. In consequence, people feel reassured by guidance, certainty, and trust rather than paralyzed by threat, bewilderment, and an unwanted personal responsibility for making judgments.[6]

Edelman thus reminds us that our political language may help us cope with the complexity and ambiguity of politics, and in doing so lull us into a false sense of security and passivity. Others find that metaphors and symbols can play a more positive role. They can be used to educate the public, to create a political identity and sense of purpose.[7] Consider the concept of "volunteerism." On the one hand it can beguile the public into thinking that voluntary efforts are sufficient to solve major social ills; on the other hand it can mobilize the energies of the public and engage them in addressing social problems in creative ways.

There are several types of abstract symbols, including metaphors, similes, analogies, and stereotypes.

Metaphors and similes. Metaphors are figures of speech in which a word or phrase ordinarily used in one context is applied in a second, different context in order to make a comparison. Metaphors make the comparison explicit ("The election was a horse race"), whereas similes insert the words like and as ("The election was like a horse race").

Metaphors and similes can help us understand something better or experience a new emotion about a subject. By establishing the similarity between two things, these figures of speech suggest that if we understand a familiar thing, we can also understand the unfamiliar. However, metaphors and similes may impede clear thinking when they make inaccurate or inappropriate comparisons. When speakers compare two events that are not really similar or that have nothing to do with the issue in question, the terms obscure rather than clarify.

Policy debates on war and strategy frequently turn on the effective use of metaphors and similes. Early in World War II, British Prime Minister Winston Churchill disagreed sharply with President Franklin D. Roosevelt over the proper site at which to open the Allies' "second front" in Western Europe. The British argued for mounting an invasion through the Mediterranean, attacking first Italy and then spreading the invasion through the rest of southern Europe. The Americans wanted to launch the invasion in France. The British view prevailed at least partly because of the metaphor used. Churchill referred to the Mediterranean coast as "the soft underbelly of Europe," dramatically underscoring its apparent vulnerability. Unfortunately, the Italian battleground proved to be not the "soft underbelly" of Europe but dangerous, difficult mountainous terrain where poor roads and scarce landing sites made the assault exceedingly dangerous. It took the Allies nearly one year to cover five hundred miles and reach Rome.[8]

What meanings are conveyed by the following commonly used synbols? Possible answers are included in note 9 at the end of the chapter, but yours may be just as valid.[9]

Poverty program described using the metaphor of a rung on a ladder.

Bag lady as a symbol for the homeless.

Glass ceiling as a metaphor suggesting that women are not promoted to the highest job levels.

Drug war as a metaphor for public policy toward drug use.

---

reasoning by analogy
Analysis of a phenomenon by reference to another; substitute phenomenon that corresponds closely to it.

Reasoning by analogy. Policy makers frequently try to understand a unique contemporary event by reasoning from an analogous historical event. They assume that if we discover a similar event from the past we can learn more about the current situation. One of the most commonly used analogies returns to an event in 1938, when Great Britain gave in to Adolf Hitler's demands that Germany be allowed to annex part of Czechoslovakia. This act of appeasement allegedly convinced Hitler that he could proceed to conquer the rest of Europe with impunity. The so-called *Munich analogy* is frequently referred to whenever someone wants to assert that others are backing off from a confrontation and in doing so are unwittingly encouraging further aggression. During the 1960s people who defended the Vietnam War often used the Munich analogy, declaring that a withdrawal of U.S. forces would only encourage further aggression by North Vietnam. And in 1988, in the wake of arms-reduction negotiations between President Ronald Reagan and General Secretary Mikhail Gorbachev of the Soviet Union, critics argued that those promoting arms reduction were in danger of forgetting the lesson of Munich, that peace comes only through strength.[10] The analogy entered the news again in 1996 when Madeleine Albright was named secretary of state. She and her family fled Czechoslovakia at the time of the original Munich accord, and this experience was commonly used to explain her strong opposition to dictatorship.

The aptness of an analogy depends on whether the points of similarity between the two events are indeed significant. In the case of Gorbachev, the question is whether the former Soviet Union was the same as Nazi Germany in its desire to dominate other nations by force. If it was not, then the Munich analogy can be misleading. Historical analogies are both appealing and dangerous precisely because the people who use such analogies seldom define the similarities they are assuming. One critic observed that "occasionally, someone emerges—Winston Churchill was perhaps the last—whose sense of historical parallels is sufficiently accurate to be a guide to statecraft. More often, those who think they're following the 'lessons' of the past are pursuing their prejudices, sound and unsound, and calling them history."[11]

Labels and stereotypes. The politician's use of metaphors, similes, and analogies illustrates the dramatic use of language in politics. Less dramatic but perhaps more significant is the use of group labels, stereotypes, and other symbols to influence decisions about who should get what. Group labels based on territorial, ethnic, or class lines commonly are used to appease those who fail to receive the tangible resources they want. In this sense, group symbols are what Charles Elliott calls "confidence mechanisms"—any social practice that distributes resources unequally, while convincing the losers that the system is essentially fair and that they lost because of their own shortcomings.[12] The best-known example is "tokenism," whereby a single representative of a minority (e.g., female, African American, Hispanic) is promoted or given special treatment. This person's good fortune is exploited to suggest to others that the system is basically fair and to turn away the frustration of other members of the minority.

Words that mask reality. Finally, language can dull our senses, blunt our awareness of unpleasant realities, or disguise the costs of policy choices. In his classic essay "Politics and the English Language," George Orwell pointed out how cliches and jargon are repeated mechanically in political speeches to obscure the truth and make mundane ideas sound creative.[13] By using phrases that are rich in texture—rhythm, symmetry, and cadence—but barren of meaning, leaders can mask the human impact of harmful policy decisions. The point of this discussion is not to say that every political statement is biased and misleading or that systematic analysis is impossible. Memorable phrases such as "I have a dream" from Martin Luther King Jr.'s famous speech in 1963, because they were anchored in specific and real experiences, can capture peoples' imaginations and give them a sense of purpose and vision. Rather the point is to heighten the importance of being careful and systematic in our use of terms. Clear definitions are central to all of the social sciences. The nature and uses of political terms are such that clarity is particularly critical and important in this arena. Thus, the book is concerned throughout with strategies for increasing the clarity and precision of the terms and definitions we use in our research.

Data Used in Political Discourse

We have noted that the language of political discourse often relies on terms that are only indirectly linked to empirical evidence and that obscure what is really occurring by oversimplifying reality or promoting a particular position. This section considers how quantitative data can also oversimplify and mislead us.

Error and Bias

Many of the data and much of the evidence we take for granted are simply erroneous. One simple reason was suggested by Sir Josiah Stamp, an official of Great Britain's Inland Revenue Department between 1896 and 1919:

> The government are very keen on amassing statistics. They collect them, add them, raise them to the *n*th power, take the cube root and prepare wonderful diagrams. But you must never forget that every one of these figures comes in the first instance from the village watchman, who just puts down what he damn pleases.[14]

We are still dependent on modern versions of the village watchman in spite of our more sophisticated technology. In the fall of 1979, for instance, the Federal Reserve Board became alarmed at a sharp increase in the money supply. It turned out that a major trust company had mistakenly reported its deposits with the Federal Reserve to be $4.5 billion more than they really were! Economists are almost totally dependent on the statistical information produced by the government, many of these data are subject to wide errors, and there is little tendency for the mistakes to cancel each other out.[15]

Reasons for the errors in government-reported data range from the complexity of the data the government collects to the fact that most data have political implications. In 1976 Congress established a blue-ribbon commission to review unemployment data. The commission's report noted that the government often relies on "extremely inaccurate statistics" to allocate aid to states and cities but concluded that there was no way to correct the deficiencies at reasonable cost.[16] During the 1980s the two highly respected congressional agencies responsible for calculating budget figures—the Congressional Budget Office and the Joint Committee on Taxation—also came under fire for inaccurate estimates. Some of the reasons for the criticism were clearly political. For example, Congress has been reluctant to face the budget deficit and thus has chosen to ignore its own budget office's gloomy estimates, preferring to be guided by the more optimistic estimates of the White House.[17]

Interpreting numbers, and even deciding which numbers to look at, depends on the assumptions you start with. Consider how Republicans and Democrats chose to talk about income during the 1980s. Republicans were more apt to talk about "average income" as a measure of national economic growth, while Democrats tended to use "median income" (the income of a person at the midpoint in a list of individuals). Their reasoning went as follows: During the 1980s the wealthy increased their income more than other groups did. Thus the Republicans, who controlled the presidency during this decade, wanted to show that income had increased. They were more apt to refer to average income because it includes the income gains of the wealthy. The Democrats, however, were more apt to refer to median income because it describes what is happening to those in the middle range of the class structure and does not include the income of the wealthy. Because it is not weighted by high income figures, it tends to be lower than average income and indicates lower economic growth.[18]

Measurement Problems

The abstract terms described earlier are hard to use in analysis because they are hard to measure. It is often equally hard to measure terms that are more concrete and that appear to be linked to empirical evidence. Consider how you would go about measuring unemployment. The Bureau of Labor Statistics takes a survey of households during one week every month, counting people as employed, unemployed, or not in the labor force. To be counted as unemployed you must be without work, actively looking for work, and available for work. If you are not working but have become discouraged and given up looking for work, or if you are working part time because there is no full-time work available, you will not be included among the unemployed. A 1985 survey in the District of Columbia found that about 2 percent of the labor force had given up looking for work and hence were not included in the government's count of unemployment.[19]

Poverty is another difficult concept to measure. The government has established a formula for computing the amount a family needs to live on, and below which people are said to be living in poverty. The formula begins with estimates of the cost of food for a family and multiplies that figure by 3 to determine what that family needs to spend to maintain a reasonable living standard. It is easy to assume that the choice of 3 as the multiplier is based on objective evidence about spending habits. In fact, it was based on a 1955 survey that determined poor people spent one-third of their income on food. More recent studies estimate the poor spend closer to one-fourth of their income on food, and one could infer therefore that the cost of food should be multiplied by 4. (Question: Would this strategy raise or lower the poverty line? If the cost of food were multiplied by 4 rather than 3, would more or fewer people be included among those living in poverty? Answer: It would raise the poverty line and include more people among those counted as living in poverty.) There is a second problem with the formula. It uses the least generous of several food budgets developed by the Department of Agriculture. (Question: If it used a more generous food budget, would more or fewer people be included among the poor? Answer: Again, more people would be included as living in poverty.) Both of these aspects of the formula reduce the amount of money that defines poverty. In 1994 the guidelines stated that a family of four with income under approximately $15,000 is below the poverty line and qualifies for assistance. The definition has important political implications. Conservatives criticize it because figures on income do not include noncash income, such as food stamps, and do not compensate for underreporting of income. If these items were included, they assert, fewer people would be identified as living below the poverty line.[20]

Another politically sensitive statistic is the level of violent crime in the nation. One source of information comes from victimization studies done by the Census Bureau. Another source relies on police records of homicides. The problem is that these two sources give very different results. A third source, and the one that is the major source of data on national crime trends, is the *Uniform Crime Reports (UCR)* published by the Federal Bureau of Investigation (FBI). The FBI faces three major obstacles in making the UCR accurate. First, the figures depend almost wholly on voluntary reports of crime submitted by citizens. Second, the figures depend on the timely submission of accurate reports by about 12,000 local law enforcement agencies. And third, many of the data submitted to the FBI are vague and based on definitions that differ from one jurisdiction to another.[21]

Or consider the ongoing debate about energy consumption in the United States and efforts to measure "wasted energy" and "energy crisis." According to one view, the United States is wasteful in its consumption of fossil fuels when compared with Europe and Japan. Presumably this wastage constitutes an energy crisis that hurts our economy and requires government action. An alternative interpretation of the same facts argues that it is inappropriate to compare energy consumption in the United States with that in Europe and Japan because of the vast size and colder northern climate of the United States. Therefore, information about energy usage in the three areas does not indicate an energy crisis, and there is no need for government action.

Manipulating Data

Finally, it is worth noting that official statistics can be used to manipulate popular opinion of government programs. Mention was already made of Congress's effort to use the most optimistic figures on the national budget, even when it means relying on White House figures rather than studies by the Congressional Budget Office. A similar point was made by former Undersecretary of the Navy James Woolsey, who pointed out that during President Jimmy Carter's administration the Department of Defense was told to predict a lower rate of inflation than that actually expected by government economists. The obvious intent was to enable the government to maintain the apparent real growth in defense expenditures without increasing the defense budget beyond 10 percent a year. Economist John Kenneth Galbraith has observed that these are common practices in the government.

> No one can seriously suppose that, in the past, official forecasts were designed to reflect what was going to happen. That, in the nature of the system, was unknown. Official forecasts were what the particular administration needed to have happen. That is why those forecasts, for anything more than the next six months, always foresaw less inflation, less unemployment, and a more vigorously expanding economy. The six-month interval is important; by rough calculation, that is the time in which any forecast will be forgotten.[22]

The Practice of Careful Research and Analysis

The Implicit Optimism in Studying Political Analysis

This book is based on an optimistic assumption: that careful attention to the meanings of concepts and to the data used by ourselves and others will improve the democratic process. As Orwell notes at the beginning of this chapter, vague language leads to sloppy thinking, but he insists that the process is reversible, that we can improve the way in which we talk and think about political ideas, events, and politics. Many contemporary observers are less optimistic than Orwell. They question whether the "slovenliness of our language" is reversible and worry that the problems are so deeply embedded in democratic practices that they cannot be easily removed. They point to tendencies in democratic elections for leaders to simplify and distort their messages. They also argue that policy problems are so complex that experts and public alike have a difficult time designing or evaluating effective policies.

There are many reasons to be troubled by current trends in democratic systems, with the growing complexity of social problems and the increasing level of conflict. There are also reasons to be cautiously hopeful. Many policy responsibilities are being decentralized, and more groups and professionals are being asked to devise new policy solutions. There is an increased willingness to experiment both with new ways to conduct the democratic process and with new policies. There is an interest in new ways both to involve members of the public in governance decisions and to provide public services jointly with other organizations in the society. Each of these innovations increases opportunities for individuals and groups to improve and apply their skills in political analysis—whether as citizens, as professionals in the public sector, or as actors in the private and voluntary sectors.

Thus, in the most general terms, the objective of this book is to help you participate more effectively in a democratic system. Because politics often relies on vague rhetoric and misleading data, as described in the preceding pages, effective participation requires thought and care as you form your opinions and marshal supporting evidence. More specifically, the book seeks to help you become educated consumers of political language and data; to make you skeptical of facile, simplistic observations and conventional wisdom about politics; and to give you the habits of thought and skills you need to carry out empirical analysis.

The Messiness of the Research Process

The following chapters approach analysis as a task of doing research and take you through the various steps of the research process. In one sense, the description of this process will seem artificial and not true to life. The reason is that you cannot follow a clear recipe to conduct research. It almost involves a number of changes and choices and trade-offs, and your finished product may not look very much like your initial plan. Chapter 14 returns to this issue and asks whether research is an orderly or messy process and affirms that it is usually very messy.

Because of the inherent messiness of the process, discussions of research design pose a dilemma. To be helpful to you, the book should provide a series of steps to design and carry out research. The problem is that such an outline inevitably suggests that the research process should be methodical and orderly. In addition, the book encourages you to be systematic and logical as you think about research on political issues. The dilemma is that while it is good to be orderly, in reality planning and carrying out research can be disorderly. If you are told to be highly systematic in designing your research, when you encounter problems and have to make detours or look for new sources of evidence, you easily may become discouraged and think that you must be going about the research in the wrong way. Or you think that you are just not bright enough to do original research. Thus the dilemma in discussing research: acknowledging the messiness of research while encouraging more systematic approaches to asking and answering questions.

Why is political research so inherently messy? This chapter has described two reasons. First, the characteristics of political discourse make political concepts hard to talk about and observe. Many of the terms we are interested in, such as *participation*, *apathy*, *power*, *relative strength*, and *development*, are vague, and it is not always clear what evidence to use to examine them. Second, the data we need often are hard to acquire, or, when available, they frequently are biased or not in a form we can use.

A third reason is that there often are multiple relationships or explanations we can examine. Poverty, for example, can be explained by a lack of jobs, by a lack of skills and education, by negative attitudes, and by a lack of good role models. Which of these is worth exploring? How do they compare with one another? What kinds of information are actually accessible to you? You may have a hunch that one of these is the most important factor to explore, but find that you don't have access to the kind of information you need. Or in the middle of a research project to examine one of these factors, you may find evidence that another is more important and decide to refocus your study. Should you try to collect information on just one of these hunches, or try to cover several even if it means you cannot go into the same depth or look at as many cases? These are all decisions you will need to make, but the trade-offs may become evident only as you proceed.

A fourth reason for the messiness of research is the lack of a single recipe for doing research. There are a number of strategies for designing research, each of which can be more or less useful depending on the question you are asking and the evidence available to you. For this reason it is difficult to select a research strategy until you have reviewed some prior research in this area, explored the kinds of evidence that are feasible to collect, and compared several strategies.

The following chapters describe elements in the research process, usually as discrete intellectual tasks. In actual research settings they are intermixed, their dividing lines are seldom neat and tidy, and their sequence seldom proceeds in a straight line from beginning to end. The discussion may err on the side of neatness and sequencing, but many of the examples will help you appreciate the realities of the research process and the potential for creativity as you apply the skills to your purposes.

Appropriateness of a Research Design

There are four broad tasks in the process of doing research. The first is to identify your subject or research question in a manner that allows you to study it empirically. The second is to consider alternative strategies for answering the question and selecting one that will tell you what you want to know and that is feasible to carry out. The third is to find evidence relevant to your question. The fourth is to analyze or interpret that evidence in a way that allows you to answer the question or at least to understand the question better. All four steps are critically important and essential elements in **research design.** Books on research often neglect the first of these. They assume that you have a question or topic and tell you how to carry out the other three steps: compare strategies, collect evidence, and analyze the evidence.

research design
Statement of research that defines terms, specifies propositions to be tested, lists data needed and how to get them, describes tests to be performed, and establishes a sequence of steps to complete project.

A key theme in this book is that initial questions are not only a very important part of research, but they also shape your research design. You can look at a given issue from many perspectives and define specific questions in a number of ways. Further, how you formulate your question will determine the best way to study it. If you are interested in voting turnout, for example, you may ask about the voting turnout in different countries and about the characteristics of those who vote and those who do not vote. Alternatively, you may seek a better understanding of the attitudes and feelings among those who do not vote. To answer the first question you would collect information that is readily available in existing documents, then analyze it using various statistical measures. To answer the second question you might interview nonvoters and then interpret their responses, probably in narrative form. The questions and related designs would give you different information and would serve quite different purposes.

The remaining chapters in Part One, chapters 2 and 3, discuss the choices you confront in formulating your research questions and designing your research. They encourage you to be clear in stating exactly what you want to find out. Because the terms in political discourse usually are vague and because the data that are available often are misleading, you will often need to be creative in following these steps.

Knowing about the various strategies for designing your research and understanding the strengths and trade-offs among them is covered in Part Two. These chapters emphasize that there is no single right way to do research, that there are several options, and that each can be valid under certain situations. They encourage you to be creative in exploring options you may not have thought of. These chapters also help you connect your own research to theories that others have developed to understand the world of politics and to encourage you to use your research to amplify these theories.

Finding relevant evidence, the third step, is also complex, as emphasized by the discussion in this opening chapter. Because the terms in political discourse usually are vague and because the data that are available often are misleading, it is difficult to link our questions with data. Part Three deals with these issues. Chapters 7, 8, and 9 compare different sources of evidence. The point is not to avoid dealing with vague concepts but to find ways to write about them clearly and meaningfully. The chapters stress that we often have to make trade-offs between data that are concrete, such as figures on voting turnout, and information that is more abstract, such as reports of alienation. Sometimes the latter can be captured in broad surveys of the voting population, and sometimes they depend on sensitive probing and interpretation of deep-seated feelings.

Parts One, Two, and Three thus deal with the logic of carrying out research—defining questions, exploring relationships, and gathering evidence; this logic is the primary emphasis of the book. To illustrate the points and to give you practice in doing research, examples are included throughout. Many of these rely on quantitative data; others use information for which numbers are irrelevant. It is important to remember that analysis can involve both kinds of information: quantitative and nonquantitative. People frequently and erroneously equate analysis with the use of quantitative information and statistics. The key to analysis does not lie in manipulating numbers; rather, it involves skills in defining research questions and finding or creating relevant evidence to answer those questions. Even when the evidence cannot be translated into numbers, it is still crucial to approach the research logically and systematically.

Despite the stress here on the logic of research design, it is nevertheless true that much of the research by others, as well as our own, does rely on evidence that can be described and analyzed numerically. Chapters 10, 11, 12, and 13 in Part Four discuss various skills in analyzing and presenting numerical data. Chapter 14 returns to the logic of research design developed throughout the book. It emphasizes the realities of designing research, particularly that you have to make trade-offs in choosing among the various tools and strategies. It underscores that there is no single, magic design for doing political research. Rather, you need to select a strategy that fits your research question. And sometimes the reverse is true: you may need to redefine your research question to match strategies that you are in a position to carry out. The central point is that questions, strategies, and evidence have to be appropriate to one another.

Throughout, the book provides concrete examples and exercises that allow you to practice the skills that are presented. Some refer to long-standing research topics in the field of political science; some draw from reports in the current media. Both of these sources are important. The discipline of political science is an effort to think systematically about the political arena, to make connections between the daily events that grab our immediate attention and more formal efforts to carry out research, and to increase our understanding of political events and our skills in formulating alternatives.

NOTES

1. This definition is based on David Easton, *The Political System* (New York: Knopf, 1959).
2. Roberto Suro, "Drug Control Strategy in Midst of a Makeover," *Washington Post*, 14 February 1996.
3. Cited in ibid.
4. Joseph Trento, *Prescription for Disaster* (New York: Crown, 1986); Malcolm McConnell, *Challenger: A Major Malfunction* (New York: Doubleday, 1986).

5. This discussion draws from an earlier one by Murray Edelman, *The Symbolic Uses of Politics*, 4th ed. (Urbana: University of Illinois Press, 1970), pp. 1–21. Edelman uses terms for political symbols different from those used here. What we call concrete symbols are, for Edelman, referential symbols. In place of his term condensation symbols, we use abstract symbols. The discussion, however, is indebted to his analysis of the uses of symbols and particularly their power to mislead the public.

6. Murray Edelman, *Politics as Symbolic Action: Mass Arousal and Quiescence* (Chicago: Markham, 1971), p. 83.

7. James G. March and Johan P. Olsen, "The New Institutionalism: Organizational Factors in Political Life," *American Political Science Review*, 78 (1984): 734–749.

8. Kenneth S. Davis, *Experience of War: The United States in World War II* (New York: Doubleday, 1965), pp. 370–371, 395.

9. Possible answers include: Poverty program as a rung on a ladder suggests that those who receive welfare will continue to climb out of poverty; overlooks the possibility that some welfare programs do not enable people to move out of poverty or that the programs may create a dependency. Bag lady as a symbol for the homeless implies that the homeless are confused and idiosyncratic old ladies rather than people who may have few options. Glass ceiling as a metaphor suggesting that women are not promoted to the highest job levels overlooks the fact that most employment discrimination against women occurs at lower job levels rather than at higher levels. Drug war as a description of public policy focuses on need for punishment rather than value of education and treatment.

10. For example, see Norman Podhoretz, "Forget Munich?" *Washington Post*, 11 October 1988, p. A19.

11. Edwin Yoder, Jr., "Munich: Lessons and Prejudices," *Washington Post*, 13 October 1988, p. A19.

12. Charles Elliott, *Patterns of Poverty in the Third World* (New York: Praeger, 1975), pp. 10–11.

13. Sonia Orwell and Ian Angus, eds., *The Collected Essays, Journalism and Letters of George Orwell*, vol. 4 (New York: Harcourt Brace Jovanovich, 1968), pp. 127–140.

14. Robert J. Samuelson, "Skeptistics: Questioning 'Inflation of Necessities,'" *Washington Post*, 30 September 1980.

15. The comment about errors in economic data is attributed to Oscar Morganstern. Leonard Silk, "Economic Scene: Flawed Data Not Uncommon," *New York Times*, 2 November 1979.

16. The commission recommended eighty-eight changes in the ways unemployment data are gathered and reported, but the cost of making the changes was estimated at more than $34 million, in contrast to the mere $2.1 million spent at that time to collect the statistics. "Aid Allocation Held Based on Faulty Statistics," *Washington Post*, 2 September 1979.

17. "Congress's Numbers-Keeping Agencies Draw Fire as Budget Deficits Prompt Unpopular Forecasts," *Wall Street Journal*, 3 May 1988.

18. E. J. Dionne, "Speeches, Statistics and Some Unsettling Facts About America's Prospects," *Washington Post*, 26 January 1992.

19. "The Understating of D.C.'s Unemployment," *Washington Post*, Business Section, 16 December 1985.

20. "Drawing the Line between Rich and Poor," *Washington Post*, 23 September 1988.

21. Brian Forst, "Violent Crime, by the Numbers," *Washington Post*, 5 May 1981.

22. John Kenneth Galbraith, "Economic Indicator: Applause," *Washington Post*, April 12, 1981.

EXERCISES

Exercise 1.1 Terms Used in Political Discourse

A. Following are concepts commonly used in political discourse. Indicate whether each is a vague term, a metaphor, or a simile. What implications does each have for our understanding of politics?

1. Descriptions of nutrition, education, and day-care programs as "investments in human resources." *metaphor/Simile*

2. Political economists often say that elections are like a marketplace and that voters are like economic consumers. *Simile*

3. Descriptions of a person as "left wing" or "right wing." *Vague*

4. Use of the concept of "family values" in political campaigns. *Vague*

5. The Pledge of Allegiance as a sign of patriotism. *Vague symbol*

B. Consider the use of the concept of "helping working people" in the 1980 election. Carter, the incumbent, wanted to demonstrate that he had improved the condition of working people and pointed to the fact that during his administration nine million jobs had been created. Reagan, the challenger, asserted that under Carter the condition of working people had gotten worse and argued that eight million were unemployed in 1980. In fact, both assertions were true. How could this be so? *different factors, unemployment, median income v average income,*

Exercise 1.2 Metaphors and Abstract Symbols

Scan copies of the *New York Times* or any other newspaper for examples of metaphors and abstract symbols used in political discourse. Choose one example of each and answer the following questions.

Metaphor

1. What was the context in which this metaphor was used? (Specify who said or wrote it, to whom, on what occasion, and so on.)

2. What are the underlying assumptions behind the use of this metaphor?

3. Does it accurately portray the comparison it seeks to make?

4. Does it shed light on the problem, or is it potentially misleading?

Abstract symbol

1. What does this symbol represent?

2. What was the context in which it was used?

3. What are the underlying assumptions behind this symbol?

4. Does it shed light on the problem, or is it potentially misleading?

Exercise 1.3 Data Used in Political Analysis

Skim the newspaper for a story that reports some empirical data that could be misleading. The textbook notes several reasons why data may not be as accurate as they appear. What questions would you like to ask of the person reporting the information?

CHAPTER TWO

Developing Research Questions

And what is the scientific method? . . . In the popular view the emphasis is on the collection of data. But not among scientists. They like to distinguish between "accumulators" and "guessers," and they're pretty much agreed that it's the guessers that are important. . . . What it comes down to is simply this: Our top scientists say we need more ideas rather than more facts; they want more Einsteins who just sit and think rather than Edisons who have a genius for tinkering in the laboratory.

—**Rudolph Flesch,** *The Art of Clear Thinking*

Asking Empirical Questions

Research and *analysis* conjure up images of tedious arguments about remote problems. All of us, however, analyze political events, often ones that closely affect us. Thinking systematically about politics frequently begins when an intriguing public event or trend catches our attention. For example, you may be curious about voting turnout in the United States because you have heard it is low. You learn that in 1996 only 49 percent of eligible voters turned out to vote in the presidential election. This figure was substantially lower than in 1992, when the turnout figure was 55 percent of eligible voters. This latter figure was an increase over recent years: in 1984 the turnout rate was 53 percent and in 1988 it was 50.1 percent. You might ask why the percentage increased or decreased at any of these times. Or conversely, if you knew that in 1960 the turnout was 64 percent, you might wonder why it was consistently lower in the 1980s and 1990s. Similarly, if you learned that voting turnout in other Western industrial nations, such as Belgium, Austria, and Australia, was around 90 percent, you might wonder why the United States ranked so low.

Notice that we moved from a general interest in voter turnout to specific questions. Questions clarify what we know and do not know, and where the interesting issues lie. This chapter introduces you to a variety of ways to frame your research questions. It is useful to consider different types of questions because they may lead you to think about events in unexpected ways. The different questions in turn shape the kind of research and analysis you design.

While questions and research designs may differ, all of the questions and approaches to research described in this book have one characteristic in common: all ask *empirical* questions, meaning that the questions can be answered with **empirical data;** that is, with observations about the world around us. Empirical questions are distinct from *normative*, or value, questions. Normative questions elicit **normative statements;** that is, value judgments or preferences that contain or imply words such as *ought* or *should*, *bad* or *good*. Examples of both kinds of questions follow:

empirical data
Data gathered directly from personal experience, experimentation, or observation.

normative statement
A statement that indicates a preference or a value about what ought to happen.

> "Do limits on campaign contributions make it more difficult for challengers to defeat incumbents?" (empirical)
>
> "Should we have a law limiting the amount of money an individual may contribute to a campaign?" (normative)
>
> "Are potential criminals less likely to commit serious crimes if they know there is a death penalty in their state?" (empirical)
>
> "Would it be *wrong* to reinstitute the death penalty?" (normative)
>
> "What impact would reductions in income taxes have on the budget deficit?" (empirical)
>
> "*Should* we reduce income taxes?" (normative)

The normative questions are not empirical because each asks for convictions, preferences, or feelings rather than evidence. People often will disagree about value statements. Some favor the death penalty; others oppose it. Because arguments on this issue may be based ultimately on convictions about the morality of killing, empirical evidence alone cannot settle the debate. In spite of these differences, however, empirical research is very relevant to normative concerns. Most of our values are based at least partly on empirical observations. We may be opposed to the death penalty because we have observed that juries and judges sometimes mistakenly find a person guilty. Yet we may ignore this evidence when stating that we are against the death penalty. By identifying and questioning the empirical assumptions behind our values, we can clarify those values and express them more effectively. It is in this very important sense that normative and empirical concerns are related to each other.

Consider the following example of a value statement about voting: "Americans should vote regularly in elections." This normative statement could be rephrased as a question that asks for empirical evidence about which groups participate most in American elections. The answers could then be used to support or question one's interest in increasing voting turnout.

> "Are lower-income groups and minorities less apt to vote than middle- and upper-income groups?"

"Do those who vote infrequently have less trust in the political system?"

"Do those who are less apt to vote also fail to participate in other forms of civic activity?"

"Do those who are less apt to vote have different policy preferences than those who do vote?"

In each case the empirical question asks for evidence that is relevant to the original value statement. Empirical evidence that supports a "yes" answer to any of the questions could provide a rationale for the original normative statement. Notice that the evidence would still be inconclusive. We would still need to decide how important these facts are to us and whether there are other points to be considered. Nevertheless, knowing that value statements usually rely on unstated empirical evidence can help us analyze our opinions more carefully.

Controversy over immigration policies is another issue that suggests both normative and empirical claims. Consider the normative statement that the United States should reduce the number of immigrants coming to this country. Again various empirical questions can lead to research that may qualify, support, or challenge the original normative statement:

"How many immigrants receive welfare?"

"What proportion of their earnings do immigrants send back to their country of origin?"

"To what extent do immigrants identify with their new country or adapt to a new culture?"

"Do immigrants compete for jobs that other groups are qualified for and would like to have?"

Evidence to support or reject these empirical statements will not settle all the debates about immigration policies, since policy will also reflect our values and priorities. Clarifying and researching these and similar questions, however, can improve the policy debates and even lead some on both sides to alter their normative positions. One useful strategy in any normative debate, therefore, is to ask all the participants to state the empirical assumptions they are making.

Describing and Explaining General Patterns

description
Information about a single case in some depth or about patterns and trends in a number of cases.

explanation
Analysis designed to determine why an event occurs.

Much of the time, empirical political questions ask for a **description**; that is, they ask us to describe general patterns and tendencies. They often go one step farther and ask about the reasons or **explanations** for the patterns. The earlier stated questions about differences in voter turnout from election to election ask us to *describe* the turnout in a variety of presidential elections to determine if there is a pattern or trend. We could go farther and ask about the most important reasons for not voting; that is, we could try to *explain* what we have found.

For instance, researchers have learned that the single factor of educational level goes a long way to predict whether or not people vote. We could compare voters and nonvoters according to the characteristics of their party identification, gender, education, social status, race, and attitude toward the candidate to see to what extent each of these was related to voting turnout.

From Descriptions to Explanations

Descriptions tell us *what* is happening. If we are interested in voter turnout, we could look for information describing turnout over the past twenty years, or we could examine the turnout of different age or income groups. Whether we collect this information ourselves or use data collected by others, we are making **observations.** These observations might describe a single case or many. If we knew someone who had chosen not to vote, we could interview the person and write a **case study** examining in some detail the person's attitudes and experiences. Or we could use election data gathered by the government and make an observation about the percentage of all citizens who voted in a given year. We could supplement this with data gathered in a broad survey to describe the characteristics of voters and nonvoters.

observation
A collection of information about an event, a person, or an activity.

case study
Study of a single unit, usually in some depth.

As noted earlier, we usually try to build on these descriptions to explain why an event or pattern occurs. The social sciences have traditionally looked for general explanations—for instance, reasons for the general decline in voter turnout—rather than learn why one particular voter did not vote. If a study does focus on explaining a specific case, this is usually because that case tells us something about a broader set of events. Studies of the *Challenger* space shuttle disaster are of obvious interest to officials who oversee space endeavors. The studies are interesting to a broader group, however, to the extent that they suggest more general explanations of the problems that arise in managing sophisticated technologies.

classify
To categorize cases into several groups according to some dimension of interest.

One way to move from description to explanation is to **classify** the cases we are describing. In studying voter turnout, for example, you could simply distinguish between those who voted and those who did not. Alternatively, you could break down the population farther and distinguish among the clusters of individuals, such as voters, those ineligible to vote, those not interested, and those who purposely choose not to vote. There is no single and correct way to classify cases. It depends on which classifications shed most light on a given question and what kinds of information you have available or decide to collect. Although in order to make the first distinction between voters and nonvoters you could easily find information on the numbers voting in national elections, you would need access to information collected in a survey of voters to carry out the second classification according to reasons for not voting. If you were interested in the characteristics of nonvoters, such survey data would be particularly useful to you.

Classifications are neither right nor wrong; rather, they are more useful or less useful for different research questions. As an example, assume you have heard that a nearby city is growing, and you wonder whether other cities in the

TABLE 2.1

Percentage Population Change in Selected Large
U.S. Cities, 1990–1994

Albuquerque	7.1	El Paso	12.4
Atlanta	0.5	Hartford	–11.1
Boise City	16.3	Los Angeles	–1.1
Chicago	–1.9	New York	.1
Cleveland	–2.5	Pittsburgh	–3.0
Dallas	1.5	Raleigh	11.6
Detroit	–3.5	Washington, DC	–6.6

Source: *Statistical Abstract of the United States, 1996*, pp. 44–46.

United States are growing or declining in population. You could simply compile a list of cities, noting any changes in population (see table 2.1).

To understand population changes more fully, you could classify the cities into groups. First, you need to consider how to group them: by size, by region, by degree of poverty. Any of these categories could be useful depending on the question you are asking. Given the information in table 2.1, it would be reasonable to divide them according to whether they were growing or declining in size.

Increasing Population		**Declining Population**	
Albuquerque	7.1	Cleveland	–2.5
Atlanta	.5	Hartford	–11.1
Boise City	16.3	Pittsburgh	–3.0
Raleigh	11.6	Detroit	–3.5
El Paso	12.4	Washington, DC	–6.6
Dallas	1.5	Chicago	–1.9
New York	.1	Los Angeles	–1.1

You can use such classifications to see if they suggest any patterns. Do those cities in each group have similar characteristics that distinguish them from the cities in the other group? No clear pattern stands out. You could decide to group them by size of population. (Population figures are commonly given in thousands; thus you should mentally add three zeroes to the numbers in each of the following categories. For example, 500 = 500,000.)

Small (Up to 500)		**Medium** (501–1,000)		**Large** (1,001 and above)	
Atlanta	.5	Detroit	−3.5	Chicago	−1.9
Albuquerque	7.1	El Paso	12.4	Dallas	1.5
Boise City	16.3	Washington, DC	−6.6	Los Angeles	−1.1
Cleveland	−2.5			New York	.1
Hartford	−11.1				
Pittsburgh	−3.0				
Raleigh	11.6				

Again, no clear patterns stand out. There are cities with declining and growing populations in each category. You could try grouping them by region.

West		**Midwest**		**South**		**East**	
Albuquerque	7.1	Chicago	−1.9	Atlanta	.5	Hartford	−11.0
Los Angeles	−1.1	Cleveland	−2.5	El Paso	12.4	New York	.1
Boise City	16.3	Detroit	−3.5	Dallas	1.5	Washington, DC	−6.6
				Raleigh	11.6	Pittsburgh	−3.0

Once we group the cities by region, we do find some patterns, suggesting that region is an important characteristic of cities. All those in the Midwest are declining, and all those in the South are growing. In both the West and East groupings there is a single exception to the dominant pattern, but note that in both cases the population change is very minor (−1.1 and .1) You could use the regional categories to collect information on more cities to see whether the same population patterns hold true as more cases are added. You could also ask whether cities in each region shared other characteristics.

The most useful explanations not only link an event with other factors but also provide a logical understanding of how they are connected. For example, it is not enough to say simply that exposure to education explains why some are more apt to vote than those with little education. We would like to understand why the two factors are linked. We may speculate that people with more education are more apt to understand the issues at stake in an election and the positions of the candidates than are those with less education. To test the adequacy of this explanation we could then ask whether people with more education have a greater understanding of political issues as well as a higher turnout rate than do people with less education.

Assume you want to understand the descriptive finding that cities in some regions are experiencing a population decline while those in other regions are not. Why are these two factors linked? Do different regions have characteristics that shape population change? To answer this we need to examine the characteristics of regions to see if any regional differences are linked to changes in population. Consider the Midwest. In the 1970s, energy costs were high; we could compare the energy costs in the Midwest and the South during this period to see if these explain the population changes listed in table 2.1. In the 1990s we would be more apt to look at employment patterns to determine whether there were more people out of work, or if there was a greater decline of industry in the Midwest as opposed to the South.

It may have occurred to you that there is no firm distinction between descriptive studies and those that attempt to explain an event or some behavior. Some of the elements used to describe an event may offer possible explanations for that event. When we classified cities by region, we referred to it as a descriptive study. As noted, once we examine characteristics of different regions, we see that region also offers a possible explanation for the different growth rates in cities. The question is whether there is some characteristic of the Midwest as a region that explains why a number of cities in that region lost population. In this manner the categories that emerge from a descriptive study may suggest an explanation. Recall the example of voting studies. In describing voters, you might observe that young people know less about politics than older people do. You could then reason that these differences in age and knowledge may explain the lower turnout by young voters. Similarly, the assertion that people with a college education are more apt to vote than those with only a grade-school education both describes the characteristics of those who vote and offers a possible explanation for voting.

We can apply this discussion of description and explanation to the phenomenon of split-ticket voting and the recent trend toward electing presidents of one party and a majority of legislators of another party. In 1952, 71 percent of the voters said they always vote for candidates from the same party, whereas forty years later in 1996 this percentage had declined to 37 percent. A common explanation for the increase in split-ticket voting begins by describing a confused electorate that is ill informed and cannot make up its mind. An alternative explanation offered by Robert Samuelson begins with a different description. Voters have lost confidence in both parties in the wake of Vietnam and Watergate. The political center has virtually collapsed as politicians have become more extreme in their views. At the same time voters have become less rigid and feel that no one represents their views. Given this portrait of voters, Samuelson proposes an explanation that says voters are actually being rational and consistent in splitting their tickets. "If you don't trust either party fully—and may share some views of both—you can hope that forcing them to bargain will create policies closer to your preferences than having either party dominate."[1] Samuelson's description of the public as fairly rational and consistent suggests a different explanation for nonvoting than is usually given.

The remainder of the book describes how to construct research to explore similar issues—especially chapter 7 on survey research. For now, take a few minutes and think how you would go about planning research to see if Samuelson is correct. A possible approach: You could survey students and community members. You could start out by asking people if they had voted, and if so whether they had split their ticket. Then ask these same people a series of questions about their attitudes toward politics: whether they trusted the parties, whether they thought there was a difference between them, and so forth. Compare the answers of those who split their tickets and those who did not and see if the result is closer to Samuelson's description of the public or to the description of the public as confused and inconsistent. Alternatively you could look at published survey results of a national sample of voters to see which of those two views of the public is consistent with their answers to a variety of attitude questions. See, for example, *The Gallup Poll* for a recent year.

Practice Exercise 2.1

Moving from Description to Explanation

Table 2.2 contains information on a randomly selected group of ten countries, which are listed in alphabetical order. (Note: GNP stands for gross national product, which is a standard measure of a country's economic productivity. The terms in parentheses tell you what the figures mean. Thus the population of Canada is 29.2 million, its GNP per capita (per person) is $19,510, and its life expectancy at birth is seventy-eight years.) Assume you are particularly interested in the life expectancies for different countries. If you were doing a descriptive study you could simply use table 2.2. Or you could make your description more useful by classifying the countries according to some relevant characteristic.

TABLE 2.2
Characteristics of Selected Countries, 1994

Country	Population (millions)	GNP per Capita (dollars)	Life Expectancy at Birth (years)
Canada	29.2	19,510	78
China	1,190.9	530	69
Ethiopia	54.9	100	49
France	57.9	23,420	78
India	913.6	320	62
S. Korea	44.5	8,260	71
Panama	2.6	2,580	73
Nigeria	108.0	280	52
United Kingdom	58.4	18,340	76
United States	260.6	25,880	77

Source: *World Development Report 1996* (Washington, D.C.: World Bank, 1996). Table 1, pp. 188–189.

Note: Population figures are expressed in millions. Since 1 million has six zeroes after the 1, you would add zeroes to the figures to the right of the decimal point until there were six figures to the right. Thus Canada has a population of 29.2 million, or 29,200,000.

Consider how to classify the countries and then use this same information to move beyond description and suggest an explanation for different life expectancies. The following three tables experiment with three ways to classify the countries. Only the first line has been filled in; complete the tables by inserting the other countries in the appropriate columns. (Answers to all the questions in Practice Exercise 2.1 are in the endnotes.)[2]

Each of the classifications in tables 2.A, 2.B, and 2.C describes something about the countries. The question is whether one or more of the classifications are more informative in understanding life expectancies than are others. Do some suggest differences better than others? Consider region, for example. If we look only at Europe, both of the countries have high life expectancies, suggesting that region may be a useful way to organize the countries. On the other

PRACTICE TABLE 2.A
Life Expectancies in Ten Countries, by Region

Europe		Africa/M. East		Asia		No./So. America	
France	78	Ethiopia	49	China	69	Canada	78

PRACTICE TABLE 2.B
Life Expectancies in Ten Countries, by Population Size

Small *(up to 100 million)*		Medium *(100 to 300 million)*		Large *(more than 300 million)*	
Canada	78	Nigeria	52	China	69

PRACTICE TABLE 2.C
Life Expectancies in Ten Countries, by Average Per Capita GNP in U.S.

Low GNP *(550 and below)*		Middle GNP *(551–10,000)*		High GNP *(10,001 and above)*	
China	69	S. Korea	71	Canada	78

hand, the North/South American region includes both the United States and Panama, which have very different life expectancies. (If we wanted to retain region, we could separate North and South America into two regions.) Population is even less useful, because each category includes a country with a high life expectancy and one with a low life expectancy.

To what extent is classification by GNP a useful way to describe the countries? Explain: _____

_____

_____

_____

Is GNP also useful in explaining life expectancy? If so, why? Is there a logical connection between GNP and life expectancy? _____

_____

_____

_____

From Explanations to Theory Building

Theories as general statements. Thus far we have noted that intriguing observations can lead to research questions and that the most interesting questions to political scientists are those that ask for explanation for a pattern of behavior. Ideally you will go one step farther and link your questions and search for answers to the ongoing process of theory building and theory testing in the social sciences. A **theory** assumes that events are not entirely random or accidental. Because a theory offers a general and logical explanation for behavior or events, it forces us to go beyond unique cases and to look for trends and relationships that apply more generally. An emphasis on theory means that we are interested in the reasons or logic connecting observations. Attention to theory also forces us to pay attention to the writings and research of others, and to determine how our research fits into the accumulated knowledge in political science.

Theories propose general explanations for events. Instead of saying simply that A occurs whenever B does, or that A explains B, a theory provides the reasons why A and B are likely to be connected. For example, consider Seymour Martin Lipset's proposition that peoples' status affects their participation in politics. Lipset's theory offers a well-developed explanation for the role that status plays. It states that lower-status groups "are less apt to participate in formal organizations, read fewer magazines and books regularly, possess less

theory
A set of proposed explanations, logically or systematically related to each other, that set out to explain or predict a phenomenon.

information on public affairs, vote less, and, in general, take less interest in politics."[3] Theory-building research would design further studies to confirm or reject this theory. Perhaps it is not as true in the 1990s as when Lipset proposed it in 1960. Perhaps it is truer for some groups than for others.

Concrete theory. In recent years, more political scientists are focusing on what Ruth Lane calls "concrete theory."[4] These researchers are less apt to look for broad general abstractions about the political system and more apt to focus on the activities of political elites. On the one hand, elites are constrained by existing political institutions; on the other hand, elites shape and change the institutions. Such a study could examine how President Clinton dealt with a congress of a different party and an electorate increasingly disillusioned with government. Or it could examine how specific governors dealt with a decline in federal resources, a suspicious public, and demands from organized interests. Studies of this type are less apt to use survey research to analyze public opinion and more apt to examine how political leaders work within the limits and opportunities posed by their political system. They are more apt to rely on case studies and interviews and analysis of government records. Lane refers to them as examples of "concrete" theory because they are grounded in empirical studies of actual behavior and specific institutions.[5]

Using research to modify theories. There is no need for you to develop new theories. In fact, most research begins with some existing theory and revisits it on a hunch that it needs to be modified or refined in some way. Consider the theory that democracies tend not to go to war with each other.[6] Edward Mansfield and Jack Snyder observe that the theory that democracies do not fight wars with each other is "as close as anything we have to an empirical law in international relations."[7] They continue that the theory may be confirmed over the long run, but it is important to look at what happens in the short run as regimes change to become more democratic. It may be that regimes act differently during periods of change than they do when they are stable.

To test the original theory and their hunch that it might not hold up, the authors classified all regimes from 1811 to 1980 as a democracy, an autocracy, or a mixture of the two. Then they collected information on all wars during this period, except civil wars. They found "considerable statistical evidence that democratizing states are more likely to fight wars than are mature democracies or stable autocracies."[8] Democracies, autocracies, and mixed states in fact are almost equally apt to go to war, but states moving from one to the other of these conditions are more apt to go to war. They conclude that it is not the kind of regime but the process of change that is related to war.

The authors did not stop with this finding, however. They drew on their research to explain *why* regimes undergoing democratic change are more likely to fight wars. Such explanations are part of building theory. They found that states moving to become democracies usually have very weak central authorities. Both old and new elites are threatened and compete with each other, but the regimes lack institutions to manage the conflict. The elites try to mobilize public support, "often through nationalist appeals, to defend their threatened positions and to stake out new ones. However, like the sorcerer's apprentice, these elites typically find that their mass allies, once mobilized, are difficult to control. When this happens, war can result. . . . "[9] This proposed explanation for the frequency of war waged by democratizing regimes is offered as a new theory. The authors conclude that eventually a world of democratic regimes should be a safer place, but in the meantime conflicts will abound and we will need policies to mitigate the turmoil during this transition.

Deciding How Many Cases to Look At

In the earlier examples we looked at a number of cities or countries and collected information about a few characteristics of each. Another approach would be to pick one or two of the cities and study them in more depth. You would be doing a descriptive case study, an intensive study of a single unit, usually in some depth. Instead of examining just a few characteristics of a number of cities, you would collect a lot of information about the one or two you selected. Here your purpose would be to describe each one more fully. You might look at the composition of the population, the percentage of minorities, and the numbers who are below the poverty line. You could collect information about the city's economy and unemployment rate. You could also gather information about its political system, its form of government, and its electoral history. Perhaps you know some people from the city and could interview them about their perceptions of it. One can either compare several cases according to a few characteristics or examine a single case in more depth. Each approach has its strengths and weaknesses. How would you assess these?

Take a minute and consider the strengths and weaknesses of each of the following:

Comparisons of a number of units:

_____

_____

_____

_____

Case studies of one or a very few units:

_____

_____

_____

_____

You probably noted that comparing a relatively large number of cases on one or two characteristics enables you to draw comparisons among units and to look for broad patterns and perhaps develop a theory. Second, because it relies on a few significant characteristics of the units you are looking at, you can link your research to other studies and to existing theories. Third, it is usually fairly easy to find specific and comparable information about a number of cases in reference books. Single case studies, by contrast, give a much fuller picture of a unit and suggest how several aspects of a case are related to each other. They do not enable you to develop comparisons among units, however. In the earlier example, if you studied just Pittsburgh you would not know that most other cities in the East were also declining in population. The point is that neither approach is right or wrong; each is more useful for certain purposes, and each answers some questions and not others.

Just as with descriptive studies, we could design research to *explain* an event either by looking at a large number of cases or by looking at a single case more intensively. A single case allows us to seek several explanations. For example, we could interview in depth one or two persons who did not vote and explore a number of possible explanations: their attitudes towards the candidates, their knowledge about the campaign, their family history of voting, their economic situation, their educational level, and so forth. This approach would give a better understanding of why these particular persons did not vote and might suggest a number of explanations we had not anticipated. On the other hand, it would not tell us whether the findings were more generally true. Thus, we have to be much more tentative about results based on a single case study.

Alternatively, we could decide to examine a few characteristics of a large number of cases. We would focus on one or two explanations that we have reason to think are important and try to arrive at generalizations about the reasons for voting. The explanations would be partial but would emphasize the factors that we believe important and likely to be generally true across a wide number of cases. For example, we could look at polling data on a sample of U.S. citizens and compare the educational level of those who indicated they planned to vote with the educational level of those who did not plan to vote. We would ignore information about family history and attitudes toward politics, even though these might also offer explanations, because we are interested primarily in learning about the extent to which education offers a general explanation for voting.

Each approach has its uses, and each leaves out information that the other provides. Case studies are most useful when we need more in-depth information; chapter 4 describes occasions when we would carry out such research. Studies that look for general explanations for a group of cases are more appropriate when theories are available to suggest which explanations are most fruitful to examine (see the next section). By now you might ask, "Why not do both?" and often that is the ideal choice. The study on democracy and war described previously began by collecting information on 890 instances of regime change and concluded that democratizing regimes are more apt to go to war than stable regimes of any type. The authors then tested their theory by studying four cases of regime change in greater depth in order to get a richer understanding of the political process during periods of democratic change.[10] The authors thus began with a larger number of cases and established a general tendency. They then looked at several cases to confirm and flesh out the theory. Conversely one could begin with several case studies to suggest possible theories, and then look at a larger number of cases to test whether these explanations apply to a larger group.

Three Strategies for Answering Research Questions

This section describes three strategies that help us describe and explain general patterns: historical narratives, comparisons, and hypothesis testing.[11] A given study may draw from one or more of these strategies.

Narrative and Historical Research

Sometimes the best way to explain patterns is to construct a narrative account of some event or series of events. Such a narrative is similar to a case study and draws on a variety of sources of information to describe what happened. This approach is often called **narrative research** or *historical research*. While narrative research is not limited to the study of past events, those using it frequently focus on the past because the passage of time enables them to gain some perspective on their research questions and findings. The point is to look for a wide range of resources and information in order to gain as full an understanding of what actually happened as possible.

narrative research
Descriptions of events drawn on multiple sources of information to understand more fully what happened.

Our interest in elections and voter turnout, for example, might lead us to describe the 1948 election, the occasion when incumbent Democratic President Harry Truman upset all predictions by defeating his Republican challenger, Thomas Dewey. A narrative study would describe the dynamics of that event. How did the candidates engage the public? What were the major issues that mobilized the public? What was the turnout for that election? Historical research can also be applied to recent and current events. Theodore White, for example, wrote histories of each of the elections in the United States beginning in 1960, descriptive accounts that drew on many sources of information and greatly enrich our understanding of the electoral process.

The best historical research draws from a range of material, including public reports, interviews, firsthand accounts by participants—anything that contributes to our understanding of what actually happened. Barbara Tuchman, the historian, reminds us that such historical research requires us to sort through the evidence we find and not to simply recite an array of facts. The main task, she writes, is to "distill." The researcher

> must do the preliminary work for the reader, assemble the information, make sense of it, select the essential, discard the irrelevant—above all, discard the irrelevant—and put the rest together so that it forms a developing dramatic narrative. *Narrative it has been said is the lifeblood of history.* To offer a mass of undigested facts, of names not identified and places not located, is of no use to the reader and is simple laziness on the part of the author.[12]

Researchers usually have a perspective on the facts they describe that enables them to "distill" and to suggest explanations for the events. Where do these perspectives and theories come from? According to Tuchman they should emerge from the history or narrative itself:

> To find out what happened in history is enough at the outset without trying too soon to make sure of the "why." I believe it is safer to leave the "why" alone until after one has not only gathered the facts but arranged them in sequence; to be exact, in sentences, paragraphs, and chapters. *The very process of transforming a collection of personalities, dates, gun calibers, letters, and speeches into a narrative eventually forces the "why" to the surface.* It will emerge of itself one fine day from the story of what happened. It will suddenly appear and tap one on the shoulder, but not if one chases after it first, *before* one knows what happened. Then it will elude one forever.[13]

Others would argue that facts do not speak for themselves, as Tuchman suggests. Instead, anyone undertaking research begins with certain preconceptions and perspectives. These in turn influence the questions asked, the resources relied on, and the conclusions drawn. One of the exercises at the end of this chapter asks you to review several narratives about the Vietnam War and determine what theory the author offers to explain U.S. participation in this Asian conflict. It is not easy to determine if these authors had the theories in mind initially or if the explanations emerged from their study of the war. Probably both played a role in their studies—their original perspectives and the evidence they describe. Errol Morris, the documentary film maker who directed the movie *The Thin Blue Line*, captures this ambiguity. He admits that his films are not totally objective, that he begins with a point of view. But, he adds, "[t]here is a world out there, and what actually happens in that world is of great importance."[14]

Comparative Research

comparative research
Systematic comparison of different units to understand their similarities and differences.

Another strategy for finding and explaining general patterns is **comparative research;** that is, to compare a number of cases and look for the similarities and differences among them. This strategy combines the advantages of single case studies with the benefits of looking at a larger number of cases. Instead of examining a case in great depth, however, the researcher selects several cases and compares them on a number of factors. The researcher begins with a question and then selects cases that vary in some interesting and important respects. To continue our example involving voter turnout, one might select and compare six senatorial races, including three states where the turnout was high and three where it was low. What was similar and different about these cases? Did those with low turnout have certain characteristics in common? Were the three states with low turnout consistently different from the three with high turnout?

Comparative studies have a very appealing logic, and they are often feasible for students to use in assigned research papers. The key to their success lies in the cases chosen to study and in the factors selected for comparing the cases. You may simply select several cases that are similar in some respect and see if they share other similarities. Crane Brinton, for example, compared four major revolutions (French, Russian, English, and American) to determine if there was a common pattern at work in spite of the differences among them.[15] Or you may begin with certain ideas you want to pursue, ideas that will influence which cases you select and how you compare them. For example, if you were curious about the influence of political controversy on voter turnout, you would compare several elections in which there was political controversy with elections in which there was little or no controversy. With reference to the information in table 2.2, you could design a number of different comparative studies, depending on your research question. You could compare the similarities and differences among Canada, the United States, and the United Kingdom, three countries that share a common heritage but that have developed in different ways. If you were interested in federalism, you could compare Canada, the United States, Nigeria, and India, all of which have federalist political institutions. What are the differences and similarities among these countries with similar political institutions but very different social and economic circumstances? Or you could compare China, India, and South Korea to examine the similarities and differences among three developing countries with low GNPs.

Consider how you could use comparative research to pursue the following questions.

> "During the 1990s, Congress devolved many policy responsibilities to the states, with limited funds to carry out the responsibilities. How has this change in responsibility altered the original policies?"

> "Many African countries are attempting a transition from authoritarian rule to democracy. Why is this transition proving so difficult?"

Hypothesis Testing

Sometimes you may have a good hunch or a fairly clear idea about what you expect to find, and you want to use this idea to structure your research. Or you are intrigued by a theory you have read and want to see if it is still supported by the evidence. When there is an available theory, you can use a third research strategy, *hypothesis testing.*

Earlier, we asked whether there is a relationship between education and voting—whether people with more education are more apt to vote than those with less education. If we have reasons to think this is so, that there is a logical reason to connect them, we can assert a **proposition** that education and voting are related to each other, that increases in education are related to increases in voter turnout. Propositions state a logical relationship between two or more concepts or phenomena. **Hypotheses** are expectations based on propositions, but stated in a way that allows us to test them empirically. Take, for example, the proposition "Highly educated people are more apt to vote than those with less education." We do not know whether this is true, but we are hypothesizing that it is

proposition
Statements that two or more factors are related to each other.
hypotheses
Propositions stated so they can be tested empirically.

for purposes of carrying out research. Specifically, we are proposing that two factors—education and voting—are related to each other. This statement asserts that education and voting are associated with each other: the more education people have, the more likely they are to vote.

The study of democracy and war discussed earlier was designed to test a prevailing theory that democracies tend not to go to war with each other. The authors observed that several contemporary states waged wars as they were developing democratic institutions. This observation became a proposition that regimes undergoing democratic change will be more prone to go to war than will stable regimes. They then converted the proposition into a research hypothesis by stating very precisely what they meant by democratic change and what they meant by going to war. (Their definitions are described in chapter 3.) Their research helped them understand the logic of the relationship between democratic change and war and enabled them to develop a theory about the relationship.

Propositions and hypotheses are particularly useful when we have some knowledge about a research topic and a specific research question to answer. They tend to be more systematic and formalized than historical and comparative studies. They also force us to be very clear about the way our research relates to existing theory and whether or not it verifies that theory. The rest of this chapter looks at hypothesis-testing research in more detail.

Example of Theory Building through Hypothesis Testing

Political researchers and politicians alike are interested to know more about the voting behavior of men and women, and specifically whether there are significant differences between the genders. Carole Gilligan developed a theory that women speak in a "different voice" from men in that they tend to be more altruistic and nurturing.[16] Does this theory apply to political behavior also? A recent study developed the following hypothesis from this theory: "Men and women activists specialize in different forms of activity, derive different gratifications from taking part, and bring different policy concerns to their participation."[17] Specifically, they hypothesized that women would be more involved in informal and local groups and more concerned with issues concerning children, human welfare, and peace than would men.

They chose to study a large number of citizens rather than a few cases. For evidence they used the results from a large-scale survey of 15,000 respondents about their political participation and followed it up with personal interviews with 2,517 of the original group. First, they found that there were few gender differences in the ways in which men and women participated. Men and women are fairly similar in the numbers who turn out to vote, work in campaigns, serve on local boards, attend protest meetings. Similarly, they found that men and women give fairly similar reasons for participating. Differences appear, however, when we examine the policy issues that men and women focus on. Women are much more apt than men to be concerned with education issues and abortion than are men. Thus the study found that there was support, but only partial support, for the hypothesis. The authors revised the original theory to take into account their finding that gender differences are not as significant in explaining political participation as the theory had suggested. Anticipating a point that will be made throughout this book, the authors noted that this result came from a particular strategy, namely a combination of a survey and short interviews. A different research strategy might enrich or slightly alter their conclusions. "Long, in-depth interviews might reveal gender differences that do not emerge from survey data—for example, in the nature of the discourse used to discuss political participation or in the propensity to engage in conflictual rather than cooperative endeavors."[18] There are different research strategies, and these in turn may shape the answers we obtain.

Theory Testing and Hypotheses

> ### HYPOTHESIS
>
> A tentative assertion linking two or more phenomena, subject to testing and proof. In political analysis, the most common and useful hypotheses are those that assert that two or more things tend to be associated with each other in some specified manner.

Characteristics of Hypotheses

Testable statements. Hypotheses are hunches, or guesses. And as the quotation at the beginning of this chapter suggests, guesses are central to the social sciences. They mean that we are not just blindly collecting information but are thinking about what our information means and what its implications are. Hypotheses are statements that may or may not be true, but that can be tested, or verified, empirically. If a statement cannot be tested empirically, it is not a hypothesis. We must be able to decide whether a hypothesis is right or wrong. A hypothesis also requires us to be precise about the evidence relevant to our question and to specify what kinds of evidence will provide a meaningful answer. The terms that it uses, therefore, must be based on evidence that we can gather.

Comparisons. Hypotheses often contain comparisons, especially in the social sciences. The statement "highly educated people vote" has limited usefulness for political analysis. Perhaps people with little education also vote. Therefore, it is more fruitful to make a statement that compares two or more phenomena: "Highly educated people are more apt to vote than less educated people." It is important to make comparisons explicit—even though they often are implied—in order to identify precisely the kind of evidence we need to verify a hypothesis.

Consider the statement "Low-income people are more apt to vote for the Democratic party." Does it mean they are more apt to vote Democratic than are wealthier people? Does it mean they are more apt to vote for Democrats than for Republicans? Does it mean they are more apt to vote Democratic now than they were a few years ago? Whichever comparison is intended must be made explicit.

States how things are related. It is not sufficient to state that two things are related, or that one influences the other. We need to state the direction of the relationship or the influence. Thus, instead of saying, "Education has an influence on voter turnout," we should say, "Education has a positive influence on voter turnout; that is, the higher one's education, the more apt one is to vote."

Linkage makes sense. Finally, it is not enough to propose that two things are related to each other; the relationship must make sense. Edward Tufte notes that there is a relationship between the price of rum in Havana and ministers' salaries: when one is high, so is the other.[19] But it would be absurd to design research to test a hypothesis that linked these two factors, because the fact that both increase is probably circumstantial. Earlier, when you were asked to consider whether education might explain voter turnout, you were also asked to consider why that might be so and whether there is an available theory that links the two. It was suggested that people with more education might better understand the issues being discussed in a campaign, and hence might be more likely to vote on election day. That may or may not be true, but it is at least plausible.

CHARACTERISTICS OF A HYPOTHESIS

Usually states a relationship between two or more things.

Is stated affirmatively (not as a question).

Can be tested with empirical evidence.

Most useful when it makes a comparison.

States how two or more things are related.

The theory or underlying logic of the relationship makes sense.

Review the earlier discussions of relationships in this chapter and reformulate them as hypotheses.

1. The relationship between region and population changes in cities:
2. The relationship between life expectancy and a country's economic productivity:
3. The relationship between the availability of jobs and unemployment:

Hypotheses and Normative Statements

Recall the earlier discussion that distinguished empirical and normative statements and concluded that values usually are based on some empirical observations. Hypotheses have to be stated so they can be tested empirically, and thus they cannot contain norms. We can, however, use empirical research to reflect on our values.

NORMATIVE STATEMENT

Expresses a value or a preference.

Example: "I think we should decentralize our public schools."

EMPIRICAL REFORMULATION AS A HYPOTHESIS

Expresses an empirical component or assumption behind a normative statement.

First cut: "Decentralized public schools would encourage more community responsibility for public education."

Better: "Parents are more involved in schools when some curriculum decisions are decentralized to the local schools."

Note that in the comparison of normative and empirical statements shown in the box, the "first cut" at reformulation does indicate the reasoning that lay behind the original normative statement. However, many of the terms are vague and could easily be misinterpreted, for instance, *responsibility*. The reformulation is much more precise, and one can actually look for information to test it empirically. The result, moreover, may qualify or strengthen our normative statement. In sum, value statements do differ from empirical statements, but we should beware of assertions that facts and values have to be kept totally separate. We can use analysis to examine the facts on which value statements are based, even if we cannot use it to state whether or not our values are true.

Common Problems in Forming Hypotheses

Vague or trivial prediction. The hypothesis predicts such a wide range of results that it is not very interesting. One way to introduce more precision is to propose a comparison between values of a variable.

> *Poor:* "Local governments are having financial difficulties."
> *Better:* "Governments in older urban areas are experiencing more financial hardship than those in recently developed areas."

Vague relationship. The relationship between two terms is vague and does not specify a direction.

Poor: "Race has an influence on elections."

Better: "Minorities are more apt to vote for Democratic nominees than for Republicans."

Value statement. The hypothesis is, or appears to be, a value statement.

Poor: "Members of Congress should not accept honoraria for speeches."

Better: "Members of Congress who accept honoraria for speeches usually support legislation favored by the groups who pay them."

Applies to individuals. The hypothesis proposes something about an individual rather than about a general behavior or activity.

Poor: "Ronald Reagan was a very popular president."

Better: "Those who serve as presidents during periods of economic prosperity are more popular than those who serve as presidents during periods of inflation."

Terms in Hypotheses: Variables

concept
Abstract term referring to a group of phenomena.

We have said that theories and hypotheses propose linkages among two or more phenomena. Many of the terms in theories are **concepts,** abstract terms that represent classes of phenomena. *Status, participation,* and *democracy* are all concepts. We have also said that hypotheses must use empirical terms. In other words, hypotheses must translate the concepts in theories into concrete terms that can be examined empirically. Finally, we said that theories and hypotheses deal with general categories of things, not with single cases. This last point means that when hypotheses translate a concept into an empirical term, they do not use a single individual, such as President Clinton. Rather, they use a more general empirical term, such as *United States president.*

value
Characteristic of a variable; or amount of a characteristic.
variable
A characteristic of a thing that can assume varying degrees or values. The variable "gender" includes the values male and female.

We can now be more precise about the terms in a hypothesis. First, they do not point to individual things; they refer to general or logical properties of individual cases—voter turnout, income, rate of employment, race, party identification, level of political interest, and position in the government are all examples. Second, these properties can all assume varying **values.** One can vote often or seldom; there are degrees of poverty and of unemployment. (In this case, value does not refer to a norm; it refers to the properties of the terms in a hypothesis.) The terms in a hypothesis are called **variables** because the properties they refer to vary, or take on different values.

But, you might say, the term *Democratic party* is a single case that cannot take on different values, and yet we often want to include such a term in a hypothesis. There are two responses. First, "Democratic party" usually is treated as a value or a characteristic of the more general variable, "political party." We could develop a hypothesis that includes the variable "political party" and compares the campaign strategies of the Democratic and Republican parties. If, however, we were studying the campaign strategies of state Democratic parties, then it would be a variable, as in the following hypothesis: "Democratic parties in the southern states receive stronger popular support than do Democratic parties in the western states."

Consider the following examples of variables and values, and fill in the blanks:

1. *Variable:* Organization size

   Values: large, small

2. *Variable:* Elected public officials

   Values: president, senator, member of Congress

3. *Variable:* Support for the president

   Values: strong, neutral, weak

4. *Variable:* Political ideology or belief

   Values: _____

5. *Variable:* _____

   Values: democracy, dictatorship

6. *Variable:* Democracy

   Values: stable, unstable

7. *Variable:* _____

   Values: Catholic, Protestant, Jew

8. *Variable:* _____

   Values: civil war, terrorist strike, guerilla war, riot

9. *Variable:* _____

   Values: "Clinton is a strong leader," "Clinton is a weak leader"

How do we select among these options? The variables and the values we select depend on the theory we are testing, the questions we are asking, or the problem we are trying to solve. In example 5, you probably indicated a variable such as "form of government" or "political regime." These variables are relevant when we are examining a theory that compares democratic and nondemocratic regimes. Alternatively, our theory might compare types of democracies, and then we would select values such as those in example 6. The purposes of the research also determine the kinds of values we choose to define. Consider the variable "family income." If our theory deals with different income levels, we would assign the values of *high*, *medium*, and *low*. If our theory deals with conditions of poverty and with the effects of welfare policy, however, we might use the values *above the poverty line* and *below the poverty line*.

Variables are important because hypotheses propose comparisons among cases with different values of a variable. We compare the voter turnout for those with a high value on education to the turnout for those with a low value on education. Sometimes a hypothesis mentions only a single value of a variable: "Large cities (population) tend to experience strikes by public employees." Refer back to the box entitled "Characteristics of a Hypothesis" and indicate which characteristic is lacking in the foregoing hypothesis. It fails to make a comparison among several values of the variable "city size." It may be that small cities also are experiencing strikes by public employees. Articles and studies often express hypotheses in this manner and imply, rather than state, a comparison. Be specific. Revise the hypothesis about strikes so that it includes a comparison between two values and is less vague about the nature of the relationship.

Consider another example: "Democracies tend to occur in economically developed countries." The variables are actually "form of government" and "economic development." The first implies the values "democracy" and "nondemocracy"; the second implies the values "economically developed" and "undeveloped." When only one value is mentioned, it is usually possible to identify a second value as an opposite condition, as in the case of "democracy" and "nondemocracy." Or you could specify degrees of the value, as in the case of "low," "moderate," and "high" economic development. Revise the statement about democracies given in the opening sentence of this paragraph as a hypothesis according to the "Characteristics of a Hypothesis" listed earlier.

_____

_____

_____

_____

_____

_____

You can introduce comparisons in a number of ways; usually your choice depends on the theory you are exploring or testing. For example, you could rephrase the original statements in the preceding two paragraphs as follows:

"Large cities tend to experience more strikes by public employees than small cities do."

"Democracy is more apt to occur in economically developed countries than in countries with undeveloped economies."

"Economically developed countries are more apt to have a democratic than a nondemocratic form of government."

Sometimes a hypothesis is complete but the values of the variable are not made specific. Often you will be able to choose which values you want to look at.

Your choice will be guided by the range of values the variable can assume, by the kinds of data you have available, and by your research interest. We will discuss this issue in more detail in following chapters. In the meantime, we simply indicate that for many variables you can choose the values you will examine. For example, refer back to table 2.2, which includes information on gross national product (GNP). Because GNP assumes varying values, it is a variable. The table reports ten values for GNP, ranging from 100 to 25,880. Table 2.C also reports information on the variable of GNP, but the values are different. Instead of ten values, there are three, and they are listed as "low," "middle," and "high" GNP rather than as numerical figures. Review table 2.C and indicate how each of the following values was defined:

Low GNP: _____

_____

Middle GNP: _____

_____

High GNP: _____

_____

While the values of "low," "middle," and "high" could have been defined differently, the classification in table 2.C was devised by the World Bank and is in common use.

Moving from theories to hypotheses, from concepts to variables, enables us to carry out research on the undefined terms in much of our political discourse. Chapter 1 noted that we need to convert abstract terms into concrete terms, or terms that refer to tangible resources. One strategy for doing this is to formulate hypotheses and select variables and sets of values at the outset of a study. Narrative research and comparative studies also use variables and values. Insofar as narratives are designed to explore which variables are important, however, this strategy is less apt to begin by defining specific variables and more apt to consider a number of factors and to consider which of the variables turned out to be the most interesting. Comparative studies are more apt to identify the variables they are using to compare cases, particularly when they also are designed to test hypotheses.

Sources for Research Questions

There are a number of ways in which we can develop ideas for research:

1. From our own observations and experiences.
2. From studies and accounts of others.
3. From theories about relationships.
4. Through logic.

Observations and Studies: Induction

We began this chapter by noting that all of us analyze political events, sometimes more systematically and sometimes less. Most of our analysis begins with personal experiences or accounts in daily newspapers and other media. These sources of information are examples of the first and second sources of hypotheses just listed, and they are both based on **induction.** With induction, we begin with particular observations or cases and develop generalizations about them. We move from the particular to the general. Throughout this chapter when you were given a series of facts and asked to develop a proposition or hypothesis, you were being asked to use induction.

induction
Practice of developing a hypothesis on the basis of our own observations or of studies carried out by others.

Most political analysis begins inductively. James Madison in *The Federalist* was one of the first to describe how Americans are divided by their economic interests. His observations have become the basis for extensive research on the political implications of a pluralist society. Tocqueville, writing in the nineteenth century, observed that Americans are "joiners" by nature, and he laid the basis for future studies on the nature and effects of participation.[20] Reflecting on his intimate knowledge of the German government at the beginning of our century, Max Weber observed that bureaucracies tend to become more hierarchical.[21] Closer to our own time, Richard Neustadt observed that the most effective presidents are those who are skillful in developing and using personal power to persuade others.[22] Theodore Lowi noted that governments often delegate powers to interest groups and concluded that in doing so they seriously compromise their own authority.[23] All of these writers were and are keen observers of the political arena who inductively developed research questions and went on to explore them in their writings.

Milton Leitenberg offers a provocative example of induction in describing a visit he made to a severely deprived area in Nova Scotia. He calls the experience "the natural birth of a hypothesis." He sat one evening observing a large group of children playing a game, a form of tag. Leitenberg observed that the game had very different rules than games commonly played in the United States:

> Quite obviously, the purpose of the chase was not at all to catch the person who was "it." . . . The chasing itself was quite a leisurely affair. . . . The pace was set to match that of the pursued. If she chose to run slower, everyone else ran slower too, and she made no attempt to outrun them. This characteristic of the sequence I am calling "cooperation" for lack of a better word.

Leitenberg speculated that this cooperative aspect of the game might be related to the community's depressed economic situation. Specifically, he hypothesized that the children had created a cooperative game to help them deal with the hardship they were experiencing.[24] He began with an interesting observation and used it to develop a hypothesis about children's behavior.

The ability to generalize from specific cases often depends on the extensiveness of our knowledge. Therefore, it may be necessary to immerse ourselves in a situation in order to develop research questions or specific hypotheses.

Consider the earlier discussion of reasons for the decline of population in urban areas. A cursory examination of information about changing employment patterns in the United States is sufficient to suggest the proposition that urban areas are declining because they offer fewer employment opportunities. However, there may be additional reasons for population loss, ones that are not immediately apparent. It is possible, for example, that more people are choosing to live in smaller, more intimate communities, or that they are choosing more simple lifestyles. These are propositions that would come only from a more in-depth knowledge of the situation.

Immersing ourselves in a situation for the purpose of collecting data in order to develop research questions and propositions is often referred to as exploratory research. For example, an exploratory case study can be used to develop hypotheses that can be tested. This more intensive approach to data collection is appropriate when we know little about a situation. As two political scientists have written, we immerse ourselves in a topic when we want to

> generate new ideas not to test preestablished hypotheses. . . . The basic strategy of exploratory research is to start by spreading as wide a net as possible, sweeping in not only the particular elements that initially seem most interesting, but also data and ideas that at first may seem irrelevant or trivial. . . . As the study progresses, the researcher will gradually discover where he is headed and which data or ideas he will use; he cannot know in advance.[25]

These authors were interested in studying the activities of urban planners who worked for local housing agencies. They believed that they did not know enough to propose a hypothesis, that they needed first to interview a wide variety of planners and learn firsthand about the planners' experiences. On that basis they could propose useful and interesting hypotheses.

Induction can be based not only on our own observations of what is going on around us but also on descriptive studies and observations made by others. Often, the inductive method uses what is called *ordinary language* to suggest hypotheses. It looks for propositions in newspaper accounts of an event, in statements by public officials, or in ordinary political discussions among citizens. The value of this approach is that it disciplines us to look for the assumptions and hypotheses that people are making, often implicitly and often without clearly defining their terms.

Theories and Logic: Deduction

deduction
Practice of developing a hypothesis from theory or logic.

Theories and logic illustrate the use of **deduction** to generate hypotheses. The Latin root of the term *deduction* means "to draw out"; hence, deduction is the act of drawing out the meaning or implications of a theory or logical argument. We begin with a theory and consider what implications it has, or we examine the premises of an argument and see what conclusions logically follow. Deduction moves from the general to the particular, from general theories to hypotheses about particular cases.[26]

A well-developed theory in political science says that presidential candidates will move toward the center of the political spectrum as the campaign progresses. The logic is that they take extreme positions in the primaries to gain the support of party members, but then move to the center in the general election to gain the support of the general electorate, who are less apt to hold strong positions. We can deduce from this general theory that, in any given election year, a candidate will moderate his stated positions between July and November. This proposition then becomes a hypothesis that we can test by studying campaign speeches. Most of the time our analyses would probably confirm the hypothesis. However, if we happened to test it by looking at the 1964 campaign, we would find that the Republican candidate, Barry Goldwater, did not move to the center. We could use this finding to qualify the theory. For example, we could propose that a few candidates may be more interested in promoting a philosophy than in winning an election and would not move to the center.

We could arrive at the same hypothesis using *logic*. Candidates want to win, and therefore they will try to appeal to the majority of the people. Because they can usually count on the support of those who agree with them, they do not need to please these people as much as they need to appeal to those who do not hold strong views. They can usually win their support by appearing moderate and avoiding extreme positions. Deduction may be useful to students because it allows them to build on existing research and theory rather than start from scratch. As the example of Goldwater's campaign suggested, new research may produce interesting qualifications or variations on long-held theories. When reading studies in political science, examine their theories and consider how you could test them.

Economic theory offers many examples of deductive theory. One variant of economic theory, known as public choice theory, begins by stating several assumptions about individual behavior. In general these theorists assume that voters behave in the political arena just as they do in the economic marketplace. In the market, individuals use their resources to get the most benefits for their money. Similarly, in the political system they use their vote in the same way, voting for the person or group of policies that will benefit them the most. One can deduce from this assumption that individuals will tend to make the same choices over time, since the policies that benefit them today will tend to do so in the future.[27] Thus a hypothesis can be deduced that individuals will vote to maximize the benefits to themselves and that they will tend to vote similarly over time.

Consider a second example in which a research hypothesis is deduced from economic theory. Albert Hirschman is interested in examining how people behave when they are unhappy with a service or policy. What do they do, for example, if they are disappointed in the public schools in their community? He notes that people can either "exit" by taking their children out of the schools or can express their "voice" by getting involved in the policy process to change the schools. Insofar as they behave according to the economic assumptions described in the last paragraph, he proposes they will choose the least costly alternative. Generally, "exit" is less costly than "voice," since the latter takes a lot of time and energy. Hirschman goes on to deduce a hypothesis that people with the resources to "exit" to private schools will do so, rather than exercise "voice" to improve the public schools.[28]

In the above two examples, an economic theory of behavior is used to hypothesize how the public behaves in the political arena. One can also draw on economic theories of rational behavior to predict how political elites will behave. Robert Bates's study of governments in Africa is one example.[29] It is interesting because he defines rationality more broadly than economists do and includes political self-interest. Bates wanted to explain why these countries so often adopt policies that are disastrous to their economies. He deduces from economic theory that elites in these countries will follow their political self-interests. Since they know their countries need to expand their industrial base, they adopt policies to protect infant industries and gain the support of industrial elites. But this is a costly strategy requiring additional resources. They obtain resources by taxing the peasants, which in turn leads peasants to grow less food and ends by making everyone worse off. Bates begins with this hypothesis and examines whether the results in African nations match the predictions of the theory.

Where We Are

This chapter has argued first that research begins by asking interesting questions, and second that the research design we use depends on the nature of the question we are asking. Sorting out the major question is the first step in any research activity. We are struck by an interesting incident or problem or we hear about a provocative theory or proposition that logically relates two or more variables. We then decide how to proceed. Does the question ask about a general pattern across many cases, or for a deeper understanding of a few cases? Does the question lead us to compare several cases? Do we need to do more exploratory research before we can even define the most interesting or useful question? Is there a reasonable theory or hunch available that we can test as a hypothesis? Often the question could lead us in several directions, and we will need to decide which is most feasible or fruitful for our purposes. The following chapters will help you make those decisions.

We conclude the chapter by quoting from a foundation's guidelines for applications for a research fellowship. The guidelines illustrate the importance of identifying a research question and designing your research around that question:

> Describe the research to be carried out. . . . This statement should identify the research questions to be asked; set those questions in intellectual context; specify the propositions or hypotheses to be evaluated, where appropriate; describe the methods to be used and the data sources to be drawn upon; and demonstrate the potential of this research for adding to knowledge.[30]

NOTES

1. Robert Samuelson, "By a Shrewd Electorate," *Washington Post*, 13 November 1996, p. A23.

2. Answers for Practice Exercise 2.1. **Table 2.A:** Europe should include United Kingdom 76; Africa/Middle East should include Nigeria 52; Asia should include S. Korea 71, and India 62; North/South America should include United States 77 and Panama 73. **Table 2.B** should include Small Ethiopia 49, France 78, S. Korea 71, Panama 73, and United Kingdom 76; Medium should include United States 77; Large should include India 62. **Table 2.C** should include Low GNP Ethiopia 49, India 62, and Nigeria 52; Middle GNP should include Panama 73; High GNP should include France 78, United Kingdom 76, and United States 77. Of the several possible ways to describe life expectancy in the countries, GNP is the most useful because the countries in each category of GNP are fairly similar and there are no countries overlapping with other GNP categories. It is most useful in describing those with high GNP because all the countries have high and similar life expectancies. It is less useful in describing life expectancy in low-income countries since there is considerable variation in that group. Would it be reasonable to propose GNP as a possible explanation for the differences? Yes, because of these patterns. You would probably decide to collect information on more countries, however, because there is no apparent pattern for the low- and middle-income countries.

3. Seymour Martin Lipset, *Political Man* (New York: Doubleday, 1960), p. 110.

4. Ruth Lane, "Concrete Theory: An Emerging Political Method," *American Political Science Review* 84, no. 3 (September 1990): 927–940.

5. Examples of concrete theory cited by Lane include: Stephen Skowronek, "Presidential Leadership in Political Time," in *The Presidency and the Political System*, ed. Michael Nelson, Washington: Congressional Quarterly; Jeffrey L. Pressman, and Aaron Wildavsky, *Implementation*, 2d edition. Berkeley: University of California Press, 1979.

6. Michael Doyle, "Liberalism and World Politics," *American Political Science Review* 80, no. 4 (December 1986): 1151–1169.

7. Edward Mansfield and Jack Snyder, "Democratization and War," *Foreign Affairs* (May/June 1995): 79–97.

8. Edward Mansfield and Jack Snyder, " Democratization and the Danger of War," *International Security* 20, no. 1 (Summer 1995): 5–38; p. 6.

9. Ibid., p. 7.

10. These cases were mid-Victorian Britain, the France of Napoleon III, Bismarckian Germany and Taisho Japan. Ibid., p. 20.

11. I am indebted to my former colleague, Torbjorn Knutsen, for suggesting these three approaches to doing research.

12. Barbara Tuchman, "In Search of History," *Radcliffe Quarterly* (May 1963): 6.

13. Ibid., p. 8.

14. P. Gourevitch, "Interviewing the Universe," *New York Times Magazine*, 9 August 1992, p. 22.

15. Crane Brinton, *Anatomy of a Revolution* (New York: Random House, 1965).

16. Carol Gilligan, *In a Different Voice* (Cambridge, Harvard University Press, 1982).

17. Kay Lehman Schlozman, Nancy Burn Sidney Verba, Jesse Donahue, "Gender and Citizen Participation: Is There a Different Voice?" *American Journal of Political Science* 39, no. 2 (May 1995): 267–293.

18. Ibid., p. 289.

19. Edward Tufte, *Data Analysis for Politics and Policy* (Englewood Cliffs, N.J.: Prentice-Hall, 1974), p. 19. The point was originally made in Darrell Huff, *How to Lie with Statistics* (New York: W.W. Norton, 1954).

20. Alexis de Tocqueville, *Democracy in America*, 2 vols. (New York: Vintage Books, 1955).

21. H. H. Gerth and C. Wright Mills, *From Max Weber* (New York: Oxford University Press, 1946).

22. Richard Neustadt, *Presidential Power* (New York: Wiley, 1960).

23. Theodore Lowi, *The End of Liberalism* (New York: Norton, 1969).

24. Milton Leitenberg, "The Natural Birth of a Hypothesis," *The American Behavioral Scientist* 7, no. 2 (1963): 3–9.

25. Martin Needleman and Carolyn Needleman, *Guerillas in the Bureaucracy* (New York: Wiley, 1974), pp. 6–7.

26. E. R. Emmett, *Handbook of Logic* (Totowa, N.J.: Littlefield, Adams & Co., 1967), ch. 4.

27. Albert Weale, "Rational Choice and Political Analysis," in *New Developments in Political Science: An International Review of Achievements and Prospects*, ed. Adrian Leftwich (Brookfield, Vermont: Edward Elgar Publishing, 1990) pp. 196–197.

28. Albert O. Hirschman, *Exit, Voice and Loyalty* (Cambridge: Harvard University Press, 1970).

29. Robert H. Bates, *Markets and States in Tropical Africa* (Cambridge: Cambridge University Press, 1983).

30. MacArthur Foundation Fellowships in International Peace and Security, Application Guidelines.

EXERCISES

Exercise 2.1 Normative Statements and Empirical Questions

Two normative statements follow. For each identify one or more empirical questions that you could use to examine the statement more concretely.

1. We should get rid of the parole system and prevent any convicted prisoner from eventually getting out on parole.

2. We should end government support for the arts because it only benefits the elites.

Exercise 2.2 Turning Vague Terms into Empirical Statements

State the proposition implicit in the following statement. Transform it into an empirical statement.

To read Morris's book about the Clinton White House is to understand why voter turnout in the United States has dropped so dramatically since 1992. In neither 1994 nor 1996 did the winning party offer the nation a Noble Vision, a Big Challenge or an Ambitious Dream."

(Mark Shields, *Washington Post*, 1 February 1997, A21.)

Exercise 2.3 Developing Hypotheses

The text described theories that can be used as the basis for your own research hypotheses. For each of the following develop a hypothesis that meets the criteria for a hypothesis stated in the text that you could use to test the theory.

1. Lipset's theory that peoples' status affects their participation.

2. Samuelson's statement that the public is rational and consistent. Develop a hypothesis that would be appropriate for testing among students.

3. The statement that men and women specialize in different forms of political activity.

4. Hirschman's theory that individuals are more apt to choose to exit than to express their voice when problems arise.

Exercise 2.4 Developing Propositions from Narrative Description

This exercise will give you practice in constructing propositions about historical events. The data you have to work with come from narrative accounts and descriptions of the Vietnam policy of President John F. Kennedy and his advisers during the early years of the war. It also gives you practice in using a single case to develop propositions about relationships among variables that can then be tested on a larger number of cases. For example, if we discovered that the president made the decision to intervene in Vietnam because of his respect for a prowar surge in public opinion, then we would formulate a proposition that leaders of democracies are more prone to go to war abroad if mass opinion at home supports the war. As you proceed with this exercise, then, keep in mind that you are not only seeking to learn more about this case but also seeking to use the case to formulate more general propositions to explain why states intervene with military force abroad. All of the narratives propose explanations for U.S. involvement in the war in Vietnam. After reading each of the following narratives, you will be asked to identify how the writer explains our involvement in Vietnam, and the proposition he is offering.

Narrative number one

Most intractable of all of President Kennedy's problems in South East Asia was the problem of Vietnam. In the end this was to consume more of the President's attention and concern than anything else in Asia. The American commitment to the Saigon government was now of nearly seven years' standing. After the Geneva Agreements of 1954 had split Vietnam along the 17th parallel, President Eisenhower had written Prime Minister Ngo Dinh Diem . . . pledging American support "to assist the Government of Viet-Nam in developing and maintaining a strong, viable state, capable of resisting attempted subversion or aggression through military means." . . .

Whether we were right in 1954 to undertake this commitment will long be of interest to historians, but it had ceased by 1961 to be of interest to policy makers. Whether we had vital interests in South Vietnam before 1954, the Eisenhower letter created those interests. Whether we should have drawn the line where we did, once it was drawn we became every succeeding year more imprisoned by it. Whether the domino theory was valid in 1954, it had acquired validity seven years later, after neighboring governments had staked their own security on the ability of the United States to live up to its pledge to Saigon. Kennedy . . . had no choice now but to work within the situation he had inherited. The Eisenhower policy left us no alternative in 1961 but to continue the effort of 1954.

(Arthur Schlesinger, Jr., *A Thousand Days: John F. Kennedy in the White House* [Boston: Houghton Mifflin, 1965], pp. 536–538, 548–550.)

Narrative number two

The argument that none of the countries in the area is absolutely essential to American defense has relatively little impact on the over-all issue that the Communists apparently have found Southeast Asia a propitious battleground where they can demonstrate U.S. inability to stand up to the enormous stresses of revolutionary war. In the first round of that war, the American-supported French lost the battle. . . .

All this spells a real challenge to the United States and one which the United States has decided to face up to in South Viet-Nam, regardless of cost. In spite of the usual press statements northern Southeast Asia has no direct military value. . . . But the "denial value" of the area is enormous.

With Southeast Asia no longer under American control, India's position would become well-nigh impossible. What Indonesia's attitude then would be is anybody's guess. In other words, the negative stake of denying the adversary access to further Southeast Asian real estate is truly an important one. It is the denial value of the area which inspires policy-makers in Washington to accept the battle on almost any terms, regardless of whether the Ngo Dinh Diem or any other regime is "popular" or not.

(Bernard B. Fall, "Southeast Asia: The West at Bay," *Current History* 43, no. 255 [November 1962]: 295–301.)

Narrative number three

Kennedy's major preoccupation was not with Vietnam but with China. . . . He was making the same judgment of China in the 1960s that his predecessors made of Russia from the mid-forties on. Even if one accepts the earlier assumptions about the Soviet Union . . . the situation in Asia was very different. . . . Yet Kennedy did not make that distinction. Communism was communism and it must be opposed wherever it might be, even at the cost of American blood and treasure. He had learned . . . that a nuclear confrontation with the Soviet Union was dangerous, but he had yet to learn of the terrible cost of intervention in revolution. He still saw a communist monolith that never existed beyond the sway of the Russian army. . . .

One more thing is evident from John Kennedy's final statements on Vietnam. Despite the rhetoric about self-determination and helping a beleaguered little nation, the Kennedy administration was not primarily interested in Vietnam and its people, but in the anti-communist war.

(Richard J. Walton, *Cold War and Counterrevolution: The Foreign Policy of John F. Kennedy* [New York: Viking, 1972], pp. 191–194.)

Narrative number four

At almost the same moment that the Kennedy Administration was coming into office, Soviet Premier Nikita Khrushchev had given a major speech giving legitimacy to wars of national liberation. The Kennedy Administration immediately interpreted this as a challenge . . . and suddenly the stopping of guerilla warfare became a great fad. . . . The President's personal interest in fighting guerillas was well publicized and the reading and writing of books on anti-guerilla warfare was encouraged.

The fascination with guerilla warfare reflected the men and the era: aggressive, self-confident men ready to play their role, believing in themselves, in their careers, in their right to make decisions here and overseas, supremely confident in what they represented in terms of excellence. . . .

A remarkable hubris permeated this entire time. . . . All of this helped send the Kennedy Administration into dizzying heights of antiguerilla activity and discussion.

(David Halberstam, *The Best and the Brightest* [New York: Random House, 1969], pp. 121–124.)

For each of the preceding narratives:

1. State the author's explanation for U.S. involvement in Vietnam.

2. Restate this explanation as a *proposition* that could be used in studying a larger number of cases to understand why states use military intervention outside their own borders.

CHAPTER THREE

Measuring Concepts and Variables

To construct a measure of the total amount of erotic affection manifested by a random sample of French lovers is not very enlightening, unless it can be known how much of it is devoted to wives and how much to mistresses.

—Philip B. Coulter, "Comparative Community Politics and Public Policy"

[One] measure of the popularity of a man is the value of his autograph in the commercial market. The supply level must be controlled, of course, but it is of some interest that the following prices held at the end of 1964.

John Hancock	*$250.00*
Winston Churchill	*225.00*
Napoleon	*185.00*
Charles Dickens	*125.00*
Calvin Coolidge	*55.00*
John Quincy Adams	*37.50*

—Eugene Webb, Donald Campbell, Richard D. Schwartz, and Lee Sechrest, *Unobtrusive Measures*

What is an American auto? Congressional leaders proposing tax credits for purchases of U.S. cars have been puzzling over what is and isn't an American car. For example:

- *The 1992 Ford Crown Victoria, widely used by police departments and federal agencies, is considered foreign under federal fuel rules because only 73 percent of its parts are U.S.-made.*
- *The Ford Festiva is made by Kia of Korea.*
- *The Mazda Navajo four-wheel-drive vehicle is really a Ford Explorer made by Ford Motor Co. in Kentucky.*

—Washington Post, 31 January 1992.

Research Questions and Empirical Evidence

You have learned about formulating empirical questions. Some questions ask you to *describe* an event or activity. Some questions ask you to *explain* why the event or activity occurred. When we want to try to explain an event, chapter 2 noted that it can be useful to develop a research hypothesis. This is a common technique for making research more precise and systematic because it forces us to be specific about what we want to know and what kinds of evidence we need. This chapter focuses on the skills we need to move from our questions, theories, and hypotheses to empirical evidence or data that we can use in our research.

Interaction of Research Questions and Sources of Evidence

The research challenge is that these two steps—formulating questions and selecting data—usually have to be taken at the same time. The questions you ask will obviously influence the kinds of data you look for. The reverse is also true, the kinds of evidence you can find, the available information or data, will influence the way in which you state your question. Assume your college or university has privatized certain services on campus such as food or the bookstore so that they are now run by private companies rather than by the university. You are assigned to do some research relevant to the changes. The way in which you formulate your research question will probably vary with the kind of information you could get. Compare the following three options:

You could focus on changes in the services produced. You would then look for information about prices under the older and newer arrangements. You might be encouraged to pursue this question if you found that back copies of the student newspaper were available and contained some price information in their ads. Or you might find that the university had reported on price differences to the state and that you could get a copy of this report. These kinds of information would fit with the following research question: *How has the price of food or books changed under the new arrangement?* If you learned that the university had formerly subsidized the food services you would hypothesize that under the new arrangement, prices will increase.

You learn that your school newspaper has run a survey of student attitudes toward the newly privatized bookstore. You change your focus and write a paper about student views using the following research question: *Do students think the services have improved under the new arrangement?*

You hear some friends complain about the services they received and decide you need more detailed information than is contained in either the information on prices or the survey on attitudes. You decide to generate your own information by interviewing students as they leave the bookstore so that you can gather individual comments. You develop the following research question: *Do students find that personnel are friendlier or more responsive to complaints than they used to be?*

In summary, the question you ask leads you to look for different kinds of information, and conversely the information that is readily at hand can help shape your research questions.

A Sample of Accessible Sources of Data

Part Three describes in some detail how to obtain three kinds of information—answers by individuals to surveys and questionnaires, qualitative information derived from interviews and observations, and information collected and reported by others in the media or in reference works. You need to be aware of these options early in the research process, while you are defining your questions and selecting your measures. To underscore this point, the chapter describes a sample of several data sources that are readily available in your library. Examples throughout the chapter will refer to these, and the exercises at the end of the chapter will ask you to find certain kinds of information using these sources.

The Statistical Abstract of the United States is published each year and, as the name suggests, it contains a great variety of data about the United States as well as other countries. It is one of several accessible sources for information about elections, both presidential and state, and covers data back to the eighteenth century. It also contains information about cities and states including population, population changes over time, and poverty. The information on population change used in chapter 2 came from this source.

The World Development Report is published each year by the World Bank. At the end of each volume it includes several tables of "basic indicators." These include population, GNP, life expectancy, adult illiteracy, access to health care, infant mortality, fertility rate, and education. The countries are conveniently grouped by low-income, lower-middle-income, upper-middle-income, and high-income economies. The information in table 2.2 on GNP, population and life expectancy was taken from this source.

The Gallup Poll: Public Opinion[1] is also published each year and reports results on national surveys carried out by the Gallup Poll. It contains information about political and social attitudes and opinions and is a rich source of information about the American public.

The Internet has become a rich source of information and is changing and expanding rapidly. This book will not teach you how to use the Internet, but for those who have learned to do so, it will indicate how to access a few of the many sources of politically relevant information. For example, many government documents can be brought onto your computer screen and even printed out. (In the following internet addresses, do not use the quotation marks.) *The Statistical Abstract of the United States* can be explored through the Internet. Go to the following Web site: "http://www.medaccess.com/census/census_s.htm#Table of Contents" to explore what is available to you. Another useful site is the University of Michigan's Documents Center. Go to the following Web site: "http://www.lib.umich.edu/libhome/Documents.center/index.htm#doctop." Explore what is available. While at the site, go to "Related Web Pages." Click on the "Statistics" link and then on "Demographics" and again explore what information is accessible.

These few references give you a sample of available data that can be used if you are starting a research project. You may also skip ahead to chapter 9 for a fuller description of comparable resources. The point is that your choices about measures, covered in this chapter, will be greatly influenced by the data you can create or access as described in chapters 7, 8, and 9. Also note the source of the information contained in tables throughout the book.

The Terms of Political Discourse: Concepts and Their Definitions

Questions about evidence and data recall the issues posed in chapter 1, and particularly the point that it is difficult to observe, measure, or compare many of the terms we want to research and analyze such as *military weakness* and *political power*. Because power cannot be directly observed, two people using the word *power* may attach very different meanings to it. As a result, political discourse often is very imprecise and even misleading. At the very least it becomes difficult to test propositions containing such terms. And yet *power* is an example of an imprecise term that points to critically important facets of our political life. Hence, it is imperative that we find ways to talk about it meaningfully and relate it to empirical evidence. This chapter considers how to establish linkages between the often imprecise terms we use in political discourse and the data we observe.

Consider the terms we use in talking about politics. We vote in a particular election and then refer to the activity as "participation." We read about the ways in which members of Congress vote on several bills and then later refer to "congressional behavior." We hear that a senator voted for a bill to extend food stamps, and we call that senator a "liberal." In each case we have observed a concrete event and then made an abstract generalization about it. When we then hear that the head of a local citizens' group favors job-training programs, we link that new knowledge to the former observation that our senator favors food stamps and then apply the term liberal to both individuals. We do not observe either of them being liberal; we observe them taking positions that we *call* liberal. These general terms or labels are referred to as concepts and, as described in chapter 1, they are the basis of our language, particularly of our political language.

Concepts do not actually exist in the external world. We cannot directly observe participation or congressional behavior, just as we cannot observe liberalism. These concepts are generalizations we draw from specific observations, and some of them remain closer to the original observation than do others. Recall that chapter 1 discussed abstract and concrete terms and told us that concrete terms are closer to reality because they refer to actual observations. Abstract terms are more remote from the original observations, and the user may even have forgotten the empirical evidence on which a concept is based. Abstract concepts thus are particularly difficult for the researcher to use and interpret. Of the terms discussed in the preceding paragraph, voting *(participation)* is fairly concrete, *congressional behavior* is somewhat more abstract, and *liberal* is very abstract.

When people speak of voting, you have a fair idea what they are referring to, even though you may not know what election they are thinking of or whether they mean that someone votes regularly or just once. When a person refers to *congressional behavior*, you can picture Congress members doing such things as meeting to discuss legislation and voting on bills. You still are not exactly sure what the speaker means by the term, however. And when someone uses the term *liberal*, you have much more difficulty imagining what that person is thinking of and what is meant by the term.

CONCEPT

A label we put on a phenomenon that enables us to link separate observations and to make generalizations. A convenience, a name we give to observations and events.

Examples: *Apathy, participation, liberalism, military strength.*

The following line ranges from "concrete" on the left to "abstract" on the right. Look at the concepts below the line and place each one on the line according to how concrete or abstract you think it is.

Concrete   Abstract

Military strength, Community involvement, Conservatism, Protest march, Development, Apathy, Economic growth, Political Interest, Grass-roots action, Voter turnout.

Of these terms, *Protest march* and *Voter turnout* would fall near the concrete end of the line since it is fairly clear what these refer to. *Military strength, Economic growth,* and *Grass-roots action* would fall nearer the middle of the line since they refer to a range of phenomena that is fairly predictable but could be defined differently depending on what information one looked at. *Conservatism, Development, Apathy,* and *Political interest* fall nearer the abstract end of the line, since they could each be used to refer to a broad range of phenomena. As a researcher you will have more decisions to make about what evidence to collect to examine these kinds of terms.

Definitions of the more abstract concepts are at the heart of many political arguments. Note the different definitions of conservatism in the following statement by the columnist George Will. He refers to the "sterile practice of defining conservatism simply as opposition to 'big government'" and then continues:

> The problem is not "bigness," it is unreasonable intrusiveness, which is a function of [bad] policy, not size. Besides, inveighing against big government ignores the fact that government is about as small as it ever will be; and obscures the fact that government, though big, is often weak.[2]

Will, a self-proclaimed conservative, goes on to say that *conservatism* to him means a strong but nonintrusive government. Thus he rebukes those who define conservatism as the desire for smaller government. His preferred definition poses a challenge for the researcher. Size of government is fairly concrete and one could use size of budget or number of personnel to measure it. "Intrusiveness" as a concept, however, is more abstract and hence harder to measure.

As noted earlier, to develop linkages between concepts and actual observations and events we have to think about the *meaning* of the concept at the same time that we consider *which data are available* for measuring the concept. Our task in this chapter is to practice being precise about the meaning we attach to our concepts, and to find ways to link them with actual data so we can examine and test political statements empirically. As we have learned in the preceding chapter, this choice depends on a number of factors, including our experiences and any theories we want to examine. In subsequent chapters we will see that it also depends on the competing hypotheses we want to compare, the model we are testing, and the relationships we are exploring.

Measuring concepts requires four steps. The first is to think through what the concept means, given our particular research and how we will define it. For instance, apathy can be defined in a number of ways, and our first task is to be clear about the aspects of apathy that are of particular interest to us. Do we mean lack of interest in politics, a failure to participate, or do we mean a conviction that politics is irrelevant?

The second step is to decide which variables we will use to measure the concept. Chosen variables need to meet two criteria: they must be relevant to the meaning of the concept we chose in step one, and they need to bring us closer to some actual data or evidence. If we are interested in studying the concept of apathy, it is not obvious what operations we would use to measure it. If we translate it into the variable "nonvoting," however, we can readily think of some evidence we could use to study it. Thus the variable "voter turnout" can be used to study the concept of apathy. More specifically, apathy would be defined as one of the values of "voter turnout," namely, the failure to vote. Turnout is relevant to the concept of apathy, and it is relatively easy to find data describing it. For example, we can obtain data that tell us the numbers of registered voters who do not vote in an election.

operational definition
A restatement of a concept so that it can be tested empirically; a reference to the operations to be used in measuring the concept.

indicator
Identifies the evidence used to describe a variable; part of an operational definition.

The third step in measuring a concept is to propose an **operational definition** or a set of **indicators** of the variables. These refer to the actual task or operations we use or the actual kinds of data that we use to measure the variable.

variable
A characteristic of a thing that can assume varying degrees or values. The variable "gender" includes the values male and female.

operational definition
A restatement of a concept so that it can be tested empirically; a reference to the operations to be used in measuring the concept.

instrument
Specific evidence used to measure a variable or concept.

concept
Abstract term referring to a group of phenomena.

For example, an indicator of nonvoting would be turnout figures for presidential elections. An indicator of which groups in the electorate turned out to vote could be responses by voters in surveys or exit polls.

The fourth step in measuring a concept is to select the actual data sets or instruments to measure the indicators we chose. For example, we could use the Gallup poll taken just after the 1996 election as an instrument to measure the indicator of citizen responses to questions about their turnout. Another instrument would be the exit poll taken by network news programs and reported in the *New York Times* the day after an election. Instruments, therefore, point to actual data sets.

We can think of the process of measurement as a funnel, with a concept at the broader end and data at the narrower end. The point is to move progressively toward the data, to redefine the concept so that we can talk about it in terms of actual evidence that we can collect and point to. Figure 3.1 depicts the steps in this process. On the left are the general steps we take. On the right the steps are applied to an analysis of participation.

Define concept. Most often we associate participation with elections. Alternatively, we could define participation as marching in rallies and attending public hearings. The first choice, voting, would be useful if we wanted to compare changes in participation before and after the 1964 Voting Rights Act, or if we wanted to look at general trends in participation over the past few decades. The second choice, rallies and hearings, would be a better definition if we were studying the variety of ways in which different ethnic groups participate in politics. There are also some people who routinely do not vote but who get very involved in politics when an issue such as gun control is placed on the ballot. If we looked at only nonvoting and voting to study participation, we would never learn how nonvoters participate in other ways. The point is that neither definition is true or false; rather, each is more or less useful depending on our research interests.

Select variables. A common way to study participation in elections is to look at voter turnout, which becomes the variable we will be using, as indicated in figure 3.1. We need to go farther, however, and specify what kinds of elections we are talking about. It is common to choose turnout for presidential elections because there is so much information available such as in *The Statistical Abstract of the United States*. Alternatively, we might select turnout for local elections if we knew a source of information about these. Local libraries often clip and save such information.

Select operational definition. Next we need to select the operations we will use to get the necessary evidence or the indicators of voter turnout. It may seem that the indicators for the variable of voting are fairly obvious, but it is still not clear what actual operations we would use to measure it. If you wanted to learn how many people in your local community voted, how would you find

FIGURE 3.1
Moving from Concepts to Data

Measurement Process		*Participation*
Define aspect of concept to study	CONCEPT	Participation in elections
Select the variables you will use	VARIABLES	Voter turnout, presidential elections
Identify evidence that tells you about the variables	OPERATIONAL DEFINITION; INDICATORS	Responses by citizens to surveys for past two presidential elections
Note actual data sets you intend to use. Have several instruments if possible.	INSTRUMENTS or MEASURES	1. Gallup poll results, November 1992. 2. Poll of students at state university, November 1992. 3. Exit polls reported by major networks on election night.

out? One possibility is to count the people who go into the polling booth, obviously very time consuming. An easier method is to go to election headquarters right after the election and ask the officials for turnout figures. Even easier is to look for a report on the turnout figures in the local newspaper. Another option is to conduct a survey and ask people whether or not they voted. Each of these choices points to a different operational definition or indicator of your variable, voter turnout. For purposes of this example, let us select the indicator "responses by citizens to a survey about their voting behavior in the past two presidential elections."

Select instruments, actual measures, data sets. The final step is to specify the actual data we will collect, or the instrument we will use to measure our indicators. In the case of voting, the instrument should point to the actual questions asked and the groups interviewed or surveyed. For example, the indicator could be a series of questions in a Gallup poll conducted just after the 1996 presidential election. It would include the actual questions, the source where they could be found, the date of the survey. In other words the instrument tells us exactly what data we would use (see figure 3.1).

Examples of the Process of Measuring Concepts

Opposition and support for the ERA. Consider a second example of the measurement process. In this case we enter the measurement at the second step, at the level of identifying the *variables* we plan to use. It concerns the defeat of the Equal Rights Amendment (ERA). During the late 1970s states voted on whether to pass the ERA to the U.S. Constitution. The allotted time for getting state support ran out in 1980 with three states too few, and the ERA died. Some proposed the defeat of the ERA was actually brought about because of opposition from women. How could we examine this proposition with actual evidence? Begin with the dependent **variable,** "action by state legislatures." A relevant **operational definition** would be the official reports of the action taken by the legislatures. A measuring **instrument** would be reports of legislative actions as published by the legislatures for a specific year. We should indicate the date, volume, and page where the information we need can be found.

The **concept** "action taken by women in support of or in opposition to the bill" is more abstract, and it is not immediately clear what we mean by "opposition" or by "support." One possibility is to select the variable "opinions about the ERA." If that were our choice, we would need to look for an operational definition that tells us about women's opinions of the ERA in a number of states. We could go to the library to see if any national poll such as the Gallup poll asked such a question. National poll data, however, are usually not reported by state. An alternative is to select the variable "organized groups" and try to identify the number of women's groups in each state that had taken a position on the ERA. The final step is to find actual data or instruments that tell us how many women's groups had taken such a position. We could look for a listing of all such groups available from the legislator who led the fight against the amendment. We would also want to know how strong the groups were. Instruments to measure the strength of the organizations could include data on membership size, budget, and number of permanent staff. Measures of active opposition could be the number of members testifying at legislative hearings as listed in official records of the legislature. Notice what these measures do and do not tell us: membership and budget figures do not tell us how active the groups were on the ERA issue, but they do indicate the potential strength of a group; data on numbers testifying point directly to the level of activity on the ERA issue itself.

Sometimes the measures are obvious once we operationally define a term; sometimes they are not. Voting, for example, is fairly close to the data, and once we decide to focus on voting and nonvoting we simply have to find a source of information on voter turnout. In the example of women's opposition to the ERA, however, the measures were not so obvious from the definition. We had to think about which data would indicate the strength of an organization and which data are accessible to us. Whenever we are forced to depend on data collected by others, we are limited in our choice of measures by the data that are available and, therefore, we need to be imaginative. (See chapter 9.) As always in using them, we need to link the variables we have chosen to specific measures and to available data.

Political development. Consider a third example of the measurement process. The concept of "political development" not only is difficult to define and measure but also has important policy implications. Thus, it is not surprising that its definition has changed as political priorities have changed. In the late 1940s analysts tended to define the concept of development as an economic process and to rely on economic variables, such as level of industrialization. The indicator most commonly used was percentage of agricultural labor: a country was developed if no more than 25 percent of the workforce was employed in agriculture. Measures of such data are commonly found in a number of reference books, including the *World Development Report.*[3]

By the 1960s analysts had redefined the concept. They worried that the emphasis on industrialization betrayed a Western bias and were also more interested in the political capacity of a nation to provide services and respond to political demands. One influential definition of *development* during this period was provided by Gabriel Almond and G. Bingham Powell. They selected the variable "distributive capacity," or the ability of a government to distribute goods to its citizens.[4]

Given Almond and Powell's definition of the concept of *development* and their selection of the variable "distributive capacity," what specific measures could they use? Before reading further, take a minute to jot down empirical terms you associate with development.

How adequate and useful are the following operational definitions of distributive capacity, and why do you think they were chosen?

1. Hectares of arable land per capita of agricultural population, c. 1960 [c. means "about"].
2. Percentage of central government budget devoted to social welfare purposes (to include health, education, social services, and so forth), expressed as an annual average for the period 1961–1965 or as close to that period as possible.
3. Percentage of total population in nonprimary grades in school, c. 1958.[5]

The author of these operational definitions notes that the second and third items are better indicators of "distributive capacity" than the first, because they point to actual government activities. The first indicator, arable land, points to how many people own how much land. Thus it tells us about the government's ability to distribute benefits, but it is less directly relevant and hence not so good an indicator as the other two.

Those who have studied development may be aware that during the 1980s the concept of development was again redefined. For some, it now refers to the capacity of people to make choices. Recent observers have focused on such variables as the distribution of economic and social benefits throughout a nation. Because this distribution can be done through the private, nonprofit, or public sectors, analysts no longer focus solely on the capacity of the government to deliver these benefits. Instead, they look for indicators of literacy, health, and income distribution and focus less on government programs and expenditures.[6]

TABLE 3.1
Empirical Definitions of Concepts

Concept	Variables	Operational Definition	Measuring Instruments
Political participation	Voter turnout in presidential elections	Responses about turnout in surveys	Reports in Gallup polls for 1984, 1988, 1992
Opposition to/support of ERA	Activity of organized groups	Groups with position on ERA, size, and budget	List of groups registered with legislature; organization records; interviews with group leaders
Political development	Economic growth	Percentage of workforce in industry	World Bank report
	Capacity of government to provide services	Per capita land holdings; budget for social welfare	World Bank report
	Distribution of social services	Health, literacy	World Bank report

Table 3.1 summarizes the definitions of participation, opposition/support for ERA, and political development.

Examples of Empirical Definitions

Concept: **political interest**

The degree to which one is concerned about political and governmental events

Variables

Level of information about politics

Degree to which one discusses politics and government

Operational definitions

Responses to survey questions that show the respondent can identify local, state, and federal officials

Responses to survey questions that show that the respondent discusses political matters with others

Instruments or measures

The actual source of responses, such as Gallup poll or poll taken by loca. newspaper

Concept: **civic involvement** or **civic society**

The degree to which citizens are invested in the public arena

Variables

Voter turnout

Level of trust in government

Time devoted to voluntary associations

Operational definitions

Media reports on voter turnout

Answers to survey questions about voting and trust in government

Answers to questions about how individuals allocate their time

Answers to questions about which concrete organizations one belongs to

Answers to questions about extent of involvement in organizations[7]

Instruments or measures

General Social Survey

Questionnaires administered by researcher

Membership records of organizations

Concept: **U.S. military capacity**

The ability of a nation to deter or win a military confrontation

Variables

Money expended on military weapons and personnel

Number of weapons and personnel of specified types available to a nation

Operational definitions

Dollars reported in the national budget

Number of specified types of weapons and personnel reported by the military

Instruments or measures

1996 budget

Reports of weapons in specific issues of a newspaper of record

Concept: **authoritarian personality**

Personality characterized by ethnocentrism, intolerance, extreme conservatism, dogmatism, and acceptance of control

Variables

Willingness to accept control by others

Operational definitions

High-level (greater than 80 percent) agreement with question on a scale developed to measure acceptance of control, such as "What this country needs, more than laws or programs, is a few dedicated, courageous leaders in whom the people can put their complete faith"

Instruments or measures

Results of specific study conducted using the "California F scale," which provides measures of an authoritarian personality and includes the question just posed

Moving from Variables to Concepts

As noted earlier, when you are defining concepts operationally, you have to keep in mind both the concept you are measuring and the data that are available. Thus far, we have begun with concepts and tried to move down the funnel toward actual data (see figure 3.1). We may want to reverse the process. Sometimes we have data available to us that were collected by others. To see if the data could be useful to us, we need to think through what concepts the data could measure. Earlier we used data on life expectancy for several countries. In addition to providing information on the number of years people in that country can expect to live on the average, do these figures point to other concepts? We could use them as an operational definition of *development*. They do not tell us all that we usually mean by the concept of *development*, but most people would argue that they are part of what we mean. Begin with the following variables, and consider what concepts they relate to.[8] Four variables are listed below. Possible concepts are suggested for the first two; what concepts would be appropriate for the third and fourth variable?[9]

Variables	Possible Concepts
Literacy rate	Educational level
	Social development
Degree of freedom of the press	Democratic regime
	Political freedom
Extent of electoral competition	_____
	_____
Newspaper circulation	_____
	_____

Validity and Reliability of Definitions

Definitions and measures need to satisfy two specific criteria: they need to be valid and they need to be reliable.

> *Validity.* Validity refers to the concept we are measuring: a valid measure provides useful information about the concept in question.
>
> *Reliability.* Reliability refers to the measure rather than the concept: a reliable measurement gives us the same result no matter who does the measuring or what the circumstances are.

Validity

validity
Extent to which an indicator tells you what you want to know about a concept or points to relevant aspects of a concept.

In moving from concepts to data we may run into difficulties. We may select a variable that actually refers to a different concept or to a relatively unimportant part of the concept. Or we may have difficulty finding indicators that tell us about a particular variable. These are problems in **validity.** And the more abstract the concept, the more difficult it is to find valid variables and indicators. For example, we discussed the concept of development earlier and proposed alternative variables, such as economic growth and distribution of services, to define it. We then proposed operational definitions for each variable (see table 3.1). Which of the variables and operational definitions come closest to telling you what you have always meant by the concept of *development?*

Variables that fit your view of development: _____

_____

_____

_____

Variables that fit your view of development less well: _____

_____

_____

_____

Select one of the variables that fits your view of development, and indicate which of the operational definitions fit your view of development. The variables and operational definitions that fit your view of development have more validity than those that do not fit it. _____

_____

_____

_____

Consider the validity of a recent effort to measure changes in political culture. Great Britain has been undergoing extensive political changes, including a decline of trust and consensus and an increase in ideological conflict. Samuel Beer argues that one explanation for these changes is the increasing populism in the political culture of the country, which he says began in the counter-culture movement of the 1960s. He is examining the concept of *populism*, which he defines as "feelings of intense individualism and romantic rejection of customary constraints on behavior." These feelings (individualism, rejection of constraints) are the variables he selects to define populism. For operational definitions of these variables he turns to the lyrics of the Beatles songs, because they reflect the sentiments he associates with populism. He argues that the popularity of the lyrics during the 1960s is an indicator of the increasing populism during that period.[10] Does this operational definition seem valid to you? To what extent do the lyrics of Beatles' songs indicate the variables of individualism and rejection of customary constraints?

Some commonly used operational definitions pose validity problems. Consider the variable of "government expenditures," often used to define the concept of government effectiveness. For example, a study to compare the effectiveness of the city governments in New York and Chicago in providing welfare benefits might well compare the expenditures on welfare in the two cities. If New York spends more on welfare per capita, it is tempting to conclude that New York is more effective in the welfare policy arena. What validity problems are raised by using the variable of "expenditures" to draw this conclusion? (Possible answers: Critics argue that money spent on welfare measures only part of what we mean by an effective welfare policy. We also have to look at the impact of the expenditures and at the way in which they are distributed. New York may have a large budget, but may spend it ineffectively and leave out some people who need welfare.)

By now it should be clear that neither variables nor their indicators are totally valid or totally invalid and that most pose some validity problems. Thus, we usually describe an indicator as fairly valid, as not very valid, or as more valid than another indicator. Because it is hard to find measures that are as valid as we would like, it is preferable to rely on two or more variables to measure our concepts and two or more operational definitions to measure our variables. Usually, no single variable can do justice to a concept or reflect its full meaning, and no single operational definition can do justice to the variables we select.

There are four ways to evaluate whether an indicator is valid: face validity, predictive validity, convergent validity, and criterion validity.[11]

concept validity, face validity
When a logical or theoretical connection exists between indicators and the concepts they are measuring

Concept validity, or face validity. Does the measure seem to make sense? Is there a logical or theoretical connection between the variable and the concept or between the variable and the indicator? For example, is freedom of the press a reasonable variable to use in discussing democracy? Is there a connection between them, and are they logically related to each other? Most people would agree they are related, that one condition for democracy is being able to express opinions openly and freely, and that this way of defining democracy does have face validity.

Predictive validity. Do the results we obtain from one variable or indicator match the results using other undisputed measures? Suppose, in order to measure the concept of conservatism, we propose a set of variables and indicators for them. Assume that some of the indicators are survey questions. Before we use the questions, we could go to a group of people who are generally accepted as conservative—perhaps the Young Conservatives on campus—and ask the questions of them. Do our questions score this group of known conservatives as conservative? In other words, do our questions predict conservatism among those we know are conservatives?

predictive validity
When the predicted result of an indicator matches known evidence

Convergent validity. This kind of validity has utility when using two or more variables for a single concept. To what extent do the different measures give the same result? For example, assume we are using "freedom of the press" and "competitive elections" as two variables defining *democracy*. If some countries have freedom of the press, but do not have competitive elections, then these indicators are not very valid. If, however, most countries that have freedom of the press also have competitive elections, then the measures have convergent validity.

convergent validity
When various indicators of a concept produce consistent results.

Criterion validity. **Criterion** validity applies when we are using two or more indicators for both the dependent and independent variables. It asks to what extent the several indicators of the dependent variable are similarly related to the several indicators of the independent variable. We could hypothesize that the variables of "economic development" and "democratic government" are related. We develop two indicators of "economic development," per capita GNP and growth in GNP, and two indicators of "democratic government," freedom of the press and competitive elections. Are changes in the latter indicators related to changes in the former? If per capita GNP is related to freedom of the press but not to competitive elections, then these measures would have some criterion validity problems.

criterion validity
When each of the indicators of a variable bears the same relationship to the indicators of a second variable.

Validity of measurements of education. We can illustrate these four kinds of validity by considering the use of educational test scores. When comparing the learning of students in different countries, observers frequently conclude that the United States ranks fairly low. Typically they use the test scores as measures of the concept of learning, or educational quality. Concept validity asks whether test scores tell us about those aspects of learning that are most important. One might argue that there are other aspects of education, not measurable on tests, that are also important. Predictive validity asks whether there are other commonly accepted measures of educational quality that match the test scores. Here one might note that the scientific output of science and engineering majors in the United States is very high, and thus the test scores do not have very high predictive validity. Convergent validity asks if test scores at different grade levels are consistent with each other. It is worth noting that, in fact, tests of twelfth-grade students often are inconsistent with tests of eighth-grade students, and hence there are doubts about their convergent validity.

Finally, criterion validity asks whether test scores that measure the dependent variable of "learning" are consistent with different measures of the independent variable, "the nature of a country's education system." The latter can be defined using the number of years that students are required to remain in school, percentage of young people who graduate from high school, and numbers who continue on to college. Do test scores relate consistently to each of these versions of the independent variable? Critics of test scores as a valid measure of learning note that many more young people attend high school in the United States than in most other countries. High school test scores may reflect the learning of those who attend high school, but they may not be a good measure of the learning of those who continue on to college, another measure of a country's educational system. For all these reasons, we could reasonably question the validity of test scores as a measure of learning among young people in different countries.

Reliability

reliability
Degree to which a measurement gives the same result under all circumstances.

Reliability problems occur at the measurement stage in selecting instruments and data sets. **Reliability** is a function of the instruments or data sets we choose, as well as of the role of the analyst in collecting the data or applying the measuring instruments. A measure is reliable if it produces the same answer no matter who is using the instrument and no matter what the circumstances are. If we ask two people to find out how much money is spent on education, we want to make sure that both of them are collecting the same information. If one person reviews the annual budget and reports that figure, and the other person asks a member of the school board for the figure, each might return with a different amount. Thus, we need to develop a measuring instrument that is reliable in the sense that both people would come back with the same amount.

Measures are unreliable if our data sets or measuring instruments are biased or misleading or inaccurate. Chapter 1 described a number of sources of information that are misleading or biased. Recall the discussions of organizations that bias data to protect their programs, of declining budgets for collecting and reporting information, of concepts that are defined to reflect the political interests of one group rather than another. Part Three describes various sources of data and discuss sources of bias and error associated with different kinds of data.

The source of reliability problems can often be traced to the operational definitions we choose. These are unreliable if they point us to unreliable instruments or to data that are easily misinterpreted or biased, or if it is difficult to devise instruments that can reliably measure the operational definitions. Indicators of government expenditures, such as annual budgets, lead us to reliable instruments because it is likely that everyone who looked at a particular budget would report the same amount. If the indicator refers us to statements by members of the board of education about expenditures, it is directing us to less reliable information. Board members may recall different figures, their memories may be faulty, they may be thinking of different periods in the budget cycle, or they may include different budget items. On the other hand, if we have reason to suspect that there were errors in the annual budget, the reports by members of the board might be more reliable.

Trade-offs between Validity and Reliability

A measure that is reliable may not be valid, and vice versa. Moreover, the quests for both reliability and validity may even work against each other. The reason is that measures have to be very exact to be reliable, but exactness may dilute the meaningfulness or validity of a variable or indicator; it may not do justice to what is important about a concept. (Recall the quotes at the beginning of this chapter. Does the commercial price of an autograph tell you what is important about John Hancock or Winston Churchill? Obviously not. On the other hand, does a comparison of the prices of several famous people tell you something interesting about them? One could argue that it provides a clue to the way they are viewed from a historical perspective.)

Review what you concluded about measures of the concept of political interest. To get a reliable measure, you would need to identify a clear variable and indicate a specific question or behavior. You could, for example, select the variable "interest in political news" and use the following question as an operational definition: "How often do you listen to the evening news on television or read the front page of the daily paper?" You could decide that anyone who reports doing one or the other behavior at least five times a week should be counted as having political interest. This is a very specific indicator, and it is likely that most people asking the question would get the same answer. Hence, it is a reasonably reliable measure.

However, the indicator may not be a totally valid way to measure the variable of "interest in political news." Some people might read a number of political journals regularly rather than rely on television news or the daily papers. Similarly, the variable "interest in political news" might not be a valid way to define the concept of political interest. Someone may be very interested in political action on behalf of the homeless and work in a soup kitchen three nights a week but pay little attention to the national news. According to your measure, that person would have no political interest, and yet that does not do justice to his or her behavior. In this case your measures are fairly reliable but have only partial validity. In general we can say that the more precise we make our variables and indicators, the greater risk we run of missing some unique characteristics of a particular event or behavior, and hence of lessening the validity of the research. The lesson is to find measures that combine and balance validity and reliability, even if they cannot do both perfectly. These choices will be raised throughout the following chapters, wherein we examine the validity and reliability problems associated with different kinds of data.

Examples of Trade-offs in Finding Valid and Reliable Measures

Democracy. It might seem that one could rather easily develop a set of measures of democracy that were reasonably valid and reliable. Measurements of democracy, however, are not as self-evident as one might think and seem to change as the number of countries aspiring to democracy increases. *The New York Times* reviewed the move toward democracy around the world and concluded, "Although more than 100 nations now call themselves democratic, the definition has never been more blurred."[12] Whereas it is common to define democracy in terms of freedom of political expression, constitutional law, and majority rule through elections, each of these conditions has run up against problems in a number of countries that consider themselves democracies. These problems can be viewed as challenges to the validity of common definitions of democracy. At the same time, there are reliability problems in defining democracy, particularly if one wants to collect information on large numbers of countries.

In keeping with the earlier comment that definitions, measures, and data all need to be looked at simultaneously, students of democracy frequently combine a discussion of the *meaning* they ascribe to democracy with a review of the literature and commonly accepted indexes or compilations of political practice. For example, several reference works include indexes of political institutions such as *Encyclopedia of the Third World* and Ted Gurr's *Polity II*.[13] Each year Amnesty International and the State Department issue reports that rate the human rights practices of each country.[14] (Chapter 9 discusses such compilations more extensively.) These data sources provide reliable measures, and assuming that researchers can find measures in these collections that deal with the meaning they ascribe to democracy, they are also valid.

Consider the research discussed in chapter 2 examining the likelihood that democratic regimes will go to war with each other. The authors of that study compared all regimes from 1811 to 1980 and classified them as either democracies, autocracies, or mixed regimes. They tried to be clear and precise about the measures they would use, as they make clear in the following statement:

> Even fairly minimal definitions of democracy require periodic elections between candidates who compete fairly for the votes of a substantial portion of the adult population, and whose outcome determines who makes state policy, including foreign and military policy. Thus, the War of 1812 does not count as a war between democracies because Britain's suffrage was too narrow. Conversely, although the German Reichstag of 1914 was elected by universal suffrage with voter turnout over 90 percent, the war between France and Germany is excluded because German cabinet officials were chosen by the Kaiser.[15]

After thinking through these validity issues the authors reviewed prior studies and the information that was readily available as far back as 1811. Relying primarily on data collected in *Polity II*, they selected as measures "the competitiveness of political participation, the strength of the rules regulating participation in politics, the competitiveness of the process for selecting the chief executive, the openness of executive recruitment, and the strength of the constraints on the chief executive's power."[16] The lesson is to be clear about the meaning of democracy and to link that meaning to easily obtained information that has been widely accepted in the literature.

Distribution of government services. Some research requires a combination of measures, some more valid and reliable than others as illustrated by a study of the distribution of government services. It is important to know if services are spread fairly equally across a community or city, or if some groups receive more than others. If the latter, why do some groups receive more? Robert Lineberry sought to answer these questions for San Antonio.[17] He began by laying out specific measures or indicators of government services in order to determine whether they were unequally distributed in the community. For example, to determine the distribution of library services he examined the distance of each census tract to a library, the number of volumes in the library per capita, the personnel per 1,000 population, the new books ordered per 1,000 population, and the library expenditures per capita.

He found that services were indeed unequally distributed, and the concept of unequal distribution became his dependent variable. He then proposed four possible independent variables or hypotheses to explain his findings: (1) the socioeconomic status of different areas, with wealthier citizens receiving more services; (2) the racial composition of different areas, with minority areas receiving less; (3) the physical quality of the area with older and more dense areas receiving less; (4) the political power of the areas. It is easy to measure the first three variables (status, racial composition, physical quality) by looking at education, income, owner-occupied housing, gross rent, percentage minority, age of housing, and so forth. Since these data are compiled by the Bureau of the Census[18] they are reliable and **feasible** to collect. They also are highly valid. It is more difficult to measure political power, however. Lineberry looked at a number of measures, including number of council members living in the tract and number of top bureaucrats residing in the tract. These are reliable and reasonably feasible, but they do not have as high a validity, in that they probably do not capture all that one usually means by political power.

Lineberry tested each of the hypotheses and found they did not explain much of the variation in the distribution of services. For example, some poor neighborhoods got the same amount of services as richer neighborhoods, while others did not. He went on to propose a fifth hypothesis, that the distribution of services reflected the way the service agencies made decisions about delivering the services. The literature on urban bureaucracies supported this proposition, but the challenge was how to measure the concept of bureaucratic decision making. Lineberry developed a number of measures. For example, he measured the amount of discretion that the bureaucracies had by determining whether the city council made any changes in the budgets submitted by the agencies. Almost no changes were made by the elected leaders, which he took as an indicator of considerable bureaucratic autonomy and discretion. He also looked at how agencies developed their decision rules—for example, their rules for determining how many books to buy for the library. Were these developed centrally or by each library, and were they in response to demand from the community or made by central librarians? To measure these more abstract concepts, Lineberry turned to analyzing departmental reports and budgets. This information was probably fairly valid, but less reliable, in that different people might interpret the reports in different ways. Lineberry concluded that

feasible
When indicators point to data that are available with a reasonable expenditure of time and effort

the decision rules that agencies developed went far to explain the unequal distribution of services. Agencies, for example, chose to focus on areas where they could be more effective, and these tended to be the more middle-class areas.

Quality of decision making. Some studies turn to more subtle variables and measures and search for evidence in narrative accounts. Consider the well-known study *Groupthink*, by Irving Janis.[19] Janis was concerned that a lot of decision-making groups failed to openly consider a wide range of options and instead tended to indulge in what he calls "groupthink." He proposed several definitions of the concept: "members tend to evolve informal norms to preserve friendly intragroup relations," "signs of high cohesiveness and an accompanying concurrence-seeking tendency interfere with critical thinking," "the members' strivings for unanimity override their motivation to realistically appraise alternative courses of action."[20] Janis then reviewed reports describing the ways in which various major decisions had been made. In order to test the power of groupthink he looked for cases where the decision-making group was cohesive and where the resulting decision was clearly a poor one. His hypothesis was that in such cases he would find evidence of groupthink. He was not able to be as systematic in identifying his indicators as some of the studies described earlier. Instead he gleaned reports of decision making and looked for evidence of the above dynamics. As proposed he found that many decisions proceeded just as he had expected.

Because Janis carefully drew on the literature of group processes and on his own experiences with small group dynamics, he was able to develop valid indicators. They were somewhat less reliable than other measures, in that other readers might interpret the reports somewhat differently. The information was feasible, since Janis was careful to draw on cases for which there was a lot of documentation and firsthand reports.

Operational Definitions and Measures Used in Public Policy Making

Chapter 1 described a number of concepts and their measures that are used by governments. Now that you have learned about the criteria of validity and reliability, we can look again at some of the measures used by governments to see how they balance these criteria.

Terrorism. An early definition of the concept terrorism by the Central Intelligence Agency (CIA) includes the following variables: "The threat of violence, individual acts of violence, or a campaign of violence designed primarily to instill fear. . . . Terrorism is violence aimed at the people watching."[21] The agency later replaced these several variables with a simpler one: violent events. Its 1976 report listed the following indicators: kidnaping, barricading, hostage taking, bombing, armed assault or ambush, hijacking, assassination, incendiary attack or arson, and "other."

One reason for the change was the difficulty in finding indicators for the first definition, which referred to the motives of those who engaged in violent acts. The initial definition had considerable validity, however, because it indicated something important about the meaning of terrorism. Yet it is very hard to develop reliable indicators of motives by using data that one can obtain easily. The second choice offers a less ambiguous definition, one that points to easily obtained measures or data sets. On the other hand, ignoring the motives that differentiate terrorism from other types of violence, one could argue, makes the new definition less valid than the original one.

Employment. Studies indicate that by the late 1970s more than half of American women were working. Journalist Andrew Hacker has questioned the definition of *work* that is commonly used in such studies. The Department of Labor, he notes, operationally defines the variable of "worker" as anyone who works one hour or more during the week. One reason is that this allows its researchers to use a fairly reliable measuring instrument: persons on a payroll. As a result, the school crosswalk guard who goes on duty for ten hours a week is counted equally with an advertising executive who puts in a ten-hour day.[22]

Unemployment. The Department of Labor defines the concept of unemployment by using the variable "available and looking for work" and relies on household surveys as its major indicator. Critics contend that the definition is invalid because it fails to include those who are discouraged and do not look for work. In 1979 an official commission rejected the complaint on the grounds that the department cannot get reliable measures of those who want to work unless they are actively seeking work.[23] The Department of Labor is willing to give up some validity in order to keep its measure reliable.

Productivity. Labor productivity refers to the amount of goods and services produced for each hour worked. More specifically it is based on the variable "output per person-hour of paid labor." It measures all non-farm economic activity and divides that figure by the number of hours worked in the non-farm part of the economy. It is useful to know if productivity is changing, in which direction, and by how much. In the 1950s and 1960s the average productivity of workers in the United States increased about 3 percent a year. Since 1973 the annual increase has stayed around 1 percent (except for 1992 when it was 3.2 percent), which leads to many claims that the productivity of the U.S. economy is declining.

Some economists, however, argue that this purported decline is actually a result of the way in which we measure productivity. One group of economists, for example, argues that we do not pick up all of the productivity gain, especially when we measure services as opposed to tangible goods. It has always been hard to measure productivity in services—education, research, tourism, and so forth. They propose an alternative measure, which reports the income producers receive rather than the amount produced. They would ask you how much you earned rather than how much you produced. In theory these should be the same, but recently income has risen faster than output. The normal productivity measure indicates that the economy grew by 0.3 percent from 1990 to 1996, a very slow growth. The income measure, however, reports a growth of 1.6 percent.[24]

Researchers at the Institute for Social Research (ISR) at the University of Michigan suggest yet another way to measure productivity: "how much people produce both on and off the job." This expanded definition would provide a far higher level of productivity than government figures report, because people do much productive work off the job. The director of ISR, F. Thomas Juster, concludes that the much-discussed productivity lag in the United States is "a simple measurement error" and that when "use of time" is included as an indicator of work output, people are far more productive than is commonly realized.[25] One could reply that it is difficult to find reliable indicators of how people use their time.

The middle class. Politicians frequently consider proposals to give tax breaks to the middle class but differ in their definition of the term **middle class.** According to Robert Reischauer, former director of the Congressional Budget Office, "Being middle class is often more a state of mind than the state of your economic circumstances. Most people consider themselves middle class, especially when someone wants to give them a tax break, and then the ranks swell."[26] Economists try to be more precise and usually define middle class as those who fall within the middle 60 percent of the income distribution, or between $19,000 and $78,000 for a family of four. Often, however, officials find it politically useful to have a much more encompassing definition, with the result that they often include groups that are close to hardship cases and others that actually are very rich.

Multiple Indicators

You may be frustrated that many of these measures do not get at the concept they are presumably measuring, in other words that they sacrifice validity. The necessity to find operational definitions that are valid, reliable, and feasible does predispose us to look for indicators that are easily measured and can readily be translated into numbers. The earlier examples of definitions used by government agencies illustrate how frequently officials sacrifice some validity in order to produce reasonably reliable and feasible data sets. You may worry that we could be seduced by numbers and ignore factors that are less tangible and less countable but yet are very important.

There are many examples of this quantitative bias. In the study of urban services discussed earlier, Lineberry noted that we are more apt to measure how much government spends on services, and less apt to measure what they do for their citizens. The reason is the kind of indicators that are accessible. It is obviously easier to say how much the government spends on public education than to determine how effective the public schools are.[27] And yet our real interest is usually with the latter, with what is actually accomplished by government services. Consider also measures of military strength. For understandable reasons, the Department of Defense collects figures on the amount spent on arms and on military personnel to measure the variable "military strength." These indicators do have a certain face validity; with some care they are reliable; and they usually are feasible to collect and report. Some people argue, however, that military strength is more subtle and involves qualitative judgment beyond the simple addition of figures:

> Nations do not go to war with money but with a particular combination of trained men and weapons. The country whose armaments are best fitted to its needs will be better off. Waste, poor planning, and lack of popular support can easily make the big spender the big loser when the final test comes.[28]

The comment criticizes the tendency in some studies to focus on quantitative measures and to ignore important qualitative dimensions of a problem.

multiple strategies
Conscious effort to pursue several different approaches to data collection

One solution is to use **multiple strategies** and draw on several measures. If both produce the same results, you can conclude there is *convergent validity*. Earlier this chapter described different sources of evidence—surveys and questionnaires, which produce quantitative information and are generally high on reliability; interviews and observations, which produce firsthand information and tend to be higher on validity than on reliability; and data found in official reports and reference works, which are high on reliability but may sacrifice some validity. Drawing on indicators from more than one of these sources of information can increase validity.

Consider research to determine whether innovations, such as new policies or new ways of delivering services, are effective. Multiple measures and data sources may be necessary to provide an overall study that is both reliable and valid.[29] Assume a local government initiated a new procedure for handling traffic violations and you are interested in whether or not the new practice is proving effective. Your major task is defining the concept of effectiveness, and you consider three strategies:

1. One indicator would measure effectiveness in terms of the number of violations handled, changes in these over time, numbers of appeals, and amount of fines collected. These indicators would be found in official reports; if the data are reported carefully these reports would be high on reliability.
2. A second indicator would use answers by government workers to a mail survey, asking specific questions about what they do differently under the new procedures and how satisfied they are.
3. A third indicator would rely on firsthand descriptions of the actual practices for handling traffic violations in several locales. You would visit a number of local governments and observe how traffic violations were being handled. You could interview people on-site, asking for their individual impressions of the effectiveness of the procedures. This third choice would probably be higher on validity than the survey, but it would probably be less reliable since another researcher might come to different conclusions or interview different people.

If any two or all three of the sets of indicators were used, drawing on different types of measures, you could be more confident that you had a valid study that gave you insight into the effectiveness of handling traffic violations. The use of multiple measures, and of different kinds of measures, gives you much greater confidence in your results.

Recent research using the Beatles' lyrics illustrates the use of two types of indicators. The study was designed to measure the emotions evoked by Beatles songs, specifically those composed by John Lennon and Paul McCartney.[30] To measure the sadness in the songs, researchers asked individuals to rate the songs of the two composers according to their sadness and pleasantness. Their indicators therefore were subjective views of the pleasantness and sadness of the actual songs. Listeners reported that Lennon wrote less pleasant and sadder lyrics than McCartney, and that over time, both composers' lyrics had become less pleasant and less cheerful. A second researcher designed a follow-up study to test these results using more objective, quantitative measures. She relied on a special dictionary that gave quantitative measures of the emotions associated with hundreds of words based on reports from a large sample of respondents. Using this dictionary, she looked up each of the words in the lyrics of Lennon and McCartney and noted its score on sadness and pleasantness. She found that, as predicted by the first study, Lennon's songs received higher numerical scores on sadness than did those of McCartney and that the lyrics of both had higher scores on sadness over time. Thus the two studies, using different kinds of measures, offered convergent validity for the findings.

In spite of a general agreement that multiple measures are preferable, researchers commonly look for quantitative measures even if these sacrifice some validity. By focusing on what is readily measurable, they may not do justice to abstract concepts and value terms. Remember, however, that you are not measuring the concepts themselves. You are looking for indicators, for measures that point to concepts and variables. Quantitative indicators may tell us something about a complex and qualitative concept even if they do not do it full justice. Recall the discussion of development, an abstract concept that involves increases in people's capacity to bring about social and economic change. In spite of this subtlety, we translated it into several measures for which we could collect concrete and numerical information. Chances are you feel these indicators do not do full justice to the concept of development. Remember, these are simply definitions, terms we assign to point to our concepts, and not reality itself.

The lessons:

1. Be imaginative in using quantitative indicators to get at qualitative concerns.
2. Take quantitative analysis as far as it can go; a little bit of knowledge is not necessarily harmful, and even a little may supplement a discussion of alternatives.
3. Try to identify several kinds of indicators, some higher on validity and some higher on reliability.
4. Remember that there are probably other aspects of your concepts that cannot be easily measured, and in your written analysis and conclusions note what these are.

5. Refine your judgment about the contributions and limitations of assertions that others make. Do not accept the conclusions of a study without noting how the author defines and measures concepts.

Choices in Selecting Measures

So far we have emphasized the importance of finding measures that link concepts to data, and that are valid, reliable, and feasible. There are two other choices that we need to make in selecting measures. One is the level of measurement and the second is the unit of analysis.

Level of Measurement

level of measurement
Amount of information an indicator provides; specifically, whether it tells the interval between cases, merely tells how they are ordered, or tells only categories into which the cases fall.

Level of measurement determines how we analyze the information we collect and what conclusions we can draw. There are three levels which, from the highest to the lowest, are ratio and interval, ordinal, and nominal.

interval measure
A variable based on a common and known unit so that we can tell the interval between different amounts of the variable.

Ratio and interval levels. We begin with the highest level because these are the easiest to understand. Both the ratio and the interval levels mean that a variable can be measured quantitatively according to how many units it contains. The units may be dollars, individuals, miles, guns, or the like. By attaching numbers to the units, we are able to state the extent to which one variable or variable value differs from another. And because we know this difference, we know the interval between the two values or variables. Examples of **interval measures** are "number of people below the poverty line," "dollars spent on defense," and "number of newspapers in a city or country." Sometimes a distinction is made between ratio and interval measures. Technically, **ratio measures** contain a meaningful zero and are used whenever there can be an absence of an item being measured. The zero point allows us to divide numbers into each other and hence derive proportions and percentages. In political analysis virtually all data that can be measured in numbers of units have a zero point, and the two kinds of measures are collapsed under the single rubric of interval-level data.

ratio measure
An interval measure in which it is possible to have zero amount.

Ordinal measures. Sometimes we can say only that one case has more or less of a value than another case has. Then we are using ordinal data that deal with relative values—with more or less—but not with the extent of the interval between them. **Ordinal measures** are used frequently in studying attitudes. A respondent could probably have said whether he was more in favor of Bob Dole or Bill Clinton in the 1996 presidential election, but he probably would have found it difficult to say exactly how much; the opinion cannot be measured at the interval level. If a respondent can say which candidate he likes more, or if he can say whether he approves or disapproves of a candidate, however, his opinion is measurable at the ordinal level.

ordinal measure
A measure allowing us to rank observations according to their order on some dimension but without knowing the number of units in each observation.

Consider another example. A researcher wanted to analyze the participation of Congress members in committees. She could have counted the number of committee meetings they attend to obtain an interval measure. She preferred to develop an ordinal measure that would include more information. So she formulated an ordinal measure in which members were ranked from low to high according to whether they did the following: attended, voted, spoke in meetings as a minor participant, spoke in meetings as a major participant, offered minor amendments, offered major amendments, played a principal agenda-setting role. It is an ordinal scale because each behavior represents a greater level of participation.[31]

nominal measure
A nonquantitative measure that can name a case only according to a category or class, such as region or race.

dichotomy
A division of values into two categories.

polyotomy
A division of values into more than two categories

Nominal measures. Finally, we may distinguish among the values of a variable without being able to attach either numbers or an order to them. In such cases we are working with **nominal measures.** "Gender," "religion," and "geographic region" are common examples of variables that are measured at the nominal level. We cannot measure the interval between male and female, for example. Nor can we say that one gender is more or less than the other. In fact, either of those statements would be meaningless. The term *nominal* means we are assigning names or categories to data rather than determining their order or measuring them in some numerical unit. We can separate nominal categories into those with only two groups and those with more than two groups. In the case of two groups, we have a **dichotomy;** with more than two groups, we have a **polyotomy** (poly means "many"). Because nominal measures do not distinguish among cases according to *more or less* or *how far apart*, we can be least precise about the conclusions we draw from data measured at the nominal level. (Part Four will emphasize the importance of this point by showing that there are limited statistics available for analyzing nominal data. It will also underscore that we can use more powerful statistical tools when we can obtain interval level data.)

Classifications actually are nominal levels of measurement. Classifications should be mutually exclusive; that is, every case should fall into some class. Dividing the United States into the regions of Northeast, Midwest, South, and West is mutually exclusive because each state fits into only one category. Classifications should also be exhaustive in the sense that there is a category for every case. Note the following commonly used classifications. To what extent are they both mutually exclusive and exhaustive?

Classifying by race: white, nonwhite
                                        white, black, Hispanic, other

Classifying by religion: Protestant, Catholic, Jew
                                        Protestant, non-Protestant
                                        Christian, Muslim, Hindu, Buddhist

Classifying by nations: industrialized, nonindustrialized
                                        developed, developing
                                        low-income, lower-middle-income,
                                               upper-middle-income, high-income

Note that there is no single or best way to classify cases. Your choice depends on (1) the most useful distinctions for your specific research question, and (2) the availability of the data that fit the categories.

Examples of Levels of Measurement

1. In chapter 6 (Practice Exercise 6.1) you will analyze information on senators and campaign finances, using variables in the following list. Indicate whether each is measured at the interval, ordinal, or nominal level:

	Measurement Level
Party	_____
Status (incumbent or challenger)	_____
Vote	_____
Percentage of vote	_____
Result of election	_____
Receipts	_____
Disbursements	_____
Money from Pacs	_____

(For Answers, see endnote 32.)[32]

2. Identify the levels of measurement in the following:

   a. List of cities grouped according to the following populations: less than 100,000, 100,000 to 1 million, more than 1 million. _____

   b. Types of bureaucratic behavior: climbers, conservers, zealots, advocates, statesmen.[33] _____

   c. City manager, commission, mayor-council forms of government.
   _____

   d. Social systems classified as organic or mechanical. _____

   e. Expenditures of ten state governments on welfare. _____

   f. Percentage of electoral turnout in the past five elections. _____

   g. Individuals listed as upper, middle, or lower class. _____

   h. National governments described as communist, democratic, or military regimes. _____

   i. Life expectancy figures for a list of countries. _____

   j. Single-party, two-party, and multiparty systems. _____

   k. Presidential roles: chief of state, chief executive, commander in chief, chief diplomat, chief legislator. _____

   l. Legislator as delegate or trustee. _____

(For Answers, see endnote 34).[34]

Selecting Levels of Measurement

Later, when we discuss how to analyze data, the importance of levels of measurement will become more evident. The higher the level—that is, choosing interval over ordinal and ordinal over nominal—the more precise we can be in analyzing the information. For this reason analysts prefer a higher level of measurement. Sometimes, however, a lower level may be sufficient for our purposes. If we are studying changes in the labor force over time, we could use nominal measures to classify workers as unskilled, blue-collar, and white-collar. If we are interested in the political attitudes of employed people, we could use ordinal measures to specify whether workers are more or less conservative. If we are interested in changes in the income of workers, however, we would probably want to collect interval-level data on salaries. As noted repeatedly throughout the book, there is no single right or wrong answer about the level of measurement we should choose. The correct choice depends on our research questions, on the data sets available, and on the kind of analysis we want to carry out.

Measuring Concepts and Variables

Practice Exercise 3.1

Assume that you want to compare how well democratic and authoritarian governments perform in providing social services to their citizens. "Type of government" is the independent variable, with two values: democratic and authoritarian. Providing social services is the dependent variable. We will look at three countries: India, Nigeria, and Venezuela.

1. *Decide how to measure the independent variable.* You could go to an encyclopedia and read a description of each country to find out what kind of government it has. You would find that India and Venezuela have multiparty democracies and that Nigeria has an authoritarian government. These are nominal-level measures.

   You could also find a score for each country on the political freedoms in that country. You could measure type of government by scores on political freedom, in which case you would be using an interval level of measurement. India has a score of 6, Venezuela a score of 7, and Nigeria a score of 4. These scores range from 1 to 10, with 1 indicating the lowest degree of political freedom and 10 the highest.[35] You could also convert these scores to an ordinal measure by coding any country scoring 1 through 5 as low and any country scoring 6 through 10 as high.

2. *Decide how to measure the dependent variable, "providing social services."* You could define this variable operationally by using the measure of infant immunization. On a range of 1 to 10, Nigeria scores 8, India scores 2, and Venezuela scores 8. These are interval-level measures. You could convert them to ordinal measures of low (India) and high (Venezuela).

   You could tabulate these data in a number of ways, including the following:

Social Progress (interval)	Type of Government (nominal)		Social Progress (ordinal)	Extent of Political Freedom (ordinal)		Social Progress (interval)	Extent of Political Freedom (interval)	
	Democratic	*Authoritarian*		*Low*	*High*		*1–5*	*6–10*
1–5			*Low*			*1–5*		
6–10			*High*			*6–10*		

See tables 3.A through 3.D, and be sure you understand why the countries were placed in each cell. Table 3.A includes a nominal-level measure of "type of government" and an ordinal measure of "social progress." Table 3.B includes two ordinal-level measures. Table 3.C presents the data from table 3.B in the form of

PRACTICE TABLE 3.A
Social Progress, by Type of Government

Social Progress	Type of Government	
	Democratic	*Authoritarian*
Low	India	
High	Venezuela	Nigeria

PRACTICE TABLE 3.B
Social Progress, by Political Freedom

Social Progress	Extent of Political Freedom	
	Low	*High*
Low		India
High	Nigeria	Venezuela

PRACTICE TABLE 3.C
Social Progress, by Political Freedom

Social Progress	Extent of Political Freedom	
	Low	*High*
Low		1 (50%)
High	1 (100%)	1 (50%)
	1 (100%)	2 (100%)

PRACTICE TABLE 3.D
Social Progress, by Political Freedom

	Extent of Political Freedom				
Social Progress	*Low* 2	*4*	*6*	*8*	*High* 10
2			India		
4					
6					
8		Nigeria	Venezuela		
10					

percentages rather than by specific countries. Table 3.D is more like a graph, with interval-level measures for both variables. Compare the kinds of information you can gather from each display.

One of the exercises at the end of the chapter asks you to do this same exercise using data on twenty-two countries; there you will be able to select the level of measurement and display that seems most useful to you.

Unit of Analysis

unit of analysis
Smallest element we are studying and about which we wish to generalize; examples are individuals, cities, nation-states.

In addition to selecting the level of measurement, we have to select the **unit of analysis** by which we are going to collect data. Commonly used units are individuals, communities, regions, neighborhoods, cities, and countries. When we ask how an individual voted, the unit of analysis is the individual. When we ask about the overall voter turnout in a city, the unit is the city. When we ask how many Hispanics voted, the unit would be the individual if we asked individual Hispanics if they had voted; alternatively, if we use the turnout figures for voting precincts with high proportions of Hispanic residents, the unit is the voting precinct and not the individual. When we compare voter turnout in California and New York, the unit of analysis is the state. If we compare voter turnout in Great Britain and France, the unit of analysis is the country.

Think of the unit of analysis as the case on which you are going to collect data or which you are going to observe. Perhaps you want to examine the relationship between income level and voting turnout; to do so you would develop table 3.2. What observations or cases will you put into each cell? Individuals? Voting precincts? Whichever you choose, you need to find information on both income and turnout for each observation. If you select voting precincts as your unit, you will need to obtain information on the average per capita income level and on turnout for each precinct.

Your research question and reasonably available data sets will influence the unit of analysis you choose. Researchers who focus on individuals are usually

TABLE 3.2
Voter Turnout by Income

Turnout	Income	
	Low	*High*
Low		
High		

interested in what factors influence individual choices, and they structure their research to compare actions by individuals with different characteristics. They often compare the political activity of whites and blacks, of men and women, or of rich and poor. Researchers who focus on geographical units are more interested in the characteristics of those units and how they influence events. They might compare rural and urban areas, or homogeneous and pluralistic communities, or states with strong and weak party organizations and ask how these characteristics influence the public policies or actions in those units.

Assume you want to study the influences on electoral outcomes. What unit would be appropriate? You could use the individual as your unit of analysis or select a more inclusive unit, such as a state. Research on more inclusive units is often called an **aggregate study** because it examines groups of individuals. Studies that use the individual as their unit of analysis might ask why individuals in the state split their tickets or why they voted for the incumbent. They would compare the votes of different kinds of individuals and would emphasize demographic characteristics of individuals and their attitudes and opinions. Studies that use cities or states as the unit would be more interested in the influence that political variables had on the outcome of the election. They would study such variables as the role of the media in the campaign, the amount of money spent on the campaign, and the issues that were raised in the campaign.

A 1987 study of voting in Democratic party primaries and caucuses used the state as the unit of analysis. The authors specifically decided not to focus on individual choices because they wanted to examine the influence of aggregate-level conditions. They studied the influence of six variables or characteristics of states, which they believe are overlooked because election studies tend to use the individual as the unit of analysis. The six variables include the sociodemographic characteristics of the state, the political context of the state, the economic conditions in the state, the electoral rules in the state, campaign expenditures in the state, and the statewide level of voter participation. The study found that contextual factors, such as the economic and ideological climate in the state, had a major influence on the outcome in states that held primary elections.[36] A study that began with the individual as the unit of analysis would be much less likely to come to that conclusion.

aggregate study
Study of groups of cases; usually involves studying them on only a few dimensions of according to only a few variables.

Identifying Units of Analysis

**Practice
Exercise 3.2**

What is the appropriate unit of analysis for the following cases? Select from individual, family, local jurisdiction, and nation-state. (Answers are in the endnote 37.)[37]

1. Comparison of crime rates in U.S. cities with populations over 50,000.

    _____

2. Actions by state legislatures on ERA. _____

3. Information on type and amount of television news coverage in the United States, Great Britain, France, and Germany. _____

4. Survey of mayors about the unemployment figures in their jurisdictions.

    _____

5. Census data on income and housing conditions. _____

6. Survey to determine attitudes toward arms control. _____

7. Per capita GNP of members of the European Common Market.

    _____

8. Campaign expenditures of senatorial candidates. _____

Where We Are

This chapter has reiterated several themes in the book. First, we need to be as clear and precise as possible in defining our terms and connecting them to empirical evidence. Second, we need to find measures and evidence that are feasible to collect and that are appropriate to our research questions and to the evidence. Third, we should select as precise a set of indicators and levels of measurement as possible assuming they have comparable validity. Fourth, there are many trade-offs in research. Here we have reviewed trade-offs in validity and reliability. Fifth, where possible it is always best to use multiple measures and data sources.

Part Two continues these points, emphasizing alternatives, tradeoffs, and appropriate choices. Chapter 4 reviews several ways to design research. You will see that in some designs the researcher is able to lay out a clear strategy in advance, while in others the process is more open-ended. As with measures, we will look for a design that connects our question to evidence and that is appropriate to our questions. Again, as we concluded in discussing measures, we will find ourselves making trade-offs and trying where possible to use more than one design. The rest of Part Two describes a variety of strategies for exploring relationships in more detail.

NOTES

1. George Gallup, Jr., *The Gallup Poll: Public Opinion, 1995* (Wilmington, Del.: Scholarly Resources, 1996), and other years.
2. George Will, "Conservatism Comes of Age," *Washington Post*, 8 January 1981, p. A17.
3. For example see Table 4, Population and Labor Force, figures for percent in Agriculture. *World Development Report*, Washington D.C.: World Bank, 1996, pp. 194–95.
4. Gabriel Almond and G. Bingham Powell, *Comparative Politics: A Developmental Approach* (Boston: Little, Brown, 1966), p. 198.
5. Robert Clark, *Development and Instability: Political Change in the Non-Western World* (Chicago: Dryden, 1974), pp. 252–253.
6. Giovanni Cornia, Richard Jolly, and Frances Stewart, *Adjustment with a Human Face*, vol. 1 (Oxford: Clarendon Press, 1987).
7. Robert Putnam argues that civic involvement is declining and uses a variety of measures of civic involvement. "The Strange Disappearance of Civic America," *The American Prospect*, (Winter 1996). Michael Schudson suggests that he has a measurement problem. Whereas Putnam asks individuals how many organizations they are involved in, Schudson argues they may belong to fewer organizations but be much more active in them. They may also be active in organizations that don't appear to be civic groups, such as Little League teams. "What If Civic Life Didn't Die?" *The American Prospect* 25 (March 1996): 17–20.
8. A useful, but somewhat dated, source for similar operational definitions is Arthur Banks and Robert Textor, *A Cross-Country Survey* (Cambridge, Mass.: MIT Press, 1963).
9. "Extent of electoral competition": Democratic regime; "Newspaper circulation": Literacy, Political development.
10. Samuel Beer, *Britain against Itself: The Political Contradiction of Collectivism* (New York: Norton, 1982).
11. Ted Gurr, *Polimetrics* (Englewood Cliffs, N.J.: Prentice-Hall, 1972), pp. 43–48; David and Chava Nachmias, *Research Methods in the Social Sciences*, 2nd ed. (New York: St. Martin's Press, 1981), pp. 140–146.
12. Barbara Crossette, "Globally, Majority Rules," *New York Times*, 4 August 1996, p. 1.
13. George T. Kurian, *Encyclopedia of the Third World*, 3 vols. (New York: Facts on File, 1992). Ted Robert Gurr, *Polity II: Political Structures and Regime Change, 1800–1996* (Ann Arbor, Mich.: Inter-University Consortium for Political and Social Research, 1990).
14. *Amnesty International Reports* for each year, London: Amnesty International. The U.S. State Department also issues annual *Country Reports on Human Rights Practices*.
15. Edward Mansfield and Jack Snyder, "Democratization and the Danger of War," *International Security* 20, no. 1 (Summer 1995), p. 8.
16. Ibid., p. 9.
17. Robert L. Lineberry, *Equality and Urban Policy* (Beverly Hills: Sage, 1977).
18. Reported in U.S. Bureau of the Census, *Metropolitan Area Statistics* (Washington D.C. Government Printing Office) annually.
19. Irving Janis, *Groupthink* (New York: Houghton Mifflin, 1982).
20. Ibid, pp. 7–9.

21. Brian Jenkins, "International Terrorism: A New Mode of Conflict," Research Paper No. 48, California Seminar on Arms Control and Foreign Policy (Los Angeles: Crescent Publications, 1975), p. 1.

22. Andrew Hacker, "Who Killed ERA? Women, Not Men," *Washington Post*, 14 September 1980, pp. C1, C3.

23. Art Pine, "Jobless Data: Modest Changes," *Washington Post*, 2 September 1979, p. A1. For the definition of employment, see Bureau of Labor Statistics, *Handbook of Methods* (Washington, D.C.: U.S. Government Printing Office, 1971), p. 8.

24. John M. Berry, "When Productivity and Income Numbers Don't Add Up," *Washington Post*, 20 February 1997, p. C1.

25. Philip Hilton, "White House Uses Social Sciences, but Cuts Funding for Research," *Washington Post*, 29 June 1981, p. A15.

26. *Washington Post*, 9 January 1992, p. A15.

27. Lineberry, *Equality and Urban Policy*, p. 67.

28. *Defense Monitor* (Washington, D.C.: Center for Defense Information, June 1979), p. 8.

29. Carol Weiss and Theodore Fuller, "On Evaluating Development Assistance Projects," *Evaluation Review* 7, no. 2 (April 1983), pp. 175–190.

30. Cynthia Whissell, "Traditional and Emotional Stylometric Analysis of the Songs of Beatles Paul McCartney and John Lennon," *Computers and the Humanities* 30 (1996), pp. 257–265.

31. Richard L. Hall, "Participation and Purpose in Committee Decision Making," *American Political Science Review* 81, no. 1 (March 1987): 105–120.

32. Party—nominal, status—nominal, vote—interval, percentage of vote—interval, result of election—ordinal, receipts—interval, disbursements—interval, money from PACs—interval.

33. Anthony Downs, *Inside Bureaucracy* (Boston: Little, Brown, 1967), pp. 79–111.

34. 1. ordinal: 2. nominal; 3. nominal; 4. nominal; 5. interval; 6. interval; 7.ordinal; 8. nominal; 9. interval; 10. ordinal; 11. nominal; 12. nominal.

35. The scores assigned in this paragraph and those in the next (on immunization) can be found in *Human Suffering Index* (Washington, D.C.: Population Crisis Committee, 1991).

36. T. Wayne Parent, Calvin Jillson, and Ronald Weber, "Voting Outcomes in the 1984 Democratic Party Primaries and Caucuses," *American Political Science Review* 81, no. 1 (March 1987): 67–82.

37. Answers to questions about unit of analysis: 1. city; 2. state; 3. country; 4. city; 5. family; 6. individual; 7. country; 8. individual.

EXERCISES

Exercise 3.1 Exploring Resources

Go to the *Statistical Abstract* and find the following:

1. How will the United States population change in the next sixty-five years? Base your answer on resident population projections from 1995 to 2050.

2. What was the infant mortality rate in 1996 for the United States? For your state?

3. How many individuals earned higher education degrees in 1950, 1960, 1970, 1980, 1990?

4. Find one other table that is of particular interest to you.

Exercise 3.2 Defining Concepts

Three commonly used political concepts are adherence to family values, violent society, national strength. For each of these do the following:

1. Give a conceptual definition.

2. Transform the definition into an empirical proposition.

3. Specify at least one variable that could be used to define it.

4. Give two operational definitions or indicators of this variable.

5. Comment on the validity of the indicators, showing you are aware of its strengths and weaknesses.

6. Suggest some instruments or data sets you might be able to use.

Exercise 3.3 Considering Measures of Educational Quality

Observers frequently comment on the low quality of education in the United States. They typically use such information as the following. Comment on the validity of these measures.

1. One-half of a national sample of college upper-class students were unable to perform cognitive tasks at a high school level; three-quarters of the faculty surveyed in a recent poll felt that their students did not meet minimum preparation standards. R. Benjamin, *The Redesign of Governance in Higher Education*, Rand Corporation, February 1993, p. 9.

2. A 1987 Gallup Poll of more than 700 college seniors found that 24 percent said that Columbus arrived in the New World after 1500; 23 percent thought that the statement, "From each according to his ability, to each according to his need" was from the U.S. Constitution.

3. The American Council on Education found that only 15 percent of universities require tests for general knowledge; only 17 percent for critical thinking, and only 19 percent for minimal competency.

4. A survey found that 50 percent of major corporations must hire people to teach college graduates how to write memos and perform relatively simple computations.

5. Numbers of graduates, faculty/student ratios, dollars spent per student, grades earned.

Exercise 3.4 Finding Indicators for Public Policies

States and local governments have been mandated to assume responsibility for helping those on welfare find work.

1. State an obvious and relatively easy indicator that you could use to determine how well the state is performing this mandate.

2. Anticipate the kinds of problems that could arise in carrying out the mandate. What indicators could you use to determine how well the state is coping with such problems?

Exercise 3.5 Measuring Democracy

Assume you work for a Congressman who has said he will oppose sending any more assistance to Haiti unless there is evidence that country is a democracy. He asks you to look for such evidence.

1. What information would you try to find for him? (Review discussion in text.)

2. Is there some information you would need to get from firsthand observers?

Exercise 3.6 Nominal and Ordinal Measures

1. Which of the following is a nominal measure? Religious affiliation, annual income, voter turnout, annual exports.

2. Which of the following is an ordinal measure? State per capita income, state rankings on innovativeness, religious affiliation, temperature.

Exercise 3.7 Selecting Indicators and Levels of Measurement

This exercise asks you to explore the hypothesis "Democracies have a better record of economic performance than do authoritarian regimes." "Economic performance" and "type of government" (democratic or authoritarian) are the variables. The tables that follow give information on twenty-two countries. Review the data and decide which indicators you want to use as measures of these two variables. Then decide what level of measurement you wish to use to report them. Develop tables to report the data. Finally, analyze whether the results support the hypothesis. Your discussion should indicate how valid and reliable you feel the measures are.

1. The data in table 3.3 are at the nominal level and describe the variable "type of government." Some of the countries are listed as liberal democracies, some as emerging democracies, some as nationalistic socialist systems, some as authoritarian nationalist systems, and some as military authoritarian systems. Decide whether to count both of the first two categories as democracies, whether to keep all of the categories separate, or

TABLE 3.3

Dominant Form of Government of Twenty-Two Selected Developing Countries

Country	Dominant Form of Government	Country	Dominant Form of Government
Bolivia	Liberal Democracy	Pakistan	Emerging Democracy
Brazil	Liberal Democracy	Peru	Liberal Democracy
Chile	Emerging Democracy	Philippines	Emerging Democracy
Colombia	Liberal Democracy	Saudi Arabia	Absolutist
India	Federal Republic	Sri Lanka	Liberal Democracy
Indonesia	Authoritarian Nationalist	Romania	Emerging Democracy
Kenya	Authoritarian Nationalist	Tanzania	Nationalistic Socialism
Malaysia	Liberal Democracy	Thailand	Emerging Democracy
Mexico	Liberal Democracy	Tunisia	Emerging Democracy
Morocco	Emerging Democracy	Uruguay	Liberal Democracy
Nigeria	Military Authoritarian	Venezuela	Liberal Democracy

Source: Derbyshire, J. Denis and Derbyshire, Ian. *Political Systems of the World*, (New York: St. Martin's Press, 1996).

whether to collapse the categories some other way. After you make your decisions note how each country scores using this indicator.

2. The data in table 3.4 are interval and also describe the variable "type of government." How could you use this information to measure type of government? Select one of these measures and divide the countries into low, medium, and high on this score. Note how each country scores using this indicator.

3. The data in table 3.5 give several indicators of economic performance at the interval level of measurement. Select one and divide the countries into three categories: low, medium and high. Note how each country scores on this variable.

TABLE 3.4

Indicators of Political Freedom in Twenty-Two Selected Developing Countries, 1991

Country	Political Freedom Index	Civil Rights Index	Country	Political Freedom Index	Civil Rights Index
Bolivia	8	5	Pakistan	5	2
Brazil	7	4	Peru	3	3
Chile	8	7	Philippines	7	4
Colombia	5	3	Romania	0	0
India	6	2	Saudi Arabia	0	1
Indonesia	4	2	Sri Lanka	5	1
Kenya	1	2	Tanzania	2	4
Malaysia	4	3	Thailand	3	4
Mexico	5	3	Tunisia	1	3
Morocco	4	2	Uruguay	9	7
Nigeria	4	4	Venezuela	7	4

Source: *The International Human Suffering Index* (Washington, D.C.: Population Crisis Committee, 1992). Based on data compiled by Freedom House, New York City.

Note: Indexes range from 1 through 10, with 10 representing greatest freedom.

TABLE 3.5

Indicators of Economic Performance of Twenty-Two Selected Third-World States, 1994

Country	Gross National Product (GNP) (Millions U.S. $)	GNP Per Capita (U.S. $)	GNP annual Rate of Growth 1985–1994	Life Expectancy (Years)
Bolivia	5,544	770	1.7	60
Brazil	472,527	2,970	−0.4	67
Chile	49,280	3,520	6.5	72
Colombia	60,621	1,670	2.4	70
India	292,352	320	2.9	62
Indonesia	167,552	880	6.0	63
Kenya	6,500	250	0.0	59
Malaysia	68,556	3,480	5.6	71
Mexico	369,930	4,180	0.9	71
Morocco	30,096	1,140	1.2	65
Nigeria	30,240	280	1.2	52
Pakistan	54,309	430	1.3	60
Peru	48,952	2,110	−2.0	65
Philippines	63,650	950	1.7	65
Romania	28,829	1,270	−4.5	70
Saudi Arabia	125,490	7,050	−1.7	70
Sri Lanka	11,456	640	2.9	72
Tanzania	4,032	140	.8	51
Thailand	139,780	2,410	8.6	69
Tunisia	15,752	1,790	2.1	68
Uruguay	14,912	4,660	2.9	73
Venezuela	58,512	2,760	0.7	71

Source: *World Development Report*, 1996 (Washington, D.C.: World Bank, 1996), Table 1, pp. 188–189.

4. Now create two tables as follows: (Make any needed adjustments in the layout depending on how you chose to measure your variables.)

Economic Performance by Form of Government
Form of Government

	Liberal democracies	Emerging democracies	Authoritarian regimes
Low			
Medium			
High			

(Economic Performance on vertical axis)

Economic Performance by Political Freedom
Political Freedom

	Low	Medium	High
Low			
Medium			
High			

(Economic Performance on vertical axis)

5. Place each country in the appropriate cell and draw conclusions based on the results. Experiment with using different indicators and see if the results vary. One of the purposes of this exercise is to illustrate that selecting measures often involves imperfect choices and judgment calls on your part. Think through your choices, be able to defend them, and indicate any trade-offs or compromises you make.

PART TWO

Designing Research to Answer Our Questions

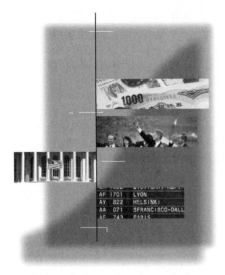

Part One examined two purposes for research—description and explanation. We noted that all of us have descriptions and possible explanations in mind as we think about political events. The major purpose of this book is to help us be more systematic in developing and examining them. We also linked explanations to the ongoing process of theory building and theory testing in our own efforts and in the literature of political science. Theories can be useful because they enable us to go beyond individual observations and look at connections among political events, exploring the logic that links them. We talked about the importance of formulating questions that focus on what we want to know, rather than simply studying general topics. Thus if you were doing a study for a class on elections, it would be preferable to ask why voting turnout in the United States has declined, rather than simply to say that you are studying participation or voting. We practiced turning such questions into research propositions, and where appropriate into hypotheses. Hypotheses and the terms they contain—variables—link our research questions to empirical evidence. This linkage, however, depends on finding appropriate definitions and measures for our variables—measures that achieve a balance between telling us what we want to know and being easy to replicate.

Part Two turns to designing research to answer these questions. You will see that there is no single way to carry out research, that there are different approaches, depending on your question, your interests and available resources. This opportunity to make choices adds considerably to the challenge and potential creativity of the research process. You need to learn about your range of options and then be clear and consistent in the strategy you choose.

Chapter 4 considers four ways to design research so that your strategy is appropriate to specific questions and the available evidence. Chapters 5 and 6 explore several ways to explore relationships, the heart of much political research and analysis. We invite you to consider a variety of relationships, applying insights and theories from a number of fields of study to enrich your understanding of politics and to look at political events in new ways.

CHAPTER FOUR

Alternative Research Designs

One day when I was a junior medical student, a very important Boston surgeon visited the school and delivered a great treatise on a large number of patients who had undergone successful operations for vascular reconstruction. At the end of the lecture, a young student at the back of the room timidly asked, "Do you have any controls?" Well, the great surgeon drew himself up to his full height, hit the desk, and said, "Do you mean did I not operate on half of the patients?" The hall grew very quiet then. The voice at the back of the room very hesitantly replied, "Yes, that's what I had in mind." Then the visitor's fist really came down as he thundered, "Of course not. That would have doomed half of them to their death." God, it was quiet then, and you could scarcely hear the small voice ask, "Which half?"

—E. E. Peacock, Jr., M.D., chairman of surgery, University of Arizona College of Medicine, cited in Edward Tufte, *Data Analysis for Politics and Policy.*

Designing a Strategy to Answer Our Research Questions

Up to this point we have discussed research propositions and relationships between two variables. We considered how some propositions can be restated as hypotheses so they can be tested empirically and how some can be stated as comparisons between two or more units or cases. We also began to explore different kinds of measures and data sets and the importance of finding appropriate measures. This chapter considers these same issues from a slightly different perspective—namely how we design our research to answer our questions. It describes four different designs and emphasizes that each has its strengths and that no single design is better than the others for every purpose. As with selecting measures, we will find that different designs are stronger on validity and reliability criteria and that in selecting among them we inevitably need to make trade-offs. You should choose a design that helps you answer the question you are interested in and that is feasible in your situation. Chapter 14 will return to this point and encourage you to develop alternative designs for researching your questions. We begin here by exploring the logic behind several designs and the trade-offs among them.

The most formal design is the *experiment*. One group of cases is treated in a special way, such as receiving a new training program. The research question would be, "Does the treatment make a difference?" To answer the question you would compare those who received the treatment with a similar, untreated group. If the two groups differ only in whether or not they receive the treatment (the independent variable), you could determine whether or not the treatment, or training in this case, made a difference. Experiments, therefore, have the advantage that they can establish causality. Their major disadvantage is that it is difficult to find or create two groups that are similar. A second design, the *quasi-experiment*, or *natural experiment*, studies the effects of a treatment in a natural or field setting. This design is typically more feasible to carry out; but because it is less rigorous, it is harder to draw conclusions about the effect of the treatment, or independent variable. A third design, called *correlation*, collects data on a large number of events or observations to determine whether there is an overall tendency for two or more variables to be related. A fourth design is the *case study*. It is more concerned with gaining a fuller understanding of a case than in establishing causality although it can be useful in suggesting possible causes. The chapter stresses that cases can be carried out in a systematic way and can complement the other designs.

The following descriptions of these designs explain their logic, offer examples, and conclude by discussing their validity. Validity includes both internal validity and external validity. **Internal validity** indicates whether a study answers the questions we are asking and whether the conclusions follow from the study. **External validity** refers to the generalizability of a study and the extent to which it tells us something about other cases and phenomena beyond those being studied.

internal validity
Extent to which conclusions follow from a study.

external validity
Extent to which a study applies to other cases and phenomena beyond those being studied.

Experiments

The Logic of Experiments

Let's say you were sick on Wednesday, took some medicine, and got well by Friday. Did the medicine actually cure you? You might have gotten better anyway, or maybe going to bed early on Wednesday helped you to recover. In this example, the dependent variable is the state of your health ("well" or "ill") and the independent variable is the medicine ("taking it" or "not taking it"). Did the medicine bring about the change in your health? The problem in answering this question is that by considering only this one event, you cannot really determine the medicine's effect. You are left with the quip that "proper treatment will cure a cold in seven days, but left to itself a cold will hang on for a week."[1]

You could, however, conduct an experiment. You begin by identifying twenty people with colds, making sure the subjects are generally similar, that is, about the same age and in otherwise good health. Give the medicine to ten of the people (the experimental group), and then a few days later compare the health of these ten with the health of the ten who did not receive the medicine. The comparison allows you to determine whether there is a relationship between taking the medicine and recovery from the cold. If the same proportion of each group recover, you can conclude that the medicine was not important; if only those in the experimental group improve, then the medicine did appear to make a difference. More than likely, the differences will not be so clear-cut; perhaps eight of those who receive the medicine get better and three of those who do not receive the medicine get better. It still seems that the medicine makes a difference, but the results are not totally explained by the medicine.

experiment
A strategy to test the effect of an independent variable by applying it to one group of cases but not to a second.

controlling
Examining a relationship for different values of a third, or control, variable.

Controls. In an **experiment,** something is done to a case or group of cases. The purpose is to find out whether this action, which becomes the independent variable, makes a difference, or brings about a change in a dependent variable. To draw that conclusion, we need to observe whether there is a change, and if there is, to rule out other causes of the change. We can rule out other possible causes by **controlling** for them. That is, we hold other variables constant by not letting them vary or change. In the example experiment about the effect of medicine, you were told to select two groups of ten people who were similar in all important respects, such as age and general health. Choosing people of the same age and health means controlling for age and health by holding them constant. The only difference in the two groups is that one group received medicine and the other did not. The group that did not receive the medicine is called the *control* group.

Random distribution of units across groups. The key element in experiments is their capacity for controlling for, or eliminating the influence of, variables other than the treatment you are interested in. You want to be able to conclude that nothing else changed and produced the result you observe. There are essentially three ways to apply controls in an experiment. In one strategy we select two groups in which characteristics relevant to the study are already *randomly* distributed. Through this technique all other influences are randomly distributed between the two groups and thus are controlled for, or removed, as possible influences.

For instance, a faculty member wants to determine if students learn research methods better when they participate in group research projects as opposed to individual projects. Group projects here is the treatment, or independent, variable, and learning is the dependent variable. The faculty member is teaching two course sections in research methods and decides to conduct an experiment by using group projects in one of the courses and not in the other. The validity of her experiment to determine which style is more effective depends on how similar the students in the two sections are. If the section assigned group projects meets at night while the other meets in the day, the characteristics of the students in the two classes might differ. Perhaps older, returning students are more apt to take the evening course; their relative maturity might have considerable influence on their performance, irrespective of whether the teacher assigns group projects. In such a case, the two courses would have different types of students, and the faculty member would not have an effective control group. If both are daytime sections, however, it is probably safe to assume that the students are randomly distributed in the two sections and hence that the two groups are essentially the same.

Assigning units to groups. Whereas the first strategy assumes the students have randomly distributed themselves, a second strategy relies on *assigning* individuals at random to two groups. For example, researchers want to determine the effectiveness of two different ways of providing services in a clinic. They establish two clinics with alternative services and receive permission to assign both patients and medical personnel at random to the two clinics. They might assign every other person who applies to group A and the others to group B. The randomness allows them to assume that the two groups are essentially similar and that the only difference would be the method of treatment in each clinic.

Matching groups. Sometimes we cannot assume people have randomly distributed themselves, and it is also difficult to assign people randomly to groups. A third control strategy begins by listing other possible influences; these are the characteristics you want to control for. Then select two groups that *match* each other on these characteristics. Again, you are controlling for these characteristics by holding them constant. To proceed with the example of clinics, you could decide that income, education, and existing health of those receiving services are important characteristics and could influence how effective the clinics are in providing services. You could then select a group in each clinic that has similar (i.e., is matched on) income, education, and health.

Examples of Experimental Design

Random assignment to groups. The following series of experiments illustrates the challenges in carrying out studies with random assignment. The studies compare majors in economics with students in other disciplines; thus the independent variable is the major field of study, economics or noneconomics, a nominal variable. The dependent variable is the extent of cooperative or self-interested behavior. The research question is whether majors in economics are less apt to be cooperative and more apt than students in other disciplines to follow the self-interest maxim, a core assumption in classical economic theory.

The first example is a hypothetical, "what-if" experiment in which students were asked to divide an imagined sum of money into two accounts, one public and the other private. The experiment was structured so that the whole group would gain if more money was put into the public account, while individuals would gain if they put their money into their own private account. The result: economics students put an average of 20 percent of their funds into the public account, while the noneconomics students put in an average of 49 percent.[2] One could conclude that the economics students were indeed more self-interested. However, one could not conclude that this difference was due to their study of economics unless the two groups were similar in every respect except their major. In fact this was not the case. The economics students were graduates and almost all male. The control group of noneconomics students were from high school and undergraduate study and a mixture of male and female, potentially important differences. Thus it is possible that the factors of age or gender could explain the finding that economic majors put more money into private accounts.[3]

Another hypothetical experiment concerned with the same question was conducted with undergraduates at Cornell University. An ethical dilemma was posed to two groups of students in introductory economics courses and to a control group in an introductory astronomy course. Students were told to imagine a case in which a lost envelope with $100 and the owner's name and address is found. They were asked first to imagine that they had lost the envelope and to estimate how likely *others* would be to return it, and second to imagine they had found such a letter and to estimate how likely *they* would be to return it. Thus the dependent variable was degrees of honesty. Students were assumed to be more "honest" according to whether they thought a stranger would return their money and whether they said they would return a stranger's money.

The design of the experiment controlled for two other factors. The students were asked to answer these questions at the beginning of the semester and then at the end of the semester. The purpose of this repetition was to determine not only if the three groups differed, but also whether the two groups taking the economics course became less likely to engage in "honest" behavior after studying economics.[4] This was a more elaborate design in that the researchers were comparing students *before and after* the study of economics and also *with and without* the study of economics. The results were consistent with the researchers' expectations that the study of economics does lead students to make "less honest" responses. Students in all three classes scored as less honest at the end of the semester, but those in the astronomy course were less honest to a much smaller degree. Again the question is whether the students were randomly distributed across the three courses and hence similar. The researchers concluded they were by noting that students gave very similar answers in the initial questionnaire at the beginning of the semester.[5]

Other researchers argued that these studies were limited because the experiments relied on class exercises rather than real-world behavior. To study actual behavior they carried out a "lost-letter" experiment. Envelopes containing ten $1 dollar bills were left lying in classrooms. The envelopes had a name and address on the front and a letter inside suggesting the money was repayment for a loan. Letters were left in thirty-two upper-level economics courses and in thirty-two upper-level history, political science, and psychology courses over the course of a year. Presumably students were randomly distributed across the classes so that the only difference was the subject matter of the course. Fifty-six percent of the letters left in economics classes were returned, while only 31 percent of the letters left in the other courses were returned. The authors concluded that this real-life experiment gave a different view of economics students. And because randomness was more likely in this study, it was more valid than the simulated experiments described earlier.[6]

Assigning units to groups. In this type of experiment, subjects are assigned to experimental and control groups in a manner to ensure the groups are similar. As an example, a recent experiment sought to determine whether negative campaigning has any effect on voting turnout.[7] Researchers established three groups each of which was shown a different ad: one with a negative message about a candidate, one with a positive message about a candidate, and one with a product advertisement having nothing to do with any candidate. Individuals were given a questionnaire at the outset to determine such factors as how likely they were to vote, their level of political interest, and socioeconomic characteristics. After watching one of the three ads they filled out a second questionnaire asking about their intent to vote, their attitude toward the campaign, their interest in voting, and so forth.

The key to the experiment was to ensure that all three groups were similar in every respect except their exposure to a different "treatment" or ad. To accomplish this the researchers, through local newspapers, invited people to participate in a study of local news programs. Individuals signed up and were assigned at random to one of three groups, each of which was shown one of the ads. The results confirmed the research hypothesis that negative campaigning has an impact, albeit a small one, on turnout. Of those who saw the positive ad, 64 percent said they intended to vote; of those who saw the product ad, 61 percent indicated an intent to vote; and of those who saw the negative campaign ad, only 58 percent said they intended to vote.

The researchers went one step farther and asked how the ads compared with other influences on turnout decisions. First, they examined whether party made a difference, that is, whether people responded to the ads according to their party affiliation. They found no evidence to support this hypothesis. Second, they examined whether the negative ad led people to feel negatively about both candidates and thus discouraged them from voting. Again they found no evidence to support this hypothesis. Third, they asked whether the negative ad seemed to create general political cynicism, which turned people off from voting. An analysis of the questionnaire results supported this hypothesis, leading them to conclude that "exposure to campaign attacks makes voters disenchanted with the business of politics as usual."[8]

Matching groups. A third strategy to ensure that the groups receiving the experimental treatment and the control groups are similar is used when random selection and assignment are not possible; it involves matching the groups on important characteristics. The researcher lists the characteristics of the subjects that are relevant to the study and selects a control and a test group that are matched or similar on these characteristics. A 1997 public policy study on the incidence of childhood cancer near electric power lines followed this strategy. Researchers found 638 children with a common form of cancer. They then identified 620 children of the same age, gender, race, and living conditions, who became the control group. For each child in both groups the researchers measured the magnetic electrical fields in their living areas. They found no correlations between electrical power lines and cancer.[9]

An interesting example of the use of the matching technique is an experiment that was carried out in Kansas City, Kansas, to determine how to improve the efficiency of the police force. The city wanted to know whether increasing police patrols would reduce crime. Crime was thus the dependent variable, and the number of police patrols was the independent variable. The researchers obviously could not assume people in different police districts were similar, nor could they randomly assign people to police districts. Instead they tried a matching strategy. They selected fifteen police beats in neighborhoods representing a variety of income levels. Three of the beats were in low-income neighborhoods that were generally similar, three were in neighborhoods one notch up in income, and so forth for five different income levels. In five of the beats, one from each income level, they assigned the regular number of patrols; in five they assigned additional patrols; and in five they reduced the patrols. This arrangement allowed for three different treatments, or three values of the independent variable (fewer patrols, same, more patrols), and applied each value to a matched set of beats.

The results were surprising. There was no difference in crime rate among the different beats. The number of patrols did not affect the incidence of crime, citizen attitudes, or police response rates.[10] The Kansas City experiment was a model type of experiment because it was possible to manipulate the independent variable—number of police patrols—and to examine the effects of changing this single factor. This simple step allowed the researchers to ask whether changes in the number of patrols preceded changes in the crime rate. In addition, by carefully controlling for different kinds of neighborhoods, the researchers were able to minimize the effects of other factors: all three levels of patrolling were tried in a poor neighborhood, for example. This process controlled for the effects of poverty and showed that any differences in crime rates were likely due to changes in the level of patrol force. (While this was a well-designed experiment, and while the results were unambiguous, it is worth noting that recent efforts in the mid-1990s to increase the number of patrols does seem to reduce crime in large cities such as New York. Thus the question of police deployment remains an important research question.)

Validity and experimental designs. While the logic of experiments is straightforward and the results can be compelling, experiments can pose serious validity problems. Internal validity asks whether the conclusions of the experiment reflect what actually occurred during the experiment. Unexpected events may influence the results; for instance, an inflammatory incident may occur close to the time an experiment is being conducted on racial attitudes. People may change during the course of an experiment; for example, they may mature in their understanding of an issue quite apart from the actual experiment. If the experiment is repeated, they may learn something from their initial experiences. People may drop out of either the experimental or the control group, a problem particularly acute for those in control groups.[11]

It is also hard to match the groups or to assign units randomly, making it difficult to be certain that the two groups are similar in all important respects.

It is rare to find people randomly distributing themselves, since they usually congregate with people like themselves. For example, if there are several sections of a university course, friends will often sign up for the same section, or athletes will tend to pick a section that does not interfere with athletic schedules. Similarly, it is difficult to get officials to agree to assign people at random to different groups. For instance, people may prefer a public school near their home, or one school may have a better reputation than another. They would strongly resist being assigned to a school that is farther away or one that does not have a positive reputation for the sake of experimental research. Finally, if we are trying to match two groups on major factors, it is easy to overlook some element that we hadn't anticipated. Any of these factors can compromise the internal validity of an experiment, making it difficult to draw clear and certain conclusions about the effect of the treatment variable.[12]

External validity refers to the generality of the results of the experiment—can the results be generalized to a larger group of cases outside of the experiment? Even if the results are valid for the experiment itself, does this tell us anything about units or relationships beyond the experiment? The major problem is that the treatment may be effective only within the context of the study. If a teacher does an experiment in a class setting and finds that a particular teaching technique makes a difference, one could always ask whether its effectiveness was dependent on other factors such as the atmosphere that had been established within that class or the personality of the teacher. The results could be very different in a different course setting or with a different instructor. External validity problems arise also with experiments that are conducted using college students as subjects, such as those testing the effect of majoring in economics. To what extent are the responses of college students a valid indicator of how other groups of people respond? Even more generally we have to ask whether any subjects would behave the same in reality as they do in an artificial situation or in a temporary experimental situation.[13]

Most of these validity problems can be avoided through rigorous controls and truly random assignment to the control and treatment groups. The problem is that these may be difficult, expensive, and time consuming to carry out in practice, thus compromising the conclusions from the experiment. There has been a decline in large-scale experiments to test social policies such as school vouchers, welfare benefits, and job training. The results are seldom clear-cut, and the designs are too easy to criticize. In the meantime, experiments can be useful on a smaller scale such as the classroom experiments described earlier, especially if they are supplemented by other designs.

Quasi-Experiments

The Logic of Quasi-Experiments

Experiments work best when the researcher is able to define the proposed cause, control who or what is affected by the experiment, and determine the control group. But as already noted, these conditions are often hard to fulfill. Analysts have developed a variation on experiments called **quasi-experiments,** because they meet some but not all of the conditions of an experiment. They are also called *natural,* or *field, experiments,* because they occur naturally—in the field, so to speak—rather than being contrived by the researcher. A quasi-experiment design can be used, for example, when a policy has been put into effect and the researcher examines what the result is, just as in an experiment. Because the policy is already ongoing, however, it is not possible to limit who is affected by the policy or to compare those affected with a similar control group. The design problem is still how to find ways to control for other variables that could also have caused the results, but this is harder when the researcher is working with a naturally occurring event and not a contrived one.

There are essentially two strategies for carrying out controls in a quasi-experiment. The first looks for a comparison group but recognizes that the two groups are probably not similar in all respects. This group is referred to as a **nonequivalent comparison group.** The second strategy is a *before-and-after strategy* and compares the characteristics or behavior of some unit before an action was taken with the characteristics or behavior of the unit after the action. The point in both is to see if the intervention or action or policy caused a change in the target population. The researcher has to determine the amount and nature of the change, as well as show whether other factors played a role in bringing about the change. Typically, a new policy may cause such a change, but other factors will also play a role. The research challenge is to sort out their relative importance.

Examples of Quasi-Experiments

Nonequivalent comparison group. This approach is also called a *cross section analysis* because it compares two or more groups. It is a *quasi* rather than a true experiment because you have little control over the composition of the two groups. The validity of the results, however, varies according to how similar the two groups are in every respect except the treatment or policy change or changed circumstance. Assume that you are studying the effects of a job training program—the independent variable. You want to know if the graduates earn more money and are more apt to retain their jobs—the dependent variable—than would be the case if they had not received the training. Typically, individuals apply for such training, so random assignment is not feasible. You could set up a *nonequivalent comparison group* study by comparing the earnings and job retention of trainees with the earnings and job history of individuals who are similar in age, gender, and work motivation but who did not receive any training. It will probably be impossible to ensure that the two groups are really similar to those who received the training, however. The more similar they are, the more confidence you can have in your results.

Consider a study of the effects of auto inspections on highway safety. Edward Tufte compared the fatality rates in states that require inspections with those that do not. He was not conducting an experiment because he had no control over which states require inspections. The comparison is limited because other factors besides inspections may enter in. Even if those states that require inspections have lower fatality rates, they may also have other characteristics, such as a public safety program or safer roads, either of which could reduce fatality rates. The challenge in this design is to compare the two groups, and then through creative analysis figure out the importance of other factors.

Tufte, who began by comparing the characteristics of states with very high and very low fatality rates, found that the latter were more likely to have required auto inspections. He then asked if the fatality rates were typical or unusual and looked at the fatality rates over several years. He found they were consistent, that states with a high number of fatalities tended to have these high numbers over a number of years. Thus he eliminated accidents of history. Tufte still wanted to determine if other factors such as bad weather had caused the higher fatality rates. He thought of all the factors that could have an impact on auto fatalities, such as density of the state, typical weather patterns, and so on. After considering which of these might be most important, he focused on population density. He controlled for density by comparing the fatality rates in high-density states with those in low-density states and concluded that while the difference is not large, inspections do reduce fatalities.[14] Note that he did not find that inspections made all the difference, nor that density had no influence. Rather, density played a role in the number of fatalities—the greater the density the higher the fatalities—but inspections also reduced their number.

Before-and-after design. This design compares the same units before and after experiencing some treatment or event rather than looking for a comparison group. The design is relatively easy to carry out, and it requires only that you be in a position to collect some information about the case or cases prior to the treatment as well as after. Without a comparison group, however, it is difficult to separate the effects of the treatment from other influences. The key is to ask if anything else happened during this same period that could have led to the result.

before-after
Compare a thing before and after an event or treatment to determine the effect of the event or treatment

The following example is based on a before-after design and also uses information on auto fatalities. The study combines a time series design with some of the features of the nonequivalent comparison group.[15] In 1955 Governor Abraham Ribicoff of Connecticut observed that traffic fatalities were very high that year. He hypothesized that the cause was highway speeding and ordered the state police to crack down on drivers exceeding the speed limit. Subsequently, fatalities declined from 324 in 1955 to 284 in 1956, and the governor declared his policy was a success. Given these figures, would you agree with his assessment? Do the results support his original hypothesis?

The answer depends largely on our ability to determine whether or not other factors could have caused the decrease in traffic deaths in 1956. What if a severe winter had been the real cause of the higher number of fatalities in 1955? If that was the case, then improved weather would explain the reduction of fatalities. To determine whether this was the case, we need to separate the effects of the speeding crackdown from those of the weather. One possible procedure is to gather data on states that experienced similar winter weather as a way to control for the effects of weather. Differences between those states and Connecticut could then be attributed to the latter's crackdown on speeders. It is reasonable to assume that adjoining states had similar weather, and thus we can control for weather by collecting accident data from the adjoining states. We can diagram the design as in table 4.1. The research design isolates the effect of the crackdown from weather and makes it easier to determine how much actual impact the speeding policy had. The adjoining states are essentially a matched control group.

A variation on a before-after study looks at several points of time prior to and subsequent to the treatment. Such multiple observations help to rule out alternative influences or explanations for an outcome. During the 1960s the Centers for Disease Control began a national program to eradicate measles and made grants to state and local health agencies to pay for immunization. By 1972 a long series of data was available on cases of measles by four-week periods. Because they could refer to these trends, researchers were able to determine the role of alternative influences and show that on balance the immunization program had been effective. Once again the researcher usually ends by showing how much influence the policy change or experimental factor has, in comparison to other influences. Seldom in the social and political arenas do we find that a single factor makes all or even most of the difference in results.

Validity and Quasi-Experiments

In comparison with experiments, quasi-experiments often are easier to design and carry out, but one cannot have as much confidence in their results. All of the internal validity problems noted earlier that can occur with true experiments are even more troublesome with quasi-experiments. And whereas experiments can overcome these problems by trying to ensure that the treatment and control groups are the same, this is more difficult to do with quasi-experiments. The internal validity in such cases depends on the rigor and logic of the analysis and the care with which alternative factors are considered and ruled out. The two earlier studies on auto fatalities are exemplary because the researchers did

TABLE 4.1

Design to Determine Effect of a Crackdown on Speeding

Group	Original Condition	Treatment	Result
Experimental group: Connecticut	1955 fatalities: 324	Crackdown	1956 fatalities: 284
Control group: nearby states	1955 fatalities: find out	None	1956 fatalities: find out

not just collect and manipulate numbers. They carried out a careful and creative analysis of the reasons for traffic fatalities and let this analysis guide their research design and data collection. Quasi-experiments may, however, rate higher on external validity than experiments. They do not depend on artificial situations and are more apt to be drawn from naturally occurring events. Here the critical question is whether or not the events studied in a natural experiment are typical, or representative, of other events.

Correlational Analysis (Nonexperimental Design)

The Logic of Correlation

nonexperimental design
When observations are made on a large number of cases under varying conditions in order to approximate the control in an experiment.

correlational analysis
Use of nonexperimental design to see whether a correlation exists between two or more variables.

Some analysts insist that experiments are the only way to establish causality and argue that we should use them more than has been done in political analysis.[16] Most political analysis, however, uses a **nonexperimental** (correlational) **design.** In experiments the analyst establishes two groups, treats one of them, and then compares the groups to see if they are different. In **correlational analysis,** data about some dependent variable (for example, voter turnout) are collected on cases with varying characteristics to see which of the characteristics, if any, are related to the dependent variable. As one of the characteristics increases in value, does the dependent variable also increase? To explain voting and nonvoting, for example, you could design a correlational analysis. You might examine the education of voters and nonvoters to see if those with more education also vote more often. An experiment, by contrast, would require you to select two groups of similar people, educate only one group, and compare their voting behavior. Obviously this approach would not be feasible.

The earlier discussion of experiments described a study that determined that negative campaigns reduced voter turnout. In the experiment subjects were assigned to one of three groups and the results compared. Following the rule to use multiple designs when feasible, the same study designed a correlational analysis using information on all thirty-four senatorial campaigns in 1992. Once again the dependent variable was voter turnout, and the independent variable was "tone of campaign." As an indicator of turnout the study computed the votes cast for each Senate seat divided by the voting-age population in that state. As an indicator of campaign tone, the researchers read media accounts of each election in general and the campaign literature of each candidate in particular. This time, instead of showing three different ads, they classified each senatorial election according to whether the tone was positive, mixed, or negative. Using statistical analyses, they asked whether turnout was lower in states with negative campaigns than it was in states with positive campaigns. They found, as predicted, that turnout was lower in states where negative ads were used and that the difference was about 4 percent in these two groups of states.[17] This approach was a model of research in that it used two different designs to examine a hypothesis. The results of the experiment and the correlation were the same. Negative campaigning does depress turnout by a relatively similar amount—4 to 6 percent.

Correlational analysis can determine if there is a relationship between political activities and socioeconomic or demographic variables such as education, age, gender, race, and income. While correlational analysis may be used to consider which factors cause a variable of interest, such as voting, it is more generally useful in helping us understand an activity or political behavior more fully. Formally it enables us to ask whether changes in one variable (voting and nonvoting) are associated with changes in another variable (low and high income). Using induction and building on our observations of voting patterns, we could explore the relationship between voting and income to see if there is any pattern. Or we could use a deductive approach and draw from others' studies the proposition that wealthy people are more apt to vote for the Republican candidate than for the Democratic candidate and that poor people are more apt to vote for the Democratic candidate than for the Republican candidate. The information in table 4.2 reports on such a correlational design. It divides people into five income groups and indicates how many of them supported the Republican candidate in two elections. After reviewing the numbers, do you see a correlation between income and vote for president? Do the data support the proposition that wealthier people are more apt to vote Republican than poorer people are? (See the endnotes.)[18]

Controls and Correlations

Earlier we saw that while experiments focus on a single causal variable—the treatment or experiment—they can indirectly look at the influence of a number of variables by holding other factors constant in some way. Usually the purpose is to show that these other factors had little or no influence on the outcome. Correlational analysis can also be designed to look at the relationships among more than two variables, and in effect it can control for additional variables. Controls are useful in two ways. First, they help us trace causal influences by enabling us to see if we can eliminate other influences besides the one we are primarily interested in. Experiments and quasi-experiments are particularly valuable for this purpose. Second, controls help us understand a relationship more fully by exploring the relative importance of several variables at the same time. Correlational studies are particularly useful for this purpose. This chapter introduces

TABLE 4.2

Republican Vote, by Income Group, 1956, 1984 (In Percentages)

Candidate, Year	Income Group				
	Poor	*Low Middle*	*Middle*	*Upper Middle*	*Affluent*
Eisenhower, 1956	59%	56%	58%	57%	75%
Reagan, 1984	32	43	57	64	75

Source: *American General Election Study, 1976* (Center for Political Studies, University of Michigan, 1976).

controls in correlations by examining how to control a relationship between two variables using a third variable. (Chapter 11 introduces statistical techniques, notably regression analysis, that allow us to examine the simultaneous effect of multiple variables.)

bivariate table
Table presenting information on two variables in a manner that shows whether they are related to each other.

multivariate analysis
Examination of relationships among three or more variables.

Analysis of propositions containing only two variables is called **bivariate analysis.** When we add control variables we are engaged in **multivariate analysis,** controlling or holding a third variable constant, that is, distinguishing several values of a third (control) variable and looking at the original relationship for each of these values. The third variable is being held constant at three different values.

Consider the following sequence: We find that variables X and Y are associated, that is, that changes in X are related to changes in Y. But perhaps there is some other factor at work, called Z, that has a stronger relationship or that affects the original relationship in some way. It is even possible that Z causes both X and Y. How can we determine if this is true? One way is to look at the relationship between X and Y when Z is present and when Z is absent. Or we can look at the relationship between X and Y when there is a small amount of Z and when there is a large amount of Z. Thus we look at the relationship for different values of Z; this is what is meant by "controlling for Z" or "holding Z constant." In steps 2 and 3, we take one value of Z and hold it constant while we examine X and Y; then we take a second value of Z and hold it constant while we examine X and Y. By looking at only one value of Z at a time, we have eliminated the chance that changes in Z are making a difference in the relationship between X and Y.

1. Are X and Y related?

2. Z present: Z absent:
   Are X and Y related?   Are X and Y related?

3. Z (small amount): Z (large amount):
   Are X and Y related?   Are X and Y related?

We can illustrate controlling a correlation by reviewing the issue of low turnout in American presidential elections. Chapter 2 cited a study that tested the proposition that registration rules can explain much of the decline in voting and found there is a relationship between these variables. In states where registration is easier, there is higher voter turnout, and the researchers concluded that ease of registration has a causal influence on voting turnout.

Others propose that voter interest in an election is more important than ease of registration. One observer, for example, noted that voter turnout is high in elections in which racial issues are at stake. He proposed that people will vote when the electoral contest raises critically important issues and that this tendency holds whether or not registration rules are easy to fulfill.[19]

We can test this proposition by looking at the relationship between turnout and registration in two kinds of elections. Turnout and registration difficulty are the two original variables. We examine the relationship between them, controlling for a third variable—intensity of interest in the election. First, we look at the relationship in elections where no particularly salient issue is posed in the campaign; this means we hold that value of the control variable constant. Second, we look at the relationship in elections in which much intense feeling was generated in the campaigns and voters believed that it made a difference who won. We are now holding this second value of the variable constant. Initially, then, we look only at elections waged over relatively trivial issues; then we look only at campaigns that generated intense conflict. By holding the control variable constant in this manner, we know that any relationship we find between registration rules and turnout cannot be the result of varying interest in the campaign. Research suggests that when important issues are at stake, registration rules do not appear to affect voting, whereas they may have more effect when the campaigns do not deal with issues of immediate salience to the voters. Thus by controlling we gained a much fuller understanding of the original relationship between voter turnout and ease of registration.

Validity of Correlation Studies

We have gone through a number of examples of research designs based on correlations, illustrating how correlational analysis can be used to explore various dimensions of a relationship. How valid is this design? Internal validity asks whether one can have confidence in the conclusions of such a study. For determining whether one variable actually causes another, correlations are fairly weak on internal validity. Compared to experiments, it is difficult to rule out other factors that may be more important. By instituting a number of controls and linking your research with prior studies and theory, however, it is possible to construct an argument that does have a measure of internal validity. For exploring relationships among a number of variables rather than establishing causes, correlations can have more internal validity, depending on the number of controlled or multivariate relationships they consider. As for external validity, referring to the generalizability of a study, correlations that rely on information drawn from a scientific sample of respondents will have greater external validity than experiments. Such samples enable us to state just how likely it is that the conclusions of a study can be generalized to a larger population (see chapter 12).

Case Study Research Designs

The Logic of Case Studies

You probably gained many insights about political events through your working knowledge of particular cases, although you have not called them "case studies." In this sense, case studies, a fourth type of research design, are closer to the way in which we normally collect information and arrive at understandings. The term is often loosely used to refer to any research about a single unit or case. Here we use case study design in a more specific sense and emphasize that case studies can and should be designed to enhance the validity of their conclusions. From this perspective, a case study is a design that allows us to be comprehensive and take the context into account. It is "a method for learning about a complex instance, based on a comprehensive understanding of that instance obtained by extensive description and analysis of that instance taken as a whole and in its context."[20] The Government Accounting Office (GAO), which developed this definition, notes that each element in the definition is important.

Method. Case studies are not simply descriptions of an event or activity. They involve a systematic presentation of the question(s) they are addressing, a clear reason for selecting the case, a rationale for focusing on particular aspects of the case, and careful delineation of the conclusions the study suggests.

Complexity. Asking whether registration rules affect voter turnout is not a complex issue. Asking why some groups are alienated from the political process is more complex and lends itself to case study design.

Based on comprehensive understanding. A case study would ask for a full understanding of such alienation and would use multiple measures and draw on a variety of kinds of evidence.

Extensive description and analysis. Cases require a variety of kinds of evidence, including direct observation and interviews, and try to integrate these several information sources. Cases achieve validity to the extent that they establish agreement or consistency among these difference sources.

Taken as a whole. Cases can deal with individuals; a specific location, such as a city; an institution, such as the State Department; a particular historical entity, such as a presidential administration; an event, such as the Persian Gulf War of 1991. These units could be studied through correlations or quasi-experiments, but the choice of a case design means that the researcher is interested in the unit as a whole, in gaining a full understanding of the many facets of the case.

In context. Cases emphasize that the context, or surroundings, of a case is critical in understanding and explaining it. A case study of the Gulf War would cover the origins of the conflict and the military strategies, as well as the political, economic, and diplomatic settings.

Types of Case Studies

Case studies include illustrative studies, exploratory studies, comparative studies, process studies, and notable exceptions.

illustrative studies
Consider a particular case of a more general theory and provide a deeper insight into the theory.

Illustrative studies. These typically consider a particular case of a more general theory and provide a deeper insight into the theory. A classic illustrative case is *Implementation* by Jeffrey Pressman and Aaron Wildavsky.[21] The authors had a theory that well-meaning and popular federal programs are often undermined at the state or local level primarily because so many competing interests get involved in implementing them. To illustrate these difficulties they selected an economic development program in the city of Oakland, California, where little was accomplished. The example was interesting because there had been no opposition to the policy and a lot of people had tried to make it work. The case analysis used interviews, observations, and government documents to trace the efforts to carry out the program. This design enabled the authors to show how the difficulties of implementation eventually overwhelmed all the actors, even though many of the conditions to ensure success were present.

exploratory study
Collecting data in order to develop research questions and propositions.

Exploratory studies. These are useful when little is known about a phenomenon. The researcher carries out a case study, often on a limited basis, to develop some questions and propositions for further study and to learn what information is available and relevant. An exploratory study of a Head Start program could be carried out prior to a quasi-experiment to learn what elements of the program appear to be most critical to its success and therefore warrant further study. In chapter 2, we read about a study of local government planning officials that used this design. The authors had observed that many planners entered their jobs with a great deal of idealism but did not stay very long. They felt they did not know enough to develop a proposition to explain the high turnover, and so they decided to do an exploratory study to find out how accurate their observation was and what some of the reasons might be. Their study, *Guerillas in the Bureaucracy*, used interviews and observations and provided a rich description of the frustrations idealistic planners face within bureaucracies and the tensions they have to deal with in the community. As a result the planners quickly burned out.[22] The exploratory study of planning units provided a number of propositions for further testing.

comparative case studies
These select two or more cases with similar circumstances but different results.

Comparative case studies. A lot can be learned from comparing two cases, especially when they differ in some interesting ways. The key issue is selecting two or more cases that are comparable in some interesting way—similar circumstances but different results, a success and a failure, contrasting circumstances but a similar result, and so forth. A recent study looked at the experiences of two cities, Charlotte and Raleigh, North Carolina, in privatizing some city services.[23] Charlotte was more successful in its efforts, and the comparison between the cities enabled the researchers to identify some likely reasons for its better record. The researchers interviewed major players in the two cities, examined reports and government records, and attended meetings to collect their information. They were able to gain insight into the political process in the two locales, the style of the leadership, and the attitudes of the public, as well as quantified information about the results.

process studies
Examine a series of
events surrounding a
decision or action.

Process studies. Process studies look at a series of events surrounding a decision or action and are often used in examining public policies. The earlier cited cases on implementation and privatization were both process studies. What is the process for crafting and enacting legislation? What is the process for implementing a public policy? What are the dynamics surrounding a particular bill? Such studies are useful because they recognize the need for collecting information over time, for understanding interactions among various policy actors, and for appreciating changing dynamics. A process case study can also be used to examine what happens when a change is introduced into an organization. What happens when computers are introduced into an organization? How do different actors respond? What problems arise? How are problems solved?

Case studies that focus on process issues can be more useful to policy actors than are the other designs in this chapter. Robert Weiss and Martin Rein compared the value of an experimental design and a case study design to examine a program to benefit minority youth. The original experimental design concluded that the program had not helped the youth in any significant way. The study wasn't useful to the administrators of the program, however. They knew the program was not working and wanted to know what they could do differently. Moreover, because the study did not deal with the questions they were facing, they were reluctant to provide the information the researchers needed. There were also many unintended results that weren't taken into account by the experimental design. While the experimental design tested whether the program was a success, the authors felt it would have been more useful to do a process study and find out why problems arose and how they were handled. A case study approach that relied on interviews, observations, and documents could have done justice to the complex process of delivering services to minority youth and could thereby have been more useful to program managers.[24]

While case studies look at particular examples, they can also contribute to more general theories about the political process. For example, chapter 2 discussed concrete theory, which examines actions by political elites. These typically draw on specific studies to develop broader theories about public officials—how they are limited by their institutions and also how they try to change their situations. Because these studies are grounded in actual experiences, they are typically case studies. And because they are looking for common elements in the cases, they can help build theories. Lane observes that the challenge of such cases is to avoid two extremes: on the one hand, not to become mere journalistic descriptions, and on the other hand, not to become formalized and lose the dynamic quality of case studies.[25]

Notable exceptions. An illustrative case study, an exploratory case, and a process case are usually chosen because they point to fairly typical events. Comparative cases are usually chosen because such cases are different from one another in some important respect. Alternatively, researchers may choose a case because it is unique. Perhaps it is a failure and there are useful lessons to be learned from it. Or it is a success and it is important to understand the conditions that produced it. Chapter 3 described Janis's study of decision making and his theory that small groups often indulge in "groupthink" and produce a false consensus in order to maintain the cohesion in the group. Several notable case studies have been done of decision making surrounding the Cuban missile crisis in 1961, precisely because it was not typical. By and large the decision makers avoided groupthink and acted responsibly and effectively.[26] The same logic could be used on a smaller scale. It is well known that in general urban public schools perform poorly. If you knew of a school marked by creative and successful leadership and a record of improved learning, it would be useful to do a case study of such a school. Instead of simply describing the school, it would be important to frame the study with analytic questions. What is unique and interesting about the case? What are the conditions that seem to explain its success? Why has it managed to succeed where many other schools are failing?

Validity and Case Studies

How do cases satisfy the criteria of internal and external validity? The more the researcher lays out the purpose of the case and the reason for selecting it, the more systematic attention is given to the aspects of the case being studied, the greater its validity is apt to be. First, the internal validity of a case study design depends on the variety of information sources about the case and the extent to which these sources are consistent. Different kinds of information can be used to check on trends, to rule out other explanations, to reinforce conclusions. For example, we could begin with official reports about a city council's decisions, follow up with interviews, and attend several open meetings. Such analyses, drawing on multiple sources of information, can rate high on validity because they can do justice to the full dimension of a case and allow the researcher some discretion to pursue what is most important. In cases, data collection and analysis go on simultaneously. We collect some information, reflect on it, analyze it, and, based on this analysis, pursue further information. If the result is a coherent and plausible study, we could propose a cause-and-effect relationship and test it through some other design.

As mentioned earlier, case study design generally is weak on external validity, although generalizability varies according to how the case or cases were selected. According to the GAO, "generalizability depends less on the number of sites and more on the right match between the purpose of the study and how the instances were selected."[27] We can select cases because they are extreme or unusual; because they offer best and worst examples; because they are typical, or representative; or because they illustrate some issue of particular interest. Obviously, if we choose representative cases, the study will have the greatest generalizability. For example, for a study of welfare policies in the fifty states, we could do case studies of three states and include states with different percentages of welfare recipients. Unusual cases and those that illustrate something of particular interest will most certainly be less generalizable; but if well designed, they can also point beyond themselves. For example, a case study of the Persian

Gulf War, an event of particular interest, could provide insights about regional wars that would be more generally applicable to other cases.

Multiple Designs and Case Studies

Chapter 3 stressed that it is always preferable to use several kinds of indicators or measures of our variables. Some may be higher on validity and others higher on reliability. We can have much greater confidence in our results if we select some indicators that pertain to the core meaning of a concept—development or democracy, for instance—and hence are valid, as well as some that are reliable and would produce the same results no matter who used them. The same point is true for research designs. The study of the impact of negative campaigning on turnout discussed earlier was noteworthy because it combined two designs—an experiment and a correlational analysis. The results of the two designs were consistent, offering greater confidence in the results of the study. Unfortunately as the authors note, it is highly unusual to combine both experimental and nonexperimental designs in the same study.[28]

Case studies, if done well, can provide a rich understanding of a relationship and can be high on validity. However, as noted, it may be hard to generalize from them and use them to learn about other cases. Case studies are particularly useful as companions to other research designs. One could do an exploratory case study to suggest propositions that are then tested through experiments or correlation studies. Or one can begin with a correlation study, then follow up with a case study to go into the relationship in more depth or to find out why a proposed relationship did not occur. If a correlation study finds that indeed incumbents are more apt to win elections than are challengers, it could be useful to follow up with a case study to understand more fully the ways in which an incumbent used his official status to mobilize voter sentiment.

Donald Campbell, a strong proponent of systematic quantitative studies and particularly of quasi-experiments, recommends using case studies also because they provide different kinds of information and understanding. "After all, man is, in his ordinary way, a very competent knower, and qualitative common-sense knowing is not replaced by quantitative knowing. Rather, quantitative knowing has to trust and build on the qualitative, including ordinary perception. We methodologists must achieve an applied epistemology which integrates both."[29] Recall the discussion about the relative merits of using a case study or an experiment to determine whether a program to benefit minority youth was successful. Campbell conceded that an experiment had not been useful in this instance. However, he said it would have been better to have used both a quasi-experiment and a historical case study to study the program. A times series study (quasi-experiment) could have provided useful information about the results of the program, and a case study would have provided a greater understanding of the process of carrying out the program.[30]

Consider an ongoing study that combines different designs. In the late 1990s a large correlational study compared student test scores on math in forty-one nations.[31] The third International Maths and Science Study administered tests to about half a million students around the world. Each country was ranked based on the average score of the thirteen-year-olds taking the test. For example, on math, Singapore was first, the United States was twenty-eighth and South Africa was forty-first. The study then analyzed correlations to explain why some countries ranked higher than others. First, they correlated the country rankings with the amount of time students spent in school. They found that test scores did not increase as students spent more time on a subject. Second, they correlated the rankings with the amount of money spent on education. Again, they did not find a correlation. Countries that spent more on education did not have higher ratings. Third, they correlated the ratings with the size of classrooms, proposing that nations with smaller class sizes would have higher scores. Again there was no correlation. The researchers then turned to case studies in which they looked at the process of teaching and at the way in which lessons were taught in each country. One researcher found that in countries with higher scores, teachers were more apt to focus on the basics of arithmetic, to teach students to do sums in their heads rather than on paper, to rely on standardized teaching manuals, and to teach to the whole class rather than work in small groups. The correlations provided some important general information about the amount and conditions of learning, while the case studies offered more specific information about the process of learning.

Where We Are

The discussion of research designs in chapter 4 compared several ways to design research to link our questions to evidence and concluded that different questions lead to different designs, and that where possible we should rely on more than one kind of evidence and more than one design. Thus the chapter has repeated two of the themes central to this book. First we should select a design that is appropriate for the questions we are asking, and second where possible we should use multiple designs. The chapter also discussed the key to all of the designs—namely sorting out the major influence or influences from the many variables associated with an event or activity. The next two chapters will discuss in more detail how to conduct this sorting out process.

NOTES

1. Darrell Huff, *How to Lie with Statistics* (New York: W. W. Norton, 1954), p. 8, attributed to Henry G. Felsen.
2. Gerald Marwell and Ruth Ames, "Economists Free Ride, Does Anyone Else?" *Journal of Public Economics* 15, no. 3 (June 1981): 295–310.
3. Robert Frank, Thomas Gilovich, and Dennis Regan, "Does Studying Economics Inhibit Cooperation?," *Journal of Economic Perspectives* 7 (Spring 1993): 159–171.
4. The researchers also controlled for the content of the economics courses. One was taught by a mainstream economist who stressed the self-interest maxim. The

second economics course was taught by a development economist who placed less emphasis on traditional economics. Those in the first economics course scored consistently less honest at the end of the semester, while those in the second economics course scored only moderately less honest at the end of the semester.

5. Frank, Gilovich, and Regan, "Studying Economics," pp. 168–170.

6. Anthony M. Yezer, Robert S. Goldfarb, and Paul J. Poppen, "Does Studying Economics Discourage Cooperation? Watch What We Do, Not What We Say or How We Play," *Journal of Economic Perspectives* 10, no. 1 (Winter 1996): 177–186.

7. Stephen Ansolabehere, Shanto Iyengar, Adam Simon, and Nicholas Valentino, "Does Attack Advertising Demobilize the Electorate?" *American Political Science Review* 88, no. 4 (December 1994): 829–838.

8. Ansolabehere, Iyengar, Simon, and Valentino, "Attack Advertising," p. 835.

9. Curt Suplee, "No Greater Cancer Risk Is Found in Children Living Near Power Lines," *Washington Post*, 3 July 1997, p. A3.

10. Richard Larson, "What Happened to Patrol Operations in Kansas City?" *Evaluation* 3, nos. 1–2 (1976): pp. 117–123.

11. A recent text lists the following potential problems with experiments: 1. Control of variables—can other factors be ruled out? 2. Time passage—do important factors change during the experiment? 3. Varying acts of measurement—are responses measured differently? 4. Statistical regression—are extreme scores an aberration? 5. Experimental mortality—do subjects drop out before experiment is completed? 6. Instrument decay—are measures carefully used the second time? 7. Selection error—are experimental and control groups equivalent? Gregory Scott, *Political Science: Foundations for a Fifth Millenium* (Upper Saddle River, N.J.: Prentice-Hall, 1997), p. 186.

12. A particularly influential discussion of validity problems is found in Donald Campbell and Julian Stanley, *Experimental and Quasi-Experimental Designs for Research* (Washington, D.C.: American Educational Research Association, 1963), pp. 5–6. See also the discussion in Earl Babbie, *The Practice of Social Research*, 3d ed. (Belmont, Calif.: Wadsworth, 1983), pp. 195–201.

13. Alice Rivlin, "Allocating Resources for Policy Research: How Can Experiments Be More Useful?" *American Economic Review* 64, no. 2 (May 1974): 346–354.

14. Edward R. Tufte, *Data Analysis for Politics and Policy*, Englewood Cliffs, N.J.: Prentice-Hall, 1974, pp. 7–30.

15. This discussion is based on an analysis by Donald Campbell, "Reforms as Experiments," *American Psychologist* 24 (April 1969): 409–429.

16. Eugene Stone, *Research Methods in Organizational Behavior* (Santa Monica, Calif.: Goodyear, 1978), p. 107.

17. Ansolabehere, Iyengar, Simon, and Valentino, "Attack Advertising," p. 833.

18. There is a relationship in that the most affluent are more apt to vote Republican. The proposition is not confirmed for 1956, however, since a majority of every income group voted for the Republican candidate. The proposition is confirmed for 1984; in this year, the more affluent one was, the greater was the probability of voting Republican.

19. Curtis Gans, "No Wonder Turnout Was Low," *Washington Post*, 11 November 1988, p. A23. Gans is director of the Committee for the Study of the American Electorate, a nonpartisan organization looking into the problem of low voter turnout.

20. U.S. Government Accounting Office, *Case Study Evaluations* (Washington, D.C.: U.S. Government Printing Office, 1990), p. 14. The discussion of cases in this section draws heavily on this excellent review of case studies as they are used in evaluations.

21. Jeffrey L. Pressman and Aaron B. Wildavsky, *Implementation* (Berkeley: University of California, 1973).
22. Martin Needleman and Carolyn Needleman, *Guerillas in the Bureaucracy* (New York: Wiley, 1974).
23. Ronnie LaCourse Korosec and Timothy D. Mead, "Lessons from Privatization Task Forces: Comparative Case Studies," *Policy Studies Journal* 24, no. 4 (1996): 641–648.
24. Robert Weiss and Martin Rein, "The Evaluation of Broad-Aim Programs: Experimental Design, Its Difficulties, and an Alternative," *Administrative Science Quarterly* 15 (March 1970): 97–108.
25. Ruth Lane, "Concrete Theory: An Emerging Political Method," *American Political Science Review* 84, no. 3 (September 1990): 927–940.
26. Irving Janis, *Groupthink* (New York: Houghton Mifflin, 1982). Graham Allison, "Conceptual Models and the Cuban Missile Crisis," *American Political Science Review* 63 (September 1969): 689–718.
27. U.S. GAO, *Case Study Evaluations*, p. 66.
28. Ansolabehere, Iyengar, Simon, and Valentino, "Attack Advertising," p. 833.
29. Donald Campbell, "Degrees of Freedom and the Case Study," *Comparative Political Studies* 8, no. 2 (July 1975): 178–193.
30. Donald Campbell, "Considering the Case Against Experimental Evaluations of Social Innovations," *Administration Science Quarterly* 15 (March 1970): 110–113.
31. "World Education League: Who's Top?" *The Economist*, March 29, 1997.

EXERCISES

Exercise 4.1 Comparing Research Designs

Develop three designs, as indicated, to carry out research on interest in politics among students at your university.

Quasi-experiment (Assume a midyear political event that affects students.)

Correlational analysis

Case study

1. For each, state your research question, a hypothesis if appropriate, your variables, and how you plan to collect information.

2. If appropriate draw a table or diagram that you could use to report your results.

3. Compare the internal and external validity of the designs.

Exercise 4.2 Analyzing Experiments

The following experiment used college students to compare two ways to make decisions. Many political decisions are made by small groups of officials who meet to discuss the decisions. This *interactive*, or typically political, approach is often criticized because a few people can dominate the process or because only a limited number of ideas may get expressed. An alternative is to *structure* the decision-making process that sets up formal procedures to ensure that everyone participates.

Julianne Mahler set up an experiment to compare students' responses after participating in one of the two approaches: interactive and structured. She assigned students in two courses randomly to groups of six. Each group was given the same task: to decide how to improve high school education in the local county. Half of the groups were told to use the interactive approach, and half were told to use a structured approach. After meeting for about forty minutes, students were each given a questionnaire and asked two questions: was their participation a positive experience, and how did they feel about the final decision of the group. Mahler's working hypothesis was that those in the interacting groups would report greater satisfaction with their participation and greater support for the group decision than those in the structured groups. The results showed that those in the interactive groups expressed a greater sense of participation, but there was no difference between the groups as to how members felt about the choices that were made. (Julianne Mahler, "Structured Decision Making in Public Organizations," *Public Administration Review* 47 [July/August 1987]: 336–342.)

1. Identify the two dependent variables.

2. What is the independent variable?

3. How does the design eliminate the role of other influences?

4. Comment on the internal and external validity of the study.

Exercise 4.3 Designing an Experiment

President David Boren of the University of Oklahoma was concerned about an apparent lack of community on the campus. He encouraged alumni to donate benches to be placed around the campus in the hopes that they would encourage students to stop and talk. As of May 1997, alumni had funded 160 benches at $1,000 each. (George F. Will, "Hyperactive U." *Washington Post*, 4 May 1997, p. C7.)

Before locating the benches, the university president asks you to design an experiment with 10 of the benches to see what effect they will have. Prepare a design for the president.

Exercise 4.4 Designing a Quasi-Experiment

U.S. officials continue to be concerned at the comparative low rate of seat belt usage. An estimated 68 percent of front-seat occupants use lap belts and shoulder harnesses regularly. While this is an increase over the late 1970s, it is far below the 90 percent usage common in many European countries. Several states are putting in place new laws that allow police to stop and ticket drivers who do not use seat belts. For example, in 1993 North Carolina enacted such a law and seat belt use went from 65 percent to 83 percent, and there have been one hundred fewer highway deaths annually. (Warren Brown, "Campaigning for Tougher Seat Belt Enforcement," *Washington Post*, 20 March 1997, p. C1.)

Assume you are asked to do research for a state that has enacted such a law. Develop an appropriate research design to determine its effectiveness. Make sure that your design controls for other factors that could affect highway deaths.

Exercise 4.5 Designing Case Studies

Welfare reform is a major issue in most states, as the officials design new programs to move welfare recipients into jobs. Many problems have arisen, including the availability of appropriate jobs, the ability of potential workers to find transportation to the available jobs, the preparation of potential workers for the jobs, a concern that they might be displacing others who currently hold the jobs, and the availability of child care. Design a case study that would give you insight into these problems and potential ways of dealing with them. Indicate your research question(s), the kind of case study you would carry out, how you would select a case or cases, and what kinds of information you would collect. How could you improve the validity and reliability of your study?

CHAPTER FIVE

Types of Relationships: Associations and Causality

"Don't light that cigarette; you know that smokers die of lung cancer!"
"Really? All of them?"
"No, of course not. I mean they tend to die of lung cancer."
"You mean that's what the majority of smokers die from?"
"No, but they're more likely to die of it."
"Oh, you mean lung cancer kills more smokers than do heart failure and auto-mobile accidents?"
"Not that either. What I mean is that more smokers die of lung cancer than do nonsmokers. In fact, the death rate from lung cancer among heavy smokers is about 1.66 per thousand deaths."
"That's very small. It's obvious that smokers don't tend to die of lung cancer."
"Yes they do. The comparative death rate among non-smokers is only .07."

—William Buchanan, *Understanding Political Variables*

Relationships

Virtually all research is concerned with examining relationships—that is determining if one or more variables are linked to each other in some way. Do education and voting turnout tend to occur together? Are they associated with each other? Is it possible to go farther and say that one causes the other? The anecdote above about smoking and lung cancer illustrates the confusing way in which we often speak of relationships. This chapter helps you explore if there is an association between two variables and describes how to be clearer and more precise about your findings. It also presents some skills for creating tables to examine relationships. The next chapter continues this discussion by looking at questions involving more than two variables.

Many of the examples in prior chapters have dealt with relationships. The discussion of the relationship between democratic regimes and a tendency to wage war in chapter 2 used a correlational design to compare characteristics of democracies and autocracies. The study of urban services in chapter 3 also used correlational analysis, combined with some case studies, to test whether there is a relationship between such factors as political power and government services. An exercise in chapter 2 asked you to compare several narrative case studies of the Vietnam War to identify what factors were associated with U.S. policies in Vietnam. Chapter 4 described an experiment to determine if specific police practices were related to decreases in crime and two quasi-experiments to determine if government policies were associated with reductions in traffic fatalities. Chapter 4 also reviewed a study about the relationship of negative campaigns to voting turnout. Most of the research in the field is asking about relationships, and it is likely that your own research will do the same.

Associations between Variables

Nature of the Relationship

associated
Indicates there is a relationship between two variables in which changes in one variable occur together with changes in the other.

correlated
When a relationship exists between two variables such that changes in one variable occur together with changes in the other.

co-vary
When a relationship exists between two variables such that changes in one variable occur together with changes in the other.

Relationships between variables can take several forms. Whenever two variables change in such a way that change in one is **associated** with change in the other, we say they are **correlated**, they are associated, or they **co-vary**. Lipset's theory to explain participation in politics, referred to earlier, proposes that people's status and their political participation are associated (or correlated, or that they co-vary). People with higher status are more apt to participate than those with lower status. As the value of one of the variables (status) increases, the value of the other variable (participation) does also. Lipset not only offers this proposition, but also bases it on a theory that explains the logic behind it and states why he expects the two variables to be correlated or associated. (Recall his theory that higher status groups are more apt to be members of organizations, to read regularly, to take more interest in politics, and hence be more apt to participate.)

The terms *association* and *correlation* describe a relationship wherein changes in one variable are accompanied by changes in the other variable.

For example, look at the information in table 5.1. What two variables are described in the table?

_____

_____

Does the evidence suggest that the two are related or associated?

_____

_____

TABLE 5.1

Giving to Charity, by Income Group

Household Income	Percentage of Income Given to Charity
Less than $10,000	2.8
$10,000–$29,999	2.5
$30,000–$49,999	2.0
$50,000–$74,999	1.5
$75,000–$99,999	1.7
More than $100,000	2.1

Source: *Washington Post*, 22 October 1988.

The information does indicate a relationship, and the pattern is consistent below the $75,000 level. As income increases, people tend to give a slightly smaller percentage of their income to charity. Finding a relationship, however, does not mean that one variable causes the other. Having a high level of income may affect the level of giving to charity somewhat; more likely there are other characteristics of those with higher income that affect their record of giving. It would not be precisely correct, therefore, to say that income actually *causes* the level of giving to charity.

Direction of the Relationship

positive association
A statement that two phenomena are related to each other in the following way: the more of one, the more of the other.

An association can be either *positive* or *negative*. In a **positive relationship** or **association** the variables change in the same direction. This can be made clearer by visualizing such a relationship. Assume you know that the years of education and income level of four individuals are as follows:

Individual	Education Completed	Income Level
A	Eighth grade	$10,000
B	Tenth grade	$15,000
C	Twelfth grade	$20,000
D	College	$30,000

Indicate on the following graph where each case would lie.

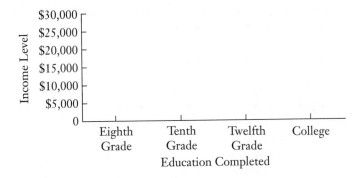

Both variables are arranged on the graph so that the values increase as one goes up (income from $5,000 to $30,000) and to the right (education from eighth grade to college). A line connecting the cases also moves up and to the right, in the same direction as the values of the variables. Thus, we say the relationship is positive: as the values of one variable increase, the values of the other variable increase.

Conversely, in a **negative relationship** or **association**, the variables change in opposite directions: one increases as the other decreases. The information in table 5.1 illustrates a negative relationship. We could use that data to project the following information about five individuals.

negative association
A statement that two phenomena are related to each other in the following way: the more of one, the less of the other.

Individual	Income	Percentage of Income Given to Charity
A	$10,000	2.8
B	$20,000	2.5
C	$30,000	2.0
D	$40,000	2.0
E	$50,000	1.5

Place these individuals on the following graph:

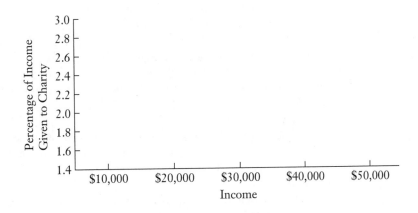

Describe the pattern you see. Both variables are arranged so they increase in value as they move up and to the right. The pattern of cases, however, moves in the opposite direction. Consequently, we say there is a negative relationship between the variables: the more of one, the less of the other. (Can you think of a possible logic behind this finding?)

Sometimes it is difficult to predict whether a relationship will be negative or positive. We might propose, for example, that the more economically developed a country is, the less apt it is to experience internal violence—a negative relationship. What is the logic behind this hypothesis? (Possible logic: as a country gains in wealth, there is more to distribute and everyone is better off, and hence there is less reason for internal violence.) Or one could propose the reverse, that the relationship will be positive. (Possible logic: the early stages of economic development are accompanied by greater wealth, increased inequity, growing resentment, and hence a greater tendency toward violence.) You could use either of these propositions as a working hypothesis.

Strength of the Relationship

How strong does a relationship need to be to allow us to say that two variables are associated? How much change does there have to be in two variables to say they are correlated? Review table 2.1 on population change in large cities. We found there was a correlation between region and population change. It was not a perfect relationship, since three of the western and two of the eastern cities did not fit the regional pattern. But most of the cities fell into a regional pattern and the two exceptions deviated by a very small amount, and thus we could say that the relationship was very strong. Now return to the data in table 4.2, which examines a relationship between income and party vote. In both elections the wealthier one is, the more apt he or she is to vote for the Republican candidate. The relationship between income and vote, however, was stronger in 1984 when Ronald Reagan was the candidate. In 1956, it was not as strong, since 59 percent of the poor voted for Dwight Eisenhower. While income was moderately related to vote, the popularity of Eisenhower spanned all income levels and thus was more strongly related to the vote than income.

In the social sciences we are unlikely to find perfect correlations, unless we are asking relatively trivial questions. The more interesting theoretical questions almost always involve less-than-perfect relationships. The reason is that the social sciences deal with human actors, who are subject to a great variety of influences. We can develop theories that predict general tendencies, but given the variation among human subjects and the great number of influences on their behavior, we are unlikely to find a theory that correctly predicts 100 percent of the behavior we observe, or even close to that amount. There will always be a few people who vote, say, even if they share all of the characteristics of those whom our theory predicts will not vote. And there will always be some who do not vote as predicted because some issues that we never took into account are important to them.

Return to the question of how strong the relationship or correlation has to be to offer support for our study. We will answer that question throughout the book as we present various techniques for reporting and interpreting information, including percentages and statistical measures. The general answer is that the preciseness of interpretation depends on the theoretical propositions we are testing and how our results compare with the findings of others. Given the number of factors that influence our behavior, we should not expect any one or two to have a preponderant influence. Thus, if we find some factor that explains as much as 10 percent of the variation in voter turnout or voting choice, we have a result that is worth noting. The language we use to describe the results becomes very important. We need to look for phrases that accurately reflect the patterns we find: "There is a strong association," "There is a relationship, but it is a weak one," and so forth.

The Null Hypothesis

A more conservative way to answer our question is to determine if we can at least reject the statement that there is *no* relationship between the variables. We do this by stating what is called a "null hypothesis" and then see if we can reject it. The null hypothesis (written as H_0) states there is a "null," or no, relationship between two variables—for example, there is no relationship between regional location and urban population changes. The first step in determining if a relationship exists is to see if the evidence allows us to reject the null hypothesis. The logic of this strategy is that we may not be able to verify a theory, but we can at least try to eliminate alternative theoretical explanations.

Apply this logic to the data in table 2.1. The null hypothesis, H_0, would state that there is no relationship between regional location and population change, that is, that cities in each region are just as likely or unlikely to experience population change as cities in other regions. The information in that table is adequate to reject the statement that there is no relationship between regional location and population changes. It shows that all three midwestern cities are declining in population, that the southern cities are increasing in size, that two out of three western cities are increasing in size, and that three out of four eastern cities are decreasing in size. Hence, we can at the very least reject the null hypothesis and state that there is some relationship.

Return to the example of charitable giving presented in table 5.1. If we had not seen the data, it would be reasonable to hypothesize that households with higher incomes give a greater percentage of their incomes to charity than do those with lower incomes.

> H_0 = There is no relationship between household income level and charitable giving.
>
> H_1 = Households with higher incomes give a greater percentage of their incomes to charity than do those with lower incomes.

The working hypothesis (H_1) assumes that H_0 is false. The data do indicate a relationship, and thus H_0 is rejected. The relationship, however, does not support the working hypothesis, and so we would have to reject that also. We were hypothesizing there would be a *positive* relationship between the variables: as one increases so does the other. There turns out to be a *negative* relationship: as one increases the other decreases. Moreover, the negative relationship is fairly strong and consistent.

It would not be enough, though, simply to report that the data lead us to reject both hypotheses. Recall that explanations and theories are based on logical understandings of the ways in which two variables are linked to each other. Accordingly, we could use these findings to return to the theory about income status and giving and rethink it. What possible logic could explain the results we have found? Are there any other studies or theories that we could consider? What further research could we carry out to understand these results better? In this manner there is a continuous interaction between research results and theoretical reformulations and further research.

Research that leads us to reject our working hypotheses can be useful. For example, it is common to assume that students perform better in private schools than in public schools. Examine the data in table 5.2. What does the table tell you that you probably didn't expect? It indicates that the percentage of twelfth-grade students who can handle high school–level material is approximately the same in all three kinds of school systems. (Specifically, the percentage of twelfth graders who can handle high school–level material doesn't exceed 5 percent in any of the school types.) There is no relationship between type of school and achievement, and hence we could not reject the null hypothesis.

Constructing Tables to Depict an Association

When we have quantitative information about two characteristics of several cases, we can treat the characteristics as variables and place the cases in a table,

TABLE 5.2

Performance in Grade Twelve, by Type of School

	Type of School		
	Public	*Parochial*	*Other Private*
Average proficiency level	295	302	301
Third-grade–level material	100%	100%	100%
Fifth-grade–level material	90%	96%	97%
Seventh-grade–level material	45%	54%	51%
High school–level material	5%	4%	4%

Source: U.S. Department of Education, National Center for Education Statistics, June 1991.

making it easier to determine whether or not the variables actually do co-vary, or correlate. First you divide the variables into several values:

Variable *A:* Value 1, Value 2

Variable *B:* Value 1, Value 2

Take either variable and determine how many cases or observations occur for each value. For example:

Variable *A*	
Value 1	*Value 2*
(number of observations)	(number of observations)

The total number of observations in each column (and in each row) are the *marginals.* They tell you how many cases have value 1 and how many cases have value 2.

To see whether there is an association between variables *A* and *B*, add the other variable to the display in order to show how the number of observations are distributed when they are related to this second variable. Each of the spaces where the values intersect is called a *cell.* Frequently tables are described by the number of rows and columns they contain; the table below is a 2×2 table, since there are two rows and two columns.

Variable B	Variable *A*		
	Value 1	*Value 2*	
Value 1	Cell A	Cell C	Number of cases (Marginal value)
Value 2	Cell B	Cell D	Number of cases (Marginal value)

Begin by looking at the number of cases in each row and column, the marginals. These tell you the total number of cases of variable *A* that assume value 1 and value 2, and the total number of cases of variable *B* that assume value 1 and value 2. The distribution of cases across the values, that is, the marginals, can tell you a lot. Do they divide 50-50? Is there a preponderance of cases on one of the two values? If a great majority of the cases assume one of the values, then you do not have much variation in the variable and will not be able to learn much about the relationship between the two variables. For example, assume that variable *A* is gender and variable *B* is education. If 90 percent of the cases are men and 10 percent are women, you will learn a lot about the gender pattern in the group you are studying, but not a lot about the relationship of gender and education. The problem is that the variable of gender does not vary in this group.

Now look at the numbers in each cell. They tell you whether and how the two variables are related to each other. Are the cases distributed across the cells fairly evenly? If so, the two variables are not related to each other. Conversely, the more cases fall into either value 1 or 2, the greater the relationship between the variables.

We could use such a table to test Lipset's hypothesis that there is an association between social status and political participation. First, we would divide both variables into two values, low and high. (We could, of course, make other divisions, such as low, medium, and high.) Second, we would place them along the top and left sides of a table, as in table 5.3. Then we would make observations of various individuals to determine both their status and the extent to which they participate in politics. Each individual would then be placed in one of the four cells. After completing all of our observations, we would indicate the total number in each cell. *A*, *B*, *C*, and *D* in table 5.3 represent these total numbers.

Lipset proposed that people with low status will participate less. He was saying that of all the observations classified as low on status, most would fall in the cell with *X* in it. We could hypothesize that the reverse is also true: high status is associated with high participation. Place a *Z* in table 5.3 to indicate where most of the cases would fall if the second hypothesis were true.

(You should have placed a *Z* beside variable *D*.)

We can illustrate how tables showing associations can be used to test hypotheses with the following research. The Justice Department reported a six-year study in 1982 that concluded that "teenagers who drive or hold jobs are more likely to run into trouble with the law." It also found that teenagers from broken homes are not more likely to break the law than are those who grow up in unbroken homes. Their initial hypotheses could be stated as follows:

H_0 Teenagers who drive are no more or less likely to run into trouble with the law than are teenagers who do not drive.

H_1 Teenagers who drive are more likely to run into trouble with the law than are teenagers who do not drive.

H_0 Teenagers from broken homes are no more or less likely to run into trouble with the law than are those from unbroken homes.

TABLE 5.3
Relationship between Status and Participation

Participation	Status	
	Low	*High*
Low	A (X)	C
High	B	D

H_2 Teenagers from broken homes are more likely to run into trouble with the law than are those from unbroken homes.

The researchers discussed possible reasons for linking these variables. Young people with jobs and access to a car have more opportunity to make contacts outside the school context than do those without jobs. This opportunity increases the chances of becoming involved with criminals. The researchers believed that the second hypothesis (H_2) did not make much sense because there is no reason to assume that teenagers from broken homes are more tempted to get into crime than those not from broken homes.

If we create tables to test these hypotheses we get the following:

For Hypothesis 1:

Variable 1: Access to car   Value 1 = yes
                                Value 2 = no

Variable 2: Trouble with law   Value 1 = yes
                                Value 2 = no

	Access to Car	
Trouble with Law	*Yes*	*No*
Yes	A	C
No	B	D

Results: The study found that variable *A* was higher than variable *C*, indicating that teenagers with access to a car were more apt to be in trouble with the law than those without access to a car. Thus, we can reject the null hypothesis and accept our first hypothesis.

For Hypothesis 2:

Variable 1: Family background   Value 1 = broken
                                Value 2 = unbroken

Variable 2: Trouble with law   Value 1 = yes
                                Value 2 = no

	Family Background	
Trouble with Law	*Broken*	*Unbroken*
Yes	A	C
No	B	D

Results: The study showed that variable *A* was about the same as variable *C*, so we cannot reject the null hypothesis. Instead, we have to reject the second working hypothesis.

Creating Tables to Show an Association

Is there a relationship between GNP and life expectancy? Is this even an interesting or logical question to ask? One would expect that the higher a country's GNP, the more resources available for basic necessities, and the greater the life expectancy. Thus there is a logic in asking if the two variables are related. It is reasonable to expect that they are related and that the association is positive. Table 5.4 contains information on these two variables for selected countries. First, state the null and research hypotheses.

H_0 _____

_____

H_1 _____

_____

These variables are at the interval level and therefore provide the highest level of measurement. If we want to display the information in a table, however, it would be cumbersome to create a table with columns and rows for each value. Therefore, we need to convert the data into the ordinal level—such as low/high or low/medium/high. Scan the data and make a judgment about a reasonable way

TABLE 5.4

Life Expectancy and Gross National Product (GNP) for Selected Countries, 1994

Country	GNP (Dollars)	Life Expectancy (Years)
Egypt	720	62
Nigeria	280	52
Burundi	160	50
Jordan	1,440	70
Philippines	950	65
Japan	34,630	79
United States	25,880	77
Brazil	970	67
Greece	7,700	78
Costa Rica	2,400	77

Source: *World Development Report, 1996* (Washington, D.C.: World Bank, 1996), Table 1, pp. 188–189.

to divide them that captures the spread of values. One possibility is to create a variable at the ordinal level with two values and designate all those cases with GNP below 2,000 as "low" and the others as "high."

> Low GNP—2,000 and below
> High GNP—above 2,000

However, it would capture the spread of values better to create three values for GNP as follows:

> Low GNP—Below 1,000
> Middle GNP—1,000 to 10,000
> High GNP—Above 10,000.

Now decide how to categorize the values for the second variable, *life expectancy*. Since you want your variable to vary, you would not designate all cases from 0 to 50 as "low" because then only one case would fall into that category. Given the distribution of cases, it is reasonable to assign a value of "low" to those below age seventy and the value of "high" to those age seventy or above. If you follow this course you will have two values as follows:

> Low life expectancy (70 and below)
> High life expectancy (above 70)

Basing your decision on the foregoing assigned values, fill in the following table, listing which value—"low," "medium," or "high"—should be assigned to each country for each variable.

Country	Value on Variable *A*	Value on Variable *B*
Egypt		
Nigeria		
Burundi		
Jordan		
Philippines		
Japan		
United States		
Brazil		
Greece		
Costa Rica		

Source: *World Development Report, 1996* (Washington D.C.: World Bank, 1996). Table 1, pp. 188–189.

TABLE 5.5
Relationship between Life Expectancy and GNP for Selected Countries, 1994

Life Expectancy (Variable *B*)	GNP (Variable *A*)		
	Low (Value 1)	*Middle (Value 2)*	*High (Value 3)*
Low (value 1)			(Total)
High (value 2)			(Total)
Total			

Complete table 5.5, indicating the proper titles for the columns and rows and filling in the cells. The result will allow you to determine quickly whether the two variables are related.

Do the data support or reject H_0? _____

Do the data support or reject H_1? _____

There clearly is a relationship between the two variables. All five countries with low GNP are also low on life expectancy scores. The two countries high on GNP are high on life expectancy. The countries with a medium GNP are split between low and high life expectancy. Thus, we would reject the null hypothesis that there is no relationship between them. As a follow-up you could do several things: You could collect information on a larger number of cases to see if the relationship held up. Recall that you worked with data on these same two variables for a different set of countries in chapter 2, table 2.2. You could include those countries in this analysis or you could go to the source for this information, *World Development Report*, and select your own sample of countries. (Chapter 7 will describe how to draw a sample.) You could go back and rethink how you set the values of "high," "medium, and "low" to see if these biased your results. You could study the four countries with middle GNP in more detail to see why some were higher on life expectancy than others. You might even do a case study of two of the countries in order to complement this analysis. Later chapters will help you consider these options further.

Explanatory and Causal Relationships

Dependent and Independent Variables

A lot of research in political science attempts to go further than describing relationships and seeks to find the causes of the events or behavior it describes.

Research commonly begins by describing some phenomenon, then considering possible causes for the phenomenon, focusing in on the most likely cause, and finally designing research to examine whether it is related to the phenomenon. But causality can be difficult to establish and involves more than saying there is a relationship between two variables. There is no clear rule that states when a relationship is more accurately described as a correlation or as a causal association. It depends on whether or not it makes sense to say that *A* causes *B*, and on whether or not other factors could have been responsible. Recall that in comparing research designs, we noted that it is easier to establish causality with experiments because the researcher has some control over the variables and the relationship. In using correlational research, it is more difficult to make a case that one variable causes another even if they are related to each other. This section introduces the terms we use to talk about causal relations and describes how to set up a table to indicate a causal relation.

Return to the question about population changes in urban areas discussed in chapter 2. There we found that large urban areas in the Midwest are losing population, and those in the South and West are increasing in size. One possible explanation or cause of this trend concerns job opportunities. If it turns out that there has been a decline in job opportunities in midwestern cities but not in southern cities, we could conclude that the loss of jobs in large midwestern cities has caused their populations to decline. Note that we are drawing this conclusion partly on the basis of the evidence and partly because it makes logical sense. This explanation could initially be stated as a research hypothesis: "Compared to cities in the South and West, large midwestern cities are losing population because they can no longer offer as many employment opportunities as cities in the South and West offer."

What are the two variables in the study of cities? One is the variable *population trend* (value 1 = increases or stays the same; value 2 = declines). This variable is called the **dependent variable.** We call it that because we want to know what it *depends on*. We are proposing that the other variable, *job opportunities* (value 1 = increases or stays the same; value 2 = declines) is the **independent variable.** We call it that because it does not depend on the first variable. Our causal hypothesis is that the population trend of cities (dependent variable) depends on the job opportunities that are present.

dependent variable
Variable we wish to explain; its value is influenced by that of the independent variable.

independent variable
Variable we propose as the cause of the dependent variable.

Refer to the earlier example about life expectancy and GNP, and name the dependent and independent variables. (Life expectancy is the dependent variable because you want to determine what it depends on. GNP is the independent variable because it is reasonable to ask if it influences the life expectancy in a country. One could argue the reverse, but it would not make as much sense.)

A third example: Recall earlier discussions about the relationship between education and voter turnout. Which of these would be the dependent variable? You would never say that one's education depends on whether or not one voted. We have already said that, strictly speaking, education does not directly cause one to vote. At the same time, we noted that educated people are more apt to understand the issues and to pay attention to differences among candidates, and in this sense it is reasonable to propose that education explains or influences voting.

VARIABLES IN A CAUSAL PROPOSITION

Dependent Variable

The variable in which we are primarily interested, and which, we assume, depends on a second variable.

Independent Variable

The variable we propose as the cause of the dependent variable. Within this particular relationship it is independent because it does not depend on the other variable(s).

Example: Changes in job opportunities have led to changes in population size in our cities. *Job opportunities* is the independent variable. It is proposed that job opportunities have an influence on changes in *population size*, the dependent variable.

**Practice
Exercise 5.2**

Finding Dependent and Independent Variables

Television and school test scores

In 1980 the California Department of Education surveyed more than half a million public school pupils in the sixth and twelfth grades about their television viewing habits. The department researchers examined the relationship between the time the youngsters spent viewing television and their test scores. Based on this description, identify the following elements of the study:

Variable 1: _____

_____

Variable 2: _____

_____

Rationale for proposing a causal relationship: _____

_____

Dependent variable: _____

_____

Hypothesis the Department of Education could have used: _____

_____

Right-turn-on-red (RTOR) laws

Congress legislated the RTOR policy in 1975, a time when energy costs were very high. Legislators assumed that RTOR would reduce the amount of time spent waiting for lights to change and hence would reduce the gasoline that cars used. The Insurance Institute for Highway Safety, however, found that RTOR had another effect also. Accidents involving cars and people on foot in cities increased by 79 percent after RTOR became law. Based on this description, identify the following elements of the study:

Independent variable: _____

_____

Two dependent variables: _____

_____

Criteria for Causality

Now that we have learned some of the terms associated with causality, we can look in more detail at the logic of causality. We have said that an association indicates that as one variable changes the other changes also. Knowing that causality is difficult to demonstrate, how can we be confident that one change brings about, or causes, the other change? The English philosopher David Hume observed that causal statements can never be proved conclusively using empirical evidence. We never can actually observe a causal link but can only assume it; therefore, we cannot demonstrate causality on the basis of evidence alone. We nevertheless continue to look for and talk about causality, and a good part of research is devoted to finding causal relations. Hubert Blalock describes causal statements as "working assumptions" that we make even if we cannot say that they actually describe reality.

> One admits that causal thinking belongs completely on the theoretical level and that causal laws can never be demonstrated empirically. But this does not mean that it is not helpful to think causally and to develop causal models that have implications that are indirectly testable.[1]

causal relationship
A relationship in which changes in one variable bring about changes in another variable.

Causal relationships must meet five conditions. First, changes in one variable must be related to changes in another one. This condition is met if the two variables are associated with each other. Second, the causal variable must precede the other in time. The causal variable may be either a previous event or a prior condition, such as a person's gender or income. Third, the linkage between cause and effect must be plausible. There must be some theoretical or logical connection between the proposed cause and effect. In other words, the nature of the relationship between two variables has to make sense. Fourth, the proposed relationship must be consistent with other evidence. Finally, it must be reasonably clear that the causal factor identified, rather than other factors, is the most important one. This last condition is probably the most significant and also the most difficult one to establish. Many of the techniques discussed throughout the rest of the book are efforts to demonstrate this. Some of them will attempt to establish that one or two factors were the most important causes. Others will look at multiple causes and try to sort out the importance of each cause.

CRITERIA FOR CAUSALITY

Variables must change together.

Change in the independent variable or causal variable must precede change in the dependent variable.

The causal process or linkage must be plausible.

The relationship must be consistent with other evidence.

While there is often more than one factor causing something, one must be reasonably certain that the proposed cause is important relative to other influences.

Consider the discussion of the defeat of the Equal Rights Amendment, which was used in chapter 3 to illustrate ways to measure concepts. One interesting causal proposition is that opposition by women rather than men led to its defeat. Using the criteria for causality listed in the nearby box, how could we test this proposition and determine if it is reasonable to assert a causal relation?

1. *Relationship.* First we could ask if the dependent variable, action by states on the ERA, changed in the same direction as the independent variable, organized action by women's groups. We would design our research to determine if the states that opposed the ERA were also the states where women were most actively organized in opposition to it. We would also determine if the states that supported the ERA were the ones where organized opposition by women was weaker. If these relations proved true, then we could say there is a relationship. To say it is causal, it would also need to meet the following criteria.

2. *Plausibility.* Is it reasonable to assume that organized groups can influence this type of legislation? (Yes, since the issue received a lot of publicity and was highly controversial.)

3. *Precedence.* If women organized themselves against the ERA prior to the legislative action, then this condition would be fulfilled.

4. *Consistency.* Is the hypothesized cause consistent with other evidence? Have women organized and been successful on other issues? Was female opinion divided on the ERA issue? Were community groups opposed to the ERA politically active? (You would need to do some background research on these questions.)

5. *Importance relative to other factors.* Does the research suggest other reasons for the defeat? For example, were the states that failed to ratify the ERA generally conservative, and did conservative philosophy play a major part in the

ERA's defeat? If so, then perhaps the role of women was not a significant cause and further analysis would be necessary.

Recall that chapter 4 dealt with the last criterion, "relative importance," in discussing experiments. The treatment, or experiment, is always the independent variable. In order to be certain that the experimental activity or policy brought about any observed difference, and not some other factor, experiments rely on control groups. To the extent that the experimental and control groups are similar except for receiving a treatment, we can be fairly certain that the experiment caused the result. For this reason, experiments can establish causality more readily than the other designs. Quasi-experiments can eliminate other factors to the extent that the treatment and control groups are similar, but this is often hard to determine with this research design. Both experiments and quasi-experiments, however, can establish whether or not the independent variable preceded the dependent variable. Correlational designs have the hardest time meeting two of the criteria: establishing which variable preceded the other and whether or not other factors besides the proposed cause were present. (Chapter 6 will describe how to include control variables in correlations in order to meet these two criteria).

Explaining Life Expectancy

Practice Exercise 5.3

Return to table 5.4 and the information you compiled in table 5.5. There you found that there is a relationship between life expectancy and GNP. Is it reasonable to go one step further and hypothesize that there is a causal relationship here, that a country's GNP influences the life expectancy in that country? Apply the criteria for establishing causality to this hypothesis. If you are not sure, indicate the information you would need in order to determine whether it met a particular criterion. (See the endnotes for answers to this exercise.[2])

1. *Relationship:* _____

_____

2. *Plausibility:* _____

_____

3. *Precedence:* _____

_____

4. *Consistency:* _____

_____

5. *Importance, relative to other factors:* _____

_____

Constructing Tables to Depict a Causal Relationship between Two Variables

When we create a table to illustrate a proposed causal relationship, we have to distinguish between the independent and dependent variables. We place the independent variable across the top, so that it labels the columns, and the dependent variable along the side so that its values are reported in the rows (see table 5.6). This is a useful convention because it allows you to test your hypothesis by comparing the columns, which is a natural way for the eye to read a table. (Some may not always follow this convention, so when reading tables prepared by others you will need to confirm that the independent variable is placed in the columns.)

Recall the earlier example in which we asked whether changes in job opportunities could explain the decline in population of some cities. We can develop a table to see if there is in fact a causal relationship (see table 5.7). Once again our observations are cities. We would collect data on the two variables and determine in which cell each city should be located. We are particularly interested in comparing variables *A* and *C*. If cities in which manufacturing jobs had left the cities were as likely to lose population as cities in which such jobs had remained, then we could not reject the null hypothesis. There would be no relationship between manufacturing jobs and population trends. On the other hand, if the percentage of cities in *A* (where manufacturing jobs left the cities) was higher than the percentage in *C* (where manufacturing jobs remained in the cities), we could conclude that there was some support for our hypothesis that job opportunities explain population trends in cities.

Note that we usually state our conclusions conservatively. These findings would not *prove* that job opportunities *cause* population trends. Rather, we developed a hypothesis that seems to make sense from all that we know about why people move. If we find evidence to support it, we can say that job markets do seem to have a positive influence on changes in population: the more jobs that are available, the more people will be drawn to an area. We can continue to look for evidence from other sources to see if this relationship continues to hold up. The more studies that confirm the causal relationship, the more confident we can be about it.

TABLE 5.6
Format of a Table Representing a Causal Relationship

	Independent Variable	
Dependent Variable	*Value A*	*Value B*
Value A		
Value B		
Total Number		

TABLE 5.7
Population Trends and Manufacturing Locations

Population Trend	Manufacturing Jobs	
	Left the Cities	*Remained in Cities*
Declined	A	C
Same or more	B	D
Total Number	A + B	C + D

Example: Exploring a Causal Relation—Civic Culture, Democracy, and TV

U.S. foreign policy is committed to encouraging democratic institutions and practices. Related to this policy concern, there is an extensive body of political science research that explores the correlates of democracy. For several decades, researchers emphasized the importance of economic development; more recently studies have returned to a much earlier concern with the role of public attitudes and values. We look here at recent research by Robert Putnam arguing that public attitudes such as trust in others and a sense of political efficacy have a positive influence on the establishment and durability of democratic regimes. Much of this research goes even farther and argues that without these attitudes, democracy will either not become established in the first place or will weaken. It is interesting for our purposes because it illustrates the importance of identifying useful concepts and finding appropriate measures, of laying out the logic of a relationship, of examining if an association between variables means there is a causal relationship, and of considering alternative influences. The example goes one step farther and proposes a second causal relationship—namely a variable that influences the degree of trust in a society. Finally, it describes some criticism of these propositions that question the ways in which the variables are measured and whether other variables have been adequately taken into account.

Putnam begins with the concept of "social capital," which he defines as the "features of social life—networks, norms, and trust—that enable participants to act together more effectively to pursue shared objectives."[3] Putnam identifies several indicators and sources of evidence to determine the amount of such "capital" in democratic societies. He looks at surveys taken over several years in which individuals recorded every activity during the day, including time spent in social and civic organizations. He looks at membership records of a variety of organizations to determine numbers of participants. He looks at national surveys that ask people about their political activities. He also looks at surveys which measure individuals' trust in others over time.[4] He concluded there has been a significant decline in civic involvement or social capital in the United States over the past several decades.

Putnam next asks what could have caused this decline. He speculates about a number of possible factors, including increased mobility in the population, the movement of people from cities to suburbs, the supposed increase in time pressures on families, economic pressures that cause people to work more, and the increase of women in the workforce. In each case, he concludes that none of these were a significant factor, since the decline in civic involvement occurred across all values of each of these variables. The decline is true of those who remain in cities and those who moved to suburbs; it is true of women who remain at home as well as those who work; and so forth. As he examines each factor he controls for the other factors, including education and gender.

One factor does stand out, namely age. Older people are more apt to involve themselves in civic activities and to trust others. But he finds no evidence that individuals become more trusting or involved as they get older. Why therefore are older people more involved and trusting? Putnam solves his puzzle by proposing that those born early in this century who came of age prior to the World War II period are more engaged in community affairs. The data support this proposition. Up until the mid-1940s people of all ages were more apt to be involved and more apt to trust others. Since then both involvement and trust have steadily declined.

Next Putnam asks what brought about this significant change. He proposes that the culprit is TV, that there is a negative relationship between civic-mindedness on the one hand and TV viewing on the other—the more TV one watches, the less that person expresses civic-mindedness.[5] Putnam states this proposition and offers a logical theory to connect the two variables. First, people spend time watching TV that they used to spend on civic activities. Second, television leads viewers to take a darker view of others and of the political arena.[6] He cites evidence for this conclusion using survey data from 1974 to 1994 that found television viewing was strongly and negatively related to social trust, group membership, and voting turnout.

Putnam's research has provoked a great deal of comment and further studies, as well as its share of criticism. Some have argued that he needs to be more precise about the variables in the relationship. Pippa Norris, for example, says that we need to distinguish between the kind of TV programs that one watches. Norris used data from a different national survey that included questions about TV viewing, attention to other media, political attitudes, and participation. After distinguishing between different TV programs, he found that "those who regularly tuned into the network news were significantly more likely to be involved in all types of political activity, and the relationship between watching public affairs programs on television and civic engagement proved even stronger."[7]

There are two relevant points here. First, we may use broad concepts (TV viewing in this case) and fail to be as precise as we need to be ("watching general TV" versus "watching TV news"). The second point is that it is difficult to use correlational research to establish that one variable causes the other. Norris illustrates the difficulty. "On the one hand it seems most plausible that watching television news or reading about public affairs would encourage people to become more active in politics. . . . On the other hand it may be that those who are already involved in public life turn to the news media to find out more about current events. The relationship is probably somewhat reciprocal. . . . "[8] In other words, even after finding a relationship, Norris said he could not conclude that one variable caused the other.

Where We Are

The last example illustrates many of the challenges and problems in researching political questions. It would be a mistake to be discouraged by the numerous criticisms of Putnam's research. He posed some important issues and sparked a lot of interest and follow-up studies. In this respect the ensuing dialogue illustrates the true nature of social science research. It is done by a community of scholars who refer to, build on, critique, and refine one another's studies. Knowing the existing literature in the field is an important element in research. For students this means that what you read in nonresearch methods courses should be examined in light of what you are learning in this book. What studies and statements are offered in other courses that interest you? How well do they observe the practices described herein? What additional studies could you carry out to add to their findings, to qualify their findings, to see if their results are applicable to a new situation or time? It also means that you are starting your research not with a blank sheet but with what others have done.

The next chapter invites you to look at the multiple ways in which others have defined and approached a research question. It will help you identify the perspective you bring to bear on a problem and encourage you to place that in a broader context. What are some of the many ways to define a problem, and how does your research fit with and complement the research of others?

NOTES

1. Hubert M. Blalock, Jr., *Causal Inferences in Nonexperimental Research* (New York: Norton, 1961), p. 7.
2. Answers to life expectancy exercise:
    1. *Relationship:* Yes, see Table 5.5.
    2. *Plausibility:* Yes, it makes sense to assume that more resources enhance life expectancy.
    3. *Precedence:* Generally, yes.
    4. *Consistency:* Yes, this proposition fits with other studies.
    5. *Importance, relative to other factors.* This is hard to determine without information on other factors such as distribution of GNP among the populace and access to health services.
3. Robert D. Putnam, "The Strange Disappearance of Civic America," *The American Prospect 24* (Winter 1996): 34–50.
4. Specific surveys used by Putnam include the General Social Survey (GSS), Gallup polls, and National Opinion Research Center information. For more on these sources see chapters 7 and 9.
5. Robert Putnam, *Making Democracy Work* (Princeton, N.J.: Princeton University Press, 1994).

6. Robert Putnam, "Tuning In, Tuning Out: The Strange Disappearance of Social Capital in America," *PS: Political Science and Politics 27*, no. 4 (December 1995): 664–683.
7. Pippa Norris, "Does Television Erode Social Capital? A Reply to Putnam," *PS: Political Science and Politics 26*, no. 3 (September 1996): 474–480.
8. Norris, "Does Television Erode Social Capital?" pp. 475–476.

EXERCISES

Exercise 5.1 Reading Tables

Read the following table, then answer the questions that follow.

TABLE 5.8

Attitudes toward Public Housing Expenditures by Income (in percentages)

Attitude toward Public Housing Expenditures	Income Group		
	Low	*Medium*	*High*
Spend more	48	35	29
Spend same	39	47	22
Spend less	13	18	49
Total	100	100	100

1. Name the two variables in this study.

2. Is there a dependent variable? If so, what is it?

3. List the values of the independent variable.

4. State a clear, brief proposition that sums up some or all of the information in the table.

5. Propose a brief explanation of the relationship you observe. Note: do not just repeat the results. *Why* do you think these results occurred? Do they make any sense from what you know? Are they logical?

TABLE 5.9
Central Government Expenditures on Defense and Social Services, 1994

Country	Defense Expenditures as % of Total Expenditures	Social Services Expenditures as % of Total Expenditures
Austria	2.2	70.1
Canada	6.9	51.4
Denmark	4.7	53.5
Finland	3.7	59.3
France	5.6	68.7
Ireland	3.2	57.3
Israel	19.2	49.1
Japan	4.2	59.2
Netherlands	4.3	69.3
Norway	6.5	55.6
Spain	3.4	48.6
Sweden	5.3	56.8
United Kingdom	10.4	52.2
United States	18.1	52.1

Source: *World Development Report, 1996* (Washington, D.C.: World Bank, 1996), table 14, pp. 214–215.

Exercise 5.2 Creating Tables to Examine Relationships

Using the information in table 5.9, create a table to determine if there is a relationship between expenditures on defense and expenditures on social services. What would you expect to find? Do countries that spend more on defense spend less on social services, as suggested by the familiar argument that countries have to choose between guns and butter? Or do those that spend a lot on one item also spend a lot on the other?

In order to place the information in a table, you will need to convert the data from the interval to the ordinal level. (In a later exercise you will analyze the information at the interval level.) Given the spread of values on defense expenditures, it is reasonable to divide the cases into three categories: low: 1–4.9 percent; middle: 5–10.9 percent; high: 11 percent and above. The values for social services fall closer together, so it would be reasonable to divide them into two categories: low: 1–55.9 percent; high: 56.1 percent and above.

1. Create a table and place the cases in the appropriate cells. Compute the percentage of cases in each cell. Be sure to include a clear title and indicate where to put 100 percent.

2. Which of the following hypotheses is best supported by the data?

H₁: There is a direct (positive) relationship between social services and defense expenditures. The more money a country spends on one, the more they spend on the other.

H₂: There is an inverse (negative) relationship between spending on social services and defense. The more money a country spends on one, the less they spend on the other.

Exercise 5.3 Creating Tables to Examine Relationships

The following information reports math scores and hours spent watching TV for thirteen-year-olds in different countries. You are asked to see if there is any relationship between these variables.

Average Math Scores of Thirteen-Year-Old Participants in IAEP*, by Country, 1991

Canada, 62; France, 64; Hungary, 68; Ireland, 61; Israel, 63; Italy, 64; Jordan, 40; South Korea, 73; Scotland, 61; Slovenia, 57; Soviet Union, 70; Spain, 55; Switzerland, 71; Taiwan, 73; United States, 55.

Percentage of Thirteen-Year-Old Participants in IAEP* Who Watch Television Five Hours or More a Day, by Country, 1991

Canada, 14; France, 5; Hungary, 13; Ireland, 9; Israel, 20; Italy, 5; Jordan, 7; South Korea, 11; Scotland, 24; Slovenia, 4; Soviet Union, 17; Spain, 10; Switzerland, 7; Taiwan, 10; United States, 20.

Source: National Center for Education Statistics, *Digest of Education Statistics* (Washington, D.C.: U.S. Department of Education, 1995), p. 431.

International Assessment of Educational Progress

1. Name the two variables contained in this information.

2. Develop a proposition and a null hypothesis about these two variables.

3. Place the information in a table that allows you to test the proposition. Be sure to include labels and an accurate title. Use your judgment to divide the values for each variable into categories that reflect the distribution of values.

4. Write a clear statement that summarizes the information in the table. If you are surprised by the results, speculate about a possible reason for them.

Exercise 5.4 Creating Tables to Examine Relationships, Continued

This exercise asks you to build on the information in Exercise 5.3. Below is information for the same countries on the percent of students in each country who read for fun every day. Create a table to see if there is a relationship between reading and math scores. Compare the two tables. Does there appear to be a stronger relationship between math scores and watching TV or between math scores and reading for fun?

Percentage of Thirteen-Year-Old Participants in IAEP* Who Read for Fun Every Day, by Country, 1991

Canada, 38; France, 40; Hungary, 44; Ireland, 41; Israel, 40; Italy, 47; Jordan, 24; South Korea, 11; Scotland, 38; Slovenia, 42; Soviet Union (former), 47; Spain, 38; Switzerland, 51; Taiwan, 19; United States, 28.

Source: National Center for Education Statistics, *Digest of Education Statistics*, (Washington, D.C.: U.S. Department of Education, 1995), p. 431.

International Assessment of Educational Progress

Exercise 5.5 Explanatory and Causal Relationships

Segregation of schools was a major public policy issue in the 1950s and has become so again in the 1990s. Below is a summary of the 1954 Supreme Court decision outlawing segregated schools. After reading it do the following:

1. Identify the causal proposition in that ruling.

2. Design research, using one of the designs studied in chapter 4, to determine whether there is support for this proposition.

In the 1954 case of *Brown* v. *Board of Education of Topeka*, the Supreme Court ruled that segregated schools were unconstitutional. Its decision was based partly on evidence offered by psychologists that segregation implies inferiority of one group. In this case, black Americans. The Court outlawed separate school systems, ruling that a sense of inferiority affects the motivation of a child to learn. Segregation with the sanction of law, therefore, has a tendency to retard the educational and mental development of Negro children and to deprive them of some of the benefits they would receive in a racially integrated school system [*Brown* v. *Board of Education of Topeka*, 347 U.S. 483, 1954].

CHAPTER SIX

Exploring Relationships: Building Theories and Causal Models

We explore the arts of developing, elaborating, contemplating, testing, and re-vising models of human behavior. The point of view is that of a person trying to comprehend the behavior around him. . . . The effort is complicated and subtle; it has a distinguished history. Aristotle, Smith, Toynbee, Marx, Malinowski, Camus, James, Weber, Dostoevsky, Freud, Durkheim, Cervantes and a host of other figures have added to our understanding of human behavior.

Despite such an impressive ancestry our ambitions are not heroic. We think that playing with ideas is fun. We think there are some interesting ideas in the social sciences. We think that an increase in the quality of speculation both in the social sciences and in everyday life would be good. We would like to contribute to an un-derstanding of models in the social sciences and to enjoyment of their pleasure.

—Charles Lave and James March, *An Introduction to Models in the Social Sciences*

The world is incomplete if seen from any one point of view and incoherent if seen from all points of view at once.

—Richard Shweder, University of Chicago

Major crime is down and nobody knows just how it happened. There's the de-mographic explanation: a drop in the number of young people reaching the age of impulse and rebellion. There's the strategic explanation: more use of community policing, forfeiture, quicker response to domestic violence and scary street crimes. There's the economic explanation: when unemployment goes down, so does crime. And there's the hang-'em-high explanation: We've finally locked up enough vio-lent offenders for long enough terms to make the world safer for the rest of us. Most likely, it's all of the above. The drop in major crime . . . has been achieved inch by inch, block by block, child by child, measure by measure.

—Editorial, Detroit Free Press, 6 June 1997

Multiple Relationships and Influences

The previous chapter described statements that propose a relationship between two variables. You learned some of the basic terms and underlying logic employed in carrying out research. We began with simple relationships that are relatively straightforward and that you can use to get started doing actual research. The material in this chapter asks you to step back, to look at your assumptions about relationships, to examine alternative theories, to develop several propositions, and to consider alternative research designs. These steps make research somewhat more complex but also more challenging and—it is hoped—more fun.

You are asked to be imaginative and speculate about a variety of relationships, to expand the number of variables and relationships you consider. Then the chapter considers techniques for reducing and simplifying the number of relationships we study. You will be introduced to model building, the design of a simplified picture of reality with a limited number of variables.[1] Throughout, the chapter refers to the measurement choices and research designs discussed in chapters 3 and 4. The central point is that the measures and evidence we select and the research designs we choose must be appropriate for the questions we are asking. It is not enough to learn different research skills; it is also important to understand how they are linked to different research questions.

Seldom is an event caused or influenced by a single factor; an event or activity or trend you are interested in usually is a product of many factors. Note the excerpt from the editorial about the reasons for the decline in crime cited at the beginning of this chapter. There are many possible reasons for the decline in crime in 1997, and probably there is some truth in all of them. How do we decide which to focus on? If explanation is viewed as a cluster of factors, or a chain of conditions, some of these conditions will be more closely linked or connected to the event we are interested in than others. And some will be things we can change more readily than others and hence may be of more interest. Sometimes we will be particularly focused on immediate or changeable factors; other times we may be more concerned with underlying factors. Figure 6.1, in which *I* represents

FIGURE 6.1

A Chain of Influences

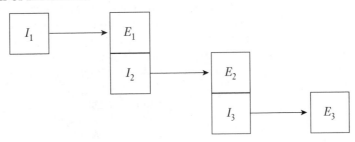

FIGURE 6.2
Influences on Crime

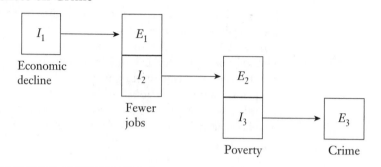

---

causal chain
Sequence of related events in which the effect of one variable becomes the cause of a third variable; multiple causes and effects.

influence and *E* represents *effects*, illustrates one hypothetical model of such a **causal chain.**[2] The figure shows how an effect in one relationship can also serve as an influence on a second effect; that is, $E_1 = I_2$, and so forth. Thus, in figure 6.2 the variable *fewer jobs* is both the effect of economic decline and an influence producing poverty. If you are interested in effect number 3 (E_3) as the dependent variable, you can choose to focus on I_1, I_2, or I_3.

 Which sequence of events you choose to study depends in part on your perspective. A chain of events leading to crime might follow the sequence shown in figure 6.2. Depending on which variables were of most interest to you, you might focus on the health of the economy, the number of jobs, or the incidence of poverty, and show how one of those factors is related to crime. You could look at all of the factors simultaneously; more often you would select one or two from the variety of possible influences. As noted in the quote at the beginning of this chapter, while "the world is incomplete if seen from any one point of view" it is also "incoherent if seen from all points of view at once."

 An analysis of teenage crime in Washington, D.C., provides an example of such a chain of influences. A newspaper account suggested a variety of influences on youth crime, and these can be diagrammed as in figure 6.3.[3]

Speculating about Different Relationships

Why do we select one set of relationships to study rather than another? Frequently the propositions we develop reflect our beliefs and values. That is, we tend to select propositions that fit our preconceptions of what relationships exist. Moreover, background and training may influence which of the several influences a researcher decides to emphasize. A scientist once observed that

> the cause of an outbreak of plague may be regarded by the bacteriologist as the microbe he finds in the blood of the victim, by the entomologist as the microbe-carrying fleas that spread the disease, by the epidemiologist as the rats that escaped from the ship and brought the infection into the port.[4]

FIGURE 6.3

Influences on Juvenile Crime

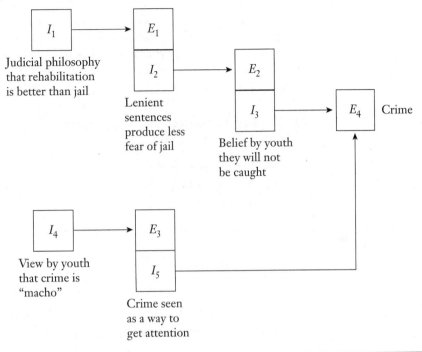

In the social sciences, similar differences can be found among the various disciplines. To understand the causes of poverty, a sociologist might focus on the pressures in the community, a psychologist might look at a person's beliefs and values, and a political scientist might emphasize the distribution of power and influence in the community.

Unfortunately it is all too natural to formulate a proposition that fits our biases and then look for evidence that confirms that proposition. The proposition may or may not be accurate, but in the meantime it leads us to look for certain kinds of evidence and to ignore others. Take a simple example. We know that scores on scholastic aptitude tests taken by high school students have generally declined. What reason do you immediately think of for the decline? Some reasons focus on the characteristics of the students themselves: their presumed disinterest, lack of ambition, and low commitment to learning. People who choose these kinds of explanations are focusing on the individuals involved. A different approach is to consider the nature of education, the quality of teaching, and the relevance of the subject matter. Perhaps students are really committed to learning, but the educational system makes it difficult for them to learn. A third approach would focus on what has been happening in the society. It might emphasize changes in the job market and the increasing demand for technical training rather than liberal arts learning. In this case the decline in scores could reflect lowered demand for the kinds of skills included on the test.

Think of your own performance in an English composition class and propose an explanation for the quality of your work. Can you think of three alternatives that match the approaches just identified: (1) characteristics of individuals, (2) characteristics of the subject matter, and (3) characteristics of one's situation or of one's expectations? Use the following questions as guides:

1. Would you describe your performance in English composition as good, fair, or poor? _____

_____

2. Was there an individual characteristic of yours that could have produced this result? _____

_____

3. Was there a characteristic of the class or subject matter that might have produced this result? _____

_____

4. Can you think of any characteristic of our culture, or of your expectations for the future, that might have contributed to this result? _____

_____

5. Which of these alternatives do you ordinarily think of first? _____

_____

Consider a second example. There is a long and important debate between those who tend to explain events by examining the characteristics of individuals and those who are more apt to propose that the characteristics of the situation explain what happens. People in the first group are more apt to hold individuals responsible for what happens to them; those in the second group are more apt to focus on the constraints and opportunities that confront individuals. To explain poverty, say, one can propose that those who remain poor are apathetic and lack a sense of the future. Alternatively, one could propose that the situation in which the poor find themselves offers few opportunities and breeds resentment and low self-esteem.[5] The debate has important policy implications. Ask yourself:

Would someone who favored spending more funds on Head Start as a way to reduce poverty be more apt to use the first or the second approach? _____

Would someone who favored a job training program be more apt to use the first or the second approach? _____

(The first approach is more compatible with Head Start, because this program seeks in part to improve children's self-image; the second approach is more compatible with job training because this program seeks to improve a person's economic opportunities. You could argue that job training also affects a person's self-image. If that is your goal, you would design the job training program somewhat differently than would someone who is interested primarily in improving a person's technical skills.)

Becoming Sensitive to Our Own Approaches and Biases

approach
Perspective we adopt in analyzing a problem; lens through which we view an event; set of assumptions.

We have been using the term **approach** to describe the way in which we initially deal with a problem. This term suggests that we view events from particular perspectives and that we look for certain kinds of data and not others. In the example of performance in English composition, persons who begin with a focus on the individual will look for and collect evidence about individual behavior and characteristics. Typically, they will not be looking for data about the way the course is taught. It is important to be aware of the view we are taking and the extent to which it influences the data we look for and find.

Approaches and biases are not unique to the social sciences. Thomas Kuhn has written an important book about scientific thinking in which he demonstrates that natural scientists also proceed from previous assumptions about reality and about what causal factors are most important.[6] Our initial assumptions and understanding of reality can cause us to look for certain kinds of evidence and not others when we frame a hypothesis. As a result, we run the risk of presenting only a partial explanation of a problem. In the earlier example of the causes of plague, the epidemiologist looks for rats in the ship, not microbes in the blood. The lesson is twofold: first, our own research represents just one view of reality; second, we need to analyze which portion of a set of influences other researchers are examining and identify how our work fits with, complements, or challenges their studies.

Our approach, or set of assumptions, affects how we view public events; it determines what we pay attention to and what questions we ask. Graham Allison has given us a classic example of the importance of our assumptions by showing how they influenced the way in which different participants and scholars viewed the Cuban missile crisis.[7] In 1962, the United States learned there were Soviet missiles in Cuba. President John Kennedy responded by imposing a blockade of Cuba, and eventually the Soviets withdrew the missiles. Many observers believed that we had narrowly missed a devastating nuclear war. Because the incident was a seminal event in relations between the United States and the Soviet Union, and because it was so well documented by participants and researchers, many students, reporters, and politicians have studied the crisis in order to gain some insight into the elements of effective decision making about foreign policy.

Allison found that the observers, like all of us, looked at the crisis from a particular perspective that led them to emphasize certain actions and not others.

Most often, he notes, analysts assume that governments have goals and behave rationally to achieve them. Using this perspective, they examined the goals of the two superpowers and analyzed how each tried to accomplish them. Allison observes, however, that this approach omits some important factors. It ignores, for example, the political dimension in the situation: the role of public opinion, and the fact that the president was a Democrat, that the Democrats had been charged with being "soft on communism," and that the president needed to demonstrate he could stand up to the Russians. The traditional approach, focusing on goals, ignores these political aspects and thereby provides an incomplete view of how the crisis was handled.

Alternative Approaches

lateral thinking
Contrasts with vertical, or logical, thinking; emphasizes speculation and imagination.

Allison concludes that we need to think of alternative ways to study a relationship. One way is to practice what Edward de Bono has called **lateral thinking**.[8] Whereas vertical thinking involves the use of logic and deduction and reasoning, lateral thinking involves imagination and speculation. We can use it to break out of traditional thought patterns and generate alternative ways of looking at a problem. Studies tell us that the mind arranges information into patterns. When new information appears, the mind relates it to something it already knows. It thus relates new ideas or data to the already existing patterns. Because of this tendency, we easily may miss the unique aspects of an event or the extent to which it indicates a new pattern or relationship. De Bono emphasizes that it requires a real effort to look at events from several different perspectives. It is something we need to practice.

Alternative propositions and research strategies. The relationships you select to study will shape the question you propose and the evidence you collect. Assume you want to study poverty and compare the merits of different proposals for improving welfare. One influential proposition states that poverty is brought about by declining economic conditions, often by the decline of manufacturing job opportunities in an area. One way to test this argument is to do a correlational study and compare the income levels and economic development figures for a number of communities over a period of years. You would probably collect information on changes in manufacturing jobs, in employment figures, and in income levels. An alternative view argues that the poor do not lack job opportunities so much as they lack an attitude that allows them to take advantage of opportunities. This proposition would require you to carry out a survey or series of interviews with lower-income individuals, some of whom fell below the poverty line. For example, you could compare the views of different minority groups in communities undergoing major economic change.

A thorough study might include both sets of questions and research approaches—economic conditions and attitudes of low-income individuals. As a student of others' research, you should be able to assess how adequately they have framed the question and how appropriate their research is for their question. As a researcher yourself you may not be in a position to study both economic realities and attitudes. Your best strategy then is to summarize the studies that others have done, and to include your own research effort and show how it fits with others' research in the area.

Example: Exploring alternative approaches to economic development. Many persistent controversies in political science result from different ways of defining problems or viewing events. We have already mentioned different perspectives on poverty. Take another example: explanations for the poor economic performance of developing nations. The following paragraph lists a number of these. Read it and select five or six that appear most important to you. Using figure 6.3 as a model, complete figure 6.4 to illustrate possible patterns of influence.

> *Proposed explanations for economic difficulties in developing nations:* corrupt leadership, widespread poverty and illiteracy, weak political institutions established during the colonial period, persistence of traditional values among the citizens such as rewarding family members, international rivalry between East and West that destabilizes the developing nations, international trade patterns that keep these countries economically dependent on the industrialized nations, unwillingness by some to encourage the private sector to be more active, ethnic rivalries and conflict, and inefficient bureaucracies.

Example: Privatization of public schools. The following example of recent research illustrates several of the themes in this chapter: comparing approaches, reasoning about alternative propositions, and identifying appropriate evidence.[9] There is considerable concern that public schools are not performing as well as they could. One proposed solution is to give students vouchers that they can use to attend the school of their choice, either public or private. The underlying assumption is that if public schools have to compete for students they will become more student centered and less bureaucratic. Critics, by contrast, fear that privatization will hurt the performance of public schools by reducing their resources and by inducing the better students to go to private schools.

FIGURE 6.4
Proposed Patterns of Influence on Developing Country Economies

How could you do research to explore these issues? The first choice is to select your unit of analysis. If you focused on the individual you would ask how individuals perform when they can choose their school as compared with those who cannot. You could perhaps design a quasi-experiment by looking for a community where some students have moved to a voucher system and compare their performance before and after the policy change. The challenge would be to control for all the other influences on their performance. Or you could select the school as your unit of analysis and study how students perform across schools, comparing schools that are part of systems that use vouchers with schools in systems that do not use vouchers. This second approach allows the researcher to go beyond the characteristics of individuals and take into account the possible influence of the organization of the school and the social characteristics of the surrounding community.[10]

As stressed earlier, your research design will be greatly influenced by the kinds of evidence that are available. In this case, the authors were able to obtain data on student performance in the fourth and eighth grades—their dependent variable—by using records available from school districts in the state of Washington. Although the state did not have a voucher system, the authors tested whether competition for students affected performance by using available information on the number of children in private schools in each community. Their hypothesis: the greater the percentage of children in private schools, the greater the competition for students and the higher the performance of students in the public schools.

Sources of alternative approaches to a problem. Recall that at the end of chapter 2 we discussed different sources for hypotheses. Some sources are deductive; the researcher draws on theories and deduces predictions about different relations. One of the reasons that most universities require students to take courses in a number of disciplines is precisely to expose them to different theories about social events and behavior. Considering alternative theories and perspectives is a useful way to force us to compare hypotheses. Other sources are inductive; the researcher develops possible relationships based on observations and prior studies. Lateral thinking, just defined, is a form of induction and is another way to force us to consider alternatives.

The Role of Political Institutions and Practices

Political scientists stress that we need to consider the possible role of political factors in addition to social and economic ones. Pluralist models of government have tended to emphasize social and economic variables to the exclusion of political and institutional factors. In addition, political variables often point to elements that we can change or shape, and hence they stimulate us to think of strategies for making improvements in our political systems.

Compare two ways of explaining ethnic conflict in the Soviet Union during 1988. The occasion was an outbreak of protest by Armenians who wanted to annex an Armenian district that was part of a neighboring Soviet republic. The *Washington Post* and *New York Times*, which gave extensive coverage to the protests, generally explained them as outbreaks of ingrained religious and ethnic tensions and hostilities. The *Post* noted that "the riots have brought to the surface deep-seated bitterness between two rival ethnic groups."[11] Both papers stressed that the conflict reflected age-old antipathies.

From another perspective, this emphasis on ethnicity presents only a partial view and one that provides limited guidance for dealing with the situation. It focuses on unyielding cultural patterns rather than specific grievances. According to one observer, "Instead of describing the character of each national claim and the origins and nature of the conflicts between them, such articles lead to the conclusion . . . that ethnic enmity is inherent in ethnic difference itself." By focusing on ethnicity, the reporters paid little attention to efforts the Soviet government had made to help the protesters. They focused on social factors and overlooked political ones. Contrast this with the analysis in the French newspaper *Le Monde*, which was far more attentive to the political dimensions of the protests and conflict. Reporters described the actual grievances of the two ethnic groups and the various political maneuvers of the Soviet leaders, and they speculated about possible compromises that could be made in the future.[12] *Le Monde's* accounts examine the political dynamics in the situation and possibilities for handling the conflict, as opposed to the suggestion, certainly unintended, that such conflicts are inevitable and that political responses are largely irrelevant.

Review figure 6.4, the diagram you completed to examine possible influences on the economies of developing nations. Underline any of the influences that point to political variables or policies that may have shaped economic development.

Studies of nonvoting provide another opportunity for speculating about the importance of specifically political factors. A recent study observes that most studies explain nonvoting by examining attitudes, values, and culture. The author proposes that political processes may be more important than attitudes in discouraging or encouraging voter turnout.[13] To test this, he compares the characteristics of elections in several industrial democracies. One of the variables he looked at is the degree of competition in electoral districts. Competitiveness is important, he suggests, because parties and candidates are more motivated to mobilize voters when they anticipate that elections will be close than when they assume elections will be one-sided. His results indicate that competitiveness does have an influence on turnout: the less competition there is, the lower the turnout. A similar study argues that voting has declined because there has been much less effort in recent years to contact voters and turn out the vote. Between 1960 and 1988 there was a drop in voter turnout of 11 percentage points. Fifty-four percent of this decline was due to a "decline in mobilization," in efforts by parties and candidates to personally contact potential voters and urge them to go to the polls.[14] Finally, recall the research described in chapter 2 that voter disaffection is influenced by press reports of political corruption. All of these studies trace current voter behavior to specific political events and institutions and suggest that adequate theories and causal models of participation need to look at political factors.

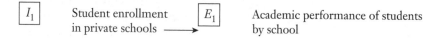

I_1 Student enrollment in private schools $\longrightarrow$ E_1 Academic performance of students by school

To test an alternative hypothesis that the social characteristics of schools (poverty, for example) affected student performance they used additional data. From census reports they found information on the median family income and the number of children in poverty in each community. From routine school reports they found information on parental education and money spent per pupil. This time, their hypothesis was that the higher the income and parental education and the more money spent per pupil, the higher the performance of students.

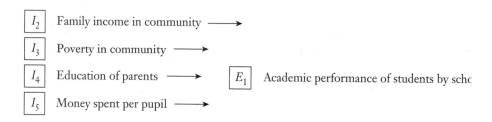

I_2 Family income in community $\longrightarrow$

I_3 Poverty in community $\longrightarrow$

I_4 Education of parents $\longrightarrow$ E_1 Academic performance of students by schc

I_5 Money spent per pupil $\longrightarrow$

The study used regression analysis (described in chapter 11) to compare the relative influence of these several independent variables. The authors found little evidence for the first hypothesis, that competition affected performance. Further, they found that education of parents and poverty in the community had a stronger relationship with performance than did either competition or resources spent per pupil.

Exploring the Process or Logic of Relationships

One way to speculate about multiple influences and relationships is to examine the logic or process that connects two variables. Earlier we noted that logic is important when we are developing propositions and hypotheses or trying to establish causality and that the connection between variables in a proposition has to be plausible. Thinking about the **process** that links several variables in a relationship may lead us to examine a number of other variables and perhaps some unexpected influences.

Consider the proposition that large organizations are more apt to be managed hierarchically than are smaller organizations. Sometimes it is sufficient

process
An examination of the logic, dynamics, and implications of a relationship between two variables.

to state this simple type of relationship: the more of one variable, the more of the other. For many purposes, however, it is useful to consider the nature of the proposed relationship more fully and to examine the process by which its terms are related. What is the basis for our reasoning? Are we suggesting that bigness *causes* hierarchy, or simply that the two conditions usually occur together? Should we consider other factors, in addition to size, that might contribute to hierarchical organization? Is hierarchy more likely in certain types of organizations than in others?[15] To answer these questions we could examine the process that links organizational size and the extent of hierarchy. We could reason in the following way: Large organizations carry out a variety of activities. Persons responsible for each activity end up specializing in it and are not very familiar with other activities. Someone has to coordinate and have authority over the different activities, and so hierarchies develop as an organization expands.

Analysis of process does several things. It forces us to be explicit about our assumptions. (For example, we are assuming that large organizations need to coordinate activities.) It suggests the kind of relationship we are expecting (for example, positive and causal). It indicates whether the relationship would be true under certain conditions and not others (for example, when an organization specializes). It tells us whether we should be considering additional variables (for example, the kinds of activities the organization carries out).

Consider the process outlined in a recent comment about organizations and the insight it provides into the relationship between size and organizational hierarchy. It proposes that most government programs benefit large organizations rather than small ones. It goes on to suggest the reason for this, or the process that explains why government programs have a bias toward large organizations.

> Suppose you've got $50 million to develop appropriate technology. . . . If you're the grants administrator, would you rather administer 50 grants to 50 little guys who have uncertain credit records, who are scattered all over God's green earth [or would you rather give the grants to large organizations, such as General Motors]? You go the safe route. There's no incentive in the bureaucracy to take risks. It's just the natural consequences of large organizations.[16]

The proposition in this reasoning is that there is a bias toward bigness because it is simpler and less risky to deal with a few companies. Research could be designed to determine whether this prediction is always accurate. If research showed that government grants tend to go to large firms, this finding would lend support to the original proposition that there is a natural bias within government toward big business.

We can use this concern for process to think more systematically about the chain of influences that explain an event. We can lay out a series of possible relationships and think through the process by means of which each is probably related to the dependent variable. Such a process approach should help us think if there are relationships we have overlooked and decide which of several relationships we want to focus on in our research.

Example: The Process of Decision Making

Thinking of underlying processes can lead us to ask if seemingly unique political events reflect more general patterns. Consider the example of presidential commissions. We read a report from one of the frequently organized commissions and assume it reflects a particular political issue and current political dynamics. Lave and March, who were quoted at the outset of this chapter, adopted a different strategy. Instead of analyzing the report of a single commission, they looked at the process by which several commissions made group decisions.[17] They found that presidential commissions, appointed by presidents to review some critical issue and offer recommendations, tend to follow a very similar pattern. This pattern holds up irrespective of the president in power or the issue in question. Commissions are set up to handle politically complex issues, and presidents appoint members from a variety of fields and points of view. In spite of the complexity of the issues and the diversity of the members, almost all commissions arrive at a final report that is critical of the government and that they support unanimously.

What is the process at work here? One possible explanation is that the members of groups representing diverse views decide to compromise with the other members. The result of this process would be a report that arrives at a middle position. Lave and March found that many commission reports did represent compromises, but they were struck by the fact that there were seldom minority reports or dissenting opinions stated later. One might expect both of these if the reports were really efforts at compromise; once away from the group, some members would want to assert their own positions.

The researchers proposed an alternative explanation, one with a different process: people with extreme views tend to moderate them when they are exposed to opposing arguments and when they are placed in positions of power. In this explanation commission members actually change their views rather than seek a compromise. This proposition suggests a number of interesting ideas. It predicts, for example, that when extremists are given responsibility, they will moderate their views. The example illustrates how we can explore the process of decision making in one situation and proceed to speculate about similar processes in other situations.

Diagramming Causal Propositions

Speculations about alternative relationships and discussions of the process linking variables can generate several propositions about relationships to examine empirically. It is often useful to take the next step and develop a model or picture of the relationships we want to examine. A model is a simplification of reality; it identifies the variables that are likely to have the most important influence on a dependent variable and specifies the direction of the influence. Models are valuable because they force us to be specific about the relationships we are examining and because they lend themselves to quantitative testing.

Models can be simple or complex in the number of variables they look at and the number of relationships they examine. Most use the following schematics:

+ or – or 0

X ————— Y

The line with the arrow represents the hypothesis that changes in variable X will bring about changes in variable Y. If there is a plus sign over the line, the hypothesis is stating that the relationship will be positive, that the changes will move in the same direction: if X increases, then Y will also increase; if X decreases, then Y will also decrease. If the sign over the line is a minus sign, then the hypothesis is proposing a negative relationship, that the changes will move in the opposite direction: if X increases, then Y will decrease, and vice versa. If there is a zero over the line, the hypothesis is essentially the null hypothesis and states that there is no relationship between the variables.

We can represent some earlier stated propositions and research findings as follows:

Electoral competition *(Y)* positively affects voter turnout *(X)*

Electoral competition *(Y)* negatively affects mobilization of voters *(X)*

Competition for students *(Y)* causes schools to improve performance *(X)*

Competition for students *(Y)* had no effect on student performance *(X)*

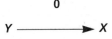

The following example illustrates model building and diagramming. An important debate in political science concerns the merits of centralized governments versus decentralized ones. Political scientists who favor centralized governments tend to argue that large governing organizations are more effective in delivering services and also more efficient. Political scientists who favor decentralization assume the opposite, that smaller organizations are more effective and more efficient. Ostrom has applied the argument to a study of police departments and illustrates a very simple modeling exercise.

Model 1 hypothesizes that a more centralized approach is preferable. Each of the arrows represents a hypothesized relationship between two variables. The three variables on the right are dependent variables. Note that the top arrow has a plus sign. This means that the model hypothesizes that there is a positive relationship between these two variables: as the size of the police department increases, citizen satisfaction with police services also increases. The middle arrow also has a plus sign, indicating the hypothesis that, as the size of the police department increases, citizen evaluation of police is more positive. The third arrow has a minus sign. This indicates that the relationship between these two variables is negative: as the size of the police department increases, the costs of services decline.

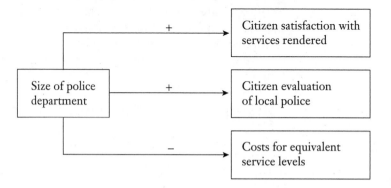

Model 2 hypothesizes that a decentralized police system is preferable.

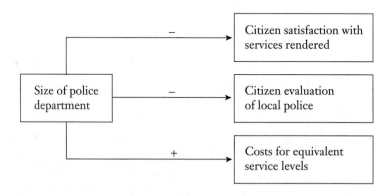

In this second model, the arrows have signs different from those in the first model. State the hypothesis implicit in each of the arrows.

Top arrow: _____

_____

Middle arrow: _____

_____

Bottom arrow: _____

_____

Ostrom argues that we should focus our research on those specific relationships where models disagree.[18] Instead of doing broad-based research on centralization and decentralization, we should analyze two contrasting theories, develop models of their arguments, and empirically test the specific points where they hypothesize different results.

At the outset of this example a few statements were offered about the general effects of centralized and decentralized governments. What do models 1 and 2 add to those statements? You could note any of the following: They make the hypothesized relations very explicit and point to exactly the kinds of quantitative results that would support or reject the hypothesis. They show the linkages among several hypotheses. They indicate the process by which the several variables are presumably linked. They make it relatively easy to test competing or alternative hypotheses. The graphics make it easier to understand the proposed relationships and to compare alternative hypotheses.

Controlling Relationships in Correlational Design

One way to look at the simultaneous effect of two independent variables, and to determine if we can isolate a significant cause of an event, is to use a control variable. Chapter 4 described how to analyze multiple relationships by using a control variable in a cross-tabulation or contingency table. (Recall that we analyzed how the proposed independent variable, *registration*, and the proposed control variable, *interest in the election*, influenced the dependent variable, *voter turnout*.) Here we look at contingency analysis in more detail to consider how controls can produce different insights into the original relationship.

Controls That Elaborate a Relationship

A study of voter turnout in the 1976 presidential election concluded that *gender* influences voting turnout. Table 6.1 shows that men are more apt to vote than women, 76.9 percent and 67.2 percent, respectively—a sizeable contrast.

Is it possible that a third factor, such as education, intrudes into this relationship? For example, is it possible that the influence of gender on voting is less within some educational levels than within others? (Can you think of a reason or process that would make this question plausible?) You could reason that as people become more educated there would be less difference in the political behavior of men and women. Their different gender experiences would become

TABLE 6.1
Voting Turnout, by Gender, 1976 (in Percentages)

	Gender	
Vote	*Men*	*Women*
Yes	76.9%	67.2%
No	23.1	32.8
	100.0%	100.0%
Number =	992	1,412

Source: *American National Election Study*, 1976 (Ann Arbor: Center for Political Studies, University of Michigan, 1976).

less important, and their enhanced knowledge base would become more important.) Table 6.2 supports this proposition. (Note that the table only lists the percentage of each group who did vote. When only two values of the dependent variable—such as "yes" and "no"—are possible, then one value can be omitted. Since the sum will always be 100 percent, a reader can compute the percentage of those with the other value.)

In the original bivariate relationship (table 6.1), there was a 10 percent difference between the turnout of men and women. When we control for education (table 6.2), we find that this difference varies substantially among educational levels. Among those who went no further than grade school, there is a 27 percent difference. The gap is much narrower among high school graduates, and it is negligible for college graduates. Education, in fact, seems to have more influence than gender on whether one voted, because the original relationship between gender and voting varies markedly with level of education. Thus the addition of a control variable enriched our understanding of the original relationship and showed it to be present under some conditions and not others.

TABLE 6.2
Relationship between Gender and Voting, Controlled for Education, 1976 (in Percentages)

	Grade School		High School		College	
Vote	*Men*	*Women*	*Men*	*Women*	*Men*	*Women*
Yes	72.1%	50.0%	69.2%	64.3%	86.4%	83.6%

Source: *American National Election Study, 1976* (Ann Arbor: Center for Political Studies, University of Michigan, 1976).

Controls and Spurious Relationships

spurious relationship
A relationship in which two variables that are not causally linked appear to be so because a third variable is influencing both of them.

Sometimes the control variable may suggest that the original relationship is only apparent, that is, that it is a **spurious relationship.** In a spurious relationship the control variable influences both of the original variables, X and Y, meaning their apparent relationship reflects the presence of Z rather than a relationship between X and Y, as shown in the following diagram.

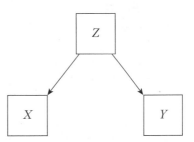

Many political debates actually are disputes over whether an observed relationship is spurious. Consider research by James Coleman in which he concluded that private schools are more effective than public schools. His conclusion was based partly on his finding that black students perform better in private schools than in public ones. Having found this relationship between type of school and educational performance, Coleman concluded that private schools cause improved educational performance as compared to public schools.[19]

Coleman's critics dispute his reasoning. They accept his findings that blacks perform better in private schools than in public ones, but they say that the private schools did not cause this result. They argue instead that the young people placed in private schools are different from those who remain in public schools and that it is this selection process that causes the better performance of the black students. Thus, according to critics, the causal relationship that Coleman found is actually a spurious one (see figure 6.5).

Voting studies also illustrate spurious relationships. We noted previously that men are more apt to vote than women (table 6.1), and that when this relationship is controlled for education, it holds in some educational levels but not others (table 6.2). When we control the relationship between gender and voting for age instead of education, however, the result is different.

Divide voters into two groups, those between ages twenty-five and sixty-five, and those over sixty-five. People over the age of sixty-five are less apt to vote than those between the ages of twenty-five and sixty-five. But within each age group similar percentages of men and women vote; that is, both men and women over age sixty-five are less likely to vote than both men and women between ages twenty-five and sixty-five. Why, then, do we find that men are more apt to vote than women when we study their voting without controlling for age? The reason is that there are far more women than men over the age of sixty-five; hence, there are more women represented in a group that has low voting

FIGURE 6.5
Arguments about the Impact of Private Schools

Coleman's Argument

Independent Variable	causes	*Dependent Variable*
Kind of school attended	$\longrightarrow$	Educational performance

Critics' Argument

Independent Variable	causes	*Dependent Variable*
Characteristics of children	$\longrightarrow$	Educational performance Kind of school attended

turnout. The apparent relationship between gender and voting is actually an association between age and voting. When controlled for age, the original relationship between gender and voting disappears, meaning it is actually spurious.

Original finding: Women less apt to vote than men.

Consider effects of age:

Age Group	
25 through 65	*Over 65*
Higher voter turnout	Lower voter turnout
Women and men roughly equal in number	More women than men in this age number group

(It is also true that women, especially older women, are more apt than men to have only a grade school education. Accordingly, their lower turnout is actually due to the combined influence of their lower level of education and their greater numbers in the over-sixty-five group).[20]

Developing Tables to Include Controls and Show Multiple Relationships

Earlier you learned to diagram alternative propositions about a variable or relationship of interest to you. You also learned some advantages of introducing a third, or control variable, into a proposed relationship. Again we use contingency tables, which are appropriate for nominal and ordinal level data. (Chapter 11 will describe how to introduce controls when using interval level data.) This section shows you how to develop tables to examine how three variables are related to each other. In the example used, you are asking whether there is a relationship between the amount of money a country spends on education and defense. In other words, you are testing the so-called guns-versus-butter argument to see whether the level of spending on social programs such as education is associated with the level of military spending. The traditional argument is that military spending is negatively related to spending for education: the more a country spends on military programs, the less it has left to spend on education. Table 6.3 contains data on these two variables for a range of countries. Note that the figures, expressed in U.S. dollars, are per capita.

We can begin by portraying the data in a **bivariate table** as was done in table 5.5. We can treat spending for education as the dependent variable, placing it along the side to label the rows and military spending as the independent variable, placing it across the top of the columns. We could have a table with twenty rows and twenty columns representing twenty values for each variable, but this arrangement would be awkward to interpret. An alternative is to divide

TABLE 6.3
Expenditures on Education and the Military, and GNP for Twenty Countries, 1990 (in U.S. Dollars per Capita)

Country	Education Spending	Military Spending	GNP Per Capita
Argentina	220	204	2,370
Bolivia	113	89	630
Brazil	142	113	2,680
Canada	594	1,494	20,470
Cameroon	115	64	960
Egypt	80	76	600
France	1,325	1,306	19,490
India	9	60	350
Indonesia	48	46	570
Italy	1,397	606	16,830
Kenya	73	29	370
Mexico	346	60	2,490
Nepal	19	10	170
Pakistan	8	117	380
Singapore	2,019	2,410	11,160
Spain	671	606	11,020
Thailand	285	246	1,420
Tunisia	235	94	1,440
Turkey	313	191	1,630
United States	370	4,925	21,790

Source: *World Development Report, 1992* (Washington, D.C.: World Bank, 1992), table 1, pp. 215–219, table 11, pp. 235–239.

the values for both variables into clusters. (Recall the discussion of establishing appropriate categories in chapter 5.) For example, we can set up two sets of values—"low" (less than $300) and "high" ($301 and greater)—producing a four-cell matrix. Place each country in the appropriate cell in table 6.4, as illustrated by the placement of Argentina. Then count the countries that fall in each cell and place these totals in their respective cells.

How would you interpret the data? What seems to be the relationship between defense spending and education spending? When the former increases, what happens to the latter? _____

_____

_____

_____

_____

TABLE 6.4

Educational Expenditures, by Military Expenditures, in Twenty Selected Countries, 1990 (in U.S. Dollars per Capita)

	Military Spending	
Education Spending	*Low* *(less than $300)*	*High* *($301 or more)*
Low (less than $300)	Argentina	
High ($301 or more)		

You should have noted that the relationship between military and education expenditures is the reverse of that posed in the original proposition: according to this information, military and education spending are related, but they rise and fall together, not in the opposite directions. It may be that a third variable produces changes in both of these variables. One possible such variable is the overall level of economic strength of the country. This conjecture gives us a new proposition: wealthy countries spend more on both military programs and education than do poor countries.

To test this proposition, we can use a multivariate table that presents the values of three variables. Table 6.5 shows how to organize a multivariate display, one with three sets of variables intersecting. In addition to the variables arrayed in table 6.4, it adds a third variable, gross national product per capita. It simply

TABLE 6.5

Educational Expenditures, by Military Expenditures, in Twenty Selected Countries, 1990, for Different Levels of per Capita GNP (in U.S. Dollars)

	Low GNP per Capita (Less Than $2,000) Military Expenditures		High GNP per Capita ($,2000 and above) Military Expenditures	
Education Expenditures	*Low (Less Than $300)*	*High ($301 or More)*	*Low (Less Than $300)*	*High ($301 or More)*
Low (Less Than $300)				
High ($301 or More)				

divides the information from table 6.3 into two sets of countries—those with low GNP and those with high GNP. We are dividing the countries into these two groups to ascertain whether the relationship we observed earlier—that military and education spending rise and fall together—holds true regardless of national wealth. Observe the way in which table 6.5 is set up, and fill in the countries in the cells based on the information in table 6.3.

Analyze these results. What is the relationship among these three variables: wealth, spending on military, and spending on education? _____

_____

_____

_____

_____

Two items are particularly interesting. First, you should have found that almost all of the countries that spend lower amounts on both military and education have a low GNP, while almost all of the countries that have high expenditures on these items have a high GNP. Thus it seems reasonable to conclude that the most important influence on spending is the amount of wealth in a country and not the amount they are spending on other items. Second, four of the countries do not fit the general pattern—Turkey, Argentina, Brazil, and Mexico. This observation could lead you to look at these four countries in more detail to understand their pattern of expenditures.

Developing Tables with Control Variables to Determine Causality

Practice Exercise 6.1

The following exercise asks you to consider the reasons for winning elections and to select among several variables. The research question is: Which variables are likely to have the greatest influence on the result of an election? The information in table 6.6 covers ten candidates from five states in the senatorial elections of 1996. There actually were sixty-eight senatorial candidates who were the major contenders for seats in thirty-four states. In the exercises at the end of the chapter you will be given data for all sixty-eight candidates to enable you to replicate this analysis for all candidates. Note that this exercise is solely designed to walk you through the steps of creating tables with control variables. The results are meaningless, since only ten candidates are included. (It should also be noted that there was a larger proportion of open seats in this election than usual, making it difficult to test the importance of incumbency.)

Examine the first line in table 6.6. It gives you information about candidate Durbin from Illinois, a Democrat. The column labeled "Status" tells you whether he was an incumbent (I), that is, presently serving in the Senate; a challenger (C) of the incumbent; or a person running in an open race (O), in which

TABLE 6.6
Electoral Results and Campaign Finance Information on Ten Senatorial Candidates, 1996

Candidate	State	Party*	Status[†]	Vote	% of vote	W/L[a]	Receipts	Disbursements	From PACs
Durbin	IL	D	O	2,384,028	55.8	W	$4,738,122	$4,838,937	$1,153,496
Salvi	IL	R	O	1,728,824	41.0	L	4,732,342	4,689,719	576,512
Harkin	IA	D	I	634,166	51.8	W	4,627,733	5,213,833	968,698
Lightfoot	IA	R	C	571,807	46.7	L	2,471,490	2,415,439	576,887
Boschwitz	MN	R	C	901,282	41.3	L	4,389,616	4,346,587	1,032,247
Wellstone	MN	D	I	1,098,493	50.3	W	5,960,925	5,950,947	568,015
Torricelli	NJ	D	O	1,519,154	52.7	W	9,144,930	9,056,398	955,070
Zimmer	NJ	R	O	1,227,351	42.6	L	8,218,597	8,220,727	1,179,138
Johnson	SD	D	C	166,533	51.3	W	2,789,488	2,911,398	802,640
Pressler	SD	R	I	157,954	48.7	L	4,083,279	4,381,920	1,466,772

Source: Federal Election Commission, http://www.fec.gov/finance/senrec.htm, http://www.fec.gov/finance/senpac.htm, http://www.fec.gov/finance/sendisb.htm; 03/11/97; and *Congressional Quarterly*, "Election Results," 15 February 1997, 447–455.

* R, Republican; D, Democratic; [†] I, incumbent; C, challenger; O, open race; [a] W, won; L, lost

neither candidate was an incumbent. The O in Durbin's column tells you that he was running for an open seat. The line then lists the votes he received, the percentage of the total vote, whether he won or lost, his campaign receipts, his campaign disbursements, and the amount of money he received from political action committees (PACs). These are the kinds of information that you can gather from the media, from the Federal Election Commission, from candidates themselves, and from various research groups.

The dependent variable, the event you want to understand or explain, is the result of the election. Note that information in three columns tells you about the result: the number of votes received, the percentage of the vote, and whether the candidate won or lost. You could measure election results using any of these indicators. Note also that the variable labeled W/L (won/lost) is an ordinal variable while vote and percent of vote are interval variables. The earlier discussion of selecting level of measurement suggested that you use as precise a measure as possible. Later when you learn some basic statistical techniques, you will be advised to use one of the interval measures (chapter 11). For now you will be comparing groups of winners and losers and creating tables, and the ordinal measure, W/L (won/lost) is more appropriate.

Which of the variables might explain why some candidates won and others lost and thus serve as independent variables? This is the point where you need to draw on your general understanding of politics, a review of the literature, a knowledge of election theory, or a sense of logic. One possibility is party; we could see if there is a relationship between party and result to ascertain if there was a national trend to vote for either party. Another possibility is incumbency; it may be that incumbents are more likely to win than challengers.

Other possible variables tell us about campaign finances. Because there does not seem to be much difference between receipts and disbursements, you could use either of these. While disbursements is a reasonable choice, you need to decide how to handle the information. It does not make much sense to compare the expenditures in Illinois, a populous state, with the expenditures in South Dakota. It would be more useful to transform these interval measures into ordinal ones and ask which of the two candidates in each state spent more than the other. Thus you could translate the information into two values for each state: "more" and "less." Following this strategy, Durbin would be listed as spending more money than his opponent, and Salvi would be listed as spending less money. We could do the same for PAC receipts. This gives us the information in table 6.7 for the ten candidates.

We can use this information to create a series of practice tables. Practice table 6.A examines whether party has an influence on winning. The information in table 6.A tells us that Democrats were more apt to win than Republicans; that is, that there is a relationship between party and winning.

It would be easier to interpret the numbers, however, if we translated them into percentages. Because party is the proposed independent variable, we are interested in the percentage of Democrats who won as opposed to the percentage of Republicans who won. So we compute percentages for the independent variables. And we make it clear to the reader that is what we are doing by putting "100%" at the bottom of each column. This gives us table 6.B, which shows

TABLE 6.7

Characteristics of a Sample of Senatorial Candidates

Candidate	W/L	Party	Status	More/Less Spent	More/Less From PACs
Durbin	W	D	O	More	More
Salvi	L	R	O	Less	Less
Harkin	W	D	I	More	More
Lightfoot	L	R	C	Less	Less
Boschwitz	L	R	C	Less	More
Wellstone	W	D	I	More	Less
Torricelli	W	D	O	More	Less
Zimmer	L	R	O	Less	More
Johnson	W	D	C	Less	Less
Pressler	L	R	I	More	More

PRACTICE TABLE 6.A

Result	Party	
	Democratic	*Republican*
Won	5	0
Lost	0	5
	5	5

PRACTICE TABLE 6.B

Result	Party	
	Democratic	*Republican*
Won	5 (100%)	0
Lost	0	5 (100%)
	5 (100%)	5 (100%)

clearly that there is a 100 percent difference between the two parties: Democrats are 100 percent more apt to win than Republicans.

An alternative proposition is that a candidate's status explains the result. Table 6.C explores this hypothesis. Here there is less of a percentage difference between the two columns (34 percent) than there was when we were examining the influence of party. Therefore, we could conclude that party affiliation seems to have more influence on the election results than incumbency does. (Recall the earlier caveat that two of the races were open with no incumbent.)

The next two tables, 6.D and 6.E, reflect the influence of money spent and PAC receipts on the election result. Determine which numbers go in the cells. Include the percentage figures for each cell, as well as the total number and 100 percent at the bottom of each column.

Spending more on a campaign has more of an influence on whether or not a candidate wins (a difference of 60 percent), while the variable PAC receipts has less of an influence (a 20 percent difference).

PRACTICE TABLE 6.C

Result	Status	
	Incumbent	*Challenger*
Won	2 (67%)	1 (33%)
Lost	1 (33%)	2 (67%)
	3 (100%)	3 (100%)

PRACTICE TABLE 6.D

	Campaign Disbursements	
Result	*More*	*Less*
Won		
Lost	____	____

PRACTICE TABLE 6.E

	PAC Receipts	
Result	*More*	*Less*
Won		
Lost	____	____

PRACTICE TABLE 6.F

	Relative Amount of Money from PACs			
	More		*Less*	
Result	*Democrat*	*Republican*	*Democrat*	*Republican*
Won	2 (100%)	0 (0%)	3 (100%)	0 (0%)
Lost	0 (0)	3 (100%)	0	2 (100%)
N =	2 (100%)	3 (100%)	3 (100%)	2 (100%)

Now select one of these relationships and determine if it remains the same when we look at the influence of a second independent variable. Recall from table 6.B that 100 percent of the Democrats won and 100 percent of the Republicans lost, suggesting that party has an influence on election outcomes. Does this relationship hold true both for those who received more money from PACs than their opponent and for those who received less money from PACs than their opponents? See table 6.F.

Table 6.F tells us that party was a more important influence on the result of the election than whether or not one received more or less money from PACs. If we just look at those who received more money from PACs, we find that all of the Democrats won and all of the Republicans lost. When we look at those who got less money from PACs than their opponents received, again we find that all of the Democrats won and all of the Republicans lost. By combining PAC money and party in this controlled analysis, we have learned something additional about the influence of these two factors that we wouldn't know from looking at only one of them at a time.

Where We Are

Chapters 1 through 6 have gone through the logic of asking interesting questions and analyzing research done by others. Part Three will go into more detail about various kinds of evidence, briefly introduced in chapter 3. Part Four will describe how to analyze and portray our evidence to communicate it more effectively. These chapters will give you additional and important skills in collecting and analyzing information. The points thus far remain critical, however. They stress the importance of the first steps we take: defining questions, considering multiple ways to approach the question, exploring prior research and available theories, and drawing on our creative imagination and common sense to support possible relationships.

The overall theme is that research is not a cut-and-dried activity with one recipe that you can follow. There are different approaches, different designs, and different kinds of evidence. Obviously some are more appropriate and useful than others for your question and the time and resources available to you. Your choices need to be laid out clearly and justified. Your research study should explain how you are defining your major concepts, on what basis you are selecting your variables and indicators, and your research design. You should also indicate how these choices fit with studies conducted by others.

You should apply these same skills when reading studies carried out by others. How do they define their terms and select their evidence? Do they use multiple designs and sources of evidence? Not all studies state their reasons explicitly, and you may need to tease out the assumptions and approaches they are making. Learn from them and evaluate their methods. What trade-offs are they making? Are they reasonable? Don't accept everything you read at face value, but don't forget that researching the social arena almost inevitably involves making hard choices and working with less than perfect measures and evidence. It is hoped this approach makes the research enterprise more interesting and challenging.

NOTES

1. Charles Lave and James March, *An Introduction to Models in the Social Sciences* (New York: Harper & Row, 1975). See especially chapters 1–3 for an introduction to model building.
2. Much of this discussion is drawn from a study by John O'Shaughnessy, who refers to the relationships as "causal chains." *Inquiry and Decision* (New York: Harper & Row, 1973); pp. 65–80.
3. "Officials Blame Courts, Community for Increase in Teenage Crime," *Washington Post*, 29 March 1981, p. A1.
4. W. I. Beveridge, *The Art of Scientific Investigations* (New York: Vintage, 1950), p. 126.
5. For an example of the first approach, see Edward Banfield, *The Unheavenly City Revisited* (Boston: Little, Brown, 1968). For an example of the second approach, see William Ryan, *Blaming the Victim* (New York: Vintage, 1971).

6. Thomas Kuhn, *The Structure of Scientific Revolutions* (Chicago: University of Chicago Press, 1962).

7. Graham Allison, "Conceptual Models and the Cuban Missile Crisis," *American Political Science Review* 63 (September 1969): 689–718. For an update on this case and literature see, Richard E. Neustadt and Ernest R. May, *Thinking in Time* (New York: Free Press, 1986), ch. 1.

8. Edward de Bono, *Lateral Thinking* (New York: Harper & Row, 1970). See also James Adams, *Conceptual Blockbusting* (New York: Norton, 1974).

9. Christopher A. Simon and Nicholas P. Lovrich, Jr., "Private School Enrollment and Public School Performance," *Policy Studies Journal* 24, no. 4 (1996): 666–673.

10. K. B. Smith and K. J. Meier, *The Case against School Choice: Politics, Markets and Fools* (Armonk, N.Y.: M. E. Sharpe, 1995).

11. *Washington Post*, 3 March 1988.

12. Mark Saroyan, "The Armenian Protests: Is It Passion or Politics?" *Nuclear Times* (July/August 1988): 8–11.

13. Robert Jackson, "Political Institutions and Voter Turnout in the Industrial Democracies," *American Political Science Review* 81, no. 2 (June 1987): 405–422.

14. Steven Rosenstone and John Mark Hansen, *Mobilization, Participation, and American Democracy* (New York: Macmillan, 1993).

15. Lave and March, *An Introduction to Models in the Social Sciences*, pp. 51–84.

16. Cited in William Greider, "Ronald Reagan, The Giantism Killer," *Washington Post*, 26 April 1981, p. C1.

17. Lave and March, *An Introduction to Models in the Social Sciences*, pp. 21–24.

18. Elinor Ostrom, "Metropolitan Reform: Propositions Derived from Two Traditions," *Social Science Quarterly* 53 (December 1972): 474–493.

19. James Coleman, "Public and Private Schools," *Washington Post*, 7 April 1981, p. A22, and Diane Ravitch, "The Way to Make Schools Good," *Washington Post*, 19 April 1981, p. C7.

20. James Clotfeler and Charles L. Prysby, *Political Choices* (New York: Holt, Rinehart and Winston, 1980), pp. 30–32.

EXERCISES

Exercise 6.1 Speculating about Alternative Propositions

Think of three propositions that explain the low turnout of voters in the United States. One explanation should focus on the characteristics or behavior of the voter; one should focus on the particular election; and one should focus on the nature of our political system or electoral process.

Based on your observations of recent elections, which of your explanations do you think would be the most fruitful and interesting to research further? Why?

Exercise 6.2 Modeling Explanations for Nonvoting

Research proposes a number of explanations for nonvoting. Some of these are as follows:

1. People are too wrapped up in their own private concerns to care about public issues.
2. Individuals feel their vote will not make a difference in the outcome.
3. The media oversimplify issues and focus mainly on the polls rather than the issues.
4. Registering to vote is too difficult.

Frances Fox Piven and Richard Cloward (*Why Americans Don't Vote* [New York: Pantheon, 1988]) stress the fourth explanation: registration barriers to voting. Nonvoting reflects difficulties that voters have in registering, problems that discourage the poor more than those in the middle class. The authors demonstrate that turnout rates are much higher in most European democracies, where registration is virtually automatic.

A reporter for the *Washington Post* disagrees with Piven and Cloward's analysis. Just prior to election day in 1988 he observed:

> In North Dakota, anyone can show up on election day and vote. But voter turnout has been dropping fast in recent elections. In Maine, Minnesota, and Wisconsin, where same-day registration has been adopted, voter turnout is still in decline. All over the United States, regardless of the ease of registering to vote, the location of the polls, or even the pizzazz of the candidates, the results are the same: voter turnout is in a downward spiral, falling, falling, falling. [Juan Williams, "Why America Doesn't Vote," *Washington Post*, 6 November 1988, p. C2.]

Data for the 1988, 1992, and 1996 presidential elections show that the states Williams cited for their easy registration rules had the following respective turnout rates: North Dakota, 60.58, 66.1, and 55.97%; Maine, 60.98, 72.9, and 71.9%; Minnesota, 65.33, 70.6, and 64.07%; Wisconsin, 61.25, 68.7, and 57.43%. The national averages were 50.1, 55.0, and 49.08%.

1. State a hypothesis based on Piven and Cloward's work:

2. State Williams's position (basically the null hypothesis):

3. Develop a model that includes these alternative positions. (Hint: make the independent variable "ease of registration.")

4. Which of these propositions do the data from 1988, 1992, and 1996 appear to support? Summarize the information and state your reasoning in a carefully worded short paragraph.

Exercise 6.3 Comparing Propositions

In 1996 voting turnout in the presidential elections was less than 50 percent. Turnout by white men, white women, and black women all declined. Interestingly, the turnout rate of black males increased significantly.

TABLE 6.8
Turnout by Gender and Race, 1996 Election

Voters	1996 vote (in Millions)	% of total vote	% change from 1992
Black men	4.8	5	+55
Black women	4.8	5	−8
White men	38.3	40	−8
White women	41.2	43	−14

Source: National Political Congress of Black Women, *Wall Street Journal*, 13 February 1997, p. A20.

Some possible explanations for the increase in voting by black men:

1. Dr. Denise Baer of the National Political Congress of Black Women suggests it was due to the Million Man March in 1995 with its stress on civic responsibility. For example, since the march more black men have been attending local PTA meetings and similar sessions.
2. Black men liked the incumbent Bill Clinton and turned out to vote for him. Clinton got 84 percent of the black vote.
3. The Democratic National Committee spent less money on registering voters, instead spending money on a massive advertising campaign. It hired black advertising firms that produced advertising that ran on stations oriented to blacks.

Select two of these propositions, and using the alternative research designs in chapter 4, design research to examine them. Indicate the kind of measures and evidence you would collect to carry out the research.

Exercise 6.4 Controlled Relationships, Percentage Differences

At the end of chapter 6 you examined data on ten senatorial candidates. Using information on the full set of sixty-eight senatorial candidates, carry out a multivariate analysis of the factors that explain why some won the election and some

TABLE 6.9
Electoral Results and Campaign Finance Information on Sixty-Eight Senatorial Candidates, 1996

Candidate	State	Party	Status	Vote	% of Vote	W/L	Receipts	Disbursements	From PACs
Bedford	AL	D	O	681,651	45.7	L	$2,413,249	$ 2,284,801	$447,820
Sessions	AL	R	O	786,436	51.9	W	3,905,870	3,862,359	936,673
Obermeyer	AK	D	C	23,977	10.3	L	NA	NA	NA
Stevens	AK	R	I	177,893	76.7	W	3,271,582	2,711,710	1,203,797
Bryant	AR	D	O	400,241	47.3	L	1,606,053	1,577,838	474,056
Hutchinson	AR	R	O	445,942	52.7	W	1,691,276	1,604,014	482,175
Allard	CO	R	O	750,325	50.7	W	2,198,131	2,233,429	1,061,594
Strickland	CO	D	O	677,600	46.3	L	2,913,066	2,894,916	395,145
Clatworthy	DE	R	C	105,088	38.1	L	1,132,167	1,126,427	71,734
Biden	DE	D	I	165,465	60.0	W	1,636,013	1,966,313	0
Cleland	GA	D	O	1,103,993	48.8	W	2,944,283	2,926,391	710,670
Millner	GA	R	O	1,073,969	47.6	L	9,917,102	9,858,955	563,120
Craig	ID	R	I	283,532	57.0	W	2,695,939	2,809,897	1,027,626
Minnick	ID	D	C	198,422	39.9	L	2,179,155	2,140,878	86,377
Durbin	IL	D	O	2,384,028	55.8	W	4,767,940	4,966,804	1,153,210
Salvi	IL	R	O	1,728,824	41.0	L	4,698,956	4,696,065	522,330
Harkin	IA	D	I	634,166	51.8	W	4,665,182	5,276,708	1,061,573
Lightfoot	IA	R	C	571,807	46.7	L	2,474,871	2,439,679	553,512
Roberts	KS	R	O	652,677	62.0	W	2,297,886	2,305,898	1,216,831
Thompson	KS	D	O	362,380	34.4	L	662,523	659,066	203,024
Brownback	KS	R	O	574,021	53.8	W	2,269,850	2,269,550	676,753
Docking	KS	D	O	461,344	43.4	L	1,145,383	1,125,844	278,924
Beshear	KY	D	C	560,012	42.8	L	1,879,343	2,073,794	229,780
McConnell	KY	R	I	724,794	55.5	W	3,840,374	4,669,642	1,293,151
Jenkins	LA	R	O	847,157	49.8	L	1,879,675	1,878,242	479,543
Landrieu	LA	D	O	852,945	50.2	W	2,689,202	2,504,815	535,736
Brennan	ME	D	O	266,226	43.9	L	978,848	976,805	321,757
Collins	ME	R	O	298,422	49.2	W	1,721,825	1,621,475	598,836
Kerry	MA	D	I	1,334,135	52.2	W	10,342,115	10,962,607	14,591
Weld	MA	R	C	1,143,120	44.7	L	8,074,417	8,002,123	800,761
Levin	MI	D	I	2,195,738	58.4	W	6,009,422	5,905,737	909,737
Romney	MI	R	C	1,500,106	39.9	L	3,175,110	3,141,502	237,575
Boschwitz	MN	R	C	901,282	41.3	L	4,399,974	4,385,982	1,035,527
Wellstone	MN	D	I	1,098,493	50.3	W	5,991,013	5,970,224	571,723
Cochran	MS	R	I	624,154	71.0	W	787,233	828,693	540,354
Hunt	MS	D	C	240,647	27.4	L	NA	NA	NA
Baucus	MT	D	I	201,935	49.6	W	3,449,478	3,748,502	1,352,466
Rehberg	MT	R	C	182,111	44.7	L	1,369,530	1,358,165	333,744
Hagel	NE	R	O	379,933	56.1	W	3,612,338	3,564,316	486,034
Nelson	NE	D	O	281,904	41.7	L	2,179,131	2,159,653	0
Smith	NH	R	I	242,257	49.2	W	1,708,376	1,718,413	875,951
Swett	NH	D	C	227,355	46.2	L	1,759,089	1,558,563	348,388
Torricelli	NJ	D	O	1,519,154	52.7	W	9,211,508	9,134,854	952,153

(continued)

TABLE 6.9 (continued)

Candidate	State	Party	Status	Vote	% of Vote	W/L	Receipts	Disbursements	From PACs
Zimmer	NJ	R	O	1,227,351	42.6	L	8,212,612	8,238,181	1,197,917
Domenici	NM	R	I	357,171	64.7	W	3,264,601	3,110,548	1,154,329
Trujillo	NM	D	C	164,356	29.8	L	155,328	155,213	12,800
Gantt	NC	D	C	1,173,875	45.9	L	8,108,548	7,992,980	406,338
Helms	NC	R	I	1,345,833	52.6	W	7,808,820	7,798,520	1,021,560
Boren	OK	D	C	474,162	40.1	L	302,633	301,621	0
Inhofe	OK	R	I	670,610	56.7	W	2,706,849	2,510,946	1,117,944
Bruggere	OR	D	O	624,370	45.9	L	3,318,883	3,301,736	406,731
Smith	OR	R	O	677,336	49.8	W	3,603,253	3,527,252	757,905
Mayer	RI	R	O	127,368	35.1	L	787,231	773,789	132,368
Reed	RI	D	O	230,676	63.5	W	2,688,136	2,732,011	1,031,702
Close	SC	D	C	510,810	44.0	L	1,919,735	1,913,574	0
Thurmond	SC	R	I	619,739	53.4	W	2,335,746	1,385,185	782,308
Johnson	SD	D	C	166,533	51.3	W	2,866,518	2,990,554	847,621
Pressler	SD	R	I	157,954	48.7	L	4,091,490	4,468,434	1,513,835
Gordon	TN	D	C	654,937	36.8	L	800,607	795,969	88,600
Thompson	TN	R	I	1,091,554	61.4	W	4,232,418	3,469,369	1,080,345
Gramm	TX	R	I	3,027,680	54.8	W	3,802,167	6,289,591	1,107,961
Morales	TX	D	C	2,428,776	43.9	L	991,290	978,862	4,539
Warner, J.	VA	R	I	1,235,744	52.5	W	5,033,390	5,196,091	1,601,460
Warner,M	VA	D	C	1,115,982	47.4	L	11,625,483	11,600,424	1,250
Burke	WV	R	C	139,088	23.4	L	NA	NA	NA
Rockefeller	WV	D	I	456,526	76.6	W	3,004,275	2,538,473	987,319
Enzi	WY	R	O	114,116	54.1	W	984,906	953,572	476,177
Karpan	WY	D	O	89,103	42.2	L	819,417	814,258	460,538

Source: Voting information and campaign receipts as reported by the Federal Election Commission, "Financial Activity of Senate Campaigns," http://www.fec.gov/1996/states, 18 June 1997; and *Congressional Quarterly*, "Election Results," 15 February 1997, pp. 447–455.

NA = No financial information available as reported by the FEC.

did not. The exercise can be done either by hand or by computer if you have learned that skill. After examining table 6.9 do the following:

Original relationship

1. Select a variable that tells whether candidate won or lost.

2. Select a variable that you anticipate has an influence on the result of the election. What is your hypothesis?

3. Tally the results and put them into a properly organized bivariate table. (Be sure the independent variable is listed across the columns. Include the totals for each column and the percentages of the total column number in each cell.)

4. Discuss the results. What is the most striking overall pattern? Does it support your hypothesis?

Controlled relationship

5. Indicate one other possible influence on the result and use it as a control. Give reasons for selecting this and state what you expect to find. Remember, you are asking how this second variable affects the first relationship.

6. Tally the results and place them in a multivariate table.

7. Again, analyze your results. (Look for patterns and relate them to your hypotheses. If the results are surprising, can you think of any reasons for them? What further research would be useful to understand the patterns better?)

Finding Information to Answer Our Questions

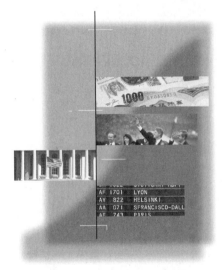

You have learned about formulating empirical questions, exploring relationships, and designing your research. The next step in doing systematic analysis is to find information to answer your questions. This is not as straightforward an activity as it may seem. You have to find a way to link the terms in your questions with the kinds of information accessible to you. The chapters in Part Three introduce you to a wide range of sources of empirical information from data you can collect yourself to sources you can find in your library and on the Internet. The problem in political analysis is not a lack of information, but an array of information that can be overwhelming.

The book throughout has emphasized the need to ensure that questions and designs and data are appropriate to each other. And chapter 3 added that you may need to adjust your research question to match data that are accessible or feasible to collect. Thus as you read these chapters you will be revisiting many of the issues raised in earlier chapters. Which indicators are relevant to the concepts you are interested in? Which relationships should you focus on? To increase the feasibility of doing research on a question of interest to you, consider carefully the range of resources available to you described in this section. Your research options will be greatly enhanced if you expand your repertoire of accessible information. And, as stressed throughout, consider if you can draw on more than one source of data, particularly if it is feasible to use two different kinds of information.

CHAPTER SEVEN

Collecting Data: Surveys and Questionnaires

Ordinary models of citizen activity—voting, writing letters, going to a protest, taking part in a campaign or a community project—. . . are voluntary, and no one has to take part and express preferences. Surveys do not let people be quiescent; they chase them down and ask them questions. If people are hard to find, the good survey looks for them, calling again and again.

—Sidney Verba, *"The Citizen as Respondent."*

. . . [H]ow do you get a random sample . . . ? The obvious thing is to start with a list of everybody and go after names chosen from it at random; but that is too expensive. So you go into the streets—and bias your sample against stay-at-homes. You go from door to door by day—and miss most of the employed people. You switch to evening interviews—and neglect the movie goers and night-clubbers.

—Darrell Huff, *How to Lie with Statistics*

Direct and Indirect Data-Gathering Techniques

As noted throughout, political analysis depends on establishing linkages between our concepts and questions on the one hand and data on the other. Further, these linkages can be developed only if we focus simultaneously on the concepts we are measuring and on possible data sources. Recall the criteria for indicators from chapter 3. Validity asks whether the data are relevant to the meaning of the concept. Does the evidence we plan to collect actually answer our questions? Reliability evaluates the data themselves. Would the same data be collected under varying conditions and by different researchers? We also stressed a third criterion—feasibility—which directs us to data that are realistically obtainable. This chapter and the next two chapters introduce a variety of strategies for obtaining data to examine propositions. After studying these strategies, you should be able to select the data most appropriate for your research questions and to evaluate the strategies that others select.

Just as there are different types of research design—experiments, quasi-experiments, correlations, and case studies, there are several ways to collect data—directly and indirectly. In **direct data gathering,** evidence is collected firsthand, either by asking questions or by observing actions and events; surveys and field research based on interviews and observations will concern us in chapters 7 and 8. **Indirect data gathering,** by contrast, relies on information others have already compiled and will be described in chapter 9. You were introduced to several indirect sources such as *The Statistical Abstract of the United States* in chapter 3 and to other sources in examples throughout Parts One and Two. Data on GNP, life expectancy, and voter turnout are examples of data that are indirect from the researcher's point of view because they have been gathered by others, independent of the research. Table 7.1 lists the approaches covered.

Direct data gathering by asking questions and making observations gives researchers more control over the data they are collecting. Such strategies allow us to examine behavior from the perspective of the actors, to ask subjects what their behavior means to them. Interviewers, for example, ask not only what people did, but also what their motives were. Observations can take into account the context of actions and capture some of the subtleties that are always involved in social events. For all of these reasons, data collected by asking and observing are often *more valid* than data collected by someone else for other purposes. They are more apt to reflect the meaning of the concepts they are designed to measure.

These direct strategies, however, may produce *less reliable* data. Directly gathered data vary according to the person who collects them. Because we view reality selectively, we may look for data that support our hypotheses. Or the researcher can get in the way and influence peoples' reactions—what they say and how they behave. The presence of someone taking notes, for example, may well influence what others say and do. In such cases, the data are described as **reactive data.**

This chapter focuses on strategies for gathering information from a sample of individuals or households or from groups of individuals. It describes surveys

direct data gathering
Collecting evidence firsthand through questions or observations.

indirect data gathering
Using data collected by others, usually for purposes different from our own.

reactive data
Data that are influenced or altered by the process of collecting them.

TABLE 7.1
Data Collection Approaches

Direct	Indirect
Surveys (chapter 7)	Data compiled by others (chapter 9)
Questionnaires, self-administered (chapter 7)	Content analysis (chapter 9)
Interviews (chapter 8)	Created indexes (chapter 9)
Observations (chapter 8)	
Field research (chapter 8)	

and questionnaires that ask individuals structured questions with a limited range of responses for the purpose of producing information in a form that can be handled quantitatively. It begins by describing the characteristics and purposes of survey research. Second, it discusses the logic of sampling, a key element in survey research. Third, it provides guidance on how to design and implement your own survey or questionnaire. Fourth, it reviews some of the pitfalls and problems that arise when using surveys—either professionally conducted surveys or your own efforts. Finally, it considers how you can use survey data compiled by others in your own research.

Characteristics and Uses of Survey Research

Recent developments in the political arena have led political leaders and researchers alike to pay more attention to the attitudes and opinions of the public. Criticisms of big government, for example, raise questions about the results of public policies and their impact on the public. Also, with the decline of political parties, candidates feel they need new means of learning about voter sentiment. At the same time, social scientists and market researchers have developed an impressive array of techniques for ascertaining public opinion on subjects ranging from hair spray to political candidates. These sophisticated methods coincide with the increased interest in public sentiment by researchers, politicians, and policy experts and have led to a growing use of survey research.[1] For some concerned about the prospects for democratic governance, the trend is a positive one. As Sidney Verba notes in the quotation at the head of this chapter, surveys can play an important role in a democracy by including the views of all citizens, not just those who choose to participate or express their views. Thus surveys can compensate to some extent for the dominant role played by organized interests by communicating broadly held sentiments.[2]

In surveys the unit of analysis is usually the individual. (The most notable exception is the United States census, which collects information about family units.) While they collect information about individuals, however, surveys are not focused on individuals as individuals. They compile information about individuals as members of a larger population or as representatives of subgroups in that larger population—women, the wealthy, minorities, and so forth.

Surveys collect information on five kinds of variables:

1. *Background* data such as age, education, and income; referred to as demographic data.
2. *Behavioral data*, such as voting or time spent reading political news. These are usually treated as dependent variables, and surveys try to explain the reasons for these behaviors.
3. *Attitudes and beliefs*, deep-seated cognitive and emotional characteristics of individuals. Typical examples are liberalism, conservatism, apathy, and alienation.

4. *Opinions* regarding immediate situations or events that usually reflect underlying attitudes.
5. *Knowledge* of political events and policies. Surveys often ask respondents the name of their representative as an indicator of their political knowledge, and where they go to vote as an indicator of how likely they are to vote. Surveys have made headlines recently describing how poorly informed the public is about geography and basic social and political facts.

Interestingly, a 1987 analysis of surveys from the preceding fifty years found a marked decline in questions about knowledge and behavior and an increase in questions about demographic facts, attitudes, and opinions.[3]

By gathering all five kinds of information, surveys can measure relationships or correlations among these variables. For example, surveys enable us to examine whether there is a relationship between the two variables *trust in government* and *partisan vote*. Whereas a case study would consider in more depth the reasons for a particular person's distrust, surveys would ask these same two questions of many individuals. They can determine broad patterns in the population, identify correlations among different sets of variables, and, by controlling relationships, identify causal patterns.

Surveys can also be used to compare subgroups in the population—say, the attitudes of women and men, of low-income and high-income groups—comparisons that are difficult to make without surveys. For example, election statistics reported by local governments indicate the number of people who voted and for whom, but they do not relate any of that information to the characteristics of the voters. To tell which kinds of people voted, it is necessary to survey behavior, attitudes, and background characteristics of individuals.

There is one exception to the foregoing statement: if a voting district is fairly homogeneous, with a high proportion of one group, then we can use the official election data from that district to describe how that group voted. When the media refer to the "black vote," they are usually basing their comments on the voting results in heavily black voting precincts. While voting precincts rather than individuals is the unit of analysis, such statements are used to describe individual behavior. A similar strategy is to characterize ZIP code areas by their dominant characteristics. Surveys ask respondents to indicate their ZIP code, and through that information they link respondents to a full set of information about their areas.[4] Many voting precincts and ZIP code areas are not completely homogeneous, however, and this strategy can produce inaccurate conclusions.

Because their purpose is to provide a profile of some population, surveys are designed to collect information that can be analyzed quantitatively. Survey answers can be nominal-level data (what party do you belong to?); ordinal-level data (do you agree or disagree?); or interval-level (how many political organizations do you belong to?). Analysts can report the distribution of responses for a single variable (see chapter 10). They can look for correlations among two or more variables by placing the information in contingency tables, using the categories from the original questions—agree or disagree for example (see chapters 5 and 6). Or they can assign numbers to each of the answers—(1) for disagree, (2) for neutral, and (3) for agree—and analyze them statistically (see chapter 11).

Survey research is broadly used in political analysis in three ways: (1) to measure public opinion and indicate trends, (2) to identify the public's view of electoral candidates and policy alternatives, and (3) by local governments, to assess citizen satisfaction with government services.

Measuring public opinion. In political science research, surveys primarily serve as a barometer of opinions and attitudes among the public and indicate trends and changes in public sentiment. And because many surveys use the same or similar questions, they can be used to report on and analyze trends. For example, a review of surveys reports interesting changes in attitudes toward women's holding public office. In 1955, 54 percent of the public said they would vote for a well-qualified woman if she were a party's nominee; in 1986, the figure was 86 percent—a significant increase.[5]

Predicting elections. The most visible use of survey research is tapping voter sentiment prior to presidential elections. Two broad conclusions about these polls tell much about survey research in general. The first is that overall the polls provide a fairly accurate picture of public sentiment.[6] As an example, table 7.2 compares the results in the Gallup survey taken just before an election with the actual result of the election. The lower accuracy in 1992 probably reflects the role of third-party candidate Ross Perot in that election. The leading national polls achieve such accuracy even though it is difficult to predict which people will actually go to the polls on election day. Some pollsters offer predictions on all registered voters, others on likely voters. Gallup usually asks each respondent about twenty questions, ten of which are designed to anticipate

TABLE 7.2

Comparison of Surveys with Election Results

Year	Gallup Final Preelection Survey		Election Result	
1992	49.0%	Clinton	43.0%	Clinton
1988	56.0	Bush	53.9	Bush
1984	59.0	Reagan	59.2	Reagan
1980	47.0	Reagan	50.8	Reagan
1976	48.0	Carter	50.0	Carter
1972	62.0	Nixon	61.8	Nixon
1968	43.0	Nixon	43.5	Nixon

Source: George Gallup, Jr. *The Gallup Poll: Public Opinion, 1990* (Wilmington, Del.: Scholarly Resources, 1991, p. xi; George Gallup, Jr. *The Gallup Poll: Public Opinion, 1992* (Wilmington, Del.: Scholarly Resources, 1992, p. 192.

whether the respondent will vote. Questions include "Do you know where your polling place is?" and "Did you cast a ballot in the last presidential election?" Still, the results are imprecise, and Gallup estimates that only about 75 percent of voters considered likely to vote actually vote on election day.[7]

Measuring policy preferences and satisfaction with local services.
Local governments use surveys to determine citizen preferences and attitudes toward local services, such as trash collection, public education, and recreation. The results can be both useful and misleading. Officials can, wittingly or un-wittingly, design surveys to collect positive information about their services. For example, recipients of social services who are asked about their satisfaction with such services could easily worry that if they voice negative opinions, these would be used against them. Or officials could phrase the questions in a way that misleads the public. For example, a town in the Southwest used the results of a citizen survey to proceed with plans to build a nuclear power plant, even though the words *nuclear* and *atomic* never appeared in the survey questions.[8] In addition, satisfaction is not necessarily an accurate indicator of how good the services actually are. Studies show that citizens do not always show greater sat-isfaction as services are improved. In fact, it appears that citizens notice when services are very good or very bad, but they make few distinctions in between these extremes.[9]

Sampling

Although you could survey all the members of a group such as your research methods class, survey research generally is used to collect information about a larger group. The power of surveys as a research tool, in fact, is their ability to provide information about large categories of individuals. They can do this be-cause researchers have established that it is possible to sample any population in such a way as to describe it fairly accurately. One of the more striking facts about sampling is that a well-chosen sample of 1,500 is adequate for generalizing about the population of the United States. If you have noticed the following kind of phrase appended to surveys, then you have already been introduced to sampling: "These results have a margin of error of plus or minus 3 percent." We will learn why a sample of 1,500 can be so informative, and what this margin of error means.

population
Group of phenomena we are studying.

A survey describes a group of people. The group, known as the **population,** could be citizens of the United States, delegates to the United Nations, or ma-jors in political science. Surveys are designed to estimate a specific characteris-tic of the population; this characteristic is called a **parameter.** We estimate the parameter by collecting data from a sample. The information we get from the sample is in turn called a **statistic.** The key issue in a survey is whether the sta-tistics collected from the sample tell us about the parameters of the entire pop-ulation being studied.

parameter
A characteristic of the population we are studying.

statistic
An estimate of a parameter based on a sample.

POPULATION

The group of phenomena we are studying.

> **Example:** Members of a political science class, Midwestern cities, registered voters, citizens of the United States of voting age.

PARAMETER

A characteristic of the population.

> **Example:** Number of women in a class, percentage of minorities in cities, number of registered voters who voted for president, number of eligible voters who are registered.

STATISTIC

An estimate of a parameter based on a sample of the population.

> **Example:** Ten women in a class of thirty, 40 percent of voters in city X are minority.

The Logic of Sampling

Assume you want to know how many members of your political analysis class regularly follow the national news in the daily papers. As your indicator, you decide to ask students if they read the editorial page, and if so, approximately how often. The choice of responses could be *almost never, sometimes,* and *often*. Because the class is your population, the resulting number and range of responses is a parameter. First, you ask each member of the class; assume the following results in a class of forty students:

Response	Number ($N = 40$)	Percentage
Almost never	15	37.5
Sometimes	17	42.5
Often	8	20.0

Second, select a sample of any five people from your class and carry out the same survey, recording the results. Draw a second sample and do likewise. Because you know the parameters in this case, you can compare the sample statistics with the known value in the total class. In all likelihood they will be different. In your first sample of five, perhaps three people, or 60 percent, will respond "sometimes." In the second sample, perhaps two people, or 40 percent, respond "sometimes." You, however, know that in the population of the entire class, 42.5 percent said "sometimes." Statisticians can help you interpret the sample results because they know how likely any given sample is. From this information we can at least determine the probability that the responses in the sample are accurate estimates of the population. This probability, or likelihood, is reported in two forms:

1. **Confidence interval.** The range of values within which the actual value falls. Based on a sample, we might be able to say that the true percentage of those who never read the paper falls in the range of 33 to 42 percent.
2. **Level of significance.** The probability that the population parameter actually falls within the confidence interval. Thus, we might say, on the basis of sampling, that the percentage of those who never read the paper falls within a range of 33 to 42 percent, 95 percent of the time.

To repeat, we draw a sample to tell us about a population. However, we can state only the probability—not the certainty—that the sample statistic reflects the parameter of the population from which the sample was taken. The sample statistic allows us to establish both the range within which the true value will fall and the probability that it will fall in that range. (Chapter 12 describes in more detail how we establish these probabilities.)

Obviously, we want to be able to report a narrow range of possible results and a high probability that the true result falls in this range. A range of 33 to 42 percent is preferable to a range of 30 to 45 percent, and a 95 percent probability is better than a 90 percent probability. The confidence interval and level of significance vary according to two characteristics of a sample: its size and the actual value of the parameter we are looking for.

The larger the sample size, the more likely it is to reflect the population and the greater the probability that any sample statistic gives accurate information. This fact should be intuitively clear. If you had drawn a sample of ten from your class in our example, you would have been more likely to draw cases from all portions of the class than you would in a sample of five. A second fact may not be so obvious, however; it is the initial increases in sample size that are most valuable in increasing the sample's accuracy. This fact is important because surveys require much time and money. It means that pollsters can increase the sample size up to a point and then stop. A sample of 1,500 is generally adequate to represent the population of the United States, and most samples are under 3,000. Increasing a sample beyond these numbers does not increase the statistical accuracy of the sample by a significant amount. It is also true that a sample of 1,500 can represent the population of the United States equally as well as it can represent the population of a city of 1,000,000. Beyond a certain threshold population size, the size of the sample and not the size of the population determines sampling error.

The appropriate size depends partly on the expected distribution of answers. If the distribution is expected to be close—for example, 48 percent of those interviewed say "yes" and 52 percent say "no"—then the sample needs to be larger to capture this small difference than it would be to capture a larger expected difference. Look back at table 7.2, and you will see that the Gallup poll was more accurate in elections in which the difference between the candidates was closer to 20 percent (1972 and 1984) than when they were more evenly matched (1976). (Compare the 0.2 percent difference in 1984 with the 2.0 percent difference in 1976.)

These points are illustrated in table 7.3, which indicates the confidence interval for different sample sizes. The numbers in the right column indicate plus or minus those numbers; thus, plus or minus three is actually a range of six. This range of plus or minus three, or four, or any number, is also referred to as the **sampling error,** because it tells us the extent to which a sample statistic could be in error. The errors in table 7.3 assume that the population is almost evenly divided. The errors would be smaller if 70 percent or more of the respondents agreed. Note that the table indicates that if you are willing to accept an error range of plus or minus four, a sample of 1,000 or even 750 is sufficient. Also, increasing the sample size from 200 to 600 considerably decreases the error, but increasing it from 1,000 to 1,500 decreases the error only slightly.

Now we can return to the kind of statement appended to most polls reported in the media: the results have a margin of error of plus or minus three points. If a pollster says that a race is tied at 50-50 and there is a margin of error of plus or minus three points, it would be equally accurate to say that one candidate leads another by 53-47 or 52-48 or 51-49. All of these possibilities have the same likelihood. Further, we now know that values will fall in this range 95 percent of the time. Most polls in the media do not add another fact, namely that the poll is likely to be accurate within the stated range 95 percent of the time, and simply wrong the other 5 percent of the time.

Putting this in a different way, we can say that the results have a sampling error or confidence interval of plus or minus 3 percent, or an error range of 6 percent. If 52 percent of the respondents say they are for the Democratic candidate, the sentiment in the population favoring the Democrats probably falls within a range of 49 to 55 percent. In other words, 52 percent is the best estimate—rather

sampling error
Degree to which a sample statistic differs from the population parameter.

TABLE 7.3
Maximum Sampling Error for Samples of Various Sizes

Sample Size	Sampling Error
1,500	3
1,000	4
750	4
600	5
200	9

Source: *Gallup Opinion Index,* April 1975, p. 30.

than the actual amount—of Democratic sentiment. The level of significance is 95 percent, meaning that the pollster is 95 percent certain that the range will contain the actual population parameter; 5 percent of the time the parameter lies outside this range of 49 to 55 percent. When the media report only a single figure from a poll, they are suggesting more accuracy than really exists, and you should remember that any figure based on a poll is accurate only within a certain confidence range.

Selecting Cases for the Sample from Large Populations

simple random sample
A sample in which each member of the population has an equal chance of being selected.

The accuracy of samples is also influenced by the manner in which the individuals (or cases) are chosen. One method is the **simple random sample,** in which each member of a population has the same chance, or probability, of being included in the sample. To satisfy this rather stringent requirement, it is necessary to have a list of everyone in the population and to select a sample randomly from the list. If you were sampling the student body at your college, you could begin by getting a list of all students from the registrar and randomly selecting a sample, perhaps by using the table of random numbers in the back of any statistics textbook. Note, however, that "a list of all students" may be hard to come by. If the registrar's list failed to include some group of students such as those who had registered late, your initial list would be inadequate. Your actual population would be the registrar's list and not the entire student body.

One interesting simulation of random sampling is random digit dialing using computer-generated telephone numbers. Callers dial each randomly generated number three or more times over a period of several days so that people who are infrequently at home will have as much chance of being included as anyone else. There are other techniques to approximate random selection. Students at one university did random dialing; each student dialed between twenty-five and fifty numbers, selecting digits at random until they got five interviews. Another group of students began with voter registration lists. Because it is illegal to copy these, students hand-copied names selected at random, and then consulted the telephone directory or called information for their phone numbers. Yet another class removed the binding of a telephone directory, and each student drew ten pages at random and then called two people selected at random from each page. In all of these cases the population consists of households with a telephone rather than all residents in the community. When the phone book was used to access numbers, the population was further restricted to those with listed telephone numbers.

stratified random sample
A sample in which the population is divided into strata, or groups, based on known characteristics, and a random sample is selected from each stratum.

With large populations, complete lists almost never exist. There is, for example, no list of all the citizens of the United States, or even of all the citizens in a local community. Even if there were, interviewing a randomly selected group by a method other than telephone would require huge travel expenses. Therefore pollsters have developed several modifications. One is **stratified random sampling,** in which the population is divided into groups, or strata, characterized by such divisions as income, race, and ethnic background. A random sample is selected from each stratum, ensuring that the sample will contain the same percentage of that group as does the population. If a town has a minority population of 15 percent, this method would ensure that 15 percent of the sample is also drawn from minorities.

cluster sample
A sample in which the population is divided into geographic clusters, and respondents are selected at random within each cluster.

A second modification of random sampling is **cluster sampling.** The population is divided into geographical clusters, such as neighborhoods, blocks, or census tracts—units of adjacent blocks. Once a city is divided into clusters, a number of the clusters are chosen at random, and then respondents are randomly selected within each cluster. Recall the warning in the heading to this chapter that it is all too easy to bias your sample.

Consider the method used for most of the national polls conducted during presidential elections. Typically these polls rely on about 1,500 respondents, selected by a combination of stratified, cluster, and random sampling. Pollsters first divide the country into geographic clusters and stratify these by region and size of community. They then randomly select about 350 sampling locations. Interviewers have to conduct their surveys within these locations; they cannot select the part of the city or county they will visit. They are given a map of sampling locations and specific directions about how to choose the respondents. Gallup, for example, divides the country into four regions (Northwest, Southwest, Northeast, and Southeast) and then divides each of these into seven types of locales: five sizes of towns and cities, rural areas, and suburbs. These divisions give Gallup twenty-eight "cells," within each of which it then interviews randomly selected residents.

During 1997 as plans were being made to conduct the national census in 2000, sampling became a highly charged political issue. Past experience showed that the census, which attempts to contact every single household rather than a sample, undercounts those households that for some reason want to avoid being counted or who are seldom home or who do not have a regular address. Such undercounting is particularly true in large cities and for poor and immigrant populations. For example, the Census Bureau estimates that in 1990 the census undercounted 5.1 percent of the population in Newark, New Jersey, and 6.3 percent of the population in Inglewood, California. Nationally the census undercounted 5 percent of Hispanics and 4.5 percent of American Indians. Looking ahead to 2000, the Census Bureau proposed conducting the census as usual and then sampling those in urban areas to get a more accurate count of the total, but many in Congress could not accept this reasoning and feared it was a political ploy by those areas which were allegedly undercounted. Questions were even raised about the constitutionality of sampling since the Constitution calls for an "actual enumeration" of the population every ten years.

Selecting Cases for a Sample of Smaller Populations

The same principles can be applied to drawing a sample from a smaller population. The general rule is that a sample should have at least thirty observations. The confidence interval is apt to be larger in small samples, and the probability that any given sample falls within this range will be smaller. The extent to which such a sample accurately reflects the population depends partly on the size of the population and also on the diversity of responses in the population.

Ideally you draw each of your cases at random so that each case has an equal chance of being included in the sample. Consider the example of the sixty-eight senatorial candidates running for election in 1996. Since the research on these candidates described in chapter 6 was collecting limited information on each candidate you should be able to include all sixty-eight in your study. However, if you needed to draw a sample in order to send a smaller group a questionnaire, you should find a way to select about thirty of them at random. The best proce-dure is to use a table of random numbers at the back of most statistics texts. It would not be ideal to select every other candidate. That would make it impossi-ble to have two candidates from the same state, contradicting the rule that each case should have an equal chance of being included in the sample.

Often you will not have a list of all the people in your population and you will have to find imaginative ways to draw a sample. Earlier we described strati-fied and cluster sampling techniques that combine convenience with random-ness, and you should try to apply these same principles to whatever units and individuals you are surveying. For example, assume you are doing research on public officials in local governments in your region and you want to submit a questionnaire to them. Locate a directory of government agencies in your local library. Select a number of agencies at random, call them, and identify the name of several people to whom you could send a questionnaire. As another example, recall the research you were asked to consider on the results of privatizing ser-vices at your university. You want to find student opinion about changes in pro-viding such services as food or books. You could position yourself where students pass by and select every tenth (or some number) student who comes by. Ask them to fill out a brief questionnaire or answer a brief series of questions. You could introduce some stratification into the sample, by making sure you did this during the day and also during evening hours to get different groups. You could also position yourself at different spots on campus to make sure you met a full range of students.

Designing and Implementing a Survey or Questionnaire

Survey research refers to structured interviews of a sample of respondents that are conducted with the intent of generalizing to a larger population. Questions can also be asked of a smaller number of people who may or may not constitute a formal sample, in which case they are typically called *questionnaires*. Question-naires can be administered in person, by telephone, or by mail to a sample or to all members of a population: delegates to a party convention, supervisors in a government agency, clients of a mental health program. The point of both surveys and questionnaires is that the questions are defined ahead of time, and respondents are typically asked to select among a limited set of answers. This section covers steps you can take to get evidence by asking individuals—

whether you are drawing a sample from your population or using a question-naire with all the members of a smaller group.

Questions as Part of Research Plan

Your actual questions need to be part of a larger research plan; they should be based on your original research question and the concepts and variables that concern you. Your plan should include at least the following:[10]

A *research question*—what you want to know

A *research hypothesis*—what you expect to find

An *instrument*—or questionnaire with the questions you will ask

A *sample plan*—a plan for selecting people whose views you want to know about

The *population*

Individual *units* in the population

The *group* from which the individual units will be chosen

The *sample*—the number and characteristics of the portion of population you select[11]

For example, your research question might concern the opinions of the student body at your school toward the political system. You could hypothesize that students in the social sciences would have the greatest political interest and political efficacy and those in the humanities and hard sciences would have the least. You would develop a series of questions. Your sample plan could include all students at the school, but you would probably do better to select four or five majors as your population and try to get as complete a list of students in each of them as possible. Alternatively, and bowing to the practical difficulties in conducting a survey, you could select two classes in each major at random and ask for permission to submit a questionnaire to department majors in each of the courses.

Developing the Questions

The questions in a survey are actually indicators of the concepts you want to know more about. To come up with valid questions, you need to make sure the questions are good measures of the variables you are studying, as discussed earlier in chapter 3. Questions can ask for four kinds of information: knowledge, opinions, experiences, and feelings. Michael Patton stresses that we need to be clear about the differences among these, making it obvious which of these four kinds of information we are interested in. "Knowledge questions imply true/false answers. Opinion questions request respondents to agree or disagree. Behavioral items ask what the respondent has actually experienced. Feeling questions should tap emotional states."[12] The cues we give tell the person which of these we are asking for. In the following examples the different sets of cues ask for different kinds of information about the same topic.

> *Knowledge cue:* "Students have an important role in governing the university."
>
>   True   False   Don't Know
>
> *Opinion cue*: "Students have an important role in governing the university."
>
>   Strongly agree   Agree   Disagree   Strongly disagree
>
> *Experience cue:* "Students have an important role in governing the university."
>
>   Always   Often   Sometimes   Seldom   Rarely   Never
>
> *Feeling cue:* "When people discuss ways to involve students in governing the university, how do you usually feel?"
>
>   Skeptical   Neutral   Sympathetic

The problem, Patton continues, is that researchers often ignore these distinctions and ask whether people agree or disagree with a statement, even if that is not precisely what they want to know.

Questions also need to be clear and unambiguous. Review questionnaires that have been used successfully in similar research, noting both their strengths and their weaknesses. Avoid complex questions that include two or more items. For example, do not ask, "Do you agree or disagree that the U.S. should spend more on defense and less on welfare?" Avoid vague terms such as "institutionalization" or "people with problems" or questions such as "How do you feel about the president?" And avoid using negatives in your questions: "Do you agree or disagree that the U.S. should not continue trade sanctions against Cuba?" is confusing.

open-ended question
A question that allows respondents to formulate their own answers.

Clarity is also important for **open-ended questions.** Eventually, you will want to group these into useful categories, and the more specific and straightforward the question, the easier it is to combine the various answers into some meaningful pattern. A question such as "How would you improve student government?" is too vague to get comparable suggestions. A more focused question, such as "What steps could the administration take to increase the number of students serving on university committees?" would be easier to analyze. You could probably group the various answers into meaningful clusters of answers.

Ask yourself if your respondents are competent to answer your question and would be familiar with the terms you are using. Avoid terms that people may not know; for example do not ask, "Do you favor the WTO?" Better to say, "Are you in favor of efforts to promote free trade with other nations?" If you are not sure what information people have, you can ask a question such as, "Are you generally familiar with current policy discussions about expanding NATO?" You would only ask a specific question about NATO if they answered "yes." Or simply ask, "Have you heard about . . . ?" Also do not presume that if they answer a question, they actually are familiar with the person or issue. Earl Babbie reports that while conducting a survey to determine peoples' opinions about their local government, he made up the name of a local leader and 9 percent of the respondents said they were familiar with him, and half of these reported seeing the fictitious person on TV.[13]

In general it is valuable to spend time asking respondents what they know as well as what they think about various political trends. A survey in late 1996 documents how much misinformation individuals have. For example, when asked, respondents estimated on average that unemployment was 1 percent, whereas in reality it was 5.4 percent. Seventy percent thought that the deficit was larger compared to five years earlier, whereas in reality it had declined from about $270 billion to just over $100 billion. The survey also showed that those with more and less accurate views of reality had different attitudes, indicating that information levels affected opinion.[14]

Avoid questions that contain biases or that encourage a particular answer. Consider the example, "Do you agree or disagree with the recent Supreme Court decision that . . ." Respondents want to appear informed and intelligent, and by indicating that the Supreme Court was positive about a decision, you are encouraging the respondent to agree with the statement.

Make your questions as nonthreatening as possible and avoid sensitive and personal questions. Thus do not directly ask people their age or income. Instead give them a series of categories to choose among. For income you could ask them to indicate whether their family income is below $20,000, $20,000–$40,000, $40,000–$60,000, or over $60,000. Normally you would ask these kinds of questions at the end of the survey because such questions can be annoying, and, if asked at the outset, could cause people to refuse to participate in the survey.

Example: Questions about Political Interest and Efficacy

At the beginning of this section you were asked to consider doing research on student opinions towards the political system, and specifically the extent of their political interest and efficacy. You could include questions such as the following:

> How much interest do you have in politics? Would you say that you are Very Interested, Moderately Interested, Not Very Interested, Not Interested At All?
>
> Do you look at a newspaper on a regular basis? Yes or No. (If "yes" ask) I would like to know which sections you look at. Answer yes or no to each:
>
>   The Front page, Local news section, Sports page, Editorial page.
>
> Do you watch one of the major network news programs on a regular basis? Yes or No.
>
> Were you eligible to vote in the last presidential election? Yes or No. (If "Yes" ask) Are you registered to vote? Yes or No. (If "Yes" ask) Did you vote for a presidential candidate?

Have you ever attended a meeting on campus related to a campaign for public office? Yes or No.

How often do you discuss politics with other students? Very often, Often, Seldom, Never.

How important are political issues to you? Very important, Some importance, Not very important, No importance.

Designing a Questionnaire to Be Completed by a Respondent

You may decide to mail your questionnaire to a group or sample of respondents, ask them to fill it out themselves, and return it in an enclosed stamped envelope. You may have received a questionnaire in the mail yourself. Try to recall what factors influenced whether or not you filled it out and returned it. The questionnaire should be preceded by a letter clearly stating who you are, the purpose of your survey, and the time it will take to fill it out. Ideally, you will arrange for the replies to be anonymous. The questionnaire's layout should be appealing to the eye. Do not cram a lot of questions onto one or two pages. Do whatever you can to encourage people to spend the time to respond.

In reporting the results, you will need to indicate the number of questionnaires sent out and the response rate. It could be as low as 10 to 20 percent, but a good return rate would be closer to 50 percent.[15] The higher the response rate to a questionnaire, the more valid the results will be. You hope that those who do respond are a random sample of those who received the questionnaire, but of course this is not likely. You can encourage a good return by calling persons who have not sent back the completed questionnaire after a certain time; by mailing a second copy; by enclosing a stamped, self-addressed envelope with each questionnaire; or by otherwise reminding the respondent and making return relatively easy.

Problems in Survey Research

A decade or so ago survey results were simply reported as straightforward percentages. Recently, more attention has been given to sampling errors and confidence intervals, both of which are routinely reported by the media. In addition, those who study polls have begun to emphasize the importance of what they call "nonsampling error." This refers to problems that can arise from the phrasing of questions, from the role of the interviewer, from the fact that people may or may not know what their own opinions are. This section examines a number of issues that can arise in interpreting survey results.[16]

Responses as Valid Indicators of Attitudes

There are a number of measurement errors that can compromise the validity of survey responses. *Validity* here refers to how well the survey responses measure the actual attitudes that respondents hold. The interview itself may produce errors if the questioner is unskilled and intentionally or inadvertently suggests which response is the appropriate one. Respondents themselves may give invalid answers if they feel certain answers are socially undesirable, such as indicating they do not intend to vote. The most important sources of error are due to the timing, phrasing, and sequencing of questions and to the interpretation of responses.

Timing. Tables reporting survey data usually note the actual question as well as the dates on which questions were asked, items that have a lot to do with the validity of the responses. For example, the timing of a question may affect people's attitudes. Regarding attitudes toward handgun control, have the percentages of people who favor stricter control changed?

1975	69%
1980	59%
1981	65%
1983	59%
1986	60%
1989	70%
1993	70%
1995	62%

The percentages remained close to 60 percent, except for periods in 1975, 1981, 1989, and 1993, when the numbers favoring control increased. It happened that the survey in 1975 was conducted just after an assassination attempt on President Gerald Ford, and the survey in 1981 just after an assassination attempt on President Ronald Reagan. These events could have led some people to change their minds temporarily.

Phrasing. The wording of the question is important also. Questions can be loaded and argumentative, or they can simply use terms that people do not understand. For example, during the Watergate scandal, the Gallup poll asked respondents if President Richard Nixon "should be impeached" and always found that less than a majority said "yes." Then Gallup realized that the question was ambiguous since the meaning of *impeach* was not specified. When the question was rephrased and asked respondents if they favored bringing President Nixon to trial before the Senate, a strong majority said "yes." As a second example, a poll on public attitudes found that two-thirds of the public felt the government spends too little on "assistance to the poor," but less than a majority felt this way when the word *welfare* was substituted for "assistance to the poor."

Decisions about different ways to phrase a question can be subtle. There has been considerable debate about the way to ask people about their party identification. The Gallup poll asks, "In politics, as of today, do you consider yourself a

Republican, a Democrat, or an Independent?" The Michigan Social Research Center (SRC) asks, "Generally speaking, do you usually think of yourself as a Republican, a Democrat, an Independent, or what?" Researchers argue that the Gallup poll, because it asks about partisanship "as of today," focuses on short-term identifications, whereas the SRC taps longer term loyalties, because it asks "generally speaking." The important question is whether or not either of these presents a misleading portrait of partisanship. Recent analysis of multiple polls concludes that both polls portray a similar picture of party identification.[17]

Sequencing. The ordering of questions also can affect the results. During the 1988 presidential election campaign, the Roper organization found that Democrat Michael Dukakis had a twelve-point lead when his name was mentioned first and only a four-point lead when Republican George Bush's name was mentioned first. The September 1988 *Washington Post* and ABC News monthly poll, however, found that both Bush and Dukakis did better when their name was mentioned second. To avoid any potential bias from the positions of names, responsible polls rotate the order in which they mention people's names.[18]

Surveys as Obtrusive Measures

Some analysts argue that we rely on surveys too readily and fail to explore other sources of data. One important study maintains that surveys provide "obtrusive" measures; that is, the survey process affects the information a researcher receives. Researchers can never be sure they are actually tapping people's opinions because they cannot help but "intrude" into the process and influence how people respond. The study notes that questions may not be valid measures or indicators of the variables, and answers may vary depending on how the questions are asked by different interviewers.[19]

Opinions—Fleeting or Stable?

Surveys may suggest that people have opinions even if they do not, or they may suggest that people's views differ more than they do in reality. People are often reluctant to admit they are unsure or have no opinion and may state a preference even if they have not really thought about an issue. Researchers call such answers "random noise."[20] When people are asked, "Did you vote in the last election?" more people respond "yes" than actually voted. In a U.S. Census Bureau survey, 59.2 percent of the electorate said they had voted in the 1980 presidential election, but election returns reported that only 53.9 percent had turned out.[21] Questions should be worded so that people feel free to say they do not know or do not have an opinion. You can also offer social support for their answers. Begin a question, "Some people say this and some people say that; how do you feel?"

A recent set of interviews with respondents following a survey provides a unique insight into the validity of the opinions that people report. In the spring of 1988 a poll was taken in Washington, D.C., to compare the opinions of whites and blacks of each other and to learn about views on discrimination. A short time later one of the pollsters interviewed several of the respondents in more depth. A number of them did not recall, or could not explain, what they had answered. A few said their answers reflected experiences they had had at the time of the survey. Others said they had changed their minds since. And some explained that they had put a particular interpretation on the questions. For example, one of the questions asked whether discrimination was a factor in keeping blacks from getting good jobs and housing; 51 percent of the blacks said it was, and 69 percent of the whites said it was not an important factor. In the interviews respondents elaborated on their answers, adding important qualifications that suggested they were not as far apart as the original "yes" and "no" answers implied.[22]

Relationship between Attitudes and Behavior

A related problem concerns the relationship between attitudes and behavior. Analysts usually study attitudes to explain and predict how people will behave. Expressed opinions, however, do not necessarily coincide with actions. "Surveys cannot measure social action; they can only collect self reports of recalled past action, or of prospective or hypothetical action."[23] In 1986, 87 percent of the voting public said they would vote for a well-qualified black candidate for president.[24] Given the controversy surrounding Jesse Jackson's candidacy for the Democratic nomination in 1984 and 1988, it is reasonable to question whether people would behave as they stated. As another example, one has to be careful in predicting votes based on surveys that report that individuals are critical of political officials. In 1992 there was widespread criticism of political officials and a general anti-incumbency mood among the public. And yet the vast majority of incumbents who ran for reelection were returned to office. The reason is simple: people often disapprove of Congress as a whole but like their congressional representative. In July 1992 a survey found that 71 percent of Americans were critical of Congress, but only 30 percent were critical of their own representative (*Washington Post*, January 13, 1996, p. A-4).

The fact that peoples' behavior and expressed opinions are not necessarily consistent was illustrated by a study carried out in 1934 to determine whether people who express prejudice against certain groups also treat them unfairly. The researcher and a Chinese couple traveled together throughout the United States, stopping at 250 hotels and restaurants. Only one hotel and no restaurant refused to serve them. Each establishment later was sent a letter asking if the proprietors would accommodate a Chinese person; of those that replied, 92 percent said "no."[25]

Bias against Political and Institutional Variables

Surveys also emphasize individual attitudes rather than political institutions or public policies. We have raised this issue several times already. For example, some argue that to understand voter turnout, researchers should not only look at people's attitudes but also pay more attention to the effect of registration rules and the role of the media on turnout. Our infatuation with polling and survey research may overlook these kinds of influences on voting and public opinions. Surveys also project a biased view of the role of public opinion and participation in a democratic system. They take a snapshot of existing opinions, whereas political leadership and political institutions can provide opportunities for individuals to debate issues, to explore new ideas, to hear new opinions. In this sense some worry that surveys place a disproportionate emphasis on existing public opinion and divert political leaders from looking for opportunities to use their position as a "bully pulpit" to inform and educate opinion.[26]

Using Others' Surveys in Your Research

Sources of Survey Data

Surveys of large populations are difficult to carry out and expensive. Many of the most professional and accurate surveys, however, are readily available. The four sources listed below report survey information about the total population or subgroups. Such surveys open up a vast range of information about public opinion, although you will be limited to the groups that the sources describe. (For example, a survey might report opinions by men and women but not give you the information according to the educational level of each gender.)

The Gallup Poll: Public Opinion is published each year. Provides information on political opinions and attitudes. Several tables in this chapter report data from this source.

The Harris Survey Yearbook of Public Opinion is also published annually. Provides results of the American opinion polls carried out by the Harris organization during the prior year.

American Public Opinion Index gives access to many surveys conducted in the United States. One section includes questions by broad subject categories; another gives the sources of polling results.

Public Opinion Quarterly is a journal that includes in each issue "The Polls" section, which gives data on opinions in the United States and elsewhere.

In addition, the national media often report surveys carried out by universities, national newspapers, and broadcasters. These reports are also given for the population as a whole or for subgroups that the media are particularly interested in. Look in indexes such as *New York Times Index* under topics you are interested in to determine if there was a survey taken.

There are two archives where political scientists can get survey information reported for individuals rather than categories of individuals: the Inter-University Consortium for Political and Social Research (ICPSR) and the

Roper Center at the University of Connecticut. You can get a list of the data available through the ICPSR in *Guide to Resources and Services,* published by the Institute for Social Research at the University of Michigan in Ann Arbor. The ISR's data are available through the computing services at many universities, although you will need additional skills to access and manipulate them. If you do have access to these data you will be able to explore many more categories of individuals than in the above sources, and you will be able to include a number of control variables that are of interest to you.

Interpreting Survey Data

closed question
A question that asks a respondent to choose among several alternative answers.

As noted earlier, surveys rely primarily on **closed questions,** in which respondents are given specific and limited alternatives from which to select. For example, in April 1995 the Gallup poll asked people the following question: "In general, do you feel that the laws covering the sale of firearms should be made more strict, less strict, or kept as they are now?" If respondents declined to select one, the interviewer would indicate "no opinion." The results are recorded in table 7.4. Because this survey also collected demographic information, it can be used to link characteristics of individuals with views on firearms and describe the relationship between types of individuals and attitudes (see table 7.5.)

Note some rules of thumb for interpreting the information in the tables. Do not begin with details but instead look for general patterns. What is the most significant fact presented in table 7.5? Two points are most striking: a majority of both men and women want stricter controls, and considerably more women feel this way than men do. After noting these general patterns, include some of the specific numbers such as the 10 percent difference between the numbers of men and women who favored stricter controls. Look at the information in table 7.6 and summarize what it tells you. Again begin with the most striking

TABLE 7.4
Attitudes toward Control of Firearms

Question: In general, do you feel that the laws covering the sale of firearms should be made more strict, less strict, or kept as they are now?"

More strict	62%
Less strict	12
Kept same	24
No opinion	2

Source: *The Gallup Poll: Public Opinion, 1995* (Wilmington, Del.: Scholarly Resources, 1996), p. 75.

TABLE 7.5
Attitudes toward Control of Firearms, by Gender

	Gender	
Attitude	*Male*	*Female*
More strict	57%	67%
Less strict	13	11
Kept same	28	20
No opinion	2	2

Source: *The Gallup Poll: Public Opinion, 1995* (Wilmington, Del.: Scholarly Resources, 1996), p. 75.

TABLE 7.6
Attitudes toward Control of Firearms, by Region

	Region			
Attitude	*East*	*Midwest*	*South*	*West*
More strict	61%	60%	65%	62%
Less strict	12	8	15	13
Kept same	24	30	19	24
No opinion	3	2	1	1

Source: *The Gallup Poll: Public Opinion, 1995* (Wilmington, Del.: Scholarly Resources, 1996), p. 70.

result; state it in its most general form first, using percentage differences to pin down your point, and then add details.

_____

_____

_____

_____

_____

_____

_____

TABLE 7.7

Most Important Problem, 1993, 1994, 1995

Question: What do you think is the most important problem facing this country today?

	January 1993	January 1994	January 1995
Crime	9%	37%	27%
Environment	3	1	1
Economy	35	14	10
Education	8	7	5
Poverty, hunger	10	11	10

Source: *The Gallup Poll: Public Opinion, 1995* (Wilmington, Del.: Scholarly Resources, 1996), p. 13; *The Gallup Poll: Public Opinion, 1994* (Wilmington, Del.: Scholarly Resources, 1995), p. 28; *The Gallup Poll: Public Opinion, 1993* (Wilmington, Del.: Scholarly Resources, 1994), p. 23.

Note: Columns do not add up to 100% because some respondents gave multiple answers or mentioned items not included here.

Researchers may include a few open-ended questions, such as the question "What do you think is the most important problem facing this country today?" Table 7.7 gives the results over a period of three years.

Again, ask yourself, What is the most striking or interesting fact presented in table 7.7? One is the remarkable consistency in opinions about most public problems; with the exceptions of crime and the economy, the figures remain fairly constant. What other facts stand out or intrigue you?

_____

_____

_____

_____

_____

_____

_____

_____

Example: Using Published Survey Data in Research

Assume that you are interested in researching public confidence in government. You could decide to do a research paper on this topic, drawing on published polls, both nationally and internationally. Some obvious questions would be: How does the American public feel about the government? Do their feelings vary according to the level of government? Has their confidence in the government changed over time? How does sentiment in the United States compare with attitudes in other countries?

Begin with an outline similar to that laid out in an earlier section that asks you to define your research question and research hypothesis. Following are some of the sources you could draw on:

1. Look in an index for a national newspaper such as the *New York Times Index* under different topics to see if a survey has been reported on your topic. For example, in March 1997, the *Washington Post* gave information from two polls about citizen confidence in government, one sponsored by the Council for Excellence in Government and the other by the research firms of Peter D. Hart and Robert M. Teeter. The *Post* reports the percentages of respondents who have various degrees of confidence in government, in other institutions such as the military, and in different levels of government. They also report some reasons given by the public for their views, and policy areas where the public has more confidence.[27] The article concludes that the survey "finds Americans optimistic that government could be more effective and work better for them." You would want to note the numbers of adults surveyed, whether any information is given about the reliability of the polls, and whether a confidence interval and probability level are given. You would also want to note the dates on which the polls were taken and ask whether any public events occurred near this time that might have influenced the results.

2. You could check how these opinions have differed over time by looking at surveys taken over several time periods by the Gallup Poll or the National Opinion Research Center. For example, *An American Profile—Opinions and Behavior, 1972–1989* summarizes opinions during the 1970s and 1980s gathered by the General Social Survey, conducted by the National Opinion Research Center.[28] To compare how the public perceives different levels of government, go to the *American Public Opinion Index, 1989* and *American Public Opinion Data, 1989* for surveys primarily from the 1980s.[29] Here you will find questions such as: "From which level of government do you get the most/least for your money?" Tables break the answers down according to different categories of respondents, including income, race, gender, employment status, region, and so forth.

3. You could then compare the results with surveys on public opinion in other countries. One relevant source is the *Index to International Public Opinion, 1994–1995*.[30] Look for comparable questions reported for other countries, again noting the information about the numbers surveyed and the confidence interval. Since these surveys would be taken by a variety of groups, you would want to note the wording of the questions and your judgment about their comparability.

Your research paper would include tables and analyses of the data in the tables, pointing first to major patterns and trends, and then illustrating these with specific figures. To what extent do the results support or refute or qualify your hypothesis? You would also review the earlier discussion of problems that can arise with surveys and discuss if any of these are relevant in this case. You would of course list all sources and relevant characteristics of the surveys you use.

Where We Are

You have now explored one source of evidence that you can draw on to answer your research questions. Recall the earlier statement that as you design your research you need to consider both what is interesting to you and what relevant information can feasibly be obtained. As you review this discussion of surveys and questionnaires, you may revise your research question to take advantage of existing information on attitudes. You may decide to focus on a narrower aspect of your original question in order to insure that you can be thorough and accurate in your findings. Or looking over the kinds of information contained in published surveys may open up interesting new research topics. It is hoped you will look in the media for current surveys and read them with a more practiced eye about what they tell you and the ways in which they might mislead you. Look for opportunities to replicate surveys that others have done to determine if their results are also true of a population of interest to you—students, for example. Look for evidence about the reliability of surveys. This chapter has emphasized that well done surveys can provide very accurate pictures of a population—does that appear to be true for the surveys you read? Finally, what are the values of surveys? Is Verba correct in his statement at the outset of this chapter that they give us a more inclusive view of public opinions than we get through direct participation? Are there some kinds of information that surveys do not provide? Chapter 8 will partially answer that question by describing a source of direct data gathering that cannot be obtained through structured questionnaires.

NOTES

1. There are many excellent treatments of survey research at the introductory level; one that discusses both survey design and interpretation is Herbert Weisberg and Bruce Bowen, *An Introduction to Survey Research and Data Analysis* (San Francisco: W. H. Freeman, 1977).
2. Sidney Verba, "The Citizen as Respondent: Sample Surveys and American Democracy," *American Political Science Review* 90, no. 1 (March 1996): 1–7.
3. Tom Smith, "The Art of Asking Questions, 1936–1985," *Public Opinion Quarterly* 51, supplement (Winter 1987): S95–S108.
4. The Claritas Corporation, for example, has divided every zip code in the United States into one of twelve groups based on predominant demographic characteristics. The groups and their percentages among voters are: young families, 14 percent; upper-middle-class families, 13 percent; small-town, blue-collar workers, 10 percent; rural mixed poor, 10 percent; rural towns, 9 percent; midscale families, 9 percent; unskilled urban, 7 percent; no kids, upscale, 7 percent; urban yuppies, 6 percent; post-kids, aging, 6 percent; urban middle-class, 5 percent; fancy suburbs 4 percent. Richard Morin, "Largest Downtowns Eluded Bush's Grasp," *Washington Post*, 25 November 1988, p. A29.
5. Glenn Norval, "Social Trends in the United States," *Public Opinion Quarterly* 51, supplement (Winter 1987): S123.
6. Most of the last preelection polls in November 1988 came within one percentage point of the actual result, an eight-point margin of victory by the Republican

candidate, Bush. *Washington Post*, 10 November 1988, p. A50. The preelection polls were equally close in 1992. *Washington Post*, 5 November 1992, p. A1.

7. *Economist* (November 1988): 14.

8. Gregory Daneke and Patricia Klobus-Edwards, "Survey Research for Public Administrators," *Public Administration Review* 39, no. 5 (September/October 1979): 421–426.

9. Brian Stipak, "Citizen Satisfaction with Urban Services: Potential Misuse as a Performance Indicator," *Public Administration Review* 39, no. 1 (January/February 1979): 46–53.

10. These steps are discussed by Gregory M. Scott, *Political Science: Foundations for a Fifth Millennium.* (Upper Saddle River, N.J.: Prentice-Hall, 1996), pp. 176–177.

11. Gregory M. Scott, *Political Science* (Upper Saddle River, N.J.: Prentice-Hall, 1997).

12. This discussion of questions is adapted from a discussion on interviews in Michael Patton, *Practical Interviewing* (Newbury Park, Calif.: Sage Publications, 1982), pp. 142–149.

13. Earl Babbie, *The Practice of Social Research*, 3d ed. (Belmont, Calif.: Wadsworth, 1983), p. 134.

14. "Statistics Do Little to Change View of Americans," *Washington Post*, 13 October 1996, p. A3.

15. Earl Babbie, *The Practice of Social Research*, 3d ed. (Belmont, Calif.: Wadsworth, 1983), p. 226. This book contains a detailed discussion of survey and questionnaire design.

16. While the large surveys taken by national research firms and academic units are remarkably reliable, this is not true for all polls. For problems associated with polling, and what the author calls "the dirty little secrets of polling," see, Richard Morin, "Behind the Numbers: Confessions of a Pollster," *Washington Post*, 16 October 1988, p. C1.

17. George Bishop, Alfred Tuchfarber, and Andrew Smith, "Question Form and Context Effects in the Measurement of Partisanship," *American Political Science Review* 88, no. 4 (December 1994): 945–954. A response says this conclusion holds except during periods of political volatility. Paul Abramson and Charles Ostrom, "Response," *American Political Science Review* 88, no. 4 (December 1994): 955–958.

18. Morin, "Behind the Numbers: Confessions of a Pollster," p. C1.

19. Eugene Webb et al., *Unobtrusive Measures* (Chicago: Rand McNally, 1969), pp. 1–34.

20. Weisberg and Bowen, *An Introduction to Survey Research and Data Analysis*, pp. 82–83.

21. "Americans Remember Voting—Even When They Didn't," *Washington Post*, 2 November 1981, p. A3.

22. Courtland Milloy, "Many Respondents Find Explaining Racial Distrust Difficult," *Washington Post*, 9 April 1988, p. A12.

23. Earl Babbie, *The Practice of Social Research.* (Belmont, Calif.: Wadsworth, 1983), p. 238.

24. Norval, "Social Trends in the United States," p. S123.

25. Robert LaPiere, "Attitudes vs Actions," *Social Forces* 13, no. 2 (1934): 230–237. Also see Irwin Deutscher, *What We Say/What We Do* (Glenview, Ill.: Scott Foresman, 1973).

26. An extreme version of this bias are the call-in "polls" sponsored by the media during U.S. presidential elections. Individuals are invited to indicate their opinion on a topic by calling a given number and pushing buttons on their phone. The results can differ significantly from scientific polls conducted at the same time. There are two major reasons for the difference. First, those who call in usually have strong

feelings about the issue and are more apt to hold extreme positions than noncallers. Second, the practice is easy to abuse. For instance, special interests can organize a response, and the same individual can "vote" many times. *Washington Post*, 9 February 1992, p. A15.

27. Stephen Barr, "Americans Gain a Small Measure of Confidence in Government," *Washington Post*, 24 March 1997, p. A17.
28. Floris W. Wood, ed., *An American Profile—Opinions and Behavior, 1972–1989* (Detroit: Gale Research Inc., 1990).
29. Both of these volumes are published in Boston: Opinion Research Service, Inc., 1990.
30. Elizabeth Hann Hastings and Philip K. Hastings, eds. *Index to International Public Opinion, 1994–1995* (Westport, Conn.: Greenwood Press, 1996).

EXERCISES

Exercise 7.1 Interpreting Surveys

Read the following information collected in a 1995 survey conducted for the Kaiser Family Foundation, Harvard University, and the *Washington Post* by Princeton Survey Research Associates. The survey of 1,514 adults age eighteen or older was conducted from Nov. 28, 1995, to Dec. 4, 1995. Write a paragraph interpreting the results. Give percentage differences where appropriate.

To begin, do you think the nation's economy is getting better, getting worse, or staying about the same?

Better	16%
Worse	39%
Staying about the same	43%

Is your personal financial situation getting better, getting worse, or staying about the same?

Better	21%
Worse	24%
Staying about the same	54%

Has there been any time in the past two years when you were unemployed, but wanted to *work*?

Yes	15%
No	51%
Not currently working	34%

Do you feel very confident, only fairly confident, or not at all confident that life for our children will be better than it has been for us?

Very confident	10%
Fairly confident	34%
Not at all confident	54%

Source: *Why Don't Americans Trust the Government?* 1995–1996 (Menlo Park, CA: Kaiser Family Foundation, 1996), pp. 1, 22.

Exercise 7.2 Exploring Correlations through Surveys

The following information from a Gallup public opinion poll reports confidence in several institutions. It also reports variation in confidence by gender, age, and political affiliation.

> Question: I am going to read you a list of institutions in American society. Would you please tell me how much confidence you, yourself, have in each one—a great deal, quite a lot, some, or very little?

TABLE 7.8
Confidence in Institutions by Gender, Age, and Party

Great Deal or Quite a Lot of Confidence in Institutions	Military (%)	U.S. Supreme Court (%)	Banks (%)	Public Schools (%)	Television (%)
All respondents	61	52	51	50	28
Male	62	53	49	50	28
Female	59	50	52	50	27
18-29 Years	57	57	46	49	33
30-49 Years	59	51	49	48	23
50 years or older	65	49	58	54	29
Republicans	70	57	56	50	25
Democrats	58	49	40	50	31
Independents	55	52	47	52	25

Develop two hypotheses that you can test using the information in the table. Develop a table to examine each hypothesis and analyze your findings. Use percentage differences, and indicate whether the results support your hypotheses. Report the most general findings first. Which of these demographic variables seems to have the greatest influence? Remember that it is just as useful to find that the null hypothesis is correct (that a variable does not make a difference) as to find that the null hypothesis is incorrect (that a variable does make a difference).

Exercise 7.3 Comparing Data from Surveys and Election Returns

Table 7.2 compared the results of a Gallup survey with the actual results in presidential elections from 1968 through 1996. Ascertain from the *Gallup Poll* for 1996 the percentage the Gallup organization predicted would vote for each of the candidates just prior to the 1996 election. How does the prediction compare with the actual results? You can find these in a number of sources, including the *World Almanac and Book of Facts 1998*.

Exercise 7.4 Analyzing Trends in Public Opinion

Every year the Gallup poll asks respondents, "In general, are you satisfied or dissatisfied with the way things are going in the United States at this time?" The results since 1988:

Satisfaction with "the way things are going," by year:

1988 (September)	56%	1992 (February)	21%
1989	N/A	1993 (December)	34%
1990 (February)	55%	1994 (November)	30%
1991 (June)	49%	1995 (July)	32%

Investigate the same question in a recent *Gallup Poll*. Look in the index under "satisfaction." The satisfaction index is probably reported several times. Be sure to refer to the question about people's satisfaction with the United States and not with their personal lives. Also select a month when the survey reports the satisfaction of different groups.

Answer the following: 1. Has the percentage who are satisfied continued to rise or decline? 2. Which groups in the society have the greatest degree of satisfaction? 3. Offer a brief analysis using percentage differences.

Exercise 7.5 Designing Questionnaires

You want to know students' views on international issues, particularly on the role of the United States in the international arena. Review the guidelines on asking questions and develop at least six questions that you could ask which would give you insight into this issue. Review the comparison of questions designed to learn about attitudes, behavior, knowledge, and opinions and include at least two of these types in your list of questions. Try out your list of questions on at least two people.

CHAPTER EIGHT

Collecting Data: Qualitative Data and Field Research

In our field (organization theory) we have always found that simpler, more direct methodologies have yielded more useful results. Like sitting down in a manager's office and watching what he does. Or tracing the flow of decisions in an organization. . . . Peripheral visits, poking around in relevant places, a good dose of creativity—that is what makes good research, and always has, in all fields.

—Henry Mintzberg, *Qualitative Methodology*

Qualitative Researcher:
"Many people these days are bored with their work and are . . ."

Quantitative Researcher (interrupting):
"What people, how many, when do they feel this way, where do they work, what do they do, why are they bored, how long have they felt this way, what are their needs, when do they feel excited, where did they come from, what parts of their work bother them most, which . . ."

Qualitative Researcher:
"Never mind."

—John Van Maanen, ed., *Qualitative Methodology*

Disorder is simply the order we are not looking for.

—Henri Bergson, quoted in David Schuman,
Policy Analysis, Education, and Everyday Life

Qualitative and Quantitative Research

Assume you are interested in recent policy debates about higher education and you have a hunch that courses and subjects that were most stimulating and valuable to people over time were not necessarily the courses that focused on career preparation. You decide to explore whether people feel that education influenced their lives and which experiences were most useful to them later. You decide the best way to determine this is to ask some recent graduates. One possible strategy is to design a survey that would be administered to a sample of college graduates. It could include such questions and possible responses as the following:

1. Do you believe that your college education has prepared you for a career (very much, somewhat, very little, not much)?
2. Of courses outside your major, which of the following fields has been most effective in stimulating you to consider new ideas (natural sciences, history, philosophy, arts, economics, social sciences)?

You might learn that 60 percent of the graduates believed their education had prepared them only "somewhat" for a career and that 40 percent believed that history courses were particularly stimulating in introducing new ideas. You might proceed to do an analysis based on your survey, in which you show that a majority of college graduates recalled that the most memorable courses with the most long-lasting effects were not the ones that specifically prepared them for a career.

Consider an alternative approach. David Schuman and Kenneth Dolbeare decided that to really understand the impact of education, they had to begin with the actual experiences of individuals. To tap this experience, they believed, they needed to engage a number of students in lengthy, open-ended conversation. Instead of asking specific questions, they encouraged students to say which issues they deemed the most important.[1] Their approach generated comments such as: "You go to college and all of a sudden you find out there aren't answers to things and you have to live the rest of your life without any answers."[2] The comment tells us a great deal about the way in which this student experienced her education and that she had to learn to deal with a loss of certainty about many aspects of her life. By documenting actual experiences, interviews can provide special insight into attitudes and behavior that cannot be gained from a survey. If you had followed this research strategy, you might write an essay on whether and how universities help students deal with uncertainty in their lives. You would not have any quantitative information about the percentage of students who experienced such uncertainty, but you would be able to report some qualitative understanding of student experiences.

structured data gathering
When data are collected according to specified categories or criteria.

unstructured data gathering
Data collected with no set criteria in mind; open-ended data collection.

Recall that chapter 6 referred briefly to debates within the social sciences about the most important questions for social science to emphasize. The survey questions discussed in chapter 7 and this study of students' educational experiences illustrate two approaches to studying social and political events. Although both collect information directly from people rather than indirectly through intermediaries, they obtain different kinds of information. The first approach, based on surveys, is called **structured data gathering;** the other, based on interviews, is an example of **unstructured data gathering.** Actually it can be misleading to think of these two approaches simply as two alternatives, because there can be varied degrees of structure, as suggested by table 8.1.

TABLE 8.1
Strategies for Direct Data Gathering

Structured			Open-ended
1	2	3	4
Survey research, questionnaires	Surveys, questionnaires with some open-ended questions	Partially structured interviews and observations	Open-ended conversational interviews and observations

open-ended question
A question that allows respondents to formulate their own answers.

field research
When researchers talk to people within their own setting; takes the context of action into account.

quantitative research
Data gathered in a form that allows the researcher to assign numbers to them.

qualitative research
Data that reflect the content and meaning of an event or the perspective of an individual; often deals with subtleties and with evidence that cannot be handled quantitatively.

Survey questions and questionnaires, described in chapter 7, provide structured data because they ask for responses that can be fitted into categories established prior to the research. Some surveys and questionnaires include only structured questions and ask for a limited number of responses; these are coded as 1 in table 8.1. When these do ask **open-ended questions,** the responses are converted into categories (supportive, neutral, nonsupportive, for example.) Some surveys include a few open-ended and less structured questions; these are coded as 2 in table 8.1. Analyses of these report the quantitative results and then add some further comments based on responses to the open-ended questions.

Interviews and observations, coded 3 or 4 in table 8.1, are commonly referred to as **field research,** because they require researchers to observe and talk with people within their own settings, to go out "into the field" so to speak, and examine what is going on there. Sometimes the researcher begins with a framework that lays out the kinds of information he or she is looking for; this kind of study is coded 3 in table 8.1 and is described as partially structured. Others, coded 4, intentionally do not decide ahead what questions will be raised and try to be completely open-ended. Proponents of this approach believe that because the questions and variables are not established prior to research, the answers are more apt to reflect the emphases and experiences of those being studied. The emphasis in this chapter is primarily on studies coded as 3 in table 8.1; these are becoming increasingly important in the literature, and they are particularly appropriate for those learning to do research.

Surveys and field research are often described, respectively, as **quantitative research** and **qualitative research.** Survey questions usually ask for a limited number of responses; the answers are assigned numbers and can be handled arithmetically, and thus they are considered to be quantitative in nature. This kind of information is useful for establishing regularities or trends in a population, for comparing the behavior and opinions of different groups, and for examining characteristics of individuals that are associated with or cause specific attitudes or behavior. Often, however, the questions we are interested in do not ask for quantitative information; rather, they ask about the meaning of different activities. Then qualitative data gained through field research are more appropriate.

Uses of Qualitative Research in Political Analysis

Meaning and Context

Qualitative research asks not only what people do but what their actions *mean* to them. There is a difference between "knowing" something directly and merely "knowing about" it. Surveys tell us something *about* a person; field research tries to get closer to the subject, to *know* an individual or group or situation more directly and fully, and to understand how that person perceives or understands the world. Qualitative research requires gathering detailed information, impressions, and feelings from the subject. Because this kind of information is often subtle in nature, and because it usually involves a small number of people, the data do not lend themselves to quantification and are described as qualitative in nature. One indication of the difference between the two types of research is that surveys refer to the people being interviewed as *respondents*, and field research refers to *subjects*. The former studies pose a fixed set of questions to which people respond; the latter emphasize more subjective types of data and attempt to interpret what these data mean to the subjects.

In addition to emphasizing the *meaning* of behavior, qualitative research often is carried out in the setting where the people are doing whatever is being studied. It is conducted "in the field." It emphasizes the *context* of behavior and links individual behavior to a situation. Field researchers usually are less interested in generalizing about the incidence of an activity or event and more interested in understanding the situation within which it occurred. It is no coincidence that anthropologists have pioneered field studies. They study the actions and attitudes of people in different societies and argue that context or culture is an important variable in understanding behavior. Many sociologists examining subcultures in a society make the same point. Their studies of gang members, of patients in mental institutions, of alcoholics, or of minorities commonly try to gain insight into the culture and norms and values in these groups as an important element in understanding their behavior. Political analysts increasingly are borrowing strategies from anthropology and sociology in order to understand the culture and norms within organizations and subgroups in the population to understand their political behavior better.

Assume that you want to understand why some people develop and retain prejudiced attitudes toward other groups. Field researchers tell us that the only way to understand prejudice is to appreciate how it develops in a certain situation or context, and the only way to learn this is through in-depth interviews. Excerpts from a series of interviews with a staunch segregationist suggest the kinds of data such interviews can produce:

> Once John and I had talked long and hard, it seemed like a whole day, and I noticed it was nearly three hours, and the length of time measured a certain trust, a certain understanding which was developing between us. I found myself knowing him, recognizing some of the hardships he had endured, not just

psychological ones, but the hunger and jobless panic which must have entered so many homes in a decade when I was scarcely born, and he yet a child.[3]

These conversations, reported by Robert Coles, produced a portrait of people with few options in their lives, with pressing responsibilities, and with little hope for the future. The study perceptively linked individual behavior with the contextual and historical events of the time, greatly enriching our understanding of such attitudes and responses. It helps political analysts appreciate how public policies are perceived by people, and in this case to understand better the effects of economic insecurity. Schuman and Dolbeare, whose research on higher education was described earlier in the chapter, also stress the link between individual behavior and its context:

> Trying to understand who we are and what we do in this way makes it impossible to concentrate wholly on either the individual or the society when we do empirical work. The two are tied in an absolute way. It is foolish to try imagining ways to do a study of individuals without paying careful attention to their history, culture, friends, work, and the like.[4]

Emphasizing the meaning and context of behavior is an important corrective to those who begin with rather simplistic theories of behavior and look for evidence to confirm their theories. Barbara Bergman, an economist, complains that economists often fall into the latter error. She offers the example of research on unemployment. An important theory in economics assumes that someone who becomes unemployed could have found a lower paying job but chooses not to take it, and thus has chosen leisure over work. Bergmann argues that we need to go out and talk to the unemployed and gain some "real-world knowledge." "What are the options that laid-off people think they face? What are their attitudes and behaviors when faced with such options?" She contends that a researcher who was truly interested in these questions "might try to interview a few dozen or a few hundred laid-off workers. The workers could be asked about how they explore their options, what they think their options are, and what their attitudes toward those options are."[5]

Process of Relationships

The discussion of relationships in chapter 6 noted that sometimes it is important to go beyond simple correlations among several variables and try to determine the *process* that links them. Qualitative approaches can be useful in this regard. Consider the example of research on the causes of poverty in ghettos. Chapter 6 described how some studies explain poverty by focusing on the poor as individuals while others focus on the conditions those individuals face. Applied to poverty, the first group tends to blame poverty on the lack of initiative among the poor, while the second group is more apt to focus on the context, particularly on the number of jobs available to the poor. William J. Wilson agrees that attitudes are important, but on the basis of extensive interviewing within poor urban areas, he concluded that the underlying cause of these attitudes is a lack of jobs. Because his interviews gave him a rich sense of the ways in which these people thought, he was able to show the *process* linking these variables (poverty, joblessness, and attitudes); namely that the disappearance of jobs has led to a lack of initiative.

> Work is not simply a way to make a living and support one's family. It also constitutes a framework for daily behavior because it imposes discipline. Regular employment determines where you are going to be and when you are going to be there. In the absense of regular employment, life, including family life, becomes less coherent.[6]

It would not have been possible to gain this broad understanding if Wilson had simply surveyed the poor with structured questions.

Understanding Political Processes

Attention to meaning and context are also useful in studying *political processes*. Compare two strategies for studying the process of developing public policy to deal with homelessness. A study of policy options would probably rely on quantitative analysis of the numbers of homeless, the costs of alternatives, and so forth. A process study, by contrast, would look at the steps in designing and enacting legislation. How did the issue get onto the public agenda? What options were considered? Which groups were active? What role did Congress play? The president? Local interest groups? Field studies of the policy process document how the various players took advantage of opportunities or were confounded by events that overtook them.[7] Typically, researchers talk to all those involved in the process of enacting a policy and reconstruct the process as it occurred. They are especially interested in understanding this process from the perspective of the players and in documenting the players' experiences.[8]

Evaluating Public Policies

Field research is also used to evaluate public policy. A traditional quantitative evaluation would begin with the goals of a policy and ask to what extent the goals were accomplished. Field research is more concerned with the problems encountered in implementing a policy. For example, quantitative approaches to evaluating a Head Start program would ask whether the program raised the performance scores of participants. A field researcher would ask what problems the teachers faced, how adequate their resources were, whether it was helpful to involve families in the program, and so forth.[9]

Recall the discussion of case studies in chapter 4 and the example of an evaluation of a program to benefit minority youth. The researchers began by doing a traditional quantitative study, spending some months collecting data on the results of the program and on the success of the program in changing the attitudes of youth. They were increasingly frustrated, however. For one thing the program had been changed drastically as it was implemented. They were reluctant, however, to call it a failure. Although it had not accomplished its original goals, it had other effects that were equally or even more significant. In the meantime the administrators were suspicious of the evaluators and were reluctant to give them the information they needed, for fear they would turn in a negative report. The evaluators argued that instead of doing a quantitative analysis of program results, they needed to do a field study in which they could describe the way the program was carried out, the shifts and changes that had occurred, the political context, and the views of the various participants. Such a field study, they believed, would offer a far more valuable insight into the worth of the program and more useful guidance to others working in the area.[10]

Organizational Studies

Field research is also used in studies of organizations, as Mintzberg comments at the beginning of this chapter. Because of its emphasis on meaning and context, field research looks at the culture and norms of an organization, at the attitudes and perceptions of those within the organization. It asks about the organization's structure and values and how these shape what people think and do. Whereas the typical quantitative study looks at organizations "from the outside," field studies look at them "from the inside," examining the organizational setting, the situation, and the demands and expectations on the individuals.[11]

For example, Meltsner designed a study of the work of policy analysts, individuals who help policy makers formulate public policies. He could have designed a structured questionnaire to measure the attitudes of policy analysts in a particular organization and to learn about the distribution of those attitudes and the behavior of individuals. Instead, he decided to ask more open-ended questions to find out how analysts view their role in the organization. He wanted to study the settings in which they worked and the demands that policy makers were placing on them. A questionnaire and quantitative analysis of the answers would not tell him about the actual experiences of individuals and their ways of coping in their immediate situations.[12]

Choices in Designing Field Research

Validity and Reliability

Field research, with its emphasis on in-depth knowledge of subjects and contexts, usually has to make trade-offs in finding measures that are both valid and reliable. Because field research can do justice to all aspects of a situation, it can provide fairly valid indicators—ones that tell us something important and relevant about the issues we are researching. At the same time such research raises serious reliability problems because different researchers might easily collect different data and thus reach different conclusions. We described Cole's qualitative study of segregationists earlier and its stress on the vulnerability of certain groups to economic problems. Another study of segregationists might not pay the same attention to the economic anxieties of people and might put more emphasis on the values that people developed in their childhood.

The methods described in this chapter tend to rate very high on validity. Researchers are able to get "close to" their subjects, and they can focus on the meaning of a concept and do not have to settle for indicators that are once removed. For example, a quantitative study of organizational effectiveness might rely on answers to questionnaires from top executives about budgets, attendance at meetings, and so forth. Compare those data with the information you would collect by directly observing a meeting of those same executives. You would probably gain some insight into the norms of the organization, the style of decision making, and the ways in which the officers used information. These observations would give you a different slant on effectiveness than you would gain through questionnaires.

Even though field research can produce valid measures and conclusions, most people would agree that unstructured strategies such as interviews and observations produce less reliable measures than do structured studies. Recall that reliability means that an indicator is coded the same no matter who does the measuring or observing and no matter what the situation is. If you ask two people to attend a meeting to analyze how effective the participants are in coming to a decision, it is easy to see that they might well come up with different judgments. One person might say that too much time was spent discussing alternatives; the other might say that the same time was well spent.

Field research is less reliable because it is easily affected by the researcher's initial biases and filters. It is all too easy to observe what you want to find and to filter out or explain away findings that do not fit your working hypotheses. We can illustrate the problem with a field study done of police. The researcher found that he was actually collecting three kinds of information:

1. What actually happened.
2. What the respondent says happened.
3. What the interviewer heard the respondent say about what happened.

He asked individual police officers to describe and explain their records in making arrests, the first kind of information. Each police officer described her or his activities in a favorable light, however, and the researcher realized he was actually getting the second kind of information: what the respondent said about the arrest record. In addition, the researcher found he was inevitably letting his own research interests affect how he interpreted what each police officer said. In other words, he was really collecting the third kind of information.[13]

It is easy to imagine that by interviewing people firsthand, by getting "into the field," we have gotten information on item 1—what actually happened. In fact, all we know is item 3, and perhaps something about item 2. Thus, field research is particularly vulnerable to the conceit that we think we have more understanding of an event than we actually do. In this sense the data we collect in field studies not only have reliability problems but may not be as high on validity as is sometimes thought.

Deciding How Much to Structure the Research

One way to increase the reliability of measures is to provide some structure, to decide ahead of time what to look for. You should be able to appreciate that if you begin with a precise list of variables to be examined and clear indicators of these variables, you will have more reliable information than if you begin with general, unspecified areas of interest. The trade-off is that the more precise your list of items, the less apt you are to uncover characteristics of the organization you did not anticipate. Many practitioners of field research are reluctant to decide ahead what is important to look for or to lay out a framework or theory and, as noted in table 8.1, studies vary on this dimension. Some begin with a very loose framework; others let the issues and questions emerge from the research study itself. Some would approach a study of the political process with a list of questions to be asked and variables to be examined. Others would do very little planning and let the conversations with policy makers define the research.

The former—the effort to provide some structure—is often referred to as the "formalization of qualitative research." Two practitioners of this approach list five characteristics of this more structured approach.[14] (1) It emphasizes *explanation* instead of description. (2) It is often carried out by *several people*, and perhaps at *several locations*; under such circumstances some structure ensures that everyone is pursuing a similar approach. (3) It begins with a *framework*, with specific questions that can be adapted, in contrast to exploratory studies in which questions emerge from the research. (4) It lays out *semistructured questions and lists of items* to observe. (5) It tries to present the *results visually* in categories, diagrams, and tables rather than simply in a narrative form. The remaining five sections of the chapter look at each of these characteristics in more detail.

Seeking Explanations

Some scholars maintain that field research is useful for describing events but not for explaining them. John Lofland, a practiced field researcher, is one who cautions against using field studies to explain events or to propose causes.[15] Causal explanations, he argues, require that the dependent variable take on several values if we are going to explain an event. For example, if we want to explain crime, we cannot get very far by studying one or two cities with the same incidence of crime. We need to compare the characteristics of cities with low and with high crime rates. Since field research often involves a single situation, researchers cannot compare it with other cases where the dependent variable differs.

Others say that field research can be designed to suggest an explanation or causal factor even if it cannot be used to prove what the cause is. And it is more apt to accomplish this if the researcher is interested in finding an explanation and not just in describing an event or trend. For example, assume you want to study the role of citizens who serve on advisory boards in local governments. We know from surveys and from media accounts that both citizens and officials usually are dissatisfied with what the citizens contribute. Another survey to describe how many people are dissatisfied would probably not add to our understanding of this problem. It would be more useful to design a study that tried to find an explanation for citizen dissatisfaction, that asks how the participating citizens feel about the experience, why they feel this way, and what they think can be done to solve those problems. Such an in-depth analysis of the problem would go a long way to explain why there is so much conflict between citizens and officials.

Comparing Multiple Sites

Increasingly field research is being conducted at several intentionally selected sites, or is done by a team of researchers, or both. In such cases some structure is important to ensure that comparable research is done at all sites and by all the researchers. If we select two or three cases that provide different values of the major variables the research will more likely be able to explain as well as to describe what takes place. (Compare the earlier discussion of case studies in chapter 4.)

comparison of cases
Selection of cases by criteria that will enable us to test a theory.

Once we decide to make a **comparison of cases,** we have to decide how to select them. Several options are possible. We could select a few sites or programs that differ in one significant respect. For example, we could look at different programs in a single community. We could also look at similar programs in different kinds of communities in order to isolate the factors that seemed most relevant to their success. Was one program run better than another? Were different kinds of people served by the programs? If we are interested in rehabilitation of criminal offenders, we could do field research on three versions of our independent variable, the treatment designed to rehabilitate them—a halfway house, a work-release program in a jail, and a job training program for offenders. Or we could look at three differing cases of the dependent variable, the degree of rehabilitation—a program known to be successful, a less successful program, and a failed program. Instead of immersing ourselves in the subtle dimensions of one program, we would be looking for contrasts and comparisons among the three programs, with an eye to what could be learned by comparing them. Until a broad range of cases is examined, the explanations will remain tentative. Nonetheless, they can offer valuable insights that other designs cannot.

Using a Framework to Provide Structure

framework
A set of categories in which to place observations.

A **framework** is a list of variables or categories to examine. It can be thought of as a set of boxes in which to place observations. Meltsner's study of policy analysts, described earlier, provides a good illustration of a study that began with a framework or set of categories within which to place information. Meltsner interviewed 116 policy analysts to learn more about their experiences. Before doing that, however, he reviewed other studies of analysts and organizations and posited that there would be three kinds of analysts: technicians, who stress the technical part of analysis; politicians, who try to respond to the demands their bosses are making on them; and entrepreneurs, who try to create a demand for their work. As he interviewed them, he placed each analyst in one of the categories and used his research to describe the common experiences of those who fell into each type.[16] In this way Meltsner brought some minimal structure to his research. It would have been far more difficult to carry out the 116 interviews and then sit down and try to make some sense out of them.

Whereas anthropologists and psychologists may decide not to use frameworks or checklists to guide their research, most of those who carry out field research in political analysis have found frameworks to be valuable. Notice the frameworks in the books and articles you read in your studies. Some are more explicit than others, but authors usually have some framework or set of categories or labels in mind when they carry out their research and present their results. Matthew Miles and A. Michael Huberman make a good case for the value of some structure in research. They ask,

> How prestructured should a qualitative research design be? Enough to reach the ground, as Lincoln said when asked about the proper length of a man's legs. It depends on the time available, how much is already known about the phenomenon under study, the instruments already available, and the analysis that will be made. Our stance lies off center, toward the structured end.[17]

Semistructured Interviews and Observations

Intensive Interviewing

There are two broad strategies for collecting information for field research. One uses intensive interviewing and is described in this section; the second uses observations and is described in the next section. Interviewing varies according to how much structure the researcher provides. Some analysts maintain we should let the subjects reveal what is important about any experience, and that researchers should avoid imposing their own expectations and ideas on the research. This approach is consistent with the comment of Henri Bergson at the head of this chapter. Bergson was suggesting that what appears to be disorderly may reflect the researcher's questions. From the subject's perspective, reality may be orderly and meaningful. Other researchers who rely on interviews find it helpful to have some ideas and questions already defined. These can provide a framework for the interviews and essentially serve as indicators linking the research questions and the actual interview data.

Planning the interview. Most people, thinking that interviewing is an extension of ordinary conversation, assume they can do it effectively with little planning. This stance seldom works, however, and almost never allows interviewers to learn all they can. Students, in particular, should begin with some structure. There are two rules of thumb in planning an interview. The first is to prepare questions ahead of time but to remain open to new ideas as the interview proceeds. The second is to structure the questions and the interviewing style to reduce the so-called social distance between the interviewer and the subject. The subject needs to feel comfortable and to trust the interviewer and not feel threatened.[18] The confrontational style epitomized by the CBS television program *60 Minutes* may work for investigative journalists but is seldom productive for social science researchers. The following list can serve as an **interview schedule** of topics, or guide, as you plan your interview.[19]

interview schedule
A list of topics to be covered in an interview.

1. *Defining the general questions and framework.* What is it that you want to know, and what are the problems to be clarified? For example, if you were doing research on the impact of budget cuts on social services, you could begin with the following points from a journalist's report:

   > Ginny Miller is a social worker whose days are filled with the dramas of the aging, the disabled, the blind, the elderly, the poor, the mentally retarded, the emotionally disturbed and, always the lonely. Miller, like all of her colleagues, has too many clients and not enough time or, increasingly, resources. But she is a good social worker and sometimes she accomplishes great things.[20]

   Based on this description, you could develop the following list of topics to cover in your interview:

   Effects:

   What kinds of effects have cutbacks had?

   Role of social workers:

   How much discretion do social workers have?

   How are decisions about cutbacks made, and specifically, do social workers have any say?

   How are social workers supervised?

   Do social workers feel they have the resources and supports they need to do a creditable job? What else do they need?

   Relations with clients

   What kinds of pressures do clients place on them?

2. *Selecting cases.* First, be clear why you choose some cases rather than others. If possible, select cases to show a range of experiences. Interview workers in two communities, one very poor and the other less so. Interview one social worker who has been in the agency at least ten years and another who has joined recently. Second, look for several ways to gain access to individuals. It is worth noting that if a manager gives you permission to interview people in the office, you will probably be perceived as acting on behalf of the administration, and you may find subjects less than candid. Yet such a step may be the only way to gain access.

3. *Making appointments.* Call ahead, introducing yourself and your purpose briefly. Practice this introduction ahead of time, because first impressions can be important. You might also write ahead, stating your purpose and indicating that you will call to set up an interview. Remember, the people you want to see are probably very busy. Often you may get no further than a secretary; if this happens, identify your purpose and ask when to call back.

4. *Preparing for the interview.* Review your planned outline of questions. Practice your introductory explanation—do not rely on the subject to remember your original phone call. Indicate how you will use the information and whether the subject will be anonymous in your report. Unless there is a particular reason to quote by name, anonymity is desirable. Plan how you will record what is said; taking notes is the most obvious method, but many interviewers believe that note taking is distracting. The alternatives are tape recorders and relying on your memory. If you are taking notes or using a tape recorder, ask the subject for his or her permission.

5. *Developing a sensitivity to the person you will be interviewing.* Plan time to collect your thoughts before the interview. Spend a few minutes anticipating how your subjects will react to you and how likely they are to feel threatened by an interview. Are they in a sensitive political position, so that they will be wary of your questions? Are they under great pressure, so that they may be reluctant to give you much time? Might they be worried that their comments will be repeated to others? Are they suspicious of people from the university or people doing research? If approached in the right manner, they may welcome a chance to describe their work. In any event, a sensitivity to the subject's perspective is a vital step in your preparation.

6. *Formulating opening questions.* The safest way to begin is to ask for background information. You might ask a civil servant, "What is the exact nature of your job?" or "What is the most time-consuming part of your job?" or "How have recent budget cuts affected this community?" Your first questions should not be threatening but should establish you as an open-minded person who is trying to get some information and is interested in the other person's point of view.

7. *Developing flexibility and probing.* You are there to ask questions and to listen. An answer may surprise you, and you may want to pursue it further. You may sense that the subject is antagonized by a given line of questioning. Be alert to ways to rephrase such questions. Respond to remarks a respondent makes, and ask for clarification when necessary. Jerome Murphy suggests four probing strategies: (1) asking for clarification of a point; (2) asking the subject to elaborate on a comment; (3) encouraging the subject to continue; and (4) remaining silent, thereby implicitly encouraging the subject to say more.[21]

8. *Eliciting specific, concrete answers.* Subjects often will answer questions in vague terms. Plan your questions to encourage specificity. If a subject is noncommittal, you might say, "How would you respond if your supervisor came out in favor of . . . ?" or "Some people have pointed out that . . . What would you say to them?" Avoid questions that can be answered with vague

generalities, and select questions that stimulate specific comments and information.

9. *Concluding the interview.* Be sensitive to the passage of time. If you sense the subject is restless, you could say, "I have just three more brief questions." Often it will be appropriate to state, "By way of concluding, can you think of any points that I have left out of our conversation that might be relevant?" or "If I have any questions later, may I call you for a clarification?"

10. *Writing up your notes.* Go over your notes as soon as possible after you leave, adding your own impressions of the interview. You may think you will remember later all that occurred, but you will not.

Asking questions. Good questions have to be thought about ahead of time. Michael Patton documents how often we fail to ask for the information we are really seeking. He describes a conversation between parents and a teenager returning home from a date:

Oh, you're home a bit late?
Yeah.
Did you have a good time?
Yeah.
Did you go to a movie?
Yeah.
Was it a good movie?
Yeah, it was OK.
I've heard a lot about it. Do you think I would like it?
I don't know. Maybe.[22]

The parents obviously had not learned how to ask what they really wanted to know. The same pattern often is repeated in interviews with public officials about programs they are administering. Interviewers often ask questions that people can answer with a simple "yes" or "no," when they really want to know what the official thought about the program. Instead of asking "Are you satisfied with the program?" (which could be answered "yes" or "no"), we probably want to know "What is your opinion of the program?"

In the same vein, our questions often make assumptions that are unwarranted. For example, we might ask an official, "How effective do you think the program is?" This phrasing assumes that the official can make such a judgment. But maybe he or she cannot. A better question would be: "Do you feel you know enough about the program to assess its effectiveness?"

Patton continues with some rules of thumb for asking good questions:[23]

1. *Make sure you ask what you want to know.* Try to avoid questions that people can simply answer with "yes" or "no." That probably is not what you want to

know, and it can make people feel like you are quizzing them. For example, instead of asking "Did you direct the program?" you probably want to know "What was your role in the program?"

2. *Ask only one question at a time.* The following question only generates confusion: "In order to help the staff improve the program we'd like to ask you to talk about the program. What are its strengths and weaknesses? What did you like and not like? What should be improved?"

3. *Avoid asking why.* That assumes there are reasons, and you may not get the kind of reason you are interested in. For example, if you ask someone who is working on a health program, "Why did you join this program?" the answer may be that he or she was between jobs or needed more money. You are probably not interested in personal reasons. A better question would be: "What is it about this program that attracted you?"

4. *Role-playing questions can be very useful.* For example you could say, "Suppose I just entered the program, and I asked you what I should do to succeed. What would you tell me?"

5. *It can be helpful to introduce questions and make them less threatening.* Instead of asking "How do you feel about the recent budget cut?" say, "Now I am going to ask you several questions about your feelings about the recent budget cuts."

Observations

A second technique for carrying out field research is to make firsthand observations of some activity or event. As with interviewing you can bring some structure to your research by specifying what you will look for ahead of time. Observing may be a one-time experience or a longer involvement in the life of a group or an organization. Observations vary not only in respect to length but also in respect to the role the observer plays: you may actually participate in the activity; you may openly observe what others are doing; or you may try to keep your role secret.

Like interviews, observations vary according to how structured they are.[24] On the one hand, it is possible to immerse yourself in a situation and let the events themselves dictate what you will look for. Or you can do some planning and listing of major questions and events ahead of time. For example, table 8.2 lists a series of items that were drawn up prior to observing a neighborhood advisory group. The purpose was to find out both how well organized the group was and how it fit into the political process in the community.

The issues listed in table 8.2, as well as those in the interview schedule, can be thought of as tentative indicators of concepts. The purpose of the interviews and observations is to refine these indicators. For example, in this study the dependent variable is *organizational effectiveness*, and the researcher needs questions that serve as indicators of effectiveness. Indicators of organizational effectiveness in table 8.2 include whether people are satisfied that something was accomplished and the extent to which issues were resolved.

Research on effective organizations can be used both to identify an effective organization and to propose possible explanations of effectiveness. Using

TABLE 8.2
Checklist of Points to Observe at Neighborhood
Commission Meeting

Facts about the Meeting
Date
Location
Purpose
Number attending

Conduct of the Meeting
Was there an agenda? Was it presented to group for approval?
Role of elected leadership and of staff

Characteristics of Those Attending
Do they represent groups in the community?
Are they there as individuals to present complaints?
Do they appear to be political activists?
Do they hold leadership positions in the community?

Substance of Meeting
What kinds of issues were dealt with?
Were any resolved?

Style of the Meeting
Would you describe the meeting as high in conflict?
Was it very orderly?
Do you think people believed that something was accomplished?

the indicators in table 8.2, one could hypothesize that organizations with links to other groups in the community are more effective than those without such links. The researcher could explore the hypothesis by conducting follow-up interviews with other community leaders and by studying additional organizations.

Analyzing and Presenting Qualitative Data

This chapter has argued that it is almost always important to do some planning of the interviews and observations. It concludes by stressing that you also need to bring some conceptual clarification and structure to your analysis of the data. It is not enough to "just go and talk to people" and "write down what you hear or observe." Even if we do not attach numbers and statistics to what we learn, we can still analyze the findings systematically, use them to supplement more quantitative studies, and suggest hypotheses for further study. Thus while field research usually is presented in narrative form, you should supplement the narrative with a more structured presentation. "The risk is *not* that of 'imposing' a self-blinding framework, but that an incoherent, bulky, irrelevant, meaningless set of observations may be produced, which no one can (or even wants to) make sense of."[25] Miles and Huberman make a persuasive case for displaying your findings visually. "Our experience tells us that narrative text alone is an extremely weak and cumbersome form of display. It is hard on analysts, because it is *dispersed*, spread out over many pages and is hard to look at; it is *sequential* rather than simultaneous, making it difficult to look at two or three variables at once; it is usually only *vaguely ordered*; and it can get monotonous and overloading."[26] Three examples of simple structures you can use to present your findings follow: a **matrix**, a **checklist**, and a **flowchart**.

matrix
Two-dimensional table that describes the interaction between two sets of variables.

checklist
List of items relevant to a research question, used to guide and report findings.

flowchart
Visual display of events or activities over time.

Matrix

A matrix is a table with two dimensions, and it can range from fairly simple to more complex. The cells in the table represent the intersection of the two dimensions. Assuming you began the research by laying out a framework, or set of issues you were looking at, you would use these to form the matrix. Assume you want to interview individuals about their reasons for voting or nonvoting. You could use the following framework, which proposes three types of reasons for nonvoting: (1) attitudes toward the political system; (2) knowledge about politics; and (3) convenience factors, such as ease of voting. In addition, it identifies two kinds of nonvoters: people who purposefully do not vote, and people who are apathetic. These distinctions give you the following matrix, which you would use to collect your data and then to present it. If your research was primarily quantitative and involved questionnaires of a number of people, you would probably place the number of those whom you interviewed who fit into each cell. Because you are conducting a qualitative study, you would probably put a few sentences or phrases in each cell that captured the reasons people gave. The "attitudes" of "intentional nonvoters" could include general alienation from politics, dislike of the candidates, anger about a recent event, and so forth.

	Reasons for Nonvoting		
Kinds of Nonvoters	*Attitudes*	*Knowledge*	*Convenience Factors*
Intentional Nonvoter			
Apathetic Nonvoter			

Checklist

An initial framework can also take the form of a checklist of items to look for. Recall that table 8.2 illustrated a checklist of items to look for in observing an advisory neighborhood commission meeting. On attending the meeting you might find that a few of the topics turned out to be irrelevant, while other items you had not anticipated were actually very important. After sorting through your notes you would revise the checklist so that it provided a good vehicle for presenting what you observed.

You could use the information gained through your checklist to develop a matrix. Assume you visited several organizations or that you are working with a team of people, each of whom visited one or two meetings. On reviewing your notes, you might observe that some meetings were attended by individuals who belonged to several other groups and were constantly referring to other activities in the community. Other organizations were more isolated, and the members did not seem to be involved in community activities. You might recall that research shows that associations with links to other groups in the community are usually more effective than associations that have few or no links. You could supplement your checklist with the following matrix.

Effectiveness of Neighborhood Associations by Links with Other Organizations

	Links with Other Community Groups	
	Members Belonged to Other Groups	*Members Belonged Only to This Group*
Issues Dealt with at Meeting		
Accomplishments of Meeting		
Effectiveness of Organization		

The layout of the matrix assumes there will be differences between the activities of two groups of associations, that the information in the cells in the first column will differ from the information in the cells in the second column. It also suggests that links are the independent variable and have an influence on issues, accomplishments, and effectiveness. You could use the matrix to organize your notes and findings. If you found out that links did not make any difference, you could rethink the matrix. The point is to look for opportunities to present your findings in a table or graph in order to highlight your conclusions and supplement your narrative description.

Flowchart

A flowchart is simply a graphic display of events that depicts how one leads to another. Earlier we described Wilson's research into the reasons for poverty and his use of in-depth interviews to talk directly to those living in poorer urban areas. While he presented his conclusions in narrative form, the following flowchart is consistent with his framework and findings. Compare this chart with the earlier paragraph summarizing his findings and consider the strengths and weaknesses of each form of presentation.

Flowchart Showing Relation between Jobs and Poverty

Jobs available	→Discipline and structure in lives of individuals	→People expect to work	→They remain connected to others in the community and to their families	→Community offers support
Disappearance of jobs	→Undermines individual discipline	→Social organizations break down and no longer support individuals	→People lose their connection to economy	→Turn to illegitimate work

Where We Are

This chapter continued the discussion begun in chapter 7 on various strategies for collecting information directly. Chapter 7 emphasized ways to collect data through structured questions; this chapter examined less structured approaches for asking questions. It emphasized in-depth interviews and observations, both of which are well suited for exploratory research and generating qualitative information. They are appropriate when the researcher wants the subjects to identify the most important issues and questions. They allow the subjects to elaborate on reasons and meanings behind their activities and attitudes and to show how the particular situation or context shapes what they do. Depending on your research question, you may decide that direct gathering is the most appropriate approach. Your choice then is to decide whether you want to stress asking a few similar questions to large numbers or whether you want to have a somewhat less structured and open-ended search for qualitative information. Because qualitative interviewing and field research are so similar to our everyday activities, it is tempting to assume we can "just go out and do a field study." One purpose of this chapter has been to make you more conscious of the steps in this method and the importance of thinking through the various steps.

> **multiple strategies**
> Conscious effort to pursue several different approaches to data collection.

Approaches that have different degrees of structure are all appropriate research strategies, depending on your questions. Once again the best course may be to combine qualitative and quantitative strategies, since studies that rely on **multiple strategies** will be even more valid than those that rely on only one approach. Thus field research can supplement other studies rather than serve as an alternative to them. For example, you could use a survey or questionnaire to document the low turnout of voters and to establish a correlation between persons who do not vote and persons who do not trust those with political power. You could then carry out some in-depth interviews with people who did not vote and ask about trust and alienation to gain more insight into the relationship and to develop some hypotheses about nonvoting. Your interviews might suggest that those who decided not to vote were critical of the role of the media. This finding could suggest a new hypothesis that you could explore further by administering a questionnaire to majors in political science. In this way field research—interviews and observations—can be used to look at quantitative research findings in more depth, and to suggest which relationships should be explored further. Political analysts increasingly are taking a more pragmatic approach to political issues and adopting whichever research strategy seems most useful for a particular question. Hence, they learn and use a number of strategies rather than assume that only quantitative or qualitative studies are the most valid way to learn about the political and social arena.

The next chapter opens up a different set of possibilities for finding information and evidence. It directs you to a variety of resources of data that are already compiled by others for other purposes than your research. It both opens up new sources of information and poses new problems. Whereas directly gathered data can be high on validity and weak on reliability, working with secondary sources can have the reverse effect.

NOTES

1. David Schuman and Kenneth Dolbeare, *Policy Analysis, Education, and Everyday Life* (Lexington, Mass.: Heath, 1982), p. 206.
2. Ibid., p. 95.
3. Robert Coles, "Public Evil and Private Problems: Segregation and Psychiatry," *Yale Review* 54, no. 4 (1964–1965): 517–518.
4. Schuman and Dolbeare, *Policy Analysis*, p. 202. The sociologist C. Wright Mills made this same point in his important study *The Sociological Imagination* (New York: Oxford University Press, 1967).
5. Barbara Bergmann, "Why Do Most Economists Know So Little about the Economy?" *Unconventional Wisdom: Essays on Economics in Honor of John Kenneth Galbraith*, eds. Samuel Bowles, Richard Edwards, and William Shepherd. (Boston: Houghton Mifflin Co., 1989), pp. 34–35.
6. William Julius Wilson, "Work," *New York Times Magazine*, 18 August 1996, p. 30.
7. One noteworthy example is Jeffrey Pressman and Aaron Wildavsky, *Implementation: How Great Expectations in Washington are Dashed in Oakland* (Berkeley: University of California Press, 1973).
8. For example, John Kingdon, *Agendas, Alternatives and Public Policies* (Boston: Little, Brown, 1984).
9. Michael Patton, *Qualitative Evaluation Methods* (Newbury Park, Calif.: Sage, 1980); Michael Patton, *Utilization-Focused Evaluation*, 2d ed. (Newbury Park, Calif.: Sage, 1986).
10. Robert S. Weis and Martin Rein, "The Evaluation of Broad-Aim Programs: Experimental Design, Its Difficulties, and an Alternative," *Administrative Science Quarterly* 15 (March 1970): 97–108.
11. R. Evered and M. Louis, "Alternative Perspectives in the Organizational Sciences: 'Inquiry from the Inside' and 'Inquiry from the Outside,'" *Academy of Management Review* 6 (1981): 385–395.
12. Arnold Meltsner, *Policy Analysts in the Bureaucracy*, 2d ed. (Berkeley: University of California Press, 1986).
13. John Van Maanen, "The Fact of Fiction in Organizational Ethnography," in *Qualitative Methodology*, ed. John Van Maanen (Newbury Park, Calif.: Sage, 1983), pp. 37–55.
14. William Firestone and Robert Herriott, "The Formalization of Qualitative Research," *Evaluation Review* 7, no. 4 (August 1983): 437–466.

15. John Lofland, *Analyzing Social Settings: A Guide to Qualitative Observation and Analysis* (Belmont, Calif.: Wadsworth, 1971).

16. Meltsner, *Policy Analysts in the Bureaucracy.*

17. Matthew B. Miles and A. Michael Huberman, *Qualitative Data Analysis* (Newbury Park, Calif.: Sage, 1984), p. 28.

18. The issue of social distance may present problems in the study of people of different backgrounds. Myron Glazer, in a book describing fieldwork in other cultures, stresses the personal and ethical dilemmas that arise, particularly when the subjects are dissident groups: *The Research Adventure: Promise and Problems of Field Work* (New York: Random House, 1972). Michael Brown notes how observers may bias their research by identifying with their subjects; see his essay, "Direct Observation: Research in a Natural Setting," in *Empirical Political Analysis*, ed. Jarol B. Manheim and Richard Rich (Englewood Cliffs, N.J.: Prentice-Hall, 1981), pp. 166–187.

19. Useful resources on the techniques of interviewing are Jerome Murphy, *Getting the Facts: A Fieldwork Guide for Evaluators and Policy Analysts* (Santa Monica, Calif.: Goodyear, 1980); Patton, *Qualitative Evaluation Methods*, pt. 2; John M. Johnson, *Doing Field Research* (New York: Free Press, 1975).

20. Sara Rimer, "Social Workers," *Washington Post*, 6 November 1981, p. A1.

21. Murphy, *Getting the Facts*, pp. 97–98.

22. Patton, *Qualitative Evaluation Methods*, pp. 213–214.

23. The following discussion is based on Patton's treatment of questions in *Qualitative Evaluation Methods*, chapter 7.

24. A very useful discussion of observation techniques is found in Brown, "Direct Observation"; he describes field research within the criminal justice system.

25. Matthew B. Miles, "Qualitative Data as an Attractive Nuisance: The Problem of Analysis," *Qualitative Methodology*, John Van Maanen, ed. (Beverly Hills: Sage, 1979), p. 119.

26. Matthew B. Miles and A. Michael Huberman, *Qualitative Data Analysis.* (Beverly Hills: Sage, 1984), p. 79.

EXERCISES

Exercise 8.1 Designing an Interview

Researchers propose a general alienation from politics, and yet we know that people feel ambivalent—they favor some government activities but also distrust the government. Design an interview through which you could learn more about students' view on the government and the political system. Because this is a very general and vague subject, identify ahead of time the issues that concern and interest you the most. Provide the following information:

1. Identify the concepts and variables you want to learn more about.
2. Make an outline of the topics to be covered in the interview (that is, a framework).
3. Write out an introduction you could use to begin the interview.
4. Write down at least six specific questions you could ask.

Exercise 8.2 Conducting an Interview

The previous exercise asked you to design an interview. Carry out two interviews; making one relatively unstructured and the second more structured. Then answer the following three questions.

1. What did you learn about people's attitudes? Organize your findings into categories instead of describing what you learned in a narrative paragraph.
2. In a paragraph, comment on the relative merits of conducting a structured interview as opposed to an unstructured one. What kinds of information does an unstructured interview give you that a more structured one would not?
3. Finally, what did you learn about the experience of conducting an interview? What would you do differently the next time?

Exercise 8.3 Interviewing

You are asked to do a case study of a college student and his/her attitude toward the media. Develop a list of concerns and questions. Carry out the interview, probing where you would like more information. Then switch the interviewer/interviewee roles. Write up your results, both what you learned about views on the media, and what you learned about interviewing.

Exercise 8.4 Field Observation

Your school has hired you to evaluate how different parts of the campus are used on Wednesday nights by people on campus. Pick one specific part of campus (e.g., library, student union, cafeteria, and so on.) Consider what kinds of questions the school would like to have answered. Make a checklist of the information you want to collect, go to the appropriate part of the campus, and observe. Write up a brief report to the head of your school.

Exercise 8.5 Planning an Observation

Table 8.2 presented a checklist of items to look for in observing a neighborhood political organization. Select some organization that has regular meetings, then attend one of them and make observations. Examples include student government meetings on campus, business meetings of fraternity and sorority groups, meetings of the faculty senate (or a comparable organization at your campus), property owners' associations in the surrounding area, citizen groups, and public hearings.

1. Develop a framework, outline, or checklist for collecting and reporting your observations.

2. How adequate was the framework, outline, or checklist in pointing to relevant observations? How would you revise or expand your framework for a subsequent observation?

Exercise 8.6 Designing Field Research

What follows are four statements about citizen participation in local government activities. After reading them, you will be asked to develop a framework for carrying out interviews or observations on citizen participation.

1. *The value of participation*

   Citizen participation is a nuisance. It is costly, it is time consuming, it is frustrating; but we cannot dispense with it for three fundamental reasons.

   First, participation, in and of itself, constitutes affirmative activity—an exercise of the very initiative, the creativity, the self-reliance, the faith that specific programs such as education, job training, housing and urban renewal, health, consumer education, and others seek to instill. . . .

   Second, citizen participation, properly utilized, is a means of mobilizing the resources and energies of the poor—of converting the poor from passive consumers of the services of others into producers of those services.

   Third, citizen participation constitutes a source of special insight, of information, of knowledge and experience which cannot be ignored by those concerned with whether their efforts are fulfilling their aims. . . . [It] offers the consumer perspective, the perspective of the person who must live day to day with the end results of those efforts. [Edgar S. Cahn and Jean Camper Cahn, "The Values of Citizen Participation," in *Citizen Participation in Urban Development*, ed. Hans C. Spiegel (Washington, D.C.: NTL Institute, 1968), pp. 218–220.]

2. *Comments by an elected local government official*

   Most of us who are now in local government were civic leaders at one time or another, and we all fostered the principle of citizen participation in local government. I guess we promoted the principle too well, because I believe that we have now gone too far in the other direction.

   The public input process has degenerated into confrontation politics, and if the public official doesn't succumb to the pressure, it provides the perfect setting for making allegations that he is in the pay of the developers, he favors the rich and ignores the poor, he has no compassion, exercises no logic, and in general lacks culture, taste and good sense. [John P. Shacochis, "Politics of Confrontation in the Suburbs," *Washington Post*, 5 May 1979, p. B1.]

3. *Co-opting citizens*

   The main purpose of citizen advisory boards is to give an agency the chance to choose who it wants to work with—to "certify" the citizens who they think are smart enough, cooperative enough. Whether it's the Mayor, or a state agency or a federal department which sets up citizen participation activity, they will pick the polite, cooperative citizens who are willing to consider things from the official perspective. They may choose one token dissenter, but they'll leave out the real radicals, the less educated, the truly innovative, the brusque, the insistent citizens. [Duane Dale, *How to Make Citizen Involvement Work* (Amherst: University of Massachusetts Press, 1978), p. 30.]

4. *Advisory boards and citizen representation*

In the health care system the consumer representative often turns out to be not "the people's" representative, but a businessman rather similar to the other board members in background and outlook. In addition, consumers on hospital boards often learn that formal entitlements do not necessarily confer real power just as stockholders long ago discovered in business corporations.

. . .The aura of expertise surrounding doctors and administrators vs. the low social status of the consumer representatives can be expected to contribute to the likelihood that the consumer representatives defer to the hospital officials. [Amitai Etzioni, "Alternative Conceptions of Accountability," *Public Administration Review* 35 (May/June 1975): 282–283.]

Based on these statements do the following: 1) State three specific research questions. 2) What is the major variable you want to know more about? 3) Identify two specific people whom you would like to interview, and design a series of questions appropriate to their role. 4) Identify a relevant activity to observe. Develop a checklist as in table 8.2.

CHAPTER NINE

Collecting Data: Working with Secondary Sources

President Clinton and congressional Republicans remain in a tug of war over how to balance the federal budget. But even as they struggle, estimates of the size of this year's deficit are shrinking.

In January, the Congressional Budget Office estimated that the federal deficit for fiscal 1997, which ends Sept. 30, would be $124 billion. Last month, the Clinton administration pegged it at a nearly identical $126 billion.

But the CBO took another look and two weeks ago said the deficit will more likely total $115 billion, largely because spending on a variety of mandatory programs such as food stamps and student loans is turning out to be less than predicted. . . .

Meanwhile, a number of private analysts are arguing that both the administration and CBO are still underestimating the amount of revenue being generated by the strong U.S. economy. These analysts predict the deficit will be no more than $100 billion—and perhaps less.

—**John M. Berry,** "As Budget Battles Rage, the Deficit is Shrinking Anyway," *Washington Post*, 20 March 1997, p. C1.

The Education Department was required to issue a report on campus crime statistics by 1995. . . . More than 10% of colleges failed to publish crime reports. . . . But critics say the biggest problem with the department's statistics is that they do not paint a true picture of campus crime. That's because the statistics don't include incidents reported to officials other than the police, such as counselors at rape crisis centers and deans, says Security on Campus, Inc., a non-profit watchdog group.

—**"Accuracy of Crime Report Questioned,"** (The Associated Press) *Broadside*, 3 March 1997, p. 6.

Secondary Sources of Information

Chapters 7 and 8 described ways to collect data directly: going to people and asking them questions, and observing behavior and events. When we are first introduced to research, these direct approaches may appear to be the easiest methods of collecting information. In fact, they are often the most time consuming and expensive, and sometimes even impossible.

There are, however, other data available: data that have already been collected. Using such data requires a different set of skills, and these kinds of data raise somewhat different problems of validity and reliability. Once you have learned the techniques, however, you will greatly expand the variety of data available to you, and you will be able to consider research questions that take you far beyond your immediate environment.

But first, some cautions. The excerpts at the top of this chapter lead us to be healthily suspicious of much of the information we find in the media and in government reports. The discussion on the federal budget suggests that officials are not necessarily misleading us—rather the concepts and information are so complex and poorly defined and the numbers so huge that they are easily misreported. And for the layperson terms such as a *million, billion,* and *trillion* can be difficult to translate into meaningful terms. One is grateful for the elementary school teacher who, wanting to make the concept of a "million" more substantial, asked her class to bring in bottle caps until they amassed a pile of 1 million caps. The second excerpt dealing with official reports on campus crime makes a somewhat different point. A watchdog group is arguing that local universities greatly underreport information when it could hurt their reputations. Nevertheless their reports are fed into official publications and are used to interpret trends in crime and to make policy decisions about the value of efforts to control crime.

The next section leads you through the reality of compiling information in order to illustrate the ways in which inaccuracies can wittingly or unwittingly enter the process.

The Flow of Information through Multiple Sources: An Example

Early in the morning of December 20, 1973, a team of young men, members of the Basque insurgent organization Basque Homeland and Freedom (ETA), assassinated the Spanish prime minister, Admiral Luis Carrero Blanco, by detonating a huge explosive charge beneath the street where the admiral's car was passing. The attack continues to be the most dramatic assault launched by the organization against the Spanish government, from which the ETA seeks to win the independence of the Basque region. The event has been featured in many media and from many points of view. For students of political analysis, the event offers an interesting example of how we come to know *about* a historical event (as opposed to know the event directly, something possible only for an extremely small group of observers). It is useful to trace the transmission of information about Carrero Blanco's assassination through four stages: primary observers, secondary interpreters, compilers, and reporters. Figure 9.1 shows in rough form how the information about the assassination passed from one stage to another.

Information about the assassination was gathered directly by only two groups, both very small. Primary observers were limited to those who staged the attack and those who witnessed it. Most of the data gathering was done by the secondary interpreters, those who obtained information from the primary observers and transmitted it to others. The ETA assassination team stated its perspective in a series of interviews with journalists. The first interview took place in southern France several days after the event, and the second one was

FIGURE 9.1

The Flow of Information about an Important Political Event

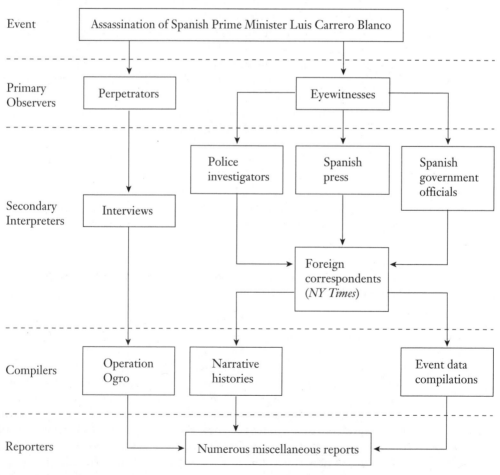

held in an undisclosed location some months later. The second interview was conducted by a Basque journalist named Julen Agirre, who later wrote it up in one of the more important compilations of material about the assassination.

The other flow of news ran through official information sources, including Spanish police investigators, Spanish government officials, and the Spanish government news agency, which released much of the information available to foreign correspondents. Through these secondary interpreters, including the Spanish mass media, foreign correspondents based primarily in Madrid developed information that was soon to produce news stories for the world's principal newspapers. Of these stories, the most significant one for U.S. audiences ran in the *New York Times* and was written by the *Times*'s Madrid correspondent, Henry Giniger. The story appeared the day after the killing, December 21, 1973. Because the *Times* is generally accepted as the newspaper of record in the United States, Giniger's story became the raw material for subsequent data gatherers.

During the next several years, people interested in Spanish politics, political violence, or related topics used these secondary interpretations to produce a third level of information about the assassination, a level that we call *compilations*. These compilations attempt to combine the many secondary reports in order to produce polished versions of the event for audiences that have neither the time nor the background to pore over primary and secondary sources. These compilations usually are considerably far removed—in time, space, and often culture and language—from the event itself. It is thus no surprise that compilations tend to introduce distortions in what is known about the event.[1] The information gathered in these third-level compilations has eventually filtered into many miscellaneous studies, which we call *reports*. And it will continue to be refined through dozens, if not hundreds, of interpretive reports and studies.

The lesson of this illustration is simple: in the case of data gathered indirectly, many layers of revision and condensation lie between the event being studied and the analyst. Between events and observers there stretches a long and often fragile line of information capable of being twisted or even broken at many different points. The wise student of political data and language will keep this fact in mind when working with data gathered indirectly.

Indirect Data-Gathering Techniques

indirect data gathering
Using data collected by others, usually for purposes different from our own.

direct data gathering
Collecting evidence firsthand through questions or observations.

Indirect data-gathering techniques differ from **direct data-gathering techniques** in a number of important respects. Some of the differences are obvious. When we gather data directly, there are no intermediaries. By contrast, indirect data gathering relies on some media intervening between us and the data. As we saw in the previous example, the intervening media may be varied and numerous. Direct techniques place the researcher close to the subject; indirect techniques presume some distance.

Beyond these fairly simple differences, however, are significant differences in the kinds of information gathered by the two techniques, the kinds of concepts that can be explored, and the kinds of questions we can answer. Indirect techniques can be used to examine large groups of individual cases or long sequences of events. Direct observation of single cases rarely can give us the information we need to test propositions about general trends and cause-and-effect relationships. Indirect techniques, just as with survey research, are useful for testing ideas about causation because they can be used to tell us about large numbers of cases. Although single cases can be useful in suggesting insights into relationships, larger samples developed from indirectly gathered data or surveys generally are needed to establish causality.

aggregate data
Empirical data that pertain to, or describe, the behavior of social units (e.g., political parties, cities) or collectivities (e.g., mobs, voters).

Indirectly gathered data often are called **aggregate data,** because they describe clusters or groups or aggregates of individual cases. They allow us to work with concepts that apply to groups or social trends rather than to individuals. For example, urbanization is a very significant phenomenon in the study of political behavior. The concept refers to a broad change in a society as people move from rural to urban areas and experience all the changes that such moves entail. Political studies often ask how urbanization affects individual attitudes or behavior, such as voting patterns. At the same time, when a particular family moves from the countryside to the city we do not say they are "urbanizing." Concepts such as urbanization refer to groups or broad social patterns and usually are only evident over time.[2]

Each kind of data-gathering approach has its utility, its strengths and weaknesses. The sections that follow describe several key issues in the application of indirect data-gathering techniques: how to find and use data gathered by someone else, how to make data, how to fill in the gaps when data are missing, and how to construct indexes.

Sources of Available Data

At the outset of any project to gather data through indirect means, you should first survey existing data sets to see whether the information you need is already available in some form. You may discover that there already is much information on your subject and good reasons for using it. The most obvious reason is cost: you save considerable time, money, and energy if you use available rather than fresh data. A second important reason is that data gathered by someone else for a purpose unknown to you are less likely to be shaped by your own biases. That is, data gathered by professional data collectors are likely to be more objective than data collected by people who intend to use the data to test a hypothesis.

This does not mean that you can use available data uncritically or that there are no costs involved in using information gathered by someone else. Data collected by people with no knowledge of your study probably will not be organized in the way you would prefer and may not address your research questions directly. In addition, although available data may not be biased in terms of your study, they may certainly be biased in other respects. Demographic data gathered in developing countries, for example, frequently are biased to reflect the government's policy objectives, yet we tend to use these figures as though they were objective. Earlier you worked with data on education expenditures in selected countries. As you worked with those figures you probably came to think of them as certain and reliable and forgot that governments probably tend to overstate the money they spend on education and understate the money they spend on the military. You probably also forgot that governments in developing countries often have very limited facilities for collecting and compiling data, and that there are always questions about accuracy.

Public Records

Available data can be found in two places: public records and private records. You should be familiar with the following public records.

Governmental sources of information on U.S. government. The following sources can be considered *primary* compilations, because they report information taken directly from government data-collection efforts. A good place to begin is to look in the following two indexes:

> *Monthly Catalogue of U.S. Government Publications*
> *Congressional Information Service Index*

Also, you may find these helpful:

> *Congressional Quarterly Almanac.* Summarizes the year's legislative activities and provides a subject analysis of important legislation.
>
> *Congressional Record.* Includes remarks made in the House and Senate. A "History of Bills Enacted into Law" section of the Daily Digest provides a brief chronological record of legislation enacted into law.
>
> *Federal Budget.* Reports presidential spending and revenue recommendations as well as information on past spending and revenue.
>
> *Department of State Bulletin.* Comprehensive source on foreign policy.
>
> *U.S. Government Organization Manual.* Describes all U.S. government organizations and lists top personnel.
>
> *Weekly Compilation of Presidential Documents.* Includes text of all statements and remarks released by the White House.

Nongovernmental sources of information on U.S. government

> *Almanac of American Politics.* An annual publication; recognized as one of the most authoritative and valuable single compilations of data on members of Congress.
>
> *CQ Weekly Report.* Published by Congressional Quarterly; an indispensable reference summarizing congressional action and developments (indexed annually). *CQ Almanac* is an annual survey covering the same areas.

National Journal. An invaluable resource on national politics; published biweekly.

Supreme Court Reporter.

Federal Reporter. Similar to above, but reports on U.S. Court of Appeals.

Governmental sources of information on the United States

Catalogue of U.S. Census Publications is a general index to specific subject areas.

Statistical Abstract of the United States. Published annually since 1878 by the U.S. Bureau of the Census.

The Municipal Yearbook. Nongovernmental publication that reports activities and statistics on U.S. cities, including demographic information, political variables such as form of government, and public expenditures.

Book of the States. Annual publication providing comparative data on the states.

County and City Data Book. Provides comparative data on counties and cities.

Current Population Surveys. U.S. Bureau of the Census.

Census of Government. Data from local government units.

Historical Statistics of the United States. Provides information from colonial period to present.

Governmental sources of information, comparing nations. The following are secondary compilations that collect information from governments.

Statistical Yearbook. A U.N. publication; reports demographic, economic, and educational data provided by nations to the United Nations.

Demographic Yearbook. A U.N. publication; contains demographic information on births, deaths, migration, and the like.

International Almanac of Electoral History. Data from twenty-four industrialized countries.

World Handbook of Political and Social Indicators. A Yale University publication; gives information over time on more than seventy-five properties for almost all countries.

World Military and Social Expenditures. Published by World Priorities, Inc.; provides data on such social factors as literacy rates, public expenditures on education, and caloric intake per capita.

World Development Report. An annual publication of the World Bank; provides such economic information as GNP and trends in manufacturing and foreign trade.

Nongovernmental sources of political information, comparing nations

The Statesman's Yearbook. Published in London.

The Political Handbook of the World. Published in the United States. This and the preceding volume contain much valuable information about the world's political systems.

Encyclopedia of the Third World. Published periodically (3 volumes, 1987); provides narrative descriptions and statistics on Third World countries.

A Cross-Polity Survey. Published by MIT Press.

The New Book of World Rankings. Published by Facts on File.

Election statistics and public opinion polls: United States

America Votes: A Handbook of Contemporary American Election Statistics. Published biannually; includes data on national elections since 1952.

American Public Opinion Index.

Gallup Poll: Public Opinion. Published annually.

Guide to U.S. Elections. Published by Congressional Quarterly; provides a complete set of data on presidential, Senate, House, and gubernatorial races since 1824.

Internet

Some of the above resources can be found on the Internet, a vast resource that is constantly expanding and changing. If you have learned how to access information on the Internet this is a resource you should explore. Begin with the following sites; most of them provide additional links to related sites. Once you find a site that is of particular interest, you can create a bookmark so that you can return to it easily.

American Political Science Association: http://www.providence.edu/polisci/rep/apsa.html

FedWorld Information Network: http://www.fedworld.gov/

Links to Political Science Resources: http://www.loyala.edu/dept/politics/polilink.html

Political Science and Sociology Online Publications: http://osiris.colorado.edu/POLSCI/RES/pubs.html

Political Science Virtual Library: http://spirit.lib.uconn.edu/PoliSci/polisci.htm

United States Federal Judiciary: http://www.uscourts.gov/

U.S. Census Bureau: http://www.census.gov/

U.S. House of Representatives: http://www.house.gov/

White House: http://www.whitehouse.gov/WH/Welcome.html

Yahoo!—Government:Politics:Indices: http://www.yahoo.com/Government /Politics/Indices/

Matching Data and Data Sources

Practice Exercise 9.1

Indicate which of the sources just listed you could use to find the following items of information. In most cases there will be more than one available source. (See the endnotes.[3])

1. Election returns for the 1996 presidential election:

   _____

   _____

2. The vote of the senators from your state on foreign aid:

   _____

   _____

3. Median family income for U.S. cities:

   _____

   _____

4. Spending on education in different countries:

   _____

   _____

5. Life expectancy in different countries:

   _____

   _____

Private Records

The second principal source of available data is private records or documents—those prepared by a private individual and usually not intended as data for political analysis. Private records include autobiographies, diaries, memoirs, letters, essays, and historical accounts of important events written by participants or direct observers. For obvious reasons, private records are both more difficult to obtain than public records and more complex to analyze than their public counterparts. In exercise 2.4 you worked with private accounts of events surrounding the Vietnam War and used them to develop hypotheses about the causes of U.S. involvement in Vietnam.

Political analysts have used private documents to analyze the institutional factors that affected a given policy decision or that helped to resolve a major crisis. A particularly interesting example, cited earlier, is the book *Victims of Groupthink*, which analyzes why the U.S. government has failed to deal effectively with several important foreign policy crises. Psychologist Irving Janis drew extensively from the memoirs or autobiographies of key participants in these decisions, including Harry Truman, Robert Kennedy, and George Kennan.[4] Janis found that tightly knit groups of like-minded individuals tend to discourage dissent and close off debate when coping with crises. He concluded that they neglect opportunities to consider whether their policy choices might fail. Political analysts have carried out similar studies of diaries and descriptions of meetings and decisions during the Cuban missile crisis.[5]

psychobiography (psychohistory) Application of psychoanalytic techniques to the lives of noted persons in order to analyze the inner dimensions of their political behavior.

Other scholars have applied psychological techniques and methods to private documents left behind by politically prominent figures to analyze their psychological predispositions. This approach, labeled **psychobiography** or **psychohistory,** has been used to analyze the motivations of such diverse figures as Mahatma Gandhi, Richard Nixon, and Vladimir Lenin. At the core of this approach lies the contention, first made by Harold Lasswell, that public figures project their private or personal needs onto public events and issues. For example, some leaders may get involved in politics to satisfy their need for esteem and approval. In other words, people's political behavior reflects their inner tensions, needs, and problems.[6] The use of private documents or records to exploit this insight is quite difficult, because it requires mastery of both psychology and political science. Nevertheless, despite considerable skepticism, it now seems to be accepted that psychohistory is a legitimate field whose findings will yield much of value to understanding the behavior of political leaders.

Using Secondary Sources of Information

Matching available data to concepts. If your research asks for voter turnout data or for information on the gross national product (GNP) or the gross domestic product (GDP), you will have no problem in identifying one or more sources. As chapter 3 discussed, however, many of the concepts we want to use in political analysis are not so concrete. Sometimes we may have to use data that "tell us about" or "serve as an indicator" of the concepts we are studying. Chapter 3 raised this issue in discussing the problem of linking concepts with reasonably available data sets. If you want to compare the development of two countries, you are not likely to find a data set labeled "development" in the sources listed earlier in this chapter. However, you will find data on life expectancy, on expenditures on education, on literacy, on growth in GNP, and so forth. You may choose to use one or more of these as an indicator of development in your research. The issue is whether the data are reliable and valid indicators of the concepts you are examining.

A caution on dates and sources. Earlier we stressed the importance of noting the dates and wording of questions in analyzing survey data. You need to be equally attentive to the dates and sources for any secondary material you use. It often takes several years to compile and publish data sets. Thus, even annual publications may report data that were collected for a prior year. Dating is even more of a problem when your data sources are not published annually. For example, the *New Book of World Rankings*, published in 1984, uses data and indexes that were gathered as many as six years earlier. Sometimes there have been major changes since the data were collected. For example, the first edition of this book, published in 1983, included tables with data on a number of countries that were described as authoritarian, and were so when it was written. Since then, in a number of countries authoritarian military regimes have been removed. In 1985 in Brazil, the military regime handed power over to civilians, a constitution was written, and presidential elections were held in 1989. Yet many publications report data about Brazil that were collected at a time when it was still governed by an authoritarian military regime. Because of rapid and frequent changes in the political arena, dates and sources for information should always be cited in your presentation of data.

Data on economic productivity. One of the commonest measures of economic productivity, and one you have already been using throughout the book, is gross national product, or GNP. A number of official sources have begun reporting a slightly different measure, gross domestic product, or GDP. The U.S. government has made this change so its reports will be more consistent with data reported by other industrial countries and to recognize changes in the international economy. GNP measures production from all assets owned *by a country's nationals*, wherever that production occurs—within or outside the country. GDP includes the total value of goods and services produced by labor and capital physically located *within* a country, no matter who owns the assets. Thus it excludes production financed by a country's citizens that takes place outside that country's borders and includes production financed by foreigners within the country's borders. In most cases there is not much difference between the two figures, given the overall size of most countries' economies. For example, in 1995, U.S. GNP was $7,237.5 billion, while its GDP was $7,245.8 billion. Why would GDP be higher than GNP? (Answer: Productivity from assets owned by foreigners located within the United States was greater than productivity from assets owned by U.S. nationals located outside the country.)

Making Data

Let us assume you have surveyed all available data sources and have found none applicable to your study. One remaining possibility, however, is to transform nonquantified information into quantified data, or, as we put it here, "to make data." This section describes three examples of making data: content analysis, counting and coding event data, and securing expert opinions, or judgmental data.

Making data offers both an advantage and a risk. The advantage is that the ingenious conversion of nonquantified information into quantified data opens up virtually the entire documented record of human history to empirical inquiry. The risk is that many techniques for transforming such material into data may lead you to draw unwarranted and biased conclusions from fragments of information. The data you gather in this way do not have the same reality as data about tanks or votes or dollars. They are data you create, leading to the gibe that "the plural of anecdote is data," meaning that it is all too easy to declare that any pieces of evidence that prove our point are "data."

Content Analysis of Documents

content analysis
Analysis of written and oral communications for the frequency with which selected words or themes are used; can be used to study the causes of the communication, the motivations of the author(s), or the effects of the communication on audiences.

Content analysis involves scrutinizing the contents of a document in order to understand its underlying structure, ideas, and concepts, and then quantifying the message it relates.[7] We do this by determining the amount of space devoted to a particular topic, theme, or idea, or by counting the frequency with which certain words or phrases are used. Content analysis can be used to delineate the characteristics of the communication itself, or circumstances of the communication, and the effects of the communication on the audience. Assuming that what people say or write bears some relationship to what they think, we can infer patterns in the minds of the authors from the patterns in their communications. Recall that chapter 3 cited a recent study of British political culture that used content analysis of the lyrics in Beatles songs as a way to describe the political culture during the 1960s.

To conduct a content analysis we formulate a set of categories into which words or phrases can be placed, select a sample of the key passages to examine, and then review the communications to see what patterns there are in the use of key words or phrases. There are two ways of recording the data. **Frequency analysis** is the simple recording of the frequency with which certain words, phrases, or themes appear in a given communication. **Contingency analysis** further records how often a word, phrase, or theme appears in conjunction with other words or ideas.

frequency analysis
Recording of the frequency with which certain words or themes appear in a communication.

contingency analysis
Recording of the frequency with which certain words or themes appear in a communication in conjunction with other selected words or themes.

Possible sources of the raw data for content analyses include newspapers, personal statements and communications, public appeals, popular culture, and electronic media (radio and television). For example, you might perform content analysis on two or more newspaper editorials on the subject of reasons for the reductions in crime in the period around 1997. To begin, you could establish the following categories: (1) "get tough" mood in the country, (2) changes in police procedures, (3) tougher sentences, (4) activities by local communities, and (5) demographic changes. To carry out a frequency analysis, you would count how many times each editorial had a phrase or sentence falling into each of these categories and then analyze the patterns you found. You might find that one editorial placed most of its emphasis on the third item, tougher sentences, while another made more references to changing patterns of police activity. Counting these references would give you a specific, numerical measure of the difference in emphasis in these two papers.

James Banks used content analysis to determine how blacks were treated in history textbooks. He looked for particular themes, such as the ways in which the texts dealt with discrimination and described the relations between the races. The themes he looked for included descriptions of discrimination, explanations for discrimination, moral issues related to discrimination, the use of stereotypes, reference to the achievements of black Americans, emphasis on violence and conflict among the races, stress on racial harmony. Banks, using these categories to analyze thirty-six textbooks, found that books published in 1968 were much more apt to mention achievements of black Americans and racial violence and conflict than books published in 1964.[8] Can you think of any reasons for this finding?

Consider a second example of content analysis, this time an analysis of items on the agenda of an urban school committee over a period of years. The researchers were interested in how the committee defined school issues. They began by interviewing school officials to learn which concerns preoccupied them and came up with the following categories: school governance, financial resources, educational program, school operations, role of citizens, and social problems in the community. They then analyzed records on eighty-eight meetings of the school committee over a three-year period to determine which issues dominated the agenda. They found that finances and education programs accounted for the greatest frequency of agenda items, 21 and 20 percent respectively.[9]

Analyzing Lists and Descriptions of Events

event data
Data about discrete historical events, transformed into numerical terms.

We can also apply *frequency analysis* to lists of events by simply counting and recording the occurrence of a particular kind of event—as well as certain details of the event. **Event data** analysis has been conducted on such phenomena as political violence, international alliances, and the exchange of diplomatic representatives. For example, one might go through an index such as the *New York Times Index* and simply count the number of occasions of violence in a particular period or location. The major concerns in analyzing data about events are developing suitable codes, choosing appropriate sources, and accurately recording observations.

Event data have been used to study public opinion. Funkhouser examined the titles of articles in magazines published during the 1960s in order to describe the major concerns and issues of the period. He began by establishing categories such as the Vietnam War, race relations, crime, and urban riots, and then consulted the *Reader's Guide to Periodical Literature* to see how many articles were listed on each subject. This allowed him to rank the issues by importance; not surprisingly, he found that the three major issues during the period were the Vietnam War, race relations, and campus unrest, but he was able to assign specific measures to each.[10] One could design a similar study that compared the incidence of articles on certain topics in two different periods as a way of comparing public opinion in the two periods.

counting and coding
A technique for transforming information about discrete historical events into a numerical format for subsequent manipulation via statistical techniques.

A frequency analysis of event data can be done by **counting and coding.** Begin by establishing a code, or a list of the categories that are relevant to your research question. A code useful to study a political demonstration could include categories such as *number involved, precipitating event*, and *major issue*. Developing a code that will effectively guide the gathering of data can be difficult. If a code is drawn too narrowly or too rigidly in the beginning, many events may be lost from the count. If the code is drawn too loosely, the count may include irrelevant events. For example, if you want to count incidents of violence, you would first have to decide exactly what you mean by a "violent act." You would need to specify the kinds of events you were including and state the characteristics that would distinguish them from other, similar events. Would a fight among neighbors be considered a case of violence? Would an armed robbery be counted as an incidence of violence? Or would you look only at cases of violence that involve larger groups of people and deal with public rather than purely private issues? Be aware, as well, that selecting codes raises validity and reliability problems. If you define the code too precisely, your study may miss some incidences of violence and hence be invalid; if your code is not precise enough, you may compromise the reliability of the study. In the latter case, different people using your directions might well code events differently.

The choice of suitable sources is likewise critical. We have basically three choices. One important source of event information is the historical study. The chief advantage of the monograph is economic. It simply is cheaper to use data sources in which someone else has already done the work of selecting the events and recording them. The principal disadvantage is, clearly, that the choice of historical studies puts us under the control of the historian, whose selection of events may not have been accurate or comprehensive.

A second major source of this kind of information is yearbooks and almanacs, some of which have been published on a more or less continual basis for years. Again, these are easy and relatively cheap to use, but they may not have been as comprehensive in their choice of events as you would like. The most comprehensive source, of course, is daily newspapers from the period you are studying, especially the major newspapers on each continent, the *New York Times*, the *Times* (London), and *Le Monde* (Paris). One of the chief advantages of the *New York Times* and the *Times* of London, apart from the quality and detail of their reporting, is their indexes, which are invaluable tools for political research.

Once a code has been developed and the principal sources identified, the last step in preparation is the design of the recording form. For example, assume you are doing a study of events of violence. You would first decide which events you wanted to include as indicators of violence. You would then decide on the source of the data and design a form for recording the incidents of violence. You could develop a code such as the following:

Political Violence Events: Data-Recording Form

Date	Location	Nature of Event	Duration	Numbers Involved	Cause	Data Source

You would then go through your sources, analyze each event, and enter the appropriate information in each column of your coding sheet. The last step would be to analyze the results.

Consider an example. You develop a hypothesis that incidents of violence that are drug-related tend to involve only a few people and that incidents of violence that arise out of problems between ethnic groups involve more people. You could then set up a table such as the following in which to enter the information from your coding sheet:

	Causes of the Violent Event	
Extent of Violence	Drugs	Interethnic Hostility
Few involved		
Many involved		

Judgmental Scores

judgmental scores
Ratings achieved by transforming narrative-format data by assigning preestablished values to decisions, events, and other types of cases.

Still a third method for making data is the use of **judgmental scores.** In this case the researcher obtains a data set by examining a number of cases (events, decisions, and so forth) and assigning values to each case according to some preestablished code or rule. There are several ways to assign values. If, say, you are studying twelve countries and want to distinguish among them, the cases could be ranked along some dimension, such as most to least democratic. You might assign the cases to categories that represent values of the variable in question, such as *democratic, partially democratic,* and *authoritarian.* Finally, you could assign specific numerical values to the cases representing their positions on a graduated scale such as one to ten, with one representing least democratic and ten representing most democratic. Whatever the case, researchers seeking to use judgmental data must ensure that the rules for assigning values to cases are set down in advance of the scoring, in writing, and as precisely as possible.[11]

Expert opinions constitute an important source of judgmental data. Researchers in a particular field consult experts in that field and record the ratings or scores that these experts award to the cases in question. Because bias or other kinds of errors are possible in this kind of assessment, researchers would be wise to consult as many experts as they reasonably can.

Tools for Indirect Data Gathering

Indicators, or Codes

coding
A technique for transforming information about discrete historical events into a numerical format for subsequent manipulation by statistical techniques.

data specifications
A set of rules indicating what to record, what to ignore, and how to classify, rate, score, or otherwise evaluate each piece of evidence.

There are two basic tools to guide the data gathering. The first is the indicators you select, the set of **codes** or **data specifications** that tell you what to record and what to ignore, and how to classify or score each piece of data. The data specifications should be as precise as needed to guide you effectively, but they should not be excessively detailed or they will make data collection more difficult. (Recall the earlier discussion of the need to make trade-offs between validity and reliability.) A single phrase or sentence may be all you need to identify your indicator. For example, if you want to study the defense budgets in Democratic and Republican administrations, you could look through budgets for the term *defense expenditures*. Your data specifications should reflect the data suggested by your propositions and operational definitions, and your principal objective should be to ensure consistency in comparing your cases.

In actual practice the development of data specifications calls for some familiarity with the data. Robert Clark, for example, was doing research on the victims of violence by insurgents in Spain. He began analyzing the daily newspapers and counting the number of persons killed in insurgent attacks. After analyzing the newspapers over a two-year period, he came to believe that his data specifications were faulty because in counting victims he had not included the wounded along with the killed. He decided that he needed to combine the wounded and the killed in a single figure and use this as an indicator or measure of victimization. He thought this would be a more valid measure because, in a number of instances, the only factor that separated the wounded from those killed was the speed with which they had been medically treated. After adjusting the data specifications to include both wounded and killed in the victim list, he had to return to the original data sources and include the new cases. One way to avoid retracing your steps is to test your measures in a trial run to see if they are well suited to your research questions. You cannot revise the data midway through the data collection process without returning to the beginning to capture all data previously overlooked.

The second essential tool is the data-recording form. You must keep in mind that eventually the data will have to be placed in graphs or tables. To facilitate both the collection and later presentation of the data, you should collect your raw data on a standard form. The form may be as simple or as complicated as need be to allow recording of the data called for in your measures. Forms for gathering simple aggregate data, such as budget figures or the size of armed forces or numbers killed in violent events, may consist of nothing more than ruled lines on notebook paper. Forms for recording event data or for judgmental coding may be much more complex and have spaces for many variables associated with each case or event. In all instances the source of the data should be noted on the recording form in case you need to return to that source later.

Dealing with Missing Data

Another practical problem involves missing data.[12] In some studies—for example, those using aggregate data such as the gross national product or political data such as voting statistics—there probably will be some gaps in the data set, as, for instance, when some countries may not be included in a listing of world GNPs. In some cases, data gaps are not a problem. If the missing data are scattered randomly throughout the data, you need not be too concerned. If, however, the gaps are clustered in just a few cases, a few variables, or a few years, then the absent data can distort your conclusions. For instance, data tend to be more available for wealthier countries than for poorer ones. If you are comparing industrialized or wealthy countries with poorer ones, then the gaps in the data could seriously affect your conclusions.

When you encounter gaps in the data set, there are several things you can do. You can delete the cases with missing data, or delete the indicators with gaps in them. If income data are missing for a number of countries, then you should probably decide to delete income as an indicator and rely on another indicator, such as education. As a last resort, you could fill in gaps with estimated values. For example, if several years of per capita income data are missing, you could insert estimates if you knew the figures both before and after the gaps, and if you had knowledge of economic conditions in the country during the period. You should take this course only when the alternative is to abandon the study, however. Further, it should be tried only with certain variables, and not others. You could estimate data on structural variables, such as government expenditures and size of the armed services, because these usually change in a predictable manner. You should not estimate data for events or interactions because they are less predictable. If you do make an estimate of data, you should indicate that in a footnote to your table.

Indexes

Now we turn to the construction of indexes. To measure change in a one-dimensional variable, such as income or literacy, is relatively simple and straight-forward. Problems arise, however, in measuring change in a complex, multi-dimensional variable, such as the economic performance of a regime. The problems arise because you need to use a number of different indicators—such as per capita GNP, industrial output, and the rates of inflation and unemployment—

to capture the several dimensions of a concept such as economic performance. One solution is to construct an index. An **index** is a single number used to measure a multidimensional phenomenon.[13] Indexes are widely used in political analyses to show trends or patterns in complex phenomena by means of a single figure that is easy to grasp and understand. The measure of unemployment discussed in chapter 3 is an example of a commonly used index. It combines in a single figure a measure of whether a person is employed, looking for work, and available for work.

Index construction is the process of combining raw data on several variables to form a summary indicator of the concept you are concerned with. The guiding principles are these: (1) the index must be *accurate* and measure the phenomenon that you want to measure; (2) the index must be *simple* and easy for the audience to understand; and (3) the index must reflect accurately the *significance* of each component factor or variable in the overall mix that produces the final index number.

The easiest way to describe the kinds of indexes used in political analysis is to survey some of the more frequently used measuring devices.[14] Among the more popular indexes are those that compare some combination of products, activities, or statistics in a given year with the same mix of variables in a **base year.** For example, the Consumer Price Index (CPI) is used by our government and governments all over the world to measure the change in the price of consumer products from one year to another. The CPI is an example of the so-called market-basket approach to indexing. The CPI represents the changing costs of a typical set of some four hundred consumer items, ranging from housing and clothing to transportation and food. Each month data collectors from the U.S. Bureau of Labor Statistics record the prices of the four hundred items in eighty-five cities across the country. The sum of the recordings is then compared to a base year. The base year is taken to equal 100, and the CPI indicates the change in the cost of the goods.[15] (In 1997 the CPI became politically controversial. A commission of economists claimed that it overstated the amount of inflation by about 1.1 percent a year and recommended that benefits such as social security that take the CPI into account be adjusted downward. Congress, however, rejected their proposal, fearing reprisal from citizens.)

Not all indexes use base years to compare current spending, production, or other variables. Some indexes use bases such as cities or countries. The International Civil Service Commission, for instance, each year calculates the Cities' Cost of Living Index to compute adjustments in the salaries of U.N. employees in various countries. The index includes costs of housing, utilities, and domestic service and compares the costs of these goods and services in several cities with what they would cost in New York City during the same year. Thus, the cost of living in New York is assumed to equal 100 for purposes of this index.

Another way to figure an index is to compute one indicator as a proportion or percentage of a second indicator, or, in other words, to express one measure as a ratio of another. In calculating an index this way, the primary measure is divided by the base measure. This kind of calculation is used when the purpose is to express a relationship between two (or more) variables by means of a single

---

index
A single number that transforms data on several different variables into a single measure that stands for the composite of the several variables taken together.

index construction
Process by which variables are weighted and combined with one another to form a summary indicator of the entire group.

base year
Year that is assigned the value of 100 in a series of annual index calculations; year to which all other annual index measurements are compared to demonstrate trends or changes over time.

number.[16] For example, we can express the number of crimes as a percentage of the population.

Other examples of indexes include the following:

Political opposition index (POI). One indicator of democracy is the existence of a viable opposition. If the largest party in a country holds 80 or 90 percent of the seats in the legislature, the opposition is not a significant force, and elections have less significance than they do in countries where the largest party holds closer to 50 or 60 percent of the seats. The political opposition index (POI) is based on this logic; it is computed by dividing the total number of seats by the seats held by the largest party in the national legislature. In this index a country with no parties would have a score of 0 and a country where the largest party holds sixty-five out of one hundred seats would have a score of 1.54 (100/65).[17]

Index of democratization. An index of democratization is based on two variables—competition and participation. Competition is measured by the share of the vote received by the smallest party. The reasoning is that the larger the vote by the smallest part, the greater the electoral competition and the greater the measure of democracy. Participation is measured by the percentage of eligible voters who turn out to vote. The index of democratization multiplies these two figures and divides the result by 100.[18]

Gini Index, Measure of Inequality. This index provides a measure of inequality within a geographic unit; it is useful for comparing how much inequality there is among several states or nations. It ranges from 0, where everyone has the same income (or resources), to 100 where one person has all of the income. Applied to the United States, the Gini Index has been steadily increasing; it was .399 in 1967 and reached .456 in 1994. To arrive at these figures, researchers used data from the *Current Population Survey* for various years, which is conducted monthly by the Census Bureau and includes detailed income questions once a year.[19] (To put this figure in perspective, an economics text notes that "the Gini [index] for countries with highly unequal income distributions typically lies between 0–50 and 0–70 while for countries with relatively equitable distributions, it is of the order of 0–20 to 0–35.[20])

Some indexes are based on judgments and in this sense are similar to the use of experts to make data, described earlier. Indexes of this kind are computed on the basis of expert judgments about various phenomena. The opinions are given numerical values and then combined into indexes. A good example is an index of power developed by Ray Cline:

National power index. For a national power index, experts are asked to indicate the perceived power of nations according to five elements: (1) population plus territory, (2) economic capability, (3) military capability, (4) strategic purpose, and (5) will to pursue national strategy.[21] Their judgments on these five elements are added together to arrive at a single index.

The last kind of index to be discussed is composed of several indicators, each of which measures data on a different scale. Before the indicators are combined into a single measure, they first must be transformed into some common scale. Then they are added (or multiplied) to obtain the final index score. You could also choose to weight one or more of the figures before adding them together. The Physical Quality of Life Index is a well-known example:

Physical quality of life index (PQLI). The physical quality of life index is based on three variables: life expectancy, infant mortality, and literacy, weighting each of these equally. Each country is rated on a scale from 1 to 100. Developed by the Overseas Development Council, the virtue of the index is that the figures are not weighted by GNP and do not involve monetary measures. In their raw form, however, the data are noncomparable. Life expectancy is expressed in years; infant mortality in numbers of deaths before the age of one year per thousand live births; and literacy in percentage of the adult population that is literate. To make the measures comparable and enable us to add them together, we have to *standardize* them, or put them each in a common scale. The PQLI does this by converting each indicator to a scale that goes from 1 to 100. The country with the highest score is given 100, and the other countries are given comparable scores. Which countries would you estimate to fall among the top ten in physical quality of life? (The answers are in the endnotes.[22])

To illustrate the actual calculation process in standardizing scores, consider an index of development based on two measures:

Country	Life Expectancy (in years)	Infant Mortality Rate (100 minus mortality rate)
United States	76	91
Soviet Union (former)	71	77
China	70	66

Source: Ruth Leger Sivard, *World Military and Social Expenditures, 1993* (Leesburg, Va.: WMSE Publications), 1993, pp. 46-49.

standardize scores
Make figures comparable by converting to the same base so they can be combined into a single index number.

To **standardize scores,** or make them comparable so they can be combined into a single index number, you would do the following in connection with the figures in the table. Because the United States has the highest life expectancy, it is assigned a score of 100. To make the other scores comparable, calculate the number that would transform the actual life expectancy into 100. To do this, divide 100 by 76, getting 1.3. Multiply the life expectancy of each of the other countries by 1.3, getting 92.3 for the former Soviet Union and 91 for China. Follow this same procedure for computing the infant mortality rates. Assign 100 to the United States, divide 100 by 91 (the actual score for the United States), getting 1.1. Multiply the score for the United States by 1.1, getting 100, the number we can assign to the United States as its standardized score. Multiply the rate of

77 for the former Soviet Union by 1.1, getting 84.7. Do the same for China and its rate of 66. We now have the following figures:

Standardized Scores for Development

Country	Life Expectancy (in years)	Infant Mortality (percentage)	Index
United States	100	100	200/2 = 100
Soviet Union (former)	92.3	84.7	177/2 = 88.5
China	91	72.6	163.6/2 = 81.8

The new index figures were obtained by adding the separate standardized scores and then dividing by 2, because we are combining two scores for each country. As with any summary figure, the validity of the index depends on whether the measures of life expectancy and infant mortality are good indicators of development.

Creating an Index

**Practice
Exercise 9.2**

Table 9.1 gives you information on six aspects of seven countries. They are taken from ten indicators used by the Population Crisis Committee to develop an index of human suffering. Select three of them to create your own index of human suffering. Select indicators that reflect effectively the human suffering in these countries to combine in a single index. Because the data are not comparable, they cannot be added together in their present form. You must convert the

TABLE 9.1
Indicators of Human Suffering of Seven Selected Countries, 1991

Country	Life Expectancy (in years)	Daily Calorie Supply (per capita)	Political Freedom (low = 1 high = 10)	GNP (per capita)	Secondary School Enrollment (percentage)	Civil Rights (low = 1 high = 10)	Inflation Rate (percentage)
United States	75	138	9	21,100	98	9	6
Soviet Union (former)	70	133	5	9,211	98	4	10
China	69	126	0	360	37	0	16
India	57	109	6	350	29	2	6
Greece	77	147	9	5,340	93	8	23
Brazil	65	128	7	2,550	38	4	2,027
Japan	79	125	9	23,730	94	7	4

Source: *The International Human Suffering Index* (Washington, D.C.: Population Crisis Committee, 1992).

sets of data to a common scale. To do this, follow the same procedures that you just used to arrive at an index of development. Assign 100 to the country with the highest number on each variable. To get the figure that shows the relationship between the actual number and 100, divide 100 by the actual number. Call this number X. Multiply every other number in the column by X. You have now standardized the figures, or made them comparable, and can add them together. Be sure to divide the sum by 3; that is, the number of items in your index.

1. Three indicators:

   _____   _____   _____

2. Standardize the scores for these three indicators:

	Variable 1	**Variable 2**	**Variable 3**
United States	_____	_____	_____
Soviet Union (former)	_____	_____	_____
China	_____	_____	_____
India	_____	_____	_____
Greece	_____	_____	_____
Brazil	_____	_____	_____
Japan	_____	_____	_____

3. Add the scores and divide by 3 (for the three variables):

United States	_____	Greece _____
Soviet Union (former)	_____	Brazil _____
China	_____	Japan _____
India	_____	

4. What do your index numbers tell you about the comparative human suffering of the countries on the list?

   _____

   _____

   _____

   _____

   _____

5. What do you gain by converting these measures into a single index? What do you lose?

_____

_____

_____

_____

_____

_____

Where We Are

Chapters 7, 8, and 9 have reviewed sources of data used in analyzing research propositions. They greatly expand your repertoire of evidence and enable you to pursue a wide variety of interesting research questions. It is clear that each is appropriate for different purposes and that each has its strengths and weaknesses. And, as the text has suggested throughout, you should draw on several sources whenever possible.

We conclude this section on data collection by giving an example of the value of multiple sources of data. Two researchers did a study of employees in the public service, using government data on employment, and found evidence that Asian Americans were not represented in the public service in proportion to their numbers in the workforce. For example, comparing Asian Americans and nonminority whites they reported a number of cases where the former are 2.6 percent of the workforce, but only 1 percent of municipal officials. As a second example, 27 percent of white men serving the federal government hold supervisory positions, but the percentage of Asian Americans in supervisory positions is only 15 percent. The authors conclude that the data suggest there is discrimination against Asian Americans.[23]

Another researcher reviewed the data and the analysis. He acknowledged the discrepancy, but observed that it is possible to think of other reasons for the discrepancy than to assume it is due to discrimination. He continued that group statistics such as these can give us important insights, but interpretations of their meaning require analysts to also look at other information, including "data from more direct sources such as surveys, focus groups, case studies, grievance records, and court documents." The employment statistics can tell us about employment patterns, but the other kinds of information are needed to determine if discrimination is the cause of the problem and to compare several possible explanations for the lower number of Asian Americans in the public service.[24]

In addition to underscoring the value of multiple sources of data, this example is a useful introduction to Part Four, which introduces statistical tools for analyzing and summarizing the data we have collected. It reminds us that statistics are not "magic bullets." They are useful only as tools within a clear research design that defines a clear question, explores alternative explanations and designs, and considers the best kind of evidence or combination of evidence for answering the question.

NOTES

1. The principal compilation based on the accounts of the perpetrators was a book written by Julen Agirre and called *Operation Ogro* (for "ogre"); it was published in Spanish in 1974 by a French company. Published in English translation in 1975 under the same title, the book has generally been accepted as authoritative. In addition, the event has been recorded in the data files of organizations that keep track of events such as political assassinations. The CIA maintains a computer file on international terrorist incidents and has published its information in annual reports since 1976. Compilations are also made by the International Institute for Strategic Studies in London and a publication called *Transnational Terrorism: A Chronology of Events, 1968–1973*. Example developed by Robert Clark.

2. For a fuller discussion of aggregate data, see Ralph Retzlaff, "The Use of Aggregate Data in Comparative Political Analysis," *Journal of Politics* 27 (1965): 797–817.

3. Some of the sources include: (1) *Statistical Abstract, CQ Almanac, America Votes*, (2) *CQ Weekly Report*, (3) *Municipal Yearbook*, (4) *World Handbook of Political and Social Indicators, World Development Report*, (5) *World Development Report, World Handbook of Political and Social Indicators*.

4. Irving Janis, *Victims of Groupthink* (Boston: Houghton Mifflin, 1972).

5. Graham Allison, "Conceptual Models and the Cuban Missile Crisis," *American Political Science Review* 63 (September 1969): 689–718.

6. Erik Erikson, *Gandhi's Truth* (New York: Norton, 1969); Bruce Mazlish, *In Search of Nixon* (New York: Basic Books, 1972); E. Victor Wolfenstein, *The Revolutionary Personality:* Lenin, Trotsky, *Gandhi* (Princeton, N.J.: Princeton University Press, 1967). For general treatments of this approach, see Jeanne Knutsen, ed., *Handbook of Political Psychology* (San Francisco: Jossey-Bass, 1973); Fred Greenstein and Michael Lerner, eds. *A Source Book for the Study of Personality and Politics* (Chicago: Markham, 1971).

7. For an interesting example of the use of content analysis, see Dina A. Zinnes, Robert C. North, and Howard E. Koch, Jr., "Capability, Threat, and the Outbreak of War," in *International Politics and Foreign Policy*, ed. James Rosenau (Glencoe, Ill.: Free Press, 1961), pp. 469–482.

8. James A. Banks, "A Content Analysis of the Black American in Textbooks," *Social Education* (December 1969): 954–957.

9. John Portz, "Problem Definitions and Policy Agendas," *Policy Studies Journal* 24, no. 3 (1996): 371–386.

10. G. Ray Funkhouser, "The Issue of the Sixties: An Exploratory Study," *Public Opinion Quarterly* 37 (Spring 1973): 260–272.

11. See Ivo K. Feierabend and Rosalind L. Feierabend, "Aggressive Behaviors within Polities, 1948–1962: A Cross National Study," *Journal of Conflict Resolution* 10 (September 1966): 249–271. This study is a good example of the use of judgmental scores.

12. Ted Robert Gurr, *Polimetrics: An Introduction to Quantitative Macropolitics* (Englewood Cliffs, N.J.: Prentice-Hall, 1972), pp. 84–87.

13. Hans Zeisel, *Say It with Figures*, 5th ed. (New York: Harper & Row, 1968), pp. 73–98.

14. Many of these can be found in a fascinating book by George Thomas Kurian, *The New Book of World Rankings* (New York: Facts on File, 1984).

15. The CPI is an extremely important index, because so much of government spending, Social Security payments, and private-sector wage contracts is tied to changes in this index. In recent years the CPI has been much criticized because the market basket of four hundred items no longer represents the items for which a typical American family spends its income. See David S. Moore, *Statistics: Concepts and Controversies* (San Francisco: W. H. Freeman, 1979), pp. 211–216.

16. For a useful discussion of the uses and misuses of index numbers, see Richard Runyon, *Winning with Statistics: A Painless First Look at Numbers, Percentages, Means and Inferences* (Reading, Mass.: Addison-Wesley, 1977), pp. 73–92.

17. The POI was computed by the Center for Social Analysis in Binghamton, New York. It was reported in George Thomas Kurian, *The Book of World Rankings* (New York: Facts on File, 1979), and was based on 1977 data. It was not updated in George T. Kurian, *The New Book of World Rankings* (New York: Facts on File, 1984).

18. Tatu Vanhanen, found in Kurian, *The New Book of World Rankings*, pp. 65–66. A more recent version of PQLI was published in 1991 using data from 1988 through 1990. Overseas Development Council, *U.S. Foreign Policy and Developing Countries* (Washington, D.C.: Overseas Development Council, 1991), pp. 37–41.

19. "Mapping Income Inequality," *USA Today*, 20 September 1996, p. 3B.

20. Michael Todaro, *Economic Development in the Third World* (New York: Longman, 1977), p. 102.

21. Ibid., pp. 55–56.

22. Ibid., pp. 331–332. On the basis of 1990 data, the top ten countries were Iceland, Japan, Netherlands, Sweden, Norway, Switzerland, Australia, Canada, Finland, and France. The United States was ranked eleventh.

23. Pan Suk Kim and Gregory Lewis, "Asian Americans in the Public Service," *Public Administration Review* 54, no. 3 (1994): 285–290.

24. Christopher Daniel, "Diminishing Returns from Statistical Analysis," *Public Administration Review* 57, no. 3 (May/June 1997): 264–266.

EXERCISES

Exercise 9.1 Using Aggregate Data

To complete this exercise you will need to go to the reference section of your library.

1. Find the *Statistical Abstract of the United States*, any recent edition.

   a. In 19_____; the gross domestic product (GDP) of the United States was _____; the GDP of Sweden was _____; and the GDP of Japan was _____.

   b. In the same year, the gross national product (GNP) of the United States was _____; the GNP of Sweden was _____; and the GNP of Japan was _____.

c. At the bottom of the table containing this information are the original sources of the data. Identify the sources.

2. The following two issues were voted on by the U.S. Senate; use *CQ Weekly Reports* for the year given. Indicate the bill number(s) and the ways the two senators from your state voted.

   a. *Fiscal 1997 Omnibus Appropriations/Passage—1996*

      Bill number: _____

      Senator and vote: _____

      Senator and vote: _____

   b. *Individuals with Disabilities Education Act Reauthorization/Passage—1997*

      Bill number: _____

      Senator and vote: _____

      Senator and vote: _____

   c. Describe what other kind of information is available on IDEA in the same year. Cite the page numbers.

3. *Municipal Year Book*, a recent edition. Select three cities of similar size.

   a. List the kinds of information you can find on these cities:

   b. Create a table in which you list information on five variables for these three cities.

4. *World Development Report*, a recent edition. Browse through the tables and select three indicators of interest to you. Select one country each within Asia, Africa, South America, and Western Europe. Indicate the score for each of the four countries on all three characteristics, as in the following table:

Characteristic	Asia	Africa	South America	Western Europe
a. _____	_____	_____	_____	_____
b. _____	_____	_____	_____	_____
c. _____	_____	_____	_____	_____

5. Pick a topic of interest to you, such as foreign aid, regulation, welfare reform, or terrorism.

   a. Look up the topic in *Library of Congress Subject Headings*, listing up to three headings you might use to find information on your topic:

   b. Using the library catalogue, find which of the sources indicated by your headings are used by your library. Put a check mark beside the sources you listed under item 5a that are in your library.

   c. Look up your topic in a bound volume of the *Reader's Guide to Periodical Literature, Social Sciences Index*, and *PAIS (Public Affairs Information Service Index)* for the past three years.

   (1) Which index has more references to your subject?

   (2) Compare the kinds of material identified in each index:

Exercise 9.2 Comparing the New York Times with Your Local Newspaper

One of the purposes of content analysis is to compare the underlying messages of two documents or communications that address the same issue. This exercise will give you practice in doing that. Because the *New York Times* is generally accepted as the newspaper of record in the United States, your university's library probably subscribes to it or has it on microfilm. In this exercise, compare the *Times* coverage of an event or issue with that in your local newspaper or in another newspaper that your library receives.

1. Choose an event or issue to which both newspapers devoted enough space (at least twenty column inches) to allow for content analysis:

2. Develop a set of categories into which you can assign words or phrases that you expect to find in the articles:

3. Review each newspaper's coverage of the selected event, noting the number of times the key words or phrases were mentioned:

4. Arrange your findings in a simple table, and write a paragraph that analyzes what you have found.

Exercise 9.3 Counting and Coding Event Data

Compare the nature of political violence in the United States in three periods: 1968, 1978, and 1988. Choose four to six variables you think are important characteristics of political disorder, such as date, duration of the violence, numbers of people involved, and causes (social, economic, racial, and so forth). Develop a data-recording form (refer to the sample data recording form). Using the *New York Times Index*, identify instances of political disorder that occurred during each of those years. Record the events and the additional data about each one on your recording sheet.

Exercise 9.4 Creating Indexes

There is a widespread assumption that the freer a country's economy is, the better its performance is. Table 9.2 reports an index created by the Heritage Foundation on economic freedom in developing countries. Note that the higher the score the less the freedom. Table 9.3 reports several indicators that can be used as measures of economic performance. Your assignment is to determine if there is a relationship between these two variables as reported in tables 9.2 and 9.3.

1. Using the data in Table 9.3 create an index of economic performance by combining two of the indicators. Remember to standardize them before combining them into a single number.
2. Now test the hypothesis that the greater a country's economic freedom, the greater its economic performance. Divide the variables of economic freedom and economic performance into a set of categories that reflects the data (e.g., high/low or high/medium/low). Remember that for the index for economic freedom the lowest scores indicate the highest freedom.

TABLE 9.2

Indicator of Economic Progress in Twenty-Two Selected Developing Countries

Country	Economic Freedom Ranking	Country	Economic Freedom Ranking
Bolivia	59	Pakistan	82
Brazil	94	Peru	65
Chile	22	Philippines	54
Colombia	78	Romania	98
India	120	Saudi Arabia	55
Indonesia	62	Sri Lanka	29
Kenya	76	Tanzania	92
Malaysia	39	Thailand	24
Mexico	96	Tunisia	49
Morocco	47	Uruguay	45
Nigeria	88	Venezuela	114

Source: *The Heritage Foundation/Wall Street Journal Index of Economic Freedom.* (Washington, D.C./New York: The Heritage Foundation/Wall Street Journal-Dow Jones & Co., 1997). The index scores the relative freedom of economies based on ten factors—trade policy, tax policy, government consumption of economic output, monetary policy, foreign investment, wage controls, price controls, property rights, regulation, and the size of the black market. For each category, a country's economy is assigned a score on a scale from one (best) to five (worst).

TABLE 9.3

Indicators of Economic Performance of Twenty-Two Selected Third-World States, 1994

Country	Gross National Product (GNP) (Millions U.S. $)	GNP Per Capita (U.S. $)	GNP Annual Rate of Growth (1985–1994)	Life Expectancy (Years)
Bolivia	5,544	770	1.7	60
Brazil	472,527	2,970	−0.4	67
Chile	49,280	3,520	6.5	72
Colombia	60,621	1,670	2.4	70
India	292,352	320	2.9	62
Indonesia	167,552	880	6.0	63
Kenya	6,500	250	0.0	59
Malaysia	68,556	3,480	5.6	71
Mexico	369,930	4,180	0.9	71
Morocco	30,096	1,140	1.2	65
Nigeria	30,240	280	1.2	52
Pakistan	54,309	430	1.3	60
Peru	48,952	2,110	−2.0	65
Philippines	63,650	950	1.7	65
Romania	28,829	1,270	−4.5	70
Saudi Arabia	25,490	7,050	−1.7	70
Sri Lanka	11,456	640	2.9	72
Tanzania	4,032	140	.8	51
Thailand	139,780	2,410	8.6	69
Tunisia	15,752	1,790 .	2.1	68
Uruguay	14,912	4,660	2.9	73
Venezuela	58,512	2,760	0.7	71

Source: *World Development Report*, 1996 (Washington, D.C.: World Bank, 1996), table 1, pp. 188–189.

3. Create a table that allows you to show the relationship of these two variables by placing the countries in the appropriate cells. Take care with the title of the table, labels of the columns and rows, and the layout of the table.

4. Comment on your findings. Do they support the original hypothesis?

Exercise 9.5 Collecting Data on the Internet

1. One of the best references for country information is the *CIA World Fact Book*. Find this on the Internet: (http://www.odci.gov/cia/publications

/nsolo/wfb-all.html). Pick a country in Asia. Select three indicators or characteristics of interest to you, and fill in their values for the Asian country you chose. Then select one country within Africa, South America, and Europe. Indicate the score for each of the countries on all three characteristics.

2. Visit the University of Michigan's Documents Center (http://www. lib.umich.edu/libhome/Documents.center/index.html#doctop). This is a wonderful reference for governmental and other statistics. Click on the "Statistics" link under "Related disciplines." Look around to see what is available. Then click on "Demographics." Click on "Congressional District Ranking Book." Answer these questions:

   a. Which district is the most Hispanic? _____

   b. Which district has the highest percentage over age 65? _____

   c. What is the source of these data? _____

3. Take a look at some historical statistics either by finding your way from the University of Michigan's Document Center, or by typing in http:// icg.harvard.edu/census/. Bring up some census data from long ago. Answer these questions:

   a. In 1790, what was the population of the state of Connecticut? _____

   b. In 1820, what was the population of New York? _____

4. Using Net Search, find your way to the Census Bureau home page. By trial and error (you'll probably find that some of the places you click will not be very helpful), find the population of your home state.

5. Search the most recent *Statistical Abstract* online. Go to http://www. medaccess.com/census/census_s.htm#Table of Contents. Click on "Comparative International Statistics." Find the correct tables and fill in the blanks below:

   a. In 19_____, the gross national product (GNP) of the United States was _____; the GNP of Sweden was _____, and the GNP of Japan was _____.

   b. In the same year, the gross domestic product (GDP) of the United States was _____; the GDP of Sweden was _____, and the GDP of Japan was _____.

   c. At the bottom of the table containing this information are the original sources of the data. Identify the sources:

Analyzing Data to Answer Our Research Questions

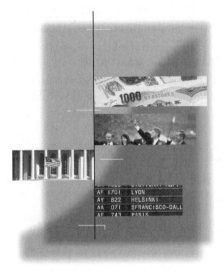

Parts One and Two introduced the logic of research. In Part One you learned how to ask empirical questions, how to define your terms so that you could collect evidence on them, and how to design your research. In Part Two you considered how to look for relationships and how to formulate hypotheses about causal relations. In Part Three you examined a variety of ways to collect information. Part Four describes techniques for analyzing and presenting the data you have collected. You will see that the kinds of questions and propositions you formulate and the kinds of data you collect have a great deal to do with the kinds of analysis that are appropriate. Recall that you learned how to develop a hypothesis that government expenditures on defense and education are associated with economic growth rates (Chapter 5). You learned to collect data and place them in a table and inspect the results to see if a hypothesis such as this is supported. A visual interpretation of tabular data may be sufficient for your purposes. However, you may wish to analyze the relationship more precisely using statistical analysis. A number of the statistical techniques you could use are introduced in Part Four.

Chapters 10, 11, and 12 cover three kinds of statistics. One kind, discussed in Chapter 10, describes patterns in the data. Assume you have collected information on economic growth rates in twenty states. This chapter shows a number of ways to describe and analyze these data: percentages, frequency distributions, central tendencies, and measures that indicate how spread out the figures are. These descriptive statistics summarize in a few numbers the patterns in data. They tell us whether the growth rates are spread out evenly across the range of growth rates or whether they cluster at the middle or at one end of this range. These measures are especially useful when we want to compare the patterns and shape of several variables.

The second kind of statistics enables us to summarize and measure the relationship between and among variables. Recall that in chapter 5 you developed tables to depict relationships and then examined these relationships by comparing percentage differences. For example, was the percentage of men who voted greater or less than the percentage of women who voted? Chapter 11 introduces techniques for measuring such relationships more precisely; some deal with relationships between two variables and some with multivariate relationships. You will learn that the kind of relationship measure you use depends in part on the kinds of data you collect.

A third kind of statistical measure is also important. In political analysis we often draw a sample of cases rather than study the entire population. The question is whether the statistics that are found to be true in the sample are significant or present in the population. Statistical measures of *significance* provide this kind of information, and will be discussed in chapter 12.

USES OF STATISTICAL MEASURES

To describe the patterns in a distribution (chapter 10).

To identify relationships between two or more variables (chapter 11).

To assess statistical significance, or whether a characteristic of a sample is also present in the population (chapter 12).

Chapter 13 deals with the visual presentation of research results. It describes specific skills for creating and interpreting tables of information. It also describes a variety of graphics that will enable you to present your findings concisely and effectively.

Chapter 14 brings together the various steps of analysis. It focuses on research designs and helps you compare strategies for designing, carrying out, and presenting your research.

CHAPTER TEN

Describing and Analyzing Variables

"Statistics show that if you place a new baby on an airplane and fly it continuously between Chicago and New York the chances are more than 50 percent that it will die of something other than a plane accident," says John Cook, an actuary at Metropolitan Life.

—The New Yorker, 19 November 1979

Ah, les statistiques! Your Secretary of Defense loves statistics. We Vietnamese can give him all he wants. You want them to go up, they will go up. If you want them to go down, they will go down.

—A Vietnamese general during the Vietnam War, reported
by Roger Hilsman in *To Move a Nation*

A few winters ago a dozen investigators independently reported figures on antihistamine pills. Each showed that a considerable percentage of colds cleared up after treatment. A great fuss ensued, at least in the advertisements, and a medical-product boom was on. It was based on an eternally springing hope and also on a curious refusal to look past the statistics to a fact that has been known for a long time. As Henry G. Felsen, a humorist and no medical authority, pointed out quite a while ago, proper treatment will cure a cold in seven days, but left to itself a cold will hang on for a week.

—Darrell Huff, *How to Lie with Statistics*

You can drown in a river whose average depth is two feet.

—Victor Cohn, former science editor, *The Washington Post*

[He] requested test scores from all 50 states and discovered that each one claimed to be "above the national average" or the statistical "norm." Newsweek *called that tendency to twist the facts to make everyone's kid look smarter the "Lake Wobegon effect."*

—John Schwartz, researcher

Describing Variables

Many interesting research questions ask us to describe patterns within single variables. Take your class in political analysis: How many are enrolled? Has this number changed in the past few years? What percentage of students take the course? What percentage of those taking the course are majoring in political science? If you surveyed class members about their career goals, which careers would they select? How many want to go into law? How many want to go into politics? How many want to work in the public sector? What career do most of the students want? How similar are they in their career goals?

Answers to these questions help us ascertain the characteristics of a group of students. There are a number of descriptive statistics and techniques we can use to summarize information about a variable and show the patterns in our data, or the lack of a pattern. They are particularly useful when we want to compare two cases or groups. How do the career goals of students in your class compare with the career goals of students in another university, or with the goals of students majoring in economics? You have already been introduced to the first technique, percentages, a very simple descriptive statistic. Instead of saying that six students want to go to law school it is probably more useful to say that 10 percent of the class want to go to law school. The second technique discussed in this chapter is frequency distributions. A frequency simply reports the number of cases in any subcategory (or value) of a variable. Frequency distributions tell us about the overall pattern or shape of the data. The third section describes ways of talking about the central tendency of the data, the center of gravity of the cases we are examining. The fourth section describes the variation or diversity in the data and offers tools for comparing the diversity in several groups. For example, it allows us to compare the diversity of a class in which most of the members want to go into the public service with the diversity in another class in which everyone has a different career goal in mind.

Percentages

percentage
A figure that reports some number of unit as a proportion of one hundred; enables us to compare numbers with different bases.

Percentages are a useful way to describe and analyze data. They not only provide a summary measure that is easily understood but also allow us to make comparisons between and among groups of different sizes. It is misleading to compare the absolute numbers in two units of very different size; the number of Hispanics in Providence, Rhode Island, and New York City, for example. Percentages, however, convert information about both groups to a proportion of one hundred, and hence permit comparison. Consider data about the number of citizens below the poverty line. We could report the absolute number of those below the poverty line for a number of years. Because the size of the population changes from year to year, however, absolute numbers would be misleading. We therefore compare the percentage of the population that is poor in each of a number of years. Similarly, if we want to compare the amount of poverty in two metropolitan areas, percentages are more useful than absolute numbers, because the populations of the two areas are undoubtedly different.

Absolute amounts and percentages may give different impressions. To appreciate this point look at the information in table 10.1. First, be sure you are clear which numbers are being reported in table 10.1. The column that reports the budget totals indicates that these figures are reported in billions of dollars. Because the figure 1,000,000,000 (one billion) is the numeral 1 followed by nine zeroes, you would (mentally) add nine zeroes to each of the figures in the first column. You therefore (mentally) add nine zeroes after the decimal point, or eight zeroes after the figure that follows the decimal point. In other words, the budget total in 1960 was $92,200,000,000, or more than $92 billion. Similarly, the budget in 1972 was $230.7 billion, or more than $230 billion.

Now let your eyes move down the first column, and describe how the budget changed over the years. It grew rapidly; in fact, during the 1980s it increased an average of more than $55 billion per year. This trend supports the common wisdom that the government's budget has gotten out of hand and, according to some, is wildly out of control. Now look at the third column, which reports the budget as a percentage of the gross domestic product (GDP) in each year. Here the result is strikingly different: there has been a very gradual increase over the years, and in some years the percentage has even dipped slightly. The obvious reason is that GDP has also been rising rapidly. By reporting the budget as a percentage of GDP, we can take this changing base into account. Be

TABLE 10.1
Federal Budget Totals as Percentage of GDP, 1960–1996

Year	Budget Total (in billions of dollars)	GDP (in billions of dollars)	Budget as Percentage of GDP
1960	92.2	504.6	18.3
1964	118.5	625.3	19.0
1968	178.1	847.7	21.0
1972	230.7	1,147.8	20.1
1976	371.8	1,684.2	22.1
1980	590.9	2,644.1	22.3
1984	851.8	3,695.0	23.1
1988	1,064.1	4,808.4	22.1
1992	1,380.9	5,921.5	23.3
1996 (est.)	1,612.1	7,407.0	21.8

Source: *Historical Tables, Budget of the United States Government, Fiscal Year 1996* (Washington, D.C.: Executive Office of the President, Office of Management and Budget, 1995), tables 1.2, 1.3.

sure you know how to compute the percentages in the fourth column of table 10.1. Express both the budget and the GDP in the same denomination of dollars (that is, billions), and then divide the budget by the GDP to determine what percentage the budget is of the GDP. For example, for 1990, with both numbers expressed in billions of dollars:

$$92.2 \div 504.6 = 0.1827, \text{ or } 18.3 \text{ \%}$$

Computing Percentages

Practice Exercise 10.1

A. In 1995 U.S. federal government expenditures totaled $1,519,133,000,000. The government paid $332,414,000,000 in interest on the general debt. What percentage of expenditures was paid in interest?

_____

B. In 1984 Zambia had a population of 6,530,000. It had 30,000 teachers. What percentage of its population was teachers? The United States had a population of 237,000,000 and 2,245,000 teachers. How does the percentage of teachers in the United States compare with the percentage in Zambia?

_____

C. In 1996 the population of the United States was 268,449,470, the number registered to vote was 127,661,000, and the turnout was 105,0017,000. What percentage of the voting age population was registered to vote? And what percentage of the registered voters turned out to vote on election day? (Answers are in endnotes.)[1]

_____

— Percentages clearly are useful in describing a variable and in showing changes over time when the base changes. But they can also be extremely misleading if you forget or obscure that the bases are different. For example, you might read that U.S. exports increased by 15 percent while imports rose only 10 percent. If you had heard that the United States has a severe trade gap, these figures would be unexpected because they suggest that U.S. exports have increased far more than imports have, and hence that the trade gap has been reduced. The problem in interpreting the percentages is that the bases of the two percentages are different. U.S. imports are almost twice as large as U.S. exports; hence a 10 percent increase in imports is greater than a 15 percent increase in exports. The trade gap is, as reported, getting bigger, not smaller.

Percentages can also be misleading if analysts select a base to produce a percentage that suits their purposes. If you are an incumbent running for national office, you naturally want to show that you have helped the economy and that, while you have been in office, people have become better off. You could compare the per capita increase in GNP between 1990 and 1995, in which per capita GNP rose $4,446, or just over 19 percent. Alternatively, you could choose the base year selectively in order to show a larger increase. For example, choosing 1989 as a base year would allow an incumbent to say that per capita GNP increased by almost 25 percent from 1989 to 1995. Compare the two percentages. (Note that you first determine the change in GNP and then divide that by the amount in the base year.)

1990 per capita GNP $23,064	1989 per capita GNP $22,042
1995 per capita GNP $27,510	1995 per capita GNP $27,510
Increase: $4,446, or 19.2 percent	*Increase:* $5,468 or 24.8 percent

Candidates who were incumbents during this period would prefer to use the second set of figures to demonstrate the benefits they had brought to the country.

One other warning when dollar amounts are used for different years: inflation means that the value of the dollar is sharply lower each year. According to one analyst, "If you give your results in 1867 dollars, a dollar could buy a lot. You could get all of Alaska for $7.2 million. Using 1987 dollars, you probably couldn't buy an ice cream company for $7.2 million."[2] All of the GNP figures in the preceding paragraph are expressed in 1992 current dollars; that is, they have been corrected for inflation.

per capita amount
Summary figure for a group or geographic unit divided by the population figure.

A commonly used statistic that is very similar to percentages is the **per capita amount.** A figure that summarizes information about a geographic unit or set of people is divided by the number in the population to show what the figure means in terms of each person in the population. Data on GNP and GDP and on military and social expenditures of nations frequently are translated into per capita amounts. Such a computation can be very useful in translating large numbers into amounts that can be grasped more readily. Often the results are striking. A 1988 study of waste in the U.S. defense budget noted that each year $45 billion is lost through waste, inefficiency, or fraud. The study went on to say that if we divide that figure by the number of taxpayers, the amount is $435 for each taxpayer.[3] A report on the amount of the enormous foreign debt owed by African countries is hard to absorb. A recent study, however, effectively converted the figure to a per capita amount: "Each one of Africa's 410 million people owed foreigners about $195, or about as much as they earned in six months of toil."[4]

Frequency Distributions

frequency
Number of cases for each value of a variable.

A second way to describe a variable is to report the **frequency** of different values. *Frequency* is a word that signifies the number of cases of each value or subcategory of the variable. Usually, we report both the number and the percentage the number is of the total. If our variable is gender, we want to know the frequency of men and the frequency of women, as well as the percentage of men and women. Gender is a nominal variable, and so it is easy to report the frequency of each value. It is also easy to report the frequency and percentage of each value for ordinal variables. If we are describing persons with low, medium, and high trust, we can report the number and percentage of persons that report each degree of trust.

It is more difficult to report frequencies and percentages for interval data. For example, if you want to report the income of one hundred people, you will probably have between eighty and one hundred different values for income, because few people earn exactly the same amount. Therefore, we often change interval-level data into ordinal-level categories and report the frequency and percentage of cases in each category. For example, annual income figures can be translated into ordinal categories such as the following, using figures that fit your data:

Low income: up to $12,000

Middle income: $12,001 to $20,000

Upper-middle income: $20,001 to $40,000

High income: $40,001 and over

Using these categories, we would then report the frequency and percentage of cases that fall into each.

Frequency distributions of nominal or ordinal data can be depicted by a **bar graph.** Each bar represents one of the values of your variable. This is a

bar graph
A graphic way of depicting changes in a variable by means of bars that rise or fall on a scale that is shown on the left (vertical) axis.

FIGURE 10.1

Changes in Size of U.S. Budget, 1960–1996

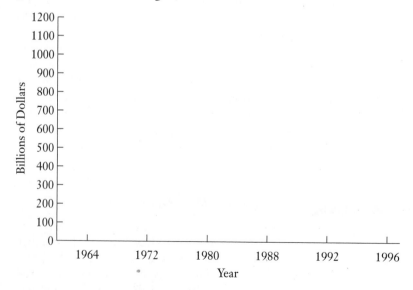

Source: *Historical Tables, Budget of the United States Government, Fiscal Year 1996* (Washington, D.C.: Executive Office of the President, Office of Management and Budget. 1995), tables 1.2, 1.3.

technique for showing changes in a variable graphically. Bar graphs compare several values by means of bars that extend to various lengths along a common scale built into the graph. Using the material in table 10.1, draw appropriate bars in the graph in figure 10.1. The bars may touch each other or be separated, but they must all be of the same width to show that length is the only dimension that varies.

line graph
A graphic depiction of change in the observed values of a single variable over time.

frequency line
Line graph depicting the frequency of values or the shape of their distribution.

If a variable is measured using ordinal- or interval-level data, you can draw a **line graph** to depict the frequency distribution. (Graphs are discussed in more detail in chapter 13; frequency lines are introduced here because they help you understand the material in this chapter.) A **frequency line** shows the general shape of the distribution of a set of values. In a graph displaying a frequency line, the values of the variable are reported along a horizontal line, and the amount or number of each value is reported on a vertical line. The amount can be expressed either in absolute numbers or in percentages. Note the following examples of frequency lines:

A. Two people score 10; three people score 20; four people score 30; and one person scores 40.

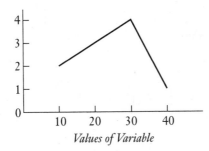

Values of Variable

B. Five percent of the class get F; 5 percent get a D; 30 percent get a C; 40 percent get a B; and 20 percent get an A.

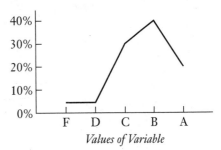

Values of Variable

C. Six cases are poor; eight cases are middle income; and four cases are wealthy.

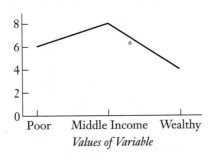

Values of Variable

D. Twenty percent score low; 40 percent score medium; and 40 percent score high.

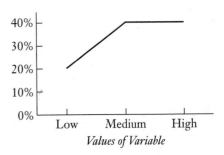

Values of Variable

As an example of data that could be used to develop a frequency line, consider the distribution of grades in your class. To draw a graph of the grade distribution, place the grades along the bottom, going from F through A (the

FIGURE 10.2
Frequency Distribution of Grades in a Class

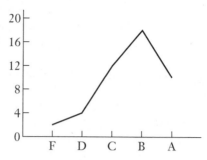

typical range). Next determine how many students have earned each of the grades; that is, how many have earned an A average, a B average, and so forth. In a class of forty-six you might get the following results: ten students with A, eighteen students with B, twelve students with C, four students with D, and two students with F. Because the numbers in each category (the frequencies) range from zero through eighteen, label the vertical line with the numerals 0 through 18 and indicate on the graph the frequency of each grade (the number of people earning each grade). (Figure 10.2 notes every fourth numeral on the vertical line to make the presentation simpler.) Then draw a line connecting the data points; this is the frequency line (see figure 10.2). Frequency lines, or frequency distributions, are useful for giving a sense of the overall shape or pattern in our data. It allows us to visualize quickly where "most" of the cases lie and which cases are relatively rare.

Frequency Distributions

**Practice
Exercise 10.2**

Frequency distributions are often used to show change over time. The dates are on the horizontal line and the amounts of the variable that is changing are on the vertical line. Draw a figure with appropriate labels and frequency lines for each of the two following sets of information. You will need to define the range and increments on the vertical line to fit the information you have.

A. The percent of the voting age population who voted in the following presidential elections was: 1972—56.0; 1976—54.3; 1980—52.6; 1984—53.1; 1988—50.1; 1992—55.09; 1996—49.08.

In this exercise the percentages are close together. On the vertical line you should identify a separate point for every percentage point between 46 and 60. (Put a number only beside the even numbers in order to make the figure less cluttered.) You would include all seven years on the horizontal line.

B. The GDP for the United States and Japan for the following years follows. United States: 1993—6259.9; 1994—6649.8; 1995—6954.8; 1996—7263.2. Japan: 1993—4275.5; 1994—4687.1; 1995—5114.0; 1996—4597.2. Note that these figures are all in billions of dollars and are at 1997 prices and exchange rates. Source: *National Accounts of OECD Countries*, 1997, volume 1.

In this second exercise you will have two frequency lines on the same figure, making it easy to compare the height and slope of these two lines. Make sure your title or heading indicates that the figures are in billions of dollars and include a note at the bottom that states that the figures are in 1997 prices and gives the source.

Measures of Central Tendency

central tendency
Value around which most of the data values are clustered; center of a series of numbers or observations.

Frequency lines visually depict the shape of the data. We can look at them and get a sense of where most of the cases lie, or where the center of gravity of the data is located. We can go one step farther and derive single and specific numerical measures to describe this **central tendency** in the data, the point where the data are most clustered. Look at figure 10.2. If you were to describe the shape of the frequency line in that figure, you might note that more people got a B than received any other single grade. Visually you could estimate that the center of the distribution was somewhere around a B– grade and that the grades ranged from F to A. Measures of central tendency and dispersion provide precise numerical values for these descriptive statements. It is also worth noting that such figures can be misleading; recall the statement at the beginning of this chapter that one could drown in a river that averages two feet of water.

Consider the students in your class. If you knew the frequency distribution of all their ages, you would probably find that the average age is nineteen or twenty. If you asked them what letter grade they anticipated receiving in the class, you could order the grades from the highest to the lowest grade and figure what the middle grade is. If you ask them whether they consider themselves Republican or Democrat, you could report which party has the most adherents. These are all measures of central tendency, and these measures vary according to the level of measurement you are working with. Age is an interval-level measure, and here the **mean** is appropriate. One's letter grade is an ordinal measure, and for that level we use the **median**. Finally, with nominal measures, such as party affiliation, we use the **mode**.

mean
Central tendency of interval-level data; obtained by totaling the observed values and dividing by the number of cases.

median
Midpoint in an ordered series of data values; used primarily with ordinal-level measures.

mode
Value that appears most frequently in a data series; used primarily with nominal measures.

MEAN

The sum of the observed values divided by the number of cases. It requires interval-level data and indicates the center of gravity of a frequency distribution. It is valuable because it takes into account all of the values in a sample.

Examples of the Mean

1. The mean value of the numbers 2, 6, 13, and 11 is

$$(2 + 6 + 13 + 11) \div 4 = 32 \div 4 = 8$$

2. In your class there are twelve students age eighteen, ten students age nineteen, eight students age twenty, and one student age twenty-four. To compute the mean age, you first multiply each age by the number in that age, then add the results, and finally divide by the total number of students.

First, multiply each age by the number of persons who are that age:

12 × 18 = 216
10 × 19 = 190
8 × 20 = 160
1 × 24 = 24
Total = 590

Then divide that "total amount of age" by the number in the class, or 31:

590 ÷ 31 = 19

Therefore, the mean age is 19.

3. Now you draw a sample of six students from your class and find the following ages:

three are eighteen years old   **3 × 18 = 54**
two are nineteen years old   **2 × 19 = 38**
one is twenty years old   **1 × 20 = 20**

The total amount of age is 112; divide that by 6, the number in the sample, and you get 18.7, which is the mean age for the sample of six students.

Thus in the entire class the mean age is 19, and in the sample of six it is 18.7.

4. The voting turnout percentages for the southeastern and northwestern states for the 1996 presidential election are as follows:

Southeastern states: Alabama, Florida, Virginia, 48; Arkansas, Kentucky, Tennessee, 47; Georgia, South Carolina, 42; Louisiana, 57; Mississippi, 45; North Carolina, 46.

Northwestern states: Colorado, 53; Idaho, 57; Montana, 62; Nevada, 38; North Dakota, 56; Oregon, 57; South Dakota, 61; Utah, 50; Washington, 55; Wyoming, 60.

Compute the average turnout for each group. First, you should multiply each turnout figure by the number of states with that turnout and then add the results together:

3 (48) + 3 (47) + 2 (42) + 57 + 45 + 46 = 144 + 141 + 84 + 57 + 45 + 46 = 517

Then divide by the number of states: 517 ÷ 11 = 47. This is the average voter turnout in the southeastern states in 1996.

Now follow the same steps for the northwestern states.[5]

Does this regional contrast surprise you? Note that the northwestern states had a considerably higher average even though one of their states, Nevada, had a much lower turnout than any of the other states.

MEDIAN

The median is the midpoint of a series of observations that have been arranged in order. The median requires ordinal rather than nominal data and may be used with interval data. If there is a large number of cases, use the following formula to locate the median value:

$$\frac{N+1}{2}$$

Examples of the Median

1. If you select three students who anticipate the grades C+, A–, and B, you would put them in order and find the midpoint: C+, B, A–. The median value is B, because there is an equal number of cases above and below B.

2. If you select six students who anticipate the grades C–, A, B, B+, C–, and A–, to find the median you could use the formula

$$\frac{N+1}{2} = \frac{6+1}{2} = \frac{7}{2} = 3.5$$

   First, place the grades in order: C–, C–, B, B+, A–, A. The formula provides the answer of 3.5. This figure means that the midway point, the median, lies between the third and fourth grades. Note that the median is not the quantity 3.5; it is the value between the third and fourth cases, between B and B+. Note also that it was necessary to put the grades in order before finding the median.

3. Assume those same six students took a quiz and got the following grades on a scale of 1 to 10: 4, 6, 7, 10, 10, 6. To find the median grade, put them in order: 4, 6, 6, 7, 10, 10. Again the 3.5 value tells you that the median is between the 6 and 7. Often it is designated 6.5 for convenience, but actually the median value is just between six and seven.

4. If you have grouped data, you would do the following to find the midpoint. Use the ages of students in the earlier-mentioned class of thirty-one: twelve students age eighteen, ten students age nineteen, eight students age twenty, and one student age twenty-four. First, put the ages in order: 18, 18, 18, 18, 18, 18, 18, 18, 18, 18, 18, 18, 19, 19, 19, 19, 19, 19, 19, 19, 19, 19, 20, 20, 20, 20, 20, 20, 20, 20, 24. Now you can apply the equation for the median:

$$\frac{31+1}{2} = \frac{32}{2} = 16$$

   Note, that 16 refers to the sixteenth value, not the age 16. Simply go to the sixteenth value in your list, which is 19 years of age. Actually, you do not need to put all 31 ages in order. You just need to begin at one end or the other until you come to the sixteenth value. There are twelve students who are eighteen; to find the sixteenth value, you need to find the fourth value following this cluster of eighteen-year-olds. The next cluster is made up of nineteen-year-olds; go to the fourth value in this cluster, the sixteenth value, which is 19.

5. If you are working with percentages, count 50 percent from either end of your distribution. That is the fiftieth percentile. The grouping that includes the fiftieth percentile is the median group or category. Consider the following two survey results. Parents and students were asked whether they thought drug abuse in local schools was a crisis or a serious problem.[6] The results were as follows:

Parents: Crisis—8%;   Serious problem—44%;   Minor problem—43%;
              Not a problem—4%

Teenagers: Crisis—6%;   Serious problem—28%;   Minor problem—51%;
              Not a problem—14%

Note: Percentages do not add to 100% because some had no opinion.

To find the median go to the category that contains the fiftieth percentile:

Parents: Serious problem
Teenagers: Minor problem

MODE

The mode is the most frequently observed value in a series. The mode is used with nominal variables, although it could be used with ordinal and interval variables.

Examples of the Mode

1. If there are more men than women in any group, then the modal value in that group is "men."
2. If there are more registered Republicans than Democrats in a community, then the modal value of *partisan registration* is "Republican."
3. If there are more students at a university majoring in business than in either liberal arts or engineering, then the modal value of majors is "business."
4. Review the example earlier of the ages of 31 students. There we found the median to be 19. The modal value, however, is 18 because there were 12 students age 18 and only 10 students age 19.

Selecting the Appropriate Measure of Central Tendency

As indicated, each of the measures—mean, median, or mode—is appropriate for a different level of measurement. You can always use a measure appropriate for lower-level data, but you cannot do the reverse and use a measure that is appropriate for a higher-level measure. Thus, you could use the median or the mode as well as the mean to analyze interval-level data. You can use only the mode to analyze nominal-level data. All other things being equal, you would use the mean to analyze interval-level data rather than the median or mode. The mean, for example, is based on information about all the specific values of the cases; the other two are not. Therefore, whenever you have interval-level measures, you would normally use the mean as your summary measure. When you have ordinal-level data, the median provides more information than the mode. The mode is appropriate only when your data are grouped into categories and you want to indicate which category has the largest number of cases.

Which measure of central tendency would you use for each of the following? (See note 7 for answers.[7])

Religion: Catholic, Protestant, Jew

Economic performance: GNP growth rate

Ideology: Very conservative, conservative, neutral, liberal, very liberal

---

There are occasions, however, when it is appropriate to select a lower measure of central tendency. For example, the median is often used for interval-level data when there are extreme values that would distort the mean. In reporting the income of a group of people, if there are a few individuals with a great deal more wealth than others, the mean would be distorted by these few high values and could be misleading. In this case the median would be a better measure of central tendency.

The following examples illustrate some of these tradeoffs. Assume you want to compare the economic development of Middle Eastern and North African nations and you decide to use per capita GNP as your measure of economic development. You collect the data contained in table 10.2 (part A). Because the data are at the interval level, it is appropriate to compute the mean per capita GNP for these seven countries. By adding the values for GNP and dividing by N (7), we get a mean of $5,316 (see table 10.2, part B). However, it might bother you that one country, Kuwait, has such a high value. Because every value is included in deriving this mean, Kuwait biases the score. As an alternative, you could decide to compute and report the median value. First, you need to arrange the countries in order (from high to low, or vice versa, it does not matter) and examine the middle value. As shown in table 10.2 (part C), the median is $1,790. Note how much lower this figure is than the mean value.

There is yet a third way to approach these data. You could decide to eliminate Kuwait from your list, because its value is so much higher than the other

TABLE 10.2
Measuring the Central Tendency of per Capita GNP in Seven Middle Eastern and North African Countries, 1994 (in U.S. dollars)

A

Egypt	720
Jordan	1,440
Kuwait	19,420
Saudi Arabia	7,050
Tunisia	1,790
Oman	5,140
Algeria	1,650

B

Mean per capita GNP = $37,210 ÷ 7 = $5,316.

C

Egypt	720
Jordan	1,440
Algeria	1,650
Tunisia	1,790
Oman	5,140
Saudi Arabia	7,050
Kuwait	19,420

The median per capita income is $1,790, the income of the fourth country, according to the formula:

$$\text{Median} = \frac{N+1}{2} = \frac{7+1}{2} = \frac{8}{2} = 4$$

D

Mean per capita GNP of six counties, omitting Kuwait = ($37,210 − 19,420) ÷ 6 = $2,965.

Source: *World Development Report, 1996* (Washington, D.C.: World Bank, 1996), pp. 188–189.

countries, and compute the mean value of the other six countries. This value is $2,965, as indicated in table 10.2 (part D). It happens to be similar to the median value for all of the countries. If you follow this course, you could report both mean values, as in table 10.3. In reporting and analyzing the data, you would compare these two figures and comment on the reasons for the contrast between Kuwait and the others.

We have discussed this example in some detail in order to emphasize that you should not routinely apply statistical measures according to set rules. Instead, examine the data, consider the purposes of your analysis, and determine which procedures are appropriate. There often is more than one way to proceed, and you will need to make a judgment. (Recall from chapter 9 that figures such as per capita income are rough approximations of the income in any nation.)

TABLE 10.3

Mean per Capita GNP, Seven Middle Eastern and
North African Nations, 1994

Seven Nations[a]	Six Poorest Nations[b]
$5,316	$2,965

Source: Data from table 10.2.

[a] Egypt; Jordan; Algeria; Tunisia; Oman; Saudi Arabia; Kuwait.
[b] Those in column one except Kuwait.

Measures of Central Tendency

**Practice
Exercise 10.3**

The answers for each question are in the accompanying endnote.

A. Do a frequency distribution, and then compute the mode, median, and mean for the following data on ground-water pollution in ten counties.[8]
County: a, 5; b, 7; c, 8; d, 9; e, 7; f, 6; g, 9; h, 6; i, 9; j, 10.

Frequency Distribution

Pollution Score	Frequency
5	_____
6	_____
7	_____
8	_____
9	_____
10	_____

Mode: _____

Median: _____

Mean: _____

B. Assume you constructed a questionnaire to determine how much people knew about current political events. Fifteen people responded and received the following scores: 5, 4, 5, 7, 6, 6, 3, 6, 7, 2,1, 6, 5, 2, 7. Do a frequency distribution of the scores, and then compute the mode, median, and mean scores.[9]

Frequency Distribution

Score	Frequency
1	_____
2	_____
3	_____
4	_____
5	_____
6	_____
7	_____

Mode: _____

Median: _____

Mean: _____

C. You sponsored a block party to raise money for a candidate running for school board. You received the following contributions: $10, $15, $12, $3, $25, $4, $2, $10, $10, $5. Compute three measures of central tendency. Compare the merits of the three measures.[10]

_____

_____

_____

D. Compute the appropriate measure of central tendency for the following data on the party affiliation of members in a political science class.[11]

Party ID	Frequency
Republican	16
Democrat	19
Independent	4
Libertarian	1

Measures of Dispersion

Variance and Standard Deviation

variance
A measure of dispersion for interval-level data; based on finding the variation around the mean.

standard deviation
A measure of dispersion for interval-level data; based on finding the variation around the mean; square root of the variance.

Variance and **standard deviation** are two versions of a second summary measure. They measure the spread of values around the central tendency. Consider the two following distributions of interval-level data:

1. 2   10   18
2. 9   10   11

In both cases the mean value is 10, but the distributions are clearly different. The values in the first distribution are much more spread out than in the second. If these numbers were people's ages, you can see the importance of the difference: a group composed of a nine-year-old, a ten-year-old, and an eleven-year-old is obviously different from a group with a two-year-old, a ten-year-old, and an eighteen-year-old. We therefore need another measure to describe a series of numbers, one that tells us how spread out around the mean the values are.

In practice exercise 10.3, part C you used some hypothetical data on contributions to a fund-raiser to compute the mean value of contributions. The answer was $9.60. It would also be interesting to know how varied the contributions were. Did most people give roughly the same amount? Or did contributions range from very high to very low? To get a precise answer, you would measure the standard deviation for these data. It makes sense that you would begin by finding the central tendency of the data and then examine how far the values are from it:

1	1	1	1		*X* 3	1		1		1				1	
2	4	6	8	10	12	14	16	18	20	22	24	26

Value of contributions ($)

This line indicates the frequency of the various contributions; the *X* on the line indicates where the mean value, 9.6, lies. You could proceed to measure the distance of each case from the mean and add these distances together. Because you would be adding the same amount of minus and positive values, however, you should see that you would always get a zero. An alternative is to square the numbers that tell you how far each value is from the mean. This procedure gives you the variance and standard deviation.[12]

Before outlining the actual sequence of steps to derive the variance and standard deviation, you need to learn the symbols used in computing them. The symbols make the formulas look forbidding until you learn what they mean.

$$X_i = \text{the value } i \text{ of variable } X$$
$$\overline{X} = \text{the mean value of variable } X$$
$$\Sigma = \text{add together}$$
$$\sigma = \text{standard deviation}$$
$$N = \text{number of cases}$$
$$\text{or } N - 1 = \text{number of cases when working with samples}$$

Now we can derive the formula for the standard deviation:

STEPS IN COMPUTING THE STANDARD DEVIATION AND VARIANCE

1. Compute the mean value: $\overline{X}$
2. Subtract the mean value from each observed value: $X_i - \overline{X}$
3. Square each of these differences: $(Xi - \overline{X})^2$.
4. Add these squared differences together: $\Sigma(Xi - \overline{X})^2$
5. Divide this sum by the number of observations. This figure is the *variance:*

$$\frac{\Sigma\left(X_i - \overline{X}\right)^2}{N}$$

6. The square root of this number is the *standard deviation:*

$$\sigma = \sqrt{\frac{\Sigma\left(X_i - \overline{X}\right)^2}{N}}$$

(The square root is used simply to return the figures to their original unit before they were squared.)

Some comments about the logic of the formula: If you simply added the differ-ences of each value from the mean, the negative and positive distances would balance out and you would get a zero. Therefore you square the differences from the mean, add them together, and divide by the number of cases. Note also that you should use $N - 1$ when you are working with a sample of cases. The result-ing number is the variance, which will be large when the cases are spread out and small when the cases are close together. But the variance is stated in squared values, which is awkward, so we use the square root to bring us back to the orig-inal units and make the final figure easier to interpret.

To illustrate the computation of the variance, we use the data about contri-butions to a political campaign from practice exercise 10.3, part C. (Since you are not using a sample, divide by N rather than $N - 1$.)

Contribution	Frequency	$\overline{X}$	$X_i - \overline{X}$	$(X_i - \overline{X})^2$
$2	1	9.60	−7.60	57.76
3	1	9.60	−6.60	43.56
4	1	9.60	−5.60	31.36
5	1	9.60	−4.40	21.16
10	3	9.60	.40	.16
		9.60	.40	.16
		9.60	.40	.16
12	1	9.60	2.40	5.76
15	1	9.60	5.40	29.16
25	1	9.60	15.40	237.17
			Sum =	426.40
			Divide by N (10) =	42.64

The result of dividing the sum by N (42.64) is the *variance*. This figure re-ports the average dispersion of values in the distribution in squared units rather than in the original units of measurement. Because the squared units are not meaningful, it is customary to convert the variance back into the original units of measurement by taking the square root of the number. This is the *standard deviation*, which is the measure of dispersion frequently reported with the mean. It is simply the square root of the variance. For our data it is the square root of

$$\sqrt{42.64} = 6.5 = \sigma$$

Standard deviations are hard to interpret by themselves. They are most use-ful when you are comparing the dispersion or standard deviations for two clus-ters of similar cases. For example, say that a friend held a block party to raise funds for the candidate in another part of the city. She took in the following contributions: $5, $5, $8, $6, $9, $4, $10, $12, $8, $10. Compute the mean value, variance, and standard deviation for these contributions:

Contribution	Frequency	$\overline{X}$	$X_i - \overline{X}$	$(X_i - \overline{X})^2$
4	1	7.7	−3.7	13.69
5	2	7.7	−2.7	7.29
			−2.7	7.29
6	1	7.7	−1.7	2.89
8	2	7.7	0.3	0.09
			0.3	0.09
9	1	7.7	1.3	1.69
10	2	7.7	2.3	5.29
			2.3	5.29
12	1	7.7	4.3	18.49

$$\text{Total} = 62.10$$
$$\text{Variance} = 62.10 \div N\,(10) = 6.21$$
$$\text{Square root of } 6.21 = 2.5 = \sigma$$

The standard deviation for the first set of contributions is 6.5, whereas for the second set of contributions, it is a much lower figure, 2.5. What does this tell us? It tells us that at the first block party there was a greater diversity or range of contributions. Some gave a lot and some gave a little. At the second block party, the range was much smaller. People gave similar amounts. If you look over the two frequencies, you will see the differences yourself.

Example of the Standard Deviation

As the preceding example indicates, the standard deviation is useful for comparing the extent of diversity or homogeneity in a set of data or group of cases. We can use it to analyze the variation in ideology among groups of senators. *Congressional Quarterly* regularly publishes studies of congressional voting behavior and frequently develops indexes of such concepts as "conservatism" and "liberalism." Each index is composed of a series of votes that the researchers believe indicates how conservative or liberal a congressional representative is. Table 10.4 reports the percentage of times in 1996 that Republican senators voted for the conservative position. The higher their score, the more conservative the senators are, according to this measure. The table groups the senators by region of the country and reports their conservatism scores.

The information in table 10.4 is hard to absorb, and it is difficult to compare the different regions. Computing the mean score on conservatism for the senators from each region makes analysis easier because it allows us to compare the conservatism of each group of senators. To compute the mean conservative score for the senators from the East, we first add:

$$86 + 81 + 79 + 89 + 92 + 89 + 92 + 66 + 68 + 59 = 801$$

TABLE 10.4
Conservative Coalition Support Scores of Republican Senators, by Region, 1996

East	Midwest	South	West
Roth, DE, 86	Coats, IN, 89	Shelby, AL, 92	Murkowski, AK, 97
Cohen, ME, 81	Lugar, IN, 92	Mack, FL, 100	Stevens, AK, 92
Snowe, ME, 79	Grassley, IA, 82	Coverdell, GA, 97	Kyl, AZ, 97
Gregg, NH, 89	Kassebaum, KS, 85	McConnell, KY, 95	McCain, AZ, 97
Smith, NH, 92	Frahm, KS, 96	Cochran, MS, 94	Brown, CO, 74
D'Amato, NY, 89	Abraham, MI, 95	Lott, MS, 97	Campbell, CO, 86
Santorum, PA, 92	Grams, MN, 92	Faircloth, NC, 89	Craig, ID, 97
Specter, PA, 66	Ashcroft, MO, 89	Helms, NC, 97	Kempthorne, ID, 97
Chafee, RI, 68	Bond, MO, 100	Inhofe, OK, 97	Burns, MT, 95
Jeffords, VT, 59	DeWine, OH, 92	Nickles, OK, 97	Domenici, NM, 94
		Thurmond, SC, 95	Hatfield, OR, 57
		Frist, TN, 97	Pressler, SD, 92
		Thompson, TN, 92	Gorton, WA, 95
		Gramm, TX, 97	Simpson, WY, 89
		Hutchison, TX, 95	Thomas, WY, 95
		Warner, VA, 89	

Source: Based on scores from *CQ Weekly Report*, 21 December 1996, p. 3470.

Then we divide by the number of senators:

$$\frac{801}{10} = 80.1 = \textit{mean score}$$

Following the same procedure for the ten Republican senators from the Midwest, we add their scores and divide by 11:

$$\frac{89 + 92 + 82 + 85 + 96 + 95 + 92 + 89 + 100 + 92 + 92}{10} = \frac{1004}{10} = 100.4$$

The two mean values furnished in table 10.5 tell us that the Republican senators from the Midwest, as a group, are more conservative than the Republican senators from the East. This fact probably does not surprise you because of what is commonly known about the two regions. Complete the table by computing the mean values for the other two regions (answers in endnotes).[13]

TABLE 10.5
Conservative Coalition Voting Scores for Republican Senators, by Region, 1987

	East	Midwest	South	West
Mean	80.1	100.4	_____	_____

Now that you know the mean scores, you can compare the relative conservatism in the different regions. Knowing the mean conservatism value is useful, but it would also be interesting to know if all of the senators in a region have the same degree of conservatism, or whether conservatism varies significantly within regions. Put another way, we are asking if there is more variation among senators in some regions than in others. It may be that in one region all of the senators have very similar scores, whereas in another region their scores vary a great deal. Before proceeding, ask yourself which regions you think will be the most homogeneous, that is, have the least variation among their senators. The standard deviation can give you a measure to verify or correct your prediction.

The following are the steps for figuring the standard deviation for the Republican senators from the East.

X_i	$\overline{X}$	$X_i - \overline{X}$	$(X_i - \overline{X})^2$
86	80.1	5.9	34.81
81	80.1	0.9	.81
79	80.1	−1.1	1.21
89	80.1	.9	9.21
92	80.1	11.9	141.61
89	80.1	8.9	79.21
92	80.1	11.9	141.61
66	80.1	−14.1	198.81
68	80.1	−12.1	146.41
59	80.1	−21.1	445.21

$$\text{Total} = 1268.90$$
$$\text{Divide by } N = 126.89$$
$$\text{Square root} = 11.26, \text{ or } 11 = \sigma$$

Now do the same for the senators from the other three regions, and compare the results (answers in endnotes).[14]

Applying the Standard Deviation

The standard deviation has many uses in analyzing data patterns. For example, it can be used to compare how much equality there is within a political unit. If everyone has an income close to the mean, then the unit has more equality than does a second unit where some are very poor and some are very rich. Thus, the lower the standard deviation of income within a political unit—the less diversity of income—the greater the income equality.[15]

Consider another use of the standard deviation. It can be used to measure how progressive a tax system is. A progressive tax system is one in which the wealthy are taxed at a higher rate than are the less wealthy. A progressive tax system would therefore have a higher standard deviation—a greater variation among tax rates or tax burdens—than a system in which everyone paid the same rate. Review the data in table 10.6, which reports the percentage of income that different income groups paid in state and local taxes in eight cities.

Compute the standard deviation for each city. That will give you a measure of the extent to which different income groups pay different tax rates. Because the tax rates increase with income group, it provides you with a measure of how progressive the tax rate is.

Because 0.84 is larger than 0.36, you can conclude that the tax rate in Atlanta is slightly more progressive than the tax rate in Baltimore. Compute the standard deviations for the other cities and enter them in table 10.7. Then draw your conclusions.[16]

TABLE 10.6
Estimated State and Local Taxes Paid by a Family of Four in Selected Large Cities, by Income Level, 1994

City	Percentage of Income by Income Level			
	$25,000	$50,000	$75,000	$100,000
Atlanta	9.0	9.7	11.0	10.9
Baltimore	10.9	11.3	11.8	11.7
Memphis	7.6	6.4	6.7	6.3
Columbus, Ohio	8.7	9.3	10.2	10.5
Los Angeles	6.7	8.0	10.7	11.2
New York City	10.6	13.5	15.2	15.6
Portland, Maine	11.8	12.7	14.7	14.6
Washington, D.C.	8.6	9.1	10.4	10.8

Source: U.S. Bureau of the Census, *Statistical Abstract of the United States, 1996* (116th edition) Washington, D.C., 1996, table 490.

Atlanta

X_i	$\overline{X}$	$X_i - \overline{X}$	$(X_i - \overline{X})^2$
9.0	10.15	−1.15	.3225
9.7	10.15	−0.45	0.2025
11.0	10.15	0.85	0.7225
10.9	10.15	0.75	0.5625

Total = 2.81
Divide by 4 = 0.7025
Square root = 0.8382
Standard deviation = .84 = σ

Baltimore

X_i	$\overline{X}$	$X_i - \overline{X}$	$(X_i - \overline{X})^2$
10.9	11.425	−0.525	0.2756
11.3	11.425	−0.125	0.0156
11.8	11.425	0.375	0.1406
11.7	11.425	0.275	0.0756

Total = 0.5074
Divide by 4 = 0.1269
Square root = 0.3562
Standard deviation = .36 = σ

TABLE 10.7

Standard Deviations for Percentage of Income
Paid in State and Local Taxes, across Income
Levels

Atlanta	.84
Baltimore	.36
Memphis	
Columbus	
Los Angeles	
New York City	
Portland	
Washington, D.C.	

Measures of Dispersion: Range, Percentiles, and Interquartile Range

range
A measure of dispersion
that indicates the difference between the lowest
and the highest values.

Another and much simpler measure of dispersion is to report the **range,** the difference between the highest and lowest value. For example, the range of conservatism scores in table 10.4 is 100 to 57. It would be interesting to compare the
range of scores within each region:

East, range is 59 to 92

Midwest, range is 82 to 100

South, range is 89 to 100

West, range is 57 to 97

According to these measures, Republican senators in the Midwest and South are
more homogeneous than those in the other two regions.

The range, however, can be misleading if there is even one unusually low or
high score. An alternative is to report one or several percentiles. X percentile is a
number such that once all the values are placed in order, x percent of the numbers
in a distribution fall below it, and the rest fall above it. The fiftieth percentile,
therefore, is the median value, and 50 percent of the cases in a distribution are
below it. Note that several cases could have the median value. For the scores 20,
40, 90, 90, 90, 95, 99, the median value is 90, but there are several scores of 90.
Thus 50 percent of the values are below the median in the rank order but not
necessarily below it in value. If you have taken the College Board or Graduate
Record Exams, your performance was reported both as a score and as a percentile. If you scored at the eightieth percentile, then 80 percent of those taking

the test had scores at or below yours, and 20 percent had higher scores. If you want to report the twenty-fifth percentile of a range of data, put the observations in numerical order, compute 25 percent of the number of observations and go to that value. To describe the dispersion in a set of data you could report the score at the twenty-fifth and seventy-fifth percentiles.

interquartile range
A measure of dispersion that indicates the difference between the lowest and the highest quarters, or fourths, of the cases.

Another name for reporting the values of twenty-fifth and seventy-fifth percentiles is the **interquartile range.** It divides the range of figures into fourths or quartiles (or groups of 25 percent) and reports the range of values in the middle two quartiles. To compute this, rank the cases in order, then divide the number of cases into quarters, or fourths. The interquartile range includes the two middle quarters. Thus, it extends from the first value of the second quarter to the final value of the third quarter. To find the interquartile range for the conservatism scores of senators, determine how many scores fall into each quartile, put the scores in order, and count up from the bottom according to the number of units in a quartile to find one end of the range and down from the top to find the other end of the range.

East: 92, 92, 89, 89, 86, 81, 79, 68, 66, 59
Each quartile includes 2½ units.
Interquartile range goes from 68 to 89

Midwest: 100, 96, 95, 92, 92, 92, 89, 89, 85, 82
Each quartile includes 2¾ units.
Interquartile range goes from 89 to 95.

South: 100, 97, 97, 97, 97, 97, 97, 97, 95, 95, 95, 94, 92, 92, 89, 89
Each quartile includes 4 units.
Interquartile range goes from 94 to 97.

West: 97, 97, 97, 97, 97, 95, 95, 95, 94, 92, 89, 86, 74, 59, 57
Each quartile includes 3¾ units.
Interquartile range goes from 86 to 97.

Based on these measures, you would conclude that there is greater variation in the East than in the other regions.

Where We Are

You have now learned some techniques for describing variables, for showing the pattern of the values of a variable, and for computing summary measures for describing the information you have collected. They are useful to help you better understand the information and to help you answer your research question. They are particularly useful when you want to compare several variables or sets of cases. Percentages enable us to compare data with different bases, and frequency distributions are helpful in describing patterns in variables. Measures of central tendency and of dispersion provide specific summary measures of information about the shape of the data—their clustering and degree of variation. They are also useful because they help you communicate what you have found to others in a memorable and comprehensible way. Always go back to your research question and ask yourself what figures are appropriate for that question. Experiment with different ways of examining and reporting the information to portray a full and accurate picture of your findings. The next chapter continues this topic by introducing additional statistics that go beyond simply describing data to tell us whether several variables are related to each other.

NOTES

1. Answers for exercise 10.1: A. 21.9 percent; B. Zambia, .4 percent; United States, .9 percent. Percent of voting age population registered to vote is 65.9 percent; percent of registered voters who turned out for all elections is 54.2 percent.
2. Nancy Spruill, "Rinse Away That Dreaded Statistic Cling," *Washington Post*, 9 February 1987, p. A16.
3. "The Business of Defense," ABC News, 1 December 1988.
4. Stephen Haykin, *Policy Reform Programs in Africa* (Washington, DC: U.S. Agency for International Development, 1987), p. 4.
5. 53 + 2 (57) + 62 + 38 + 56 + 61 + 50 + 55 + 60 = 549 (10) = 54.9
6. Richard Morin and Mario Brossard, "Communication Breakdown on Drugs," The *Washington Post*, 4 March 1997, p. A1.
7. Religion, mode; economic performance, mean; ideology, median.
8. Mode, 9; median, 7.5; mean, 7.6. Note the median is between the fifth and sixth values. Since these are different, the median is between 7 and 8. Note to arrive at the mean, add the values to get 76; divide by 10; the result is 7.6.
9. Mode, 6; median, 5; mean, 4.8. The formula for the median directs you to the eighth value; put the numbers in order; the eighth value is 5. To get the mean add the values, getting 72; divide by the number of values, which is 15; the mean is 4.8.
10. Mode, $10; median, $10; mean, $9.60. The formula for the median gives you 5.5, which directs you to a value between the fifth and sixth contributions; since both are 10, the median value is $10. To get the mean add the figures, getting 96; divide by 10; the mean value is 9.6. These figures are all very close together, suggesting that the contributions are fairly spread out across the range of contributions. The two low ones are balanced by the high one, which causes the mean value to be close to the median value.
11. You would use the mode, and you would report that the modal value is Democratic. It would be inappropriate to use either of the other measures of central tendency.
12. These measures are useful because they can be linked with probability theory and used in other statistical procedures. David and Chava Nachmias, *Research Methods in the Social Sciences*, 2d ed. (New York: St. Martin's Press, 1981), pp. 310–312.
13. South = 1520/16 = 95; West = 1354/15 = 90.
14. Mean for South = 95; West = 90; Standard deviation for East = 11; Midwest = 10; South = 3; West = 11.

15. Compare the Gini Index, which also measures inequality and was described in chapter 9. The lower the Gini Index, the great the equality.
16. Memphis, .5; Columbus, .7; Los Angeles, 1.87; New York, 1.97; Portland, 1.24; Washington, .9. Los Angeles and New York have the largest diversity of tax rates, presumably more progressive.

EXERCISES

Exercise 10.1 Describing Trends in Opinion of Most Important Problem

The following are data from Gallup surveys asking respondents about their opinions on the most important problems facing the United States. The data report the dates on which the surveys were taken and the percentage of respondents mentioning each problem.

Problem	May 1989	April 1990	April 1991	March 1992	January 1993	January 1994	January 1995
Unemployment		3	8	25	22	17	15
Crime	6	2		5	9	49	27
Ethics, moral decline	5	1	4	5	7	8	6
Education	3	1	6	8	8	6	5
Economy (general)	34	7	20	42	35	17	10
Poverty	10	11	13	15	15	9	10
Budget deficit		6	6	8	13	8	14

Source: Gallup polls reported in annual collections, *The Gallup Poll.*

Note: Totals do not add to 100 percent because some respondents gave multiple answers, and not all answers are reported here.

1. Select two issues that would be interesting to compare. Do a frequency line for each on the same graph, indicating changes in the percentage of respondents reporting it as the most important problem. Hint: Put "years" along the bottom axis and "percentage of respondents" on the vertical axis. Label each line according to the problem it represents.
2. Select two other issues that would be interesting to compare. Compute the mean percentage reporting them as the most important problem over the years and the standard deviation. Interpret your findings.

Exercise 10.2 Measures of Central Tendency and Dispersion

Table 10.8 presents data on adult literacy for two groups of nations selected at random.

TABLE 10.8

National Adult Literacy Rates, by Income, 1995

Middle-Income Countries		Low-Income Countries	
Saudi Arabia	63	Pakistan	38
Thailand	94	Burma (Myanmar)	83
Bolivia	83	Kenya	78
Morocco	44	Haiti	45
Jordan	87	Rwanda	60
Turkey	82	Sierra Leone	31
Chile	95	Nepal	27
Algeria	62	India	48
Colombia	91	Egypt	51
Panama	91	Bangladesh	38

Source: *World Development Report, 1996* (Washington, D.C.: World Bank, 1996), pp. 188–189.6.

1. What is the best measure of central tendency for these data? Compute it for each set.
2. Select a second measure of central tendency you could use, and compute it.
3. What is the best measure of dispersion of the data? Compute it and interpret what it tells you.
4. What is the range and interquartile range for each set of data?

Exercise 10.3 Computing Central Tendencies and Dispersion

The following are turnout figures for three kinds of elections. Compute the appropriate measures of central tendency and dispersion, and write a short analysis of your findings. The presidential election data and U.S. House of Representatives off-year election data are taken from the *Statistical Abstract of the United States, 1996*, except for the 1996 turnout figure, which was reported by the Federal Election Commission (http://www.fec.gov/pages/96to.htm). The turnout data for elections around the world are taken from the *Journal of Democracy* and media reports.

U.S. Presidential elections: 1960, 62.8%; 1964, 61.9%; 1968, 60.9%; 1972, 55.2%; 1976, 53.5%; 1980, 52.6%; 1984, 53.1%; 1988, 50.1%; 1992, 55.1%; 1996, 49.1%. (Note: The percentage turnout reported here refers to those who voted in the presidential election in 1996 and is smaller than the overall percentage reported by the Census Bureau as having voted in 1996. Compare this to the information in practice exercise 10.1.C.)

U.S. House of Representatives, off-year elections: 1962, 45.4%; 1966, 45.4%; 1970, 43.5%; 1974, 35.9%; 1978, 34.9%; 1982, 38.0%; 1986, 33.4%; 1990, 33.1%; 1994, 36%.

Selected parliamentary and legislative elections worldwide, July 1995–May 1997: Algeria, 75%; Armenia, 37.8%; Bangladesh, 10%; Belarus, 52%; France, 68%, Ghana, 77%; Haiti, 27.9%; Mongolia, 87.3%; South Korea, 63.9%; United Kingdom, 71.3%.

1. Compute the mean and median for each set. Is the median more appropriate than the mean for any of the sets?
2. Compute the interquartile range for each set.

CHAPTER ELEVEN

Measures of Relationships

Formal statistics provide the investigator with tools useful in conducting thoughtful research; these tools are not a substitute for either thinking or working. A major goal for the statistical training of students should be statistical thinking rather than statistical formulas.

—Frederick Mosteller and Robert Bush, "Selected Quantitative Techniques," in *Handbook of Social Psychology*, ed. Gardner Lindzey

Measuring Relationships

The preceding chapter showed you how to compute measures to describe single variables. As you recall from earlier chapters, however, often in political analysis we want to examine relationships between and among variables. We want to determine if two variables are associated with each other and if one causes the other. This chapter describes a number of techniques we can use to describe and measure relationships. We begin with two fairly simple techniques: percentage differences and comparison of central tendencies. The next section describes measures we can use to describe associations among nominal- and ordinal-level variables. The third section describes regression analysis, appropriate for interval-level data. The emphasis is on the logic and purpose in applying the different measures. Some formulas are presented so that you can compute a few of the measures. For the most part we assume you can generate the measures on a computer or can refer for more details to one of many texts that emphasize statistical analysis.

Percentage Differences

percentage difference
Difference between the percentage values of the dependent variable for different groups of the independent variable.

The simplest way to demonstrate the strength of a relationship is to compute the **percentage difference** between two categories of the independent variable. You were introduced to this technique in chapter 5. Assume there are eighteen people in your class who live on campus and twelve who commute. You want to

307

TABLE 11.1

Voter Turnout of Students, by Place of Residence

Turnout	Dormitories	Off-Campus
No	8	4
Yes	10	8

know if place of residence has an influence on voter turnout. *Turnout* is the dependent variable and *residence* is the independent variable. The latter has two values: "dormitories" and "off-campus." You hypothesize that commuters are more apt to vote than those who live on campus. You reason that they are more apt to live at home and hence to be involved in local politics. You find that ten of those who live in dorms voted and eight of those who commute voted (see table 11.1). Is there a relationship between residence and turnout? Does residence make a causal difference? Are commuters more apt to vote?

One way to answer these questions is to compare the percentages of those who voted among dormitory and off-campus residents; that is, compare the values of the dependent variable for each category of the independent variable. Review the rules for setting up tables. Forty-four percent is the percentage of those who live in dormitories who did not vote. Recall that it is the convention to compute the percentages of the column total rather than of the row total. The "100%" at the bottom of each column reminds you that the numbers in the cell were computed in this way. Note also that the table indicates the number *(N)* of respondents on which the percentages are based. Thus, readers can compute the number in each cell if they want to. To determine the column percentages, divide each cell by the total in that column. Complete table 11.2.

TABLE 11.2

Voter Turnout of Students, by Place of Residence (in percentages)

Turnout	Dormitories	Off-Campus
No	44%	_____
Yes	_____	_____
	100%	100%
	N = 18	*N* = 12

TABLE 11.3
Citizen Contact of Government Officials, by Satisfaction with Services

Contact	Satisfaction	
	Yes	*No*
Yes	21%	33%
No	79	67
	100%	100%
	N = 4,293	304

Source: *The Fulton County Survey*, 1976 (Atlanta: Georgia State University, n.d.).

TABLE 11.4
Percentage of Citizens Reporting Contact of Government Officials, by Satisfaction with Services

	Satisfaction	
	Yes	*No*
	21%	33%
	N = 4,293	304

Source: *The Fulton County Survey*, 1976 (Atlanta: Georgia State University, n.d.).

The percentage difference tells you that more off-campus students or commuters voted, confirming the hypothesis. The figure does not establish causality, however. That conclusion comes only from the theory and a logical interpretation of the data.

Percentage difference is _____

Hypothesis confirmed _____ not confirmed _____ .

If the table is fairly simple, with either two-by-two or three-by-three rows and columns, then it is usually sufficient to report the numbers at the bottom of each column. If the table has more cells, you may choose to report the N in each cell. In that case, the convention is to place the N in parentheses just below or beside the percentage in each cell. Sometimes tables can be further simplified. If you have only two values of the dependent variable to report, such as "yes" and "no," or "Republican" and "Democrat," once you know the percentage of one of the values, the other will automatically be 100 percent minus that percentage. Therefore, you will often see tables in which only one of the values is reported. Examine tables 11.3 and 11.4, and satisfy yourself that they are expressing the same information.[1] Note also that the title of table 11.4 is changed from that of table 11.3.

Percentage differences are useful when there are only two values of the independent variable, as is true in tables 11.3 and 11.4. Then it is clear that you subtract the figure for one value of the independent variable from the second value. If there are more than two values of the independent variable, however, it is not clear which columns to compare. Assume that satisfaction was coded "A lot," "Some," and "None," and the percentage of voters in each category was as follows:

	Satisfaction	
A Lot	*Some*	*None*
18	28	33

You could compare the lowest and the highest categories of the independent variable or subtract the two columns of most relevance to the theory you are using. A single percentage difference, however, cannot capture all of the information you are given in the table.

Comparing Central Tendencies

difference of means or medians
Comparison of the appropriate central tendency in two groups.

A second way to examine relationships is to compare the central tendency of each value of the independent variable, or to compute the **difference of means or medians.** If your study examines whether gender has an influence on earning power, you could compare the mean or median income of women with that of men. This choice is appropriate when the dependent variable is an interval or ordinal measure and you can compute either a median or mean value for each category of the independent variable. Recall that earlier you compared the economic growth patterns of democratic and authoritarian political systems. You relied on percentage differences to analyze the data and compared the percentage of each group of countries that ranked high on economic growth. Now that you know how to compute measures of central tendency, you could compare the median or mean values of economic growth for both democracies and authoritarian political systems.

The following study uses central tendencies to analyze data. It compares how local political executives spend their time. Studies of political executives often note that they play a variety of roles. Some emphasize management and administration; some focus on legislation and policy issues; some emphasize political relationships. Questionnaires were sent to local officials asking them how much time they spent on each of these roles; 559 were returned. The results were reported according to the status of the leader—elected mayor or appointed city manager—and according to the size of the jurisdiction. Thus the study controls for changes in these two variables—status quo and size—by holding them constant. That is, it focuses first on all small cities, and then on a second group, all medium-size cities, and so forth. The results are reported in table 11.5.

It would be reasonable to hypothesize first that mayors are more apt to emphasize a political role than managers do, while managers are more apt to play an administrative role. A second reasonable hypothesis is that executives of either type—manager or mayor—play a greater political role the larger the jurisdiction. The logic is that there would be more competing interests in a larger unit and political bargaining among them would be more important. Be certain you

TABLE 11.5
Mean Percentage of Time Spent in Roles by Municipal Chief Executives

	Mayors			City Managers		
	Size of Jurisdiction			*Size of Jurisdiction*		
Role	*Small*	*Medium*	*Large*	*Small*	*Medium*	*Large*
Manager	49%	49%	38%	52%	50%	51%
Policy	25	24	26	30	34	33
Political	27	27	35	18	16	19
	100%	100%	100%	100%	100%	100%

Source: Adapted from Charldean Newell and David N. Ammons, "Role Emphases of City Managers and Other Municipal Executives," *Public Administration Review* 47 (May/June 1987): 246–253.

Notes: Figures may not add to 100 percent due to rounding.

know what the figure in each cell represents. For example the figure 49 percent in the first column says that mayors in small jurisdictions spend nearly half their time on management. Given your hypotheses it would be fruitful to examine the average time that city managers and mayors spend on politics compared to each other and compared across different sized jurisdictions. Ask yourself what the data tell you.

_____

_____

_____

_____

_____

_____

_____

_____

(Some patterns you might note: Both mayors and city managers spend more of their time on management than on either of the other two roles, especially those serving in small and medium jurisdictions. In large jurisdictions, city managers spend most of their time on management roles, about 50 percent; while mayors emphasize both management and political roles, 38 and 35 percent, respectively. Overall, mayors spend more of their time on political roles than managers do, especially in large jurisdictions. Size of jurisdiction does not seem to influence how managers spend their time, but it does have an influence on how mayors spend their time.)

Practice Exercise 11.1

Computing Percentage Differences and Measures of Central Tendency to Measure Relationships

Return to the data in table 10.5 reporting conservatism scores of Republican senators. Analyze the relationship between the two variables, *region* and *conservatism score*. State a null and working hypothesis that posits a relationship between these two variables. (The null hypothesis states that conservatism does not vary by region. As a working hypothesis you might propose that Republican senators from the West and the South are more conservative than those from the East and the Midwest.)

Now test your hypothesis by examining percentage differences and comparing mean scores. Use the information in table 10.4 on conservatism among Republican senators, by region. The information reported there is at the interval level but can easily be converted to ordinal scores as follows: very conservative, 90–100; moderately conservative, 80–89, less conservative, below 80. This change allows you to count, by region, the numbers of senators who fall into each category:

	East	Midwest	South	West
Very conservative	2	6	14	11
Moderately conservative	4	4	2	2
Less conservative	4	0	0	2
Total	10	10	16	15

TABLE 11.6
Degrees of Conservatism of Republican Senators, by Region, in Percentages

	East	Midwest	South	West
Very conservative	20%	_____	_____	_____
Moderately conservative	40%	_____	_____	_____
Less conservative	40%	_____	_____	_____
	100%	_____	_____	_____
	N =10	_____	_____	_____

TABLE 11.7

Mean Conservatism Scores of Republican
Senators, by Region

	East	Midwest	South	West
$X =$	80.1	———	———	———
$N =$	10	———	———	———

Based on these data, compute the percentage of senators in each category, and then complete table 11.6. Next, using the information from table 10.5 on mean conservatism scores for the senators from each region, complete table 11.7.[2]

Comment on the value of these two types of summary measures. Do they help you see patterns and draw comparisons?

_____

_____

_____

_____

_____

_____

_____

_____

Percentage differences and comparisons of central tendencies are easy to compute, are readily understood by others, and give you an immediate feel for any patterns there may be. For these reasons they are good places to begin your analysis, and they may even be sufficient for your purposes. The next sections introduce additional and somewhat more precise measures.

The Logic of Strength of Relationship

strength of relationship
Extent to which changes in one variable are accompanied by changes in another variable.

We can supplement percentage differences with single statistics that indicate the strength of a relationship by summarizing the overall pattern of the data in a table. **Strength of relationship** indicates whether changes in one variable are accompanied by changes in a second variable and by how much. Consider the following hypothetical tables. You can assume they are reporting the percentage of men and women who say "yes" or "no" as follows:

	Men	Women
Yes		
No		

We follow the convention that the cells are in the following order:

a	c
b	d

(1)	100%	0%	(2)	95%	10%	(3)	40%	55%	(4)	0%	100%
	0	100		5	90		60	45		100	0
	100%	100%		100%	100%		100%	100%		100%	100%

Table (1) depicts a perfect positive relationship between the two variables; all of the values in each column coincide with one of the values of the dependent variable. (All of the men say "yes" and all of the women say "no.") We say there is a strong (or perfect) relationship between these two variables. Table (4) depicts a perfect negative relationship; tables (2) and (3) depict variations in between, with (3) depicting the weakest relationship. Note that the strongest relationship occurs when all of the cases are in cells a and d and none in b and c, or vice versa. We can build on this fact to talk about the strength of a relationship, noting that the higher the percentage of cases that fall in a and d (or in b and c), the stronger the relationship.

It would be useful to devise a single measure that describes how the cases fall in these four tables. Such a measure would allow us to summarize the strength of each relationship and to compare the relationships with one another. One way to proceed is to take the number of cases that show a positive relationship and subtract the number of cases that show a negative relationship.

The symbol Q stands for a measure of strength of relationship that is based directly on this logic. (Also known as **Yule's Q.**) The formula for Q is:

> **Yule's *Q***
> Statistical measure for nominal-level data with only two values.

$$Q = \frac{ad - bc}{ad + bc}$$

The formula shows you one way to manipulate the figures to express a relationship between the number of cases that show a positive relationship and those that show a negative relationship. Take the product of the cases that fall into cells a and d, those that indicate a positive relationship. Subtract the product of the cases that fall in the opposite direction, b and c, those that indicate a negative relationship. Divide this number by the sum of the same two products. The resulting number tells you how strongly the two variables are related.

The resulting number, or the value of Q, has several characteristics. It varies from -1.00 to $+1.00$, a number telling how strong the relationship is. The closer the number is to either -1.00 or $+1.00$, the stronger the relationship; .9 is stronger than .3, which is stronger than .1. Similarly, $-.8$ is stronger than $-.2$ or $+.3$. The signs tell you whether the direction of the relationship is negative or positive. Q is used primarily with nominal variables, which means there is no necessary way to order the values. If the independent variable is gender, either male or female could be placed in the left column. As a result, the sign of Q (– or +) is purely a function of how the variables are ordered. Confirm this point in the following tables, which report Q values of +.71 and −.71. Both of these values tell us that gender has a strong influence on one's answer and that women are more apt than men to answer "yes."

	Men	Women		Women	Men
No	6	2	**No**	2	6
Yes	4	8	**Yes**	8	4

$Q = +.71$ $Q = -.71$

There is one other characteristic of Q that illustrates an important lesson about statistical measures: even if a measure is appropriate, given the number of cells and the level of measurement, it may not be appropriate for the distribution of cases. In the case of Q the formula requires that you multiply the frequencies in the cells by each other. The result is that if there is a zero in any one of the cells, you will compute a perfect relationship. For example:

$$\begin{matrix} 6 & 0 \\ 4 & 10 \end{matrix} \quad \frac{(6 \times 10) - (4 \times 0)}{(6 \times 10) + (4 \times 0)} = \frac{60}{60} = +1.00$$

In reality it is not a perfect relationship, because four cases out of twenty do not fit it. In such cases you may choose not to use Q. You need always to examine the pattern in your data to determine if a given relationship measure seems to be fitting.

We can think of the logic behind strength of relationship in a second, closely related way. Such measures tell us whether knowledge about the values of the independent variables helps us to predict the value of the dependent variable. Assume you know there are twenty people in a room, and that eight of them oppose a proposal and twelve support it. If you were asked to guess how one of the people, Sam, voted, you would be wise to guess he supported it, since you would be right twelve out of twenty times.

Now let's say you are given the information in the preceding table about the numbers of men and women who say "yes." You learn that the men are more apt to say "no." Do the new data improve your chances of being correct? Because Sam is a man, should you change your guess? Yes. Because the men were more apt to vote "no" than were the women, you would guess that Sam opposed the measure, and you would be right six out of ten times. If the same proportion of men and women had supported the measure, you should stay with your original guess, since the new information would not improve your chances of guessing correctly. If the new information about the independent variable helps you improve your guess, we can say the variables are related. The more the information helps, the stronger the relation.

Consider the question of how much support for the president there is in Congress. One indicator of support is the number of congressional votes favoring the president's position on a bill. It happens that 66 senators opposed President Bill Clinton's position on the constitutional balanced budget amendment in 1997 and 34 senators supported him. If we want to estimate how a senator from our state voted, we would guess that he or she opposed the president's position. We would be right 66 times and wrong 34 times.

Is there any other variable that is probably related to support for or opposition to the president's position and that could improve our ability to guess how our senator voted? You might have thought of *party*. It is reasonable to hypothesize that Democratic senators would be more apt to support Clinton, a Democrat, than would Republican senators. Research gives us the information in table 11.8. We could collect similar information on a second bill, as reported in table 11.9.

A casual glance at the data in tables 11.8 and 11.9 tells us that party does seem to make a difference, but it affects the two votes differently. It is difficult to use the raw figures in the two tables to tell how much influence party affiliation has and to compare its influence on the two issues. We can ask whether information about the party affiliation of a senator helps us guess how he or she voted, and if so, by how much. If it does improve our ability to guess our senator's vote for a particular bill, then there is a relationship. If it does not, we would have to conclude that party does not appear to have a relationship or that it is very weak.

Use this logic to compare the information in tables 11.8 and 11.9. In studying the constitutional balanced budget amendment vote, if we knew nothing about party vote, we might guess that our senator supported the amendment in opposition to the president's position, and we would be correct 66 times and wrong 34 times. Once we know the votes by party affiliation, however, we could improve our guess. If we know that our senator is a Democrat, we would guess that he or she voted to oppose the amendment and support the president's position and we would be right 34 times and wrong 11 times. If we knew that our senator was a Republican, we would guess that he or she opposed the president's

TABLE 11.8

Senate Support for Constitutional Balanced Budget Amendment, by Party, 1997 (President Opposed Amendment)

	Republican	Democrat
Supported	55	11
Opposed	0	34

Source: *CQ Weekly Report*, 8 March 1997, p. 604.

TABLE 11.9
Senate Support for President on Chemical
Weapons Treaty, by Party, 1997

	Republican	Democrat
Supported	29	45
Opposed	26	0

Source: *CQ Weekly Report*, 26 April 1997, p. 979.

position and we would be right 55 times and wrong zero times. Not knowing the party affiliation produced a chance of being wrong 34 times; knowing the party affiliation reduced the chances of error to 11 times. The fact that knowing the party affiliation led to a reduction in errors means that party does have an influence on a senator's support for or opposition to the president's position.

Follow this logic for guessing support for the president on the chemical weapons treaty. (Answers in the endnotes.[3])

A. Estimate based on information about number supporting the president:

_____

B. Chances of making an error:

_____

C. Estimate based on information about support by party:

　　1. If our senator is a Democrat: _____

　　2. If our senator is a Republican: _____

D. Chances of making an error:

_____

E. Reduction in chances of making an error due to having information about party:

_____

Knowing party affiliation on the constitutional balanced budget amendment vote reduced the chances of making errors from 34 to 11, or by 23. Knowing party affiliation on the chemical weapons treaty vote did not reduce our chances of making errors. Party made much more of a difference on the first vote, and hence we would say that the relationship of party to vote on the constitutional balanced budget amendment vote is stronger than on the chemical weapons treaty vote and in fact was nonexistent in the latter case.

measure of reduction in error
Extent to which we can reduce possible errors in estimating the value of a case if we know its value on a second variable.

The following word formula for the **measure of reduction in error** expresses the logic behind the relationship measures described in the rest of the chapter:

$$\frac{\text{Number of errors not knowing values of independent variable} - \text{Number of errors knowing values of the independent variable}}{\text{Number of errors not knowing values of independent variable}}$$

Relationship Measures for Nominal and Ordinal Variables

relationship measures
Single numbers indicating how strongly two or more variables are related to each other; examples include Q, lambda, gamma, tau$_b$, and tau$_c$.

correlation coefficient
A measure of relationship.

A number of **relationship measures,** or **correlation coefficients,** (including Q) are based on this same logic. They indicate whether knowing the value of one variable reduces the chance of error (or improves the success rate) when guessing the value of another variable.[4] Like Q, these measures vary from −1.00 to +1.00 and indicate the strength and direction of a relationship. The appropriate statistics vary according to the level of measurement, the number of values, and the patterns in the data. This section describes how to compute two commonly used measures—lambda and gamma—and discusses when it is appropriate to use each.

Nominal-Level Measure: Lambda

lambda
Relationship measure for nominal-level data.

Recall the discussion of support for the president as reported in tables 11.8 and 11.9. It would be helpful to develop a single measure for each of the bills to compare the relationships. We could use Yule's Q because these tables use dichotomies and nominal-level variables. **Lambda** is a second measure for nominal variables that can also be used in tables larger than two-by-two. The first step is to determine how many errors we would make in estimating the value on one variable without knowing about the other. In using any nominal variable, if we want to guess the value of any single case, we would guess the modal value of the variable. If there are more Republicans than Democrats in a gathering, we would guess that any single individual is a Republican, the modal value, and be right more times than if we had guessed Democrat. Lambda is a measure that allows us to determine the influence of a second variable, and the extent to which it reduces the errors we make without knowing that variable. Essentially, it compares the modal value for each value of the independent variable. Lambda is based on this formula:

$$\frac{\text{Number of errors not knowing values of independent variable} - \text{Number of errors knowing values of the independent variable}}{\text{Number of errors not knowing values of independent variable}}$$

For example, consider hypothetical data in which the dependent variable is *voting behavior* and the independent variable is *degrees of cynicism*. Because the dependent variable is a nominal variable ("yes" or "no"), and because there are more than two values of the independent variable, you would be on safe grounds to compute a lambda measure.

| | **Cynicism** | | | |
Vote	*Low*	*Medium*	*High*	**Row Total**
Yes	7	9	4	20
No	3	10	12	25

The row totals tell you the values for the dependent variable, *vote*, if you do not know anything about *cynicism*. If you do not have information about the independent variable, you would guess "no" and be wrong twenty times. If you knew the values of *vote* by degrees of *cynicism*, you could improve your guess by choosing the most frequent vote in each group (yes, no, no). You would be right 7 + 10 + 12 = 29 times out of 45. You would be wrong 3 + 9 + 4 = 16 times. Using the preceding formula, you would get:

$$\frac{20-16}{20} = \frac{4}{20} = .2$$

The interpretation of .2 depends on your theory, on prior research on cynicism, and on what other influences you are looking at. It would be easier to interpret if you were comparing the influence of *cynicism* in two different groups, or if you were comparing the influence of *cynicism* with the influence of other variables, such as *trust* and *political interest*.

Consider a second example, using the following data. The table allows you to determine whether one's religion has an influence on one's support for a particular policy. You could compute the percentages of different religions that support a policy; you could figure the median value and compare these. Because religion is a nominal variable and because there are more than two values, lambda could also be used.

| | **Religion** | | | |
Support	*Protestant*	*Catholic*	*Jew*	**Row Total**
High	5	6	15	26
Medium	6	18	4	28
Low	20	7	3	30

If you have no information about religion and only knew the row totals, you would guess that a single case had the support value of "low," because 30 is the modal value among the row totals; you could be in error 26 + 28 = 54 times. Now you are given the information about support for different religious groups. Now you could guess the values low (20 cases), medium (18 cases), and high (15 cases). And you would be wrong $(5 + 6) + (6 + 7) + (3 + 4) = 31$ times. Return to the formula:

$$\text{lambda} = \frac{54 - 31}{54} = .43$$

Just as we noted with Q, there are certain patterns of the data when lambda would not be appropriate even if the variables are nominal level. This would occur if the modal values for one of the variables had the same value on the other variable. For example, assume that the preceding table read as follows:

	Religion			
Support	*Jew*	*Catholic*	*Protestant*	**Row Total**
High	8	2	2	12
Medium	4	2	4	10
Low	10	27	25	62

The modal value for Jew, Catholic, and Protestant is the same—low support. In this case the formula would provide a 0 value for lambda even though there is some relationship and even though other measures would indicate a relationship:

$$\text{lambda} = \frac{(12 + 10) - (12 + 4 + 6)}{(12 + 10)} = 0$$

As with Q you need to examine the patterns of your data to see if lambda appears appropriate.

Ordinal-Level Measures: Gamma and Tau and Somer's *d*

gamma
Relationship measure for ordinal-level data; tends to be higher than other measures because it does not count cases tied on a value.

Gamma and **tau** and **Somer's *d*** are used for ordinal-level variables. Whereas lambda guesses the exact value of a variable (whether Catholics had low or medium trust, in the preceding example), these measures are based on the order of the values. They resemble Yule's Q; in fact, Q and gamma are identical for two-by-two tables. Whereas lambda counts the modal frequencies for each value of the independent variable, gamma is based on the order within pairs of cases. Conceptually, it lists all the possible pairs of cases, and for each pair determines if their ordinal ranking on one variable is the same as their ordinal ranking on the other variable; if they are tied, then they are not counted. Tau and Somer's *d* follow the same logic, but they include the pairs in which the cases are tied with each other (have the same ordinal ranking).

Assume you question individuals about their political trust and their political interest. You sort them according to whether they are low, medium, or high on each variable, as follows:

	Political Interest		
Trust	*Low*	*Medium*	*High*
Low	Haley		Andrew
Medium	Cameron	Sam	Sarah
High		Molly	Emily

Now look at each pair of individuals, a pair at a time. The question is whether a case that is higher on one variable is also higher on the other variable. If so, the two variables are related. The same is true if both members of the pair are lower on both variables. Therefore, for each pair, determine whether one case is ordered the same as the other case on both variables. For example, for the pair of Haley and Sam: Sam ranks higher than Haley on both variables; thus the two variables have the *same* ordering for this pair. Similarly Emily ranks higher than Sam on both variables; so this pair also would be counted as having the *same* ordering. Now consider the pair of Sam and Andrew: Sam is higher than Andrew on trust, but lower than Andrew on interest. Thus the ordering of the variables for this pair would be counted as *different*. Pairs for which the ranks are the same on either variable (for instance, Molly and Emily) are not counted.

Take each pair of individuals and indicate whether the variables are ordered the same (S) or different (D) or whether they are tied.

Pair	**S**	**D**	**Tied on Either Variable**
Haley and Andrew			tied on trust
Haley and Cameron			tied on interest
Haley and Sam	yes		
Haley and Sarah	yes		
Haley and Molly	yes		
Haley and Emily	yes		
Cameron and Andrew		yes	
Cameron and Sam			tied on trust
Cameron and Sarah			tied on trust
Cameron and Molly	yes		
Cameron and Emily	yes		
Sam and Sarah			tied on trust
Sam and Molly			tied on interest
Sam and Emily	yes		
Sam and Andrew		yes	
Molly and Andrew		yes	
Molly and Sarah		yes	
Molly and Emily			tied on trust
Andrew and Emily			tied on interest
Andrew and Sarah			tied on interest
Sarah and Emily			tied on interest

Just as with Q, we subtract the number of pairs on which the variables have different orderings from the number of pairs on which the variables have the same ordering, and then divide by the sum of these two figures.

$$\text{gamma} = \frac{\text{pairs in same order} - \text{pairs in different order}}{\text{pairs in same order} + \text{pairs in different order}}$$

$$\text{gamma} = \frac{7-4}{7+4} = \frac{3}{11} = .27$$

Gamma reports the number of similarly ordered pairs of cases as a proportion of all relevant pairs; that is, all pairs for which the cases are not tied on one or the other variable. In our example, ten of the pairs were not counted, since they had ties.

Computing gamma. The formula for gamma is:

$$\text{gamma} = \frac{N_s - N_d}{N_s + N_d}$$

where N_s is the number of pairs in which the cases have the same ordering on the two variables, and N_d is the number of pairs in which the cases have a different ordering on the two variables.

If the table is set up so that the lowest value for each variable is in the upper left cell (as in our example) you can find N_s and N_d as follows. N_s pairs are obtained by multiplying each cell total by the number of cases *below and to the right* of it. In our example, there is one case in the upper left cell (Haley) and four cases below and to the right of it (Sam, Sarah, Molly, and Emily). Thus you would multiply 1×4. You would *not* multiply the number in the cell where Haley is located by the numbers in the cells where Cameron and Andrew are located, since, by the logic of gamma, the tie on one value cannot tell us anything about a relationship between the two variables. N_d pairs are obtained by multiplying each cell by those cases in cells *above and to the right.*

Now follow the formula in a similar table in which there is more than one case in each cell:

Political Interest

Trust	Low	Medium	High
Low	2	4	
Medium	3	11	5
High	9	3	2

$N_s = 2(11 + 5 + 3 + 2) = 42$
$+ 4(5 + 2) = 28$
$+ 3(3 + 2) = 15$
$+ 11(2) = 22$
$= 107$

$N_d = 9(11 + 4 + 7 + 5) = 243$
$+ 3(7+5) = 36$
$+ 3(4 + 7) = 33$
$+ 11(7) = 77$
$= 389$

$$\text{gamma} = \frac{N_s - N_d}{N_s + N_d} = \frac{107 - 389}{107 + 389} = \frac{-282}{496} = -.57$$

You are asking whether changes in political interest are related to changes in trust. Specifically, you want to know whether one is more apt to trust the political system as one's level of political interest increases.

Begin with the cell in the upper left corner. It tells you that two cases are low on trust and also low on interest. Thus, the variables are positively related. Now list all the cases below and to the right of 2 and multiply by 2; you are adding the pairs of cases that are also positively related and ignoring the ties. That gives you:

2(11 + 5 + 3 + 2) = 42

Now move to the next cell, which has a 4, and multiply that by all the numbers to the right and below it. This gives you:

4(5 + 2) = 28

There is nothing to the right of 7, so you do not use that. Now move to the next cell, where there are figures below and to the right. It contains a 3. Multiply it by the numbers below and to the right:

3(3 + 2) = 15

Now move to the next cell, with an 11, and multiply it by the number in the cell below and to the right:

11(2) = 22

Add these four results together:

42 + 28 + 15 + 22 = 107

Follow the same procedures in looking at the pairs in which the cases are differently related. This time begin at the lower left corner with number 9; that is, the number who rank low on political interest and high on trust. The result is 389. Completing the computations, your result is negative, −.57.

The negative sign tells you that the two variables are negatively related to each other. You have to look back at the table and the way in which the values are ordered to interpret this statement. For this table, because both variables go from low to high, it means that the higher the value of the independent variable, the lower the value of the dependent variable. As the values of political interest increase, trust declines.

Again, you have to understand gamma and your data to interpret −.57 as a measure of strength of the relationship. If there are many tied values, gamma will be higher than other correlation measures. If there are many tied values, you could use another measure, or you could try to increase the number of values of your variables so that there would be fewer ties. Perhaps you could code political interest into very low, low, medium, medium high, and high.

tau_b, tau_c
Relationship measures for ordinal-level data, for square and rectangular tables, respectively; tends to be lower than gamma because it counts pairs in which cases have the same value on one variable.

Tau_b and Tau_c. Tau_b is a similar measure, but it includes tied pairs in the denominator because it assumes that tied pairs can tell us something about the strength of a relationship. In a perfect relationship, in which the independent variable fully explains the dependent variable, all cases would fall on the diagonals. Pairs that do not fall on the diagonals show that the relationship is not perfect (for example, Molly and Sarah). Whereas gamma ignores such pairs, tau_b includes them among the total of relevant pairs and reports the number of similarly ordered pairs as a proportion of this larger group of pairs. In the formula for tau_b the number of ties increases the size of the denominator, which lowers the value of the correlation measure. It thus cautions us that the independent variable does not fully explain the dependent variable and that the relationship may not be as strong as gamma would suggest. If your data have a large proportion of pairs with tied values, gamma would be higher than other measures and could be misleading. Use it only if your hypothesis applies to units that differ on both x and y, that is only to cases that *differ* on both trust and political interest in the earlier example.

The discussion thus far refers to tau_b, which is used for square tables. A variation, tau_c, is used when the number of rows and the number of columns are not the same. Since it is based on the numbers of rows and columns rather than on the number of pairs, it is harder to interpret. Instead of measuring the number of similarly ordered pairs as a proportion of all relevant pairs, tau_c can only be used to say which of two tables of similar proportions is stronger.

Somer's d
Relationship measure for ordinal-level data; useful for causal analysis.

Somer's d. Somer's *d* is another relationship measure similar to gamma and the tau measures. Like tau, the numerator equals the number of pairs with a positive association minus the number of pairs with a negative association. The denominator sums these two figures plus the number of pairs that are tied only on the dependent variable. Thus Somer's *d* also produces a smaller relationship measure than gamma. Because it includes ties on the dependent variables, it focuses on pairs of cases where the independent variable changes, allowing us to observe the effects of the independent variable. It looks at the number of similarly ordered pairs as a proportion of all pairs for which the independent variable assumes different values. In the earlier example exploring the relationship between trust and political interest, Somer's *d* would again count the numbers of similarly and differently ordered pairs for the numerator, but would include in the denominator the pairs for which individuals were tied on the dependent variable, or had the same amount of trust but different amounts of interest. Because it focuses on cases where the independent variable changes, Somer's *d* is particularly useful when we are exploring a causal relationship.

The formula for Somer's *d* is:

$$\text{Somer's } d = \frac{N_s - N_d}{N_s + N_d + T_Y}$$

where T_Y is the number of pairs tied on Y (the dependent variable) but not on X (the independent variable). To compute T_Y, multiply the number in each cell by the numbers in other cells in that row and add together: Return to the data used to compute gamma on page 322. To that denominator you need to add:

$$T_Y = 2(4 + 7) + 4(7) + 3(11 + 5) + 11(5) + 9(3 + 2) + 3(2) = 204$$

Thus,

$$\text{Somer's } d = \frac{N_s - N_d}{N_s + N_d + T_Y} = \frac{107 - 389}{107 + 389 + 204} = \frac{-283}{700} = -.40$$

Because gamma omits all ties, it gives the highest measure of relationship. Somer's *d* includes some ties in the denominator and thus gives the next-highest measure. Tau includes more ties in the denominator and thus provides the lowest measure.

SELECTED RELATIONSHIP MEASURES AND LEVEL OF MEASUREMENT

Q **(also known as Yule's** *Q***):** For nominal-level data arrayed as a dichotomy (two values only).

Lambda: For nominal-level data. If table has one nominal and one ordinal variable, use a measure for nominal variables, such as *Q* or lambda.

Gamma: For ordinal-level data; tends to be higher than other measures because it does not count pairs tied on a value.

Tau$_b$ and Tau$_c$: For ordinal-level data; for square and rectangular tables, respectively. Use with nominal data when lambda is inappropriate. Similar to gamma, but counts pairs in which cases have same value on one variable, and thus tends to be lower.

Somer's *d***:** For ordinal-level data; can be used with nominal-level data. Similar to gamma, but counts pairs that are the same on the dependent variable, but vary on the independent variable, making it useful in causal analysis.

Selecting and Computing Measures of Relationship (Answers in endnotes.[5])

A. Assume you are testing a hypothesis that there is a relationship between *party identification* and *support for term limits for members of Congress* (strongly agree, agree, not sure, disagree, strongly disagree). What is an appropriate statistical measure of association between the variables as long as the cases do not cluster in one of the values of *support for term limits?*

_____

B. Calculate the relevant statistic for the following data.

_____

Degree of Party Identification	Status	
	Low	*High*
Low	10	1
Medium	5	5
High	1	10

C. To test a version of the "gender-gap" hypothesis of voting in the 1996 presidential election, look at the relationship between *gender* and *party vote*. Compute the appropriate statistic, and interpret your finding.

_____

Party Vote	Gender	
	Male	*Female*
Republican (Dole)	44	37
Democratic (Clinton)	44	54

Source: *Washington Post*, 6 November 1996, p. B7.

Interpreting Ordinal Measures of Relationship

As noted earlier, relationship measures are most useful when they can be used to compare different influences or relationships. Consider tables 11.10 and 11.11, which present information from surveys conducted at the time of the 1996 presidential election (Clinton versus Dole).[6] They enable us to compare how a person's income and view on the economy affects their vote for president. It is well known that the higher one's income the more apt one is to vote for the Republican candidate, in this case Dole. Remembering that candidate Clinton was promising to continue his policies for a second term, however, it is possible that

TABLE 11.10
Presidential Vote, by Family Income, 1996

	Income			
	Low	*Middle*	*Upper*	*High*
Clinton	56%	49%	47%	41%
Dole	33	40	44	50
Perot	10	10	7	6
	99%	99%	98%	97%

N = 16,338

gamma = 0.096

those who thought the economy was getting better or was about the same would be more likely to support Clinton, irrespective of their income. Which do you anticipate would have a stronger influence on a person's vote, *income* or *view on the economy?*

Since table 11.10 has four columns, it is hard to answer the question by using percentages. The gamma relationships are clearer, especially in comparing the two influences rather than in asserting specific numerical relationships. The tables tell us that both *income* and *view on the economy* are associated with how a person votes. *View on the economy* has a much stronger influence on one's vote, however, with a gamma of .53 compared to .096.

TABLE 11.11
Presidential Vote, by View of Economy, 1996

	View on Economy	
	Excellent/Good	*Not so Good/Poor*
Clinton	63%	32%
Dole	30	51
Perot	5	14
	98%	97%

N = 16,338

gamma = 0.533

Measures of Relationship for Interval-Level Variables

Measures of relationship for interval-level variables are also based on the logic of reducing errors in estimating values. Like Q and lambda and gamma, they measure how much we are able to reduce possible errors when we estimate the value of a case based on information about a second variable. The procedures are altered to take into account the properties of interval-level data, however. When variables are measured at the nominal level, the best guess of the value of any single case on the dependent variable is the mode, or the value in which the largest number of cases fall. That is, if we know there are more Republicans than Democrats in our community, we would guess that any one individual is a Republican, the modal value, and we would be right more often than not. When we are working with interval measures, the best guess is the mean. We come closer to being right using the mean value than relying on any other figure. Measures of relationship for interval-level data compare the errors we would make if we use the mean to estimate the value of a variable with the errors we would make if we had information about the relation of the variable to a second variable.

Pearson's *r* Correlation Coefficient, r^2

Pearson's correlation, *r* A measure that indicates the strength of relationship between interval-level data.

Pearson's correlation, known as *r,* is the relationship measure used for interval-level variables. It tells us how likely it is that an estimate (of the value of a case within the dependent variable) will be more accurate than the mean value when that estimate is based on additional information about a second variable. For example, assume you took a survey in your community and want to estimate the income of one of the respondents. If you know the mean income for the community from census data, you could guess that the income of any given person is going to be more or less close to that figure. Now assume that you know which education level that particular person attained. If education is related to income—presumably if the more educated respondents tend to be the higher-income respondents—then knowing a person's education would enable you to make a more accurate estimate of income than if you used the mean value of income alone. In this example, a relationship measure tells how much you can improve your estimate of a person's income once you know how much education he or she has had. On the one hand, it is unlikely that you would be able to estimate the *exact* income of a person. On the other hand, you want to do more than say it would be close to the mean value. Pearson's *r* and r^2 tell *how closely* we can guess the value of one variable by knowing its value on another variable, or how much variation in one variable can be explained by changes in another variable.

Regression Lines

scatterplot A graphic used to depict bivariate data when both variables are measured on an interval or ordinal scale; each bivariate observation is represented by a data point with a horizontal value equal to the value of the first variable and a vertical value equal to the value of the second variable.

We can visualize the relationship between two interval-level variables by developing a type of graph known as a **scatterplot.** Assume you have information on five cases (e.g., individuals, countries) and that you know their scores on two different variables (e.g., *education* and *income*, or *literacy rate* and *GNP*). Place one variable along the bottom of the graph, on the horizontal line, and the other along the side of the graph, or the vertical line. Then locate each of the cases on the graph, and examine the pattern to see if there appears to be a relationship between the two variables.

If the dots are spread out seemingly at random over the entire graph, then the two variables probably are not related. If they fall in a pattern, however, they probably are related to some extent. Draw a line that best fits the dots. This is the **regression line, *b*.** There are three elements to look for in the graph: direction, slope, and closeness of fit. The direction of the line tells you if the relationship is positive or negative. The slope, or steepness, of the line tells you how much change in one variable is associated with how much change in the other variable. The closeness of fit of the line to the dots tells you how strong the relationship is. The regression line itself indicates the direction and slope. Pearson's *r* measures how closely the cases fit this line, or how strong the relationship is between the two variables. The closer the dots are to the regression line, the stronger the relationship between the two variables and the higher the value of the Pearson's correlation.

regression line, *b* On a graph, a line that shows how much change occurs in the dependent variable *(Y)* for a given change in the independent variable *(X).*

Visualizing a Regression Line and Correlation Measure

Use the following steps, employing these hypothetical data:

Case	X	Y
A	3	4
B	4	4
C	1	2
D	3	3
E	0	1

Step 1. Do a scatterplot. Locate the values of *X* and *Y* on the following graph.

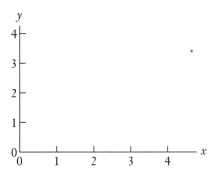

Step 2. Draw a straight line that comes as close as possible to all of the observations. This is the regression line that describes the relationship between X and Y. Although most of the values do not lie exactly on the line, it should be drawn so that the differences between the actual cases and the line are minimized. A regression line can be thought of as a prediction. Based on the line, we could predict that if an individual has a score of 2 on variable X, he or she would have a score of 2.5 on variable Y.

Step 3. To determine the strength of the relationship between X and Y, we would compare the estimate of Y based on the regression line with estimates we would make if we relied only on the mean value for variable Y. Compute the mean of the Y values. Compare the Y values on the regression line with the mean value for Y. Does the regression line improve the chances of successfully predicting values for Y? Pearson's r is the measure that could be used to answer this question (answers in endnotes.[7])

Computing the Regression Line

The formula for the regression line is based on the general formula for relationships. (Note that Y denotes the dependent variable, and X denotes the independent variable.)

$$Y = f(X),$$

This says that the values of Y can be explained by changes in the value of X. This formula can be restated as

$$Y = a + bX$$

where a is the value of Y when X is 0, and b is the amount of change in X. Thus, the formula tells you how much the Y variable (the dependent variable) changes

FIGURE 11.1
Mean and Regression Line

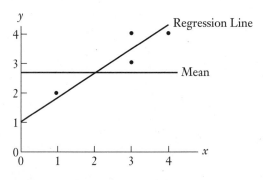

for every unit change in X (the independent variable). It looks forbidding, but it is based on the same logic and computations as the standard deviation. Like the standard deviation or like σ, the regression line (known as b) is computed by finding the extent to which cases deviate from the mean. In regression, the formula specifies a line that comes closest to all of the points. It is based on finding the extent to which each case deviates from the means of both the dependent and the independent variables (the Y and the X values).

FORMULA FOR SLOPE OF REGRESSION LINE

$$b = \frac{\Sigma\left(X_i - \overline{X}\right)\left(Y_i - \overline{Y}\right)}{\Sigma\left(X_i - \overline{X}\right)^2}$$

Using the hypothetical data listed on p. 329, compute the regression line for the following data.

	X_i	$\overline{X}$	$(X_i - \overline{X})$	$(X_i - \overline{X})^2$	Y_i	$\overline{Y}$	$(Y_i - \overline{Y})$	$(X_i - \overline{X})(Y_i - \overline{Y})$
A	3	2.2	+.8	.64	4	2.8	+1.2	$.8 \times 1.2 = .96$
B	4	2.2	+1.8	3.24	4	2.8	+1.2	$1.8 \times 1.2 = 2.16$
C	1	2.2	−1.2	1.44	2	2.8	−.8	$-1.2 \times -.8 = .96$
D	3	2.2	+.8	.64	3	2.8	+.2	$.8 \times .2 = .16$
E	0	2.2	−2.2	4.84	1	2.8	−1.8	$-2.2 \times -1.8 = 3.96$
				10.80				8.20

$$b = \frac{8.20}{10.80} = .76$$

The figure .76 means that the regression line has a slope in which Y, or the dependent variable, increases by .76 of one unit for every one-unit change in the independent variable.

How do we interpret this figure? It depends wholly on the units in which both variables are measured. Assume that the X variable is *government expenditures on social services*, and the Y variable is *number of people served*. Let one unit of $X = \$1$ million on social services and one unit of $Y = 100$ people served. Then .76 means that for every increase of \$1 million spent on social services, seventy-six additional people are served. If, however, we let X equal a much smaller amount, or \$1,000 spent on social services, then .76 means that for every increase of a thousand dollars in social services, seventy-six additional people are served. The implications of the two different units are obviously very different.

Now that we know the slope, we need to have one more piece of information: we need to know where the line crosses the Y axis, or what the value of Y is when *X* is zero. This is the *a* value, also called the **intercept, *a*.** It often is difficult to interpret *a* for a particular research question. It may or may not make sense to say that if zero dollars were spent on social services a certain number of people would be served; the meaning would depend on the kinds of data we had collected and whether our measures of "being served" included activities by volunteer groups in the community. Again the point is that you have to be clear about the measures and the data you have collected in interpreting particular measures.

$$a = \overline{Y} - b\overline{X}$$

Using the same data, we get the following value for *a*:

$$a = 2.8 - .76 \,(2.2)$$
$$= 2.8 - 1.67$$
$$= 1.13$$

Return to figure 11.1 and you will see that these values for *a* and *b* closely match the placement of the regression line.

Computing Pearson's *r*, a Correlation Coefficient, and *r²*, the Variance

The direction and slope of the regression line tell us only part of what we want to know. We also want to know whether this line is a good fit, or how strong the relationship is between the two variables. Look back at figure 11.1. You can imagine a series of cases that is much more scattered throughout the graph but still has the same slope. Thus, we want to know how closely the cases fit the regression line and the strength of the relationship.

The measure of close fit is called Pearson's correlation coefficient, or Pearson's *r*. This number tells us how closely the actual cases fit the regression line. More precisely, it indicates to what extent estimates based on the line are closer to the actual cases than estimates based on the mean. It is often called the "least-squares" measure because it asks whether the squared distances of the cases from the regression line are *less than* the squared differences of cases from the mean. Pearson's *r* and *r²* is based on the following logic:

1. Compute the distance of actual values from the mean.
2. Square and sum these distances to calculate the *total variance*.
3. Compute the distance of actual values from the regression line.
4. Square and sum these distances to calculate the *unexplained variance*.
   Distances from the regression line indicate the extent to which the independent variable does not explain all of the changes in the dependent variable, and hence is the *unexplained variance*.

5. Subtract the unexplained variance from the total variance to calculate the *explained variance*, the extent to which changes in the independent variable are associated with or predict changes in the dependent variable.

$$r^2 = \frac{\text{Total variance} - \text{Unexplained variance}}{\text{Total variance}}$$

6. Note that research studies commonly report *adjusted r* and r^2 scores when they deal with samples to take into account that r^2 slightly overstates the variance in Y explained by X, although the difference is minimal in samples over fifty.

These steps follow the same logic used throughout the chapter. Like other correlation measures, r and r^2 indicate how much we can improve our ability to estimate values on one variable by knowing its relation to a second variable. The greater the distance between the cases and the regression line, the lower the value of r and r^2. The closer the cases fit the regression line, the higher the value of r and r^2. Note that r does not tell you the slope of the line, or how much change in Y is associated with a change in X. It tells you how closely or strongly the cases fit the regression line. You could have a very slight slope with cases clustered tightly around it, or a very steep slope with cases broadly spread out.

To find r^2 we begin with the following formula for r, which uses many of the notations and elements already used to find the regression line.

FORMULA FOR PEARSON'S *r*

$$r = \frac{N \sum XY - \sum X \sum Y}{\sqrt{\left[N \sum X^2 - (\sum X)^2\right]\left[N \sum Y^2 - (\sum Y)^2\right]}}$$

---

r^2, variance
A measure of the extent to which variation in Y, the dependent variable, is explained by variation in X, the independent variable.

We compute r because the result can be either negative or positive, and it is important to know the direction of the relationship. It is difficult to verbalize what this value means, however; r^2, **(variance)** has more meaning. It tells us that the amount of the variance that can be explained by the relationship between X and Y is equal to the square of the r coefficient for the association. Thus the r^2 symbol tells us how much of the variation in Y is attributable to variation in X. It does not necessarily mean that X causes Y to change; it means that we can use the known pattern of cases that fall outside the regression line to estimate the value of Y, given any value of X. It tells us to what extent knowing X enables us to predict Y. If we find $r = .60$, we square that value to get $r^2 = .36$. This figure tells us there is an equation that relates X and Y, and that if we use that we can reduce our errors in predicting Y by 36 percent. Or we can say that this equation (or regression line or changes in the value of X) accounts for 36 percent of the changes we observe in Y. Sixty-four percent of the change in the dependent variable is still unaccounted for and therefore must be due to other factors.

Drawing Regression Lines and Computing Correlations

A. Ten counties in your state are experimenting with ways to reduce Medicare costs. The costs of their efforts are listed as values of variable X and are reported in hundreds of thousands of dollars. The second variable, Y, is the amount of increase in Medicare costs in the ten counties. You want to see if spending more money on cost-saving activities leads to a lower increase or a reduction in costs. You hope that the number is negative, that the more money spent, the less costs will increase.

First, draw a scatterplot and locate the ten counties on the graph. Speculate about the relationship you observe. Second, compute the Pearson's correlation and r^2, and interpret these figures. (Answers appear in endnotes.)[8]

County	Amount Spent on Reducing Costs, X (in hundreds of thousands of dollars)	Amount of Increase in Medicare Costs, Y (in hundreds of thousands of dollars)
A	1	6
B	1	7
C	2	4
D	2	5
E	3	5
F	3	4
G	4	3
H	4	3
I	5	2
J	6	1

B. You have carried out an analysis to see if state expenditures on primary school education are related to higher SAT scores in the state. You get a Pearson's correlation of $r = .50$. Determine r^2 and interpret what it means. As a policy maker deciding on future expenditures on education, what would you conclude (answers in endnotes.[9])

Multivariate Relationships and Multiple Independent Variables

Multivariate Relationships

multivariate relationship
Relationship among more than two variables; usually examines the influence of several independent variables on a single dependent variable.

multiple regression
Regression analysis expressing the influence of more than one independent variable on a dependent variable.

multiple correlation, R, R^2
A measure that indicates how closely observations fit the regression line; R is the measure expressing this cumulative influence.

Most dependent variables of interest in political analysis are related to more than one independent variable (recall Chapter 6). Therefore we usually need to analyze relationships with three or more variables either to test the effect of a third or control variable on a relationship or to test the simultaneous effects of several independent variables. In these cases, we are looking at **multivariate relationships.** We may, for example, want to know how much influence income, degree of political interest, and level of trust have on voter turnout. If these are all measured at the interval level, we could do **multiple regression** and **multiple correlation (R, R^2)** analyses.

Multiple correlation figures indicate two kinds of information. First, they tell us the cumulative influence of all of the independent variables on the dependent variable; these influences are reported as R and R^2. As with r and r^2, R^2 is the meaningful number. It tells us what percentage of change in the dependent variable is due to changes in the independent variables taken together. In other terms it tells us how much of the variance in the dependent variable is accounted for by all of the independent variables.

$$R^2 = \frac{\text{Total variance} - \text{Unexplained variance}}{\text{Total variance}}$$

partial correlation coefficient
Strength of relationship between the dependent variable and one of several independent variables when the other independent variables are controlled.

Second, multiple correlation figures give us a separate r for each independent variable, known as a **partial correlation coefficient.** This coefficient tells us how much a change in each independent variable is related to a change in a dependent variable when changes in all of the other independent variables are controlled or held constant. It is thus a mathematical technique for carrying out controls. Recall that chapter 6 described how to control a relationship for the influence of a third variable. We created tables showing a relationship for each value of the control variable. We have since learned that you can examine the influence of this control variable through such analytic techniques as percentage differences, comparisons of central tendencies, and computing correlation measures such as lambda and gamma. When we want to control for several variables at the same time, and when we are working with interval-level data, we can perform this same analysis through partial correlations.

The basic formula for multiple regression and correlation extends the formula used earlier.

$$Y = a + b_1X_1 + b_2X_2 + b_3X_3 + e$$

X_1, X_2, and X_3 refer to three independent variables (e.g., *income, interest,* and *trust*); b_1, b_2, and b_3 refer to the formulas for the slope of each of these independent variables; and e refers to the unexplained variance, or measurement error, remaining after the influence of all three of these variables has been taken into account.

It is helpful to consider one other term useful in interpreting multiple regressions. Assume you are examining the multiple influence of income, interest, and trust on participation. In addition to computing a multiple regression and a multiple correlation that tell you about the combined effects of these variables, you compute the partial influence of each of these variables controlled for the other two. Because income and interest and trust are reported in different units with different variances, it is hard to compare them. Thus, it is common to **standardize scores.** You do this by making each unit equivalent to one standard deviation from its mean. The result is ß or the **beta coefficient,** which varies from +1.00 to −1.00 and enables you to compare the influence of several independent variables. For example, a beta coefficient of .5 tells you that for every one unit change in income, participation increases by one-half unit. It can then be compared with standardized scores for both trust and political interest.

Tables reporting regression studies may include any of the following:

standardize scores
Translating scores into comparable units, such as an amount of the standard deviation of each score.

beta coefficient, ß
Measure of a regression slope in terms of the standard deviation for that variable; allows us to compare the influence of several variables.

b Regression slope. Amount of change in dependent variable associated with a one-unit change in the independent variable.

$ß$ Beta score (standardized slope). Reports slope in units such that each unit is one standard deviation from the mean. Allows you to compare relationship among variables.

r Correlation measure, degree of association. When used in multiple correlations it may indicate the relationship of one independent variable, controlled for the others. The latter may also be referred to as a *partial correlation.*

r^2 Explained variance; indicates the percentage of change in one variable that can be explained by changes in the other.

R Combined correlation measure for multiple variables.

R^2 Variance explained by all independent variables acting together.

Comparing Simple and Partial Correlation Measures

We have said throughout that causality is difficult to establish and that one of the criteria for establishing causality is to eliminate the effects of alternative relationships. If we hypothesize that income *(X)* causes participation *(Y)*, then we need not only to establish a relationship between income and participation but to show that income has an effect even after the effects of alternative influences are taken into account. One way to accomplish this is by examining the *partial* effects of variables, with the effects of other variables removed.

An analysis of a survey of citizens in Ghana illustrates the use of these techniques. The survey asked several questions to determine how knowledgeable citizens were about political events and institutions in their country.[10] It also included questions about the characteristics of the respondents—age, gender, and so forth. The research problem was to determine which of these characteristics had the strongest bearing on a person's political knowledge.

Table 11.12 presents the results of the research. Be sure you understand what the columns are reporting. The column labeled "Pearson's *r*" is looking at each independent variable, one at a time, and stating how strongly it is related to the dependent variable, political information. The column labeled "Partial correlation coefficient" is reporting the results of a multiple correlation analysis. It again looks at the influence of each independent variable, but this time the effects of the other independent variables have been removed. Note the values for education. The Pearson's *r* value is .34, showing that education has an influence on the amount of information a person has, as you would probably expect. But education overlaps with some of the other variables, such as mobility and economic position. That is, educated people are generally more mobile and have a higher economic position. So the partial correlation coefficients are computed by holding the values of these other variables constant. We are removing the influence of these other variables by holding them constant or by controlling the relationships. We are looking at the influence of education after removing the influence of other variables, such as mobility and economic position. The partial coefficient of .18 states the influence of education all by itself, with the effect of the other variables removed.

We know from the correlation measure for education (.34) that as a person's education increases, so does his or her political information. We square this value to derive the r^2 for education, getting a value of .12, which tells us that 12 percent of the variation in information is attributed to changes in education. When education is controlled for all of the other factors, the relationship measure drops from .34 to .18, making it still one of the more important factors. Taken all together, the eleven variables in table 11.12 have an R of .60 and an R^2 of .36, meaning that 36 percent of the variation in a person's political knowledge can be explained by the complex of factors considered in this particular study.

TABLE 11.12

Relationships between Political Information and Demographic Variables, Ghana

Demographic Variable	Pearson's *r*	Partial Correlation Coefficient	
Education	.34	.18	
Occupation	.32	.06	
Age	−.31	−.21	
Mobility	.23	.13	
Town size	.30	−.09	
Gender	−.42	−.27	$R = .60$
Urban	.28	−.02	$R^2 = .36$
Economic position	.13	−.06	
Ethnic group:			
Northern	.13	−.06	
Ewe	−.27	−.10	
Southern	.11	−.03	
$N = 115$			

Source: Adapted from Fred Hayward, "A Reassessment of Conventional Wisdom about the Informed Public: National Political Information in Ghana," *American Political Science Review* 70 (1976): 439, table 8.

Examine table 11.12 further. Which factors other than education have a large influence on political knowledge? Which of the factors change the most when entered into a multiple correlation? For example, occupation has a strong relationship, an *r* of .32; however, when it is controlled for all of the other factors, its relationship measure is reduced to .06. Carrying out this kind of analysis can help us in our efforts to state which relationships are more apt to be causal.

Time Series Analysis

There is one other use of correlation and regression worth noting. Regression lines often are used to analyze changes over time. When you have a series of figures for a succession of years, you may want to see whether there is any trend in the data and to make predictions, assuming that trends continue. You can begin by creating a scatterplot in which the horizontal axis marks off the years or some other measure of time and the vertical axis measures the variable that changes over time. A regression line can be computed from the location of the observations. It can then be extended to predict the value of *Y* in coming years. This technique is called **time series analysis.** In addition to predicting the future, this technique also deals with the problem of missing values discussed in chapter 9. If we lack data for certain years, and if we can assume that there were

time series analysis
Use of regression analysis to examine whether there is a trend over time and to use the trend to extrapolate data for other years.

no unique conditions operating then, we can draw a regression line and interpolate the value for the intervening years based on what we know about events prior to and following those years.

Time series analysis can also be used to make predictions and assist in policy planning. For example, if we want to predict the number of new homes that will be built over the next few years, we can create a graph with *years* on the horizontal axis and *number of new homes built* on the vertical axis. We simply plot the number of new homes that were built each year. After observing the data, we determine whether the changes in number of homes built approximate a straight line. If so, and if we have reason to believe that the same trend will continue, we can compute the regression line and use it to project the numbers of homes that will be built in future years. There is one important assumption behind all such analysis: all other conditions are staying the same. If, say, there is a recession or a change in the tax code, either could affect the numbers of new homes built, and the prediction based on the regression line would almost certainly be in error. To the extent that we can assume relatively stable conditions, time series analysis can be helpful in anticipating needs and problems for the purpose of making policy.

Interpreting Strength of Relationship

There are several ways to verbalize what relationship measures tell us. We can refer to the strength of the relationship. We can also say that we want to explain the variance in the dependent variable. If the dependent variable, such as the GNP of developing nations, varies, then one way to describe our research is to say that we want to explain which factors influence this variation. The study of Ghana found that its residents had different amounts of political information: some more, some less. The author was researching which factors (age, gender, and so forth) account for that variation. Some of the factors obviously explain more of the variation than do others. In other words, they have a stronger relationship with increases in the amount of information a person has.

We have been using the term *strength of relationship* rather loosely. Is it possible to be any more precise and state what number corresponds to a strong relationship or explanation, and what number corresponds to a weak relationship or explanation? Can we be more specific in stating what a relationship measure of .40 means? Is .40 strong or weak? This is a difficult question, and there is no precise answer. The answer depends partly on the data and partly on the supporting theory and logic. Another part of the answer is that both strong and weak relationships can be of interest. If existing studies report a relatively strong relationship between two variables, and you find a particular country or period of time in which the relationship is quite weak, then that is an important finding, worth reporting and studying further.

A common rule of thumb states that any r over .30 is considered to be fairly strong. An r of .30 has an r^2 variance of .09 ($.30^2$), meaning that changes in one variable explain 9 percent of the change in the other variable. It may surprise you that this small relationship is of any interest. Yet, if you remember that any social event or behavior usually is influenced by a vast array of factors, finding one that explains as much as 9 percent of the variation usually is worth noting. For example, why do you vote as you do? Your social and economic background, your gender, your parents' party affiliation, your particular experiences with salient policy issues, your optimism about the future, and your level of information and interest in politics all influence your vote. If you find any one factor out of all these that explains 9 percent of the variation in voter turnout, the discovery would be quite interesting and certainly worth reporting.

Relationship measures are particularly useful when you are comparing measures of two or more relationships. You would report the measures for each relationship and compare them to each other. If you found that income has an r^2 value of .15 and gender an r^2 value of .05, you would report the two measures and note that income has the greater influence. In other words, men and women do not differ very much in their behavior, but wealthy and poor people do differ in their behavior. It is just as interesting to know that gender has little influence as it is to know that income has more influence. In this case the null hypothesis, that gender differences do not affect behavior, is a valuable piece of information.

Where We Are

This chapter has described a number of measures for stating the relationship among variables. They range from simple measures, such as percentage differences and comparisons of means, to more complex measures such as lambdas, gammas, and Pearson's correlation coefficients. The logic behind all of them is fairly straightforward. Essentially, they are asking whether we can improve our guess about the value of a case if we have information about its value on a second variable. For instance, can we guess how senators will vote if we know what party they belong to? The answer is seldom an absolute yes or no. Rather, we can state some figure less than one as a measure of how much knowledge of the second variable will improve our ability to guess the value of a case.

The statistics described throughout the chapter are appropriate for different levels of measurement. Thus one should have interval level data to carry out regression analysis, to determine correlations and variance. Many studies, however, do not meet these requirements. For example, Pearson's r is frequently applied to ordinal data by assigning numbers to the different categories. For example, you could code a question about your level of political interest so that Very is (3) and Some is (2) and Not much is (1). While there are reasonable grounds for doing this, and while you may learn something about your data based on the analysis, you should not overlook the assumptions you made in attaching numbers to the survey results.

Finally, it is important to remember that any of these measures are meaningful only in the context of your research questions, existing theories, and findings in the literature. The importance of a relationship measure has to be judged according to prior expectations and findings. Recall the finding that negative campaigning reduced voting turnout by about 4 percent (chapter 4). That may seem like a small figure, especially in light of the earlier comment that a relationship of .3 is considered fairly strong. However, given the multiple influences on voting, prior studies in the literature, and the interest in increasing voter turnout, 4 percent is actually a noteworthy number.

NOTES

1. Throughout this chapter, where appropriate, examples of statistics were calculated from a survey of Atlanta residents carried out in 1976: *The Fulton County Survey, 1976* (Atlanta: Georgia State University, n.d.). The figures are based on responses by 5,503 Atlanta residents.
2. Table 11.6: Midwest: very conservative—60%; moderately conservative—46%; South: very conservative—88%; moderately conservative—13%; West: very conservative—73%; moderately conservative—13%; less conservative—13%. Table 11.7. Mean values: Midwest—100.4; South—3; West—11.
3. (a) supported; (b) 26; (c1) supported; (c2) supported; (d) 26; (e) 0.
4. This logic often is referred to as *PRE*, or *proportional reduction of error*.
5. A. Lambda, because one of the variables is a nominal variable.
   B. Use gamma as long as both variables are ordinal:

$$N_s = 10(5 + 10) + 5(10) = 10(15) + 5(10) = 150 + 50 = 200$$
$$N_d = 1(5 + 1) + 5(1) = 1(6) + 5(1) = 6 + 5 = 11$$

$$gamma = \frac{200 - 11}{200 + 11} = \frac{189}{211} = .895, \text{ or } .90$$

   C. $Q = \dfrac{ad - bc}{ad + bc} = \dfrac{2376 - 1628}{2376 + 1628} = \dfrac{748}{4004} = .19$

   This value tells us that females are slightly more apt to vote for the Democratic candidate than are males. Thus, there is a gender gap, although according to this measure it is not large.
6. "Election 1996: The States and the Region—A Closer Look at the Voters: *Washington Post Exit Poll*," *Washington Post*, 6 November 1996, p. A7.
7. A line for the cases in this example would be similar to the line depicted in figure 11.1. The figure also contains a line for the mean value of 2.8. With the exception of case D (3,3), all of the cases are closer to the regression line than they are to the mean. Thus, the regression line is a better estimate of the Y values than is the mean.
8. A. Scatterplot shows a strong negative relation: the more spent on cost-cutting measures, the lower the increase the Medicare costs. The dots fall in a line that slopes up and to the left.

$$r = \frac{(10 \times 98) - (31 \times 40)}{\sqrt{[10(121) - 961][10(190) - 1,600]}} = \frac{980 - 1,240}{\sqrt{249 \times 300}} = \frac{-260}{273.3} = -.95$$

$$r^2 = .83$$

Thus, the results confirm and give a precise measure to what you observed in the scatterplot. The cost-cutting measures explain 83 percent of the decline in Medicare costs. That is an unusually high value for r^2. As a policy maker you would do well to continue your cost-cutting program.

9. B. $r^2 = .25$. Because it is a positive number, you know that expenditures do relate to SAT scores: the higher the expenditures, the higher the SAT scores. And you know that state expenditures explain 25 percent of the variation in the scores. That means that a number of other factors, such as socioeconomic level of students and size of classroom, also have a lot to do with SAT scores. However, for expenditures to have that much influence is a very positive sign for policy makers, and would probably encourage you to continue state assistance.

10. Fred Hayward, "A Reassessment of Conventional Wisdom about the Informed Public: National Political Information in Ghana," *American Political Science Review* 70 (1976): 433–451.

EXERCISES

Exercise 11.1 Computing Measures of Relationship

Return to tables 6.1 and 6.2. The first table presents information on voting turnout by gender, and the second table controls that relationship for education. At that time you were asked to examine the percentage differences in the tables. Now you will compute Yule's Q for each of the tables, one for table 6.1 and three for table 6.2. Note that in table 6.2 you will need to figure out the implicit second line in the tables. To find out how many said "no," you should subtract the percent saying "yes" from 100 percent.

The accompanying text in chapter 6 analyzes the results on the basis of the percentage differences. Do the same using the Q measures, and compare the merits of the two measures.

Exercise 11.2 Computing Measures of Relationship

The following two sets of figures can be used to determine if gender or age has more influence on a person's vote.

TABLE 11.13
Vote by Gender, 1996

Vote	Gender	
	Men	*Women*
Clinton	44	54
Dole	45	37
Perot	10	7

Source: "Election 1996: The States and the Region—A Closer Look at the Voters: *Washington Post* Exit Poll," *Washington Post*, 6 November 1996, A7.

Note: Percentages do not always add to 100 because of rounding and because of additional candidates.

Table 11.14
Vote by Age, 1996

Vote	Age			
	18–29	*30–44*	*45–59*	*60+*
Clinton	53	49	49	49
Dole	34	41	41	43
Perot	10	9	9	7

Source: "Election 1996: The States and the Region—A Closer Look at the Voters: *Washington Post* Exit Poll," *Washington Post*, 6 November 1996, A7.

Note: Percentages do not always add to 100 because of rounding and because of additional candidates.

1. Develop a hypothesis relevant to each table.
2. Compute percentage differences for each.
3. Select an appropriate measure of relationship for each table and compute it. (Hint: you will probably use a different measure for each table.)
4. Use the percentage differences and relationship measures to analyze the hypotheses.

Exercise 11.3 Selecting Measures of Relationship

You are doing research to see if there is a relationship between *per capita expenditure on education* (coded "low," "medium," and "high") and *percentage of workforce in industrial and manufacturing jobs* (coded "low," "medium," and "high") for ten countries.

1. What level of data do you have for each variable?
2. Propose a hypothesis stating the expected relationship between the variables, and give a brief explanation of your expectation.
3. Which is the dependent variable?
4. Which statistics would be useful to examine your data? Why would you select these?

Exercise 11.4 Computing a Relationship Measure

The following table reports information on quality rating of schools in three types of jurisdictions. Select the most appropriate statistic to analyze the relationship between these two variables. Compute it, and write a brief statement interpreting what you find.

TABLE 11.15
Quality of Schools by Type of Jurisdiction

	Type of Jurisdiction		
Quality Rating of Schools	*Suburb*	*Small Town*	*City*
Excellent	10	0	0
Adequate	20	25	5
Poor	0	15	25

Exercise 11.5 Computing Relationship Measures

Exercise 5.3 asked you to analyze data on math scores and watching TV for fifteen countries. You converted the information to the ordinal level and developed a table. Here you again analyze those same data. This time retain the data at the interval level, create a scatterplot, compute a measure of relationship appropriate for the interval level, and interpret your findings. (The data are repeated below.)

The following information reports math scores and hours spent watching TV for thirteen-year-olds in different countries. You are asked to see if there is any relationship between these variables.

Average Math Scores of Thirteen-Year-Old Participants in IAEP*, by Country, 1991

Canada, 62; France, 64; Hungary, 68; Ireland, 61; Israel, 63; Italy, 64; Jordan, 40; South Korea, 73; Scotland, 61; Slovenia, 57; Soviet Union, 70; Spain, 55; Switzerland, 71; Taiwan, 73; United States, 55.

Percentage of Thirteen-Year-Old Participants in IAEP Who Watch Television Five Hours or More a Day

Canada, 14; France, 5; Hungary, 13; Ireland, 9; Israel, 20; Italy, 5; Jordan, 7; South Korea, 11; Scotland, 24; Slovenia, 4; Soviet Union, 17; Spain, 10; Switzerland, 7; Taiwan, 10; United States, 20.

Source: National Center for Education Statistics, *Digest of Education Statistics* (Washington, D.C.: U.S. Department of Education, 1995), p. 431.

* *International Assessment of Educational Progress*

CHAPTER TWELVE

Determining the Significance of Our Results

Lucy: "How about it, Charlie Brown? I'll hold the ball and you come running up and kick it."

Charlie Brown: "Boy, it really aggravates me the way you think I'm so stupid."

Lucy: "I guarantee that the only thing that will make me pull the ball away this year will be an involuntary muscle spasm! Now, you certainly will agree that the odds must be astronomical against such an involuntary muscle spasm occurring at the very moment you try to kick the ball."

Charlie Brown: "She's right! This year has to be the year I kick that ol' ball! SO HERE I GO! AAUGH!"

Lucy: "I've looked it up, Charlie Brown. The actual odds against such an involuntary muscle spasm occurring at that precise moment were ten billion to one!"

—**Charles M. Schulz,** *"Peanuts"*

Statistical Significance

We have discussed two kinds of statistical measures thus far: techniques for describing variables, in chapter 10, and techniques for measuring the relationships between and among variables, in chapter 11. There is a third kind of statistical technique we need to be familiar with, namely, measures of statistical significance. Often in doing analysis, we draw a sample from the total set of cases we are interested in. We need to know whether the measures we arrive at, be they means or gammas or correlation coefficients, are true of the total population and not just true of the sample. For example, chapter 11 reported correlation measures between different kinds of political participation in a sample of U.S. citizens. It is important to know whether these sample statistics accurately represent characteristics of all citizens. Measures of statistical significance help us answer this question.

The chapter begins by recapping the discussion in chapter 7 that discussed samples and survey research. Then it revisits sampling distributions in somewhat more detail and describes several distributions that can tell us the statistical significance of relationship measures. It will show you how to compute one commonly used measure of significance, chi square. This could be useful in your own research and will also give you a sense of the reasoning behind significance measures. It concludes by describing two other measures and showing you how to interpret them. The purpose of the chapter is to give you a sense of what statistical measures of significance mean when you come across them in studies, or when a computer statistical program you are using reports them.

Recall the earlier and similar discussion in chapter 7. In both contexts we are asking what the probability is that the measure we have arrived at by examining a sample would turn up if there was no relationship or difference in the broader population. Notice how this question is phrased. We are not proving a particular relationship exists. We are asking how likely we would be to find a certain characteristic of the sample if the characteristic was not present in the population. Chapter 7 said that we can state this probability in terms of a **confidence interval** and a **level of significance.** A confidence interval tells us the range within which we can be confident that the value in the population falls, while the level of significance tells us how likely it is to fall within that interval. In large national samples it is common to hold to a standard of a confidence interval of plus or minus three points and a level of significance of .05. This would mean that there is only a 5 percent chance that we would have gotten the result we did if there was no relationship in the population. Researchers often are willing to accept a 5 percent standard, but frequently they look for and report significance measures of one out of a hundred, or .01 significance, meaning that there is only one chance in a hundred that the characteristic of the sample would have turned up if there was no evidence of such a characteristic in the population. Lucy's standard of less than one out of 10 billion is clearly in another league.

confidence interval
Numerical range within which an estimated value is likely to fall; tells us the extent to which the characteristics of a whole population will match those of a smaller sample of that population.

level of significance
Probability that the population parameter falls within the confidence interval we have established; hence, the likelihood that we can draw a conclusion about the population from which the sample is drawn.

normal curve
A symmetrical, bell-shaped curve in which the distribution of values bears a direct and known relationship to the size of the standard deviation: a given percentage of cases are within one, two, and three standard deviations from the mean.

Sampling Distributions

These assumptions are based on the statistical concept of probability distributions. We begin with the distribution known as the **normal curve.** ("Normal" is simply the name of the curve and does not mean that it is typical.) The normal distribution is a valuable tool because we know its standard deviation—the spread of values around the mean. If we keep drawing individual cases or observations at random we would find that they fall in a predictable pattern. The largest number of cases is located in the center of the distribution, and the number of cases tapers off on both sides at a symmetrical rate. Beyond this general statement, we can describe precisely the shape of the distribution, how many cases fall close to the mean, and how many lie within specific distances from the mean value. When we can assume the cases fall in a normal curve, we can say that 34 percent of the values lie within one standard deviation of the mean and that 48 percent (47.7 to be precise) of the values fall within two standard deviations of the mean. Thus we can say that just over 95 percent of the samples we draw (2 × 47.7) fall within plus or minus two standard deviations of the mean value. See figure 12.1.

Assume that we draw a random sample from a population and that 62 percent of the sample respondents say they voted. Assume further that the standard deviation of this sample is 3. Now we know some useful information. We know that if we kept drawing samples from the population and measuring the voter turnout, 95 percent of the samples would show a turnout within two standard deviations of the sample statistic of 62 percent. Because the standard deviation is 3, we know that 95 percent of the samples would indicate a voter turnout of 62 percent plus 6 (2 × 3) or minus 6 (2 × 3). The 95 percent confidence interval therefore is the interval from 56 percent to 68 percent, and we can be sure that 95 percent of the samples would indicate a voter turnout within this interval.

The normal curve allows us to determine how confident we can be that a sample reflects the population. If we kept drawing samples and calculating the mean for each one, they would form a sampling distribution. This distribution also has a mean and a standard deviation just like any distribution. The standard deviation of the sampling distribution is called the **standard error** and is based on two factors—the standard deviation of the sample and the size of the sample. Consider each factor in turn.

First, the standard error varies with the standard deviation of the sample, or the measure of diversity in the sample. Compare two distributions taken from two different populations, one with a mean of 15 and a standard deviation of 3, and the second with a mean of 113 and a standard deviation of 38.5. The second sample clearly has a greater diversity than the first. In both of these samples, 34 percent of the cases would fall within plus or minus one standard deviation of the mean. Thus in the first instance we assume that 34 percent of the cases lie between 15 and 18 and in the second instance that 34 percent of the

standard error
The standard deviation of the sampling distribution; it depends on the standard deviation in the sample and the size of the sample.

FIGURE 12.1
The Normal Curve

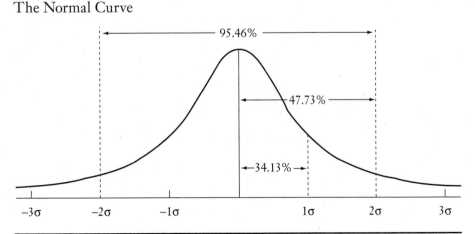

cases lie between 113 and 151.5. Thus the amount of variation in the sample determines how much confidence we can have that the sample mean is close to the population mean. See the two examples in figure 12.2. The less the variation among the cases, the greater the chances the sample statistic is close to the population statistic. Similarly the stronger a correlation measure, the greater the chances that the sample correlation measure is close to the relationship in the population, and hence the greater the confidence we can have in its significance.

In summary, we draw a sample, we compute the mean and standard deviation, and then use these to talk about the full range of cases in the sample. Notice in figure 12.2 that a few cases will lie at the extremes. This means that if we keep drawing cases from our population most will lie near the mean but a few will fall at the extreme. In asking whether our sample reflects the population we are asking what the chances are that the characteristics of our sample could be one of those extreme values. We would like to be able to say that the chances are less than one out of one hundred chances but are often willing to accept five out of one hundred chances.

The second critical characteristic of the sampling distribution and its standard error is its relationship to the size of the sample. The standard error of the sampling distribution of means equals the standard deviation of the population, divided by the square root of the sample size. This is an important piece of information. It means that as the sample size increases, the size of the standard error becomes smaller and the distribution will be narrower. See figure 12.3.

To repeat, we obviously do not know the characteristics of the population, and we usually do not draw many samples. Instead we draw one sample and let it substitute for the characteristics of the population. Because we assume that the many samples would form a normal distribution, we compute the standard error based on the sample we have drawn. The standard error in turn is based on the standard deviation or diversity in the sample and the size of the sample. We can now state the confidence interval and the level of confidence we can have that our findings based on the sample reflect the population. The smaller the standard error the greater confidence we can have that our finding is true of the population.

Consider a numerical example: Assume you have taken a sample and computed the mean and standard deviation of the sample. The mean is 12 and the

FIGURE 12.2
Standard Deviations and Sampling Distributions

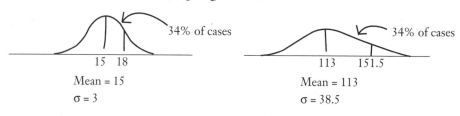

34% of cases   34% of cases

15   18   113   151.5

Mean = 15   Mean = 113

σ = 3   σ = 38.5

FIGURE 12.3
Sample Size and Sampling Distributions

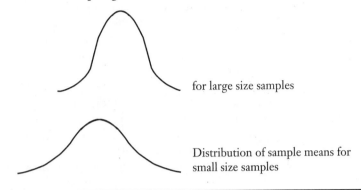

for large size samples

Distribution of sample means for
small size samples

standard deviation is 1.1. We use this sample as an estimate of the population. Assume further that the standard error in this sampling distribution is .20, based on the distribution of values in the sample and the size of the sample. We can now say that a sample mean of 12 lies within plus or minus $1.96 \times .20$ of the real mean, or plus or minus .39. This means that we can be 95 percent confident that the sample mean falls within a confidence interval of 11.61 to 12.39. Thus the larger the number in the sample and the less the diversity in the sample, the greater the level of confidence in the sample statistic or its statistical significance. These same principles apply when we want to determine whether a measure of relationship in a sample indicates a relationship in the population. The larger the number in the sample and the stronger the relationship, the more confidence we can have that there is a relationship in the population.

Statistical Significance and Strength of Relationship

Note that this concern with confidence in our results is different from the one we discussed at the end of chapter 11. There we asked whether relationships were strong or weak. We said that relationships of .30 generally are considered to be influential. We also said that even weaker relationships can be interesting, particularly when we are comparing them with other factors. This chapter is asking a different question; namely, is the relationship we find in a sample, whether strong or weak, also true of the broader population from which the sample was taken? Confusion may be introduced because analysts often use the term *significant* for both questions. When we want to know if a relationship is strong, we often ask, "Is it significant?" That is an incorrect usage. Strictly speaking, *significance* refers to the extent to which we can say that a sample statistic is true of a population. That is our concern in this chapter.

   In the social sciences we usually want to be able to say there is a 95 percent chance that there is a relationship in the larger group. When we state this confidence, however, it usually is phrased in reverse. We say that we are willing to tolerate an error of one out of twenty, or 5 percent; this is expressed as $p = .05$. This statement means that if there is a relationship in a sample, the probability is less than 5 percent that it would have turned up by chance if there is no relationship in the population. Similarly, $p = .01$ means that the probability that there is no relationship in the population is 1 percent or less.

While strength of relationship and statistical significance are different in their essential meanings, they are related concepts. Recall the earlier point that a greater diversity in the sample means a greater standard deviation in the sample and a greater standard error in the sampling distribution. And these in turn mean a lower confidence level or significance for the sample statistic you compute. Or put another way, the greater the homogeneity in the sample, the higher the confidence level. Similarly, the stronger a relationship measure in a sample, the greater the confidence that it is close to the relationship in the population. In this sense strength of relation is connected to statistical significance.

For example, an important study of participation by Verba and Nie reported correlation coefficients among different acts of participation.[1] Citizens were asked if they had voted in the 1964 and 1968 elections. Based on a random sample, the authors reported that the correlation between these two actions has an r of .71. (Recall that if we square this number to get r^2 or .50, we can say that whether or not one voted in 1964 explains 50 percent of the variation in whether or not one voted in 1968.) How confident can we be that there is a similar relationship between these variables in the population? It is possible there is no relationship among all citizens. Given the dependence of the standard error of the sampling distribution on the diversity in the sample and on the size of the sample, we can say that the large relationship measure ($r = .71$) and the large number in the sample ($N = 549$) allow us to be very confident that there is a relationship between these two variables in the population. If the sample had been very small (say, fifty people) and the relationship had been only $r = .04$, then we could not have had as much confidence that there is a relationship in the population. Because of this connection among these characteristics of the sample, it is easy to see why the term *significance* is applied to both strength of relationship and representativeness of the sample. A stronger relationship is more apt to be statistically significant than a weaker one.

These points are related to the earlier discussion of the null hypothesis. Strictly speaking, we cannot prove there is a relationship between two variables. Thus, we undertake the simpler task of rejecting the null hypothesis that there is no relationship. The same logic is applied in determining the significance of statistical measures. To determine whether there is a relationship in the population, statisticians propose the hypothesis that there is not a relationship and then ask how confident they can be that they are wrong. This procedure appears unnecessarily roundabout, but it illustrates how conservative statistical measures of significance are. These measures do not guarantee what the relationship in the population is, but say only how confident researchers can be in *rejecting* the hypothesis that a relationship in a sample turned up only by chance when there is *no relationship* in the population. To repeat, the larger the sample size and the stronger the relationship, the easier it is to reject the hypothesis of no relationship and to conclude instead that there is a relationship.

Determining Sample Size

Statisticians have developed tables that tell us, for different sample sizes, how strong a relationship has to be for us to be confident that it is significant at different levels. Consider the statistic of percentage differences. Assume we find a 10 percent difference between reported voter turnout of men and of women. Is this difference large enough to disprove the hypothesis that there is no difference between the turnout of men and of women? Will this difference in percentages produce a *p* value of .05 or less? By this latter point, we mean that we want to be able to say that in only five out of each one hundred chances could we be wrong—that no relationship will occur in only five of each one hundred cases.

To answer this question, let us assume we interviewed 100 men and 150 women. Table 12.1 gives us the information we need to make a judgment. The figures in the table indicate that the amount of difference needed for the difference to be significant decreases as the sample size increases. If you interviewed two groups of fifty persons each, you would need a difference of 20 percentage points between them in order to be 95 percent certain that there is a difference between the groups in the population. In this example we are working with sample sizes of 100 and 150. The table indicates that we need a difference of 14 percentage points in order to say that the difference is statistically significant at the .05 level. (We read down the column for 90, because it is the figure closest to 100, and across the row for 150.) Because we found only a 10 percent difference, it is not significant in a statistical sense, and we would have to report n.s. (for "not significant").

There is one other term we need to learn, the difference between one- and two-tailed tests. *Tail* refers to one-half of the distribution curve as it tapers off.

TABLE 12.1

Significant Percentage Differences, by Sample Size, at .05 Level of Confidence

Minimum Size of Group B	Minimum Size of Group A				
	50	*90*	*150*	*300*	*600*
50	20	18	16	15	15
90	18	15	14	12	12
150	16	14	12	10	9
300	15	12	10	8	7

Source: William Buchanan, *Understanding Political Variables*, 3d ed. (New York: Scribner's, 1980).

Note: Figures are based on chi square values.

A one-tailed test says that we are only interested in values that fall above *or* below the mean, but not both. A two-tailed test looks at values that fall above and below the mean. It is obviously easier to conclude that you are not likely to find many values above *or* below the sample statistic than to say you won't find many values that are either above or below. Thus to attain a confidence level of .05, you would need a higher significance value if you were carrying out a two-tailed test than if you simply were interested in a one-tailed test. In the latter case you would be looking for the probability of a sample statistic only on one-half of the normal curve. For example, you are told that student participation in the last election was 20 percent, but you believe that it is higher than that. Since you are only asking if the turnout was higher than 20 percent you are looking for a one-tailed test of significance. You take a sample and find that 30 percent of the students in your sample voted. How likely are you to draw such a sample if the real turnout rate was only 20? If 20 percent of the population voted, there is a very small probability of drawing a sample indicating that 30 percent voted. The sample would fall within the "tail" of the normal distribution. The actual probability would depend on the number in your sample and you would find it in a table of significance values under the listing of values for a one-tail test of significance. You would probably conclude that the original estimate of 20 percent was unlikely. You would answer this question by looking at a table of significance values, and for values for a one-tail test of significance.

Consider an example of research reporting significance levels. The data in table 12.2 report the results of a study comparing how citizens evaluate services

TABLE 12.2

Mean Ratings by General Public of Selected Publicly and Privately Provided Services

	Mean	N	St. Dev.	One-Tailed Significance
Public Services				
Fire department	80	333	16.9	.311
U.S. Post Office	72.8	386	19.6	.015*
Municipal trash	70.2	314	19.9	.004**
Public transportation	65.1	192	27.2	.000**
Private Services				
Private mail carriers	81.2	369	16.2	.008*
Banks	71.2	364	22.7	.000**
Auto repair	61.2	334	24.5	.000**
Fast food restaurants	68.9	355	23.1	.424

*Significant at .05 level

**Significant at .01 level

provided by the public sector with services provided by the private sector. (The data were collected in a telephone survey of Georgia residents in 1992, using random digit dialing. The response rate was 66 percent, yielding a total sample of 805.)[2] The table reports information on only a few of the services studied.

The data show that taken as a whole, mean ratings of services are generally quite positive, although they range from the 60s to the 80s. The next question concerns how much confidence the authors could have in these mean values based on the sample. Remember that the answer varies according to the standard deviation in the sample and the size of the sample. The authors were using a one-tailed test because they were examining how confident they could be that the services were not rated lower than the sample indicates. Look at the right hand column in table 12.2. The top figure, .311, has no asterisk, so it is not considered significant at an acceptable level. The next value has a single asterisk, and the key at the bottom of the table indicates this means that there is less than five out of one hundred chances that this mean would have turned up unless the value in the population was fairly close. The next two figures have two asterisks, indicating an even higher confidence; there is less than one out of a hundred chances that this mean would have turned up unless the value in the population was fairly close. Note that three of the significance levels are .000, which says there is virtually no chance that this mean would have turned up unless the actual value in the population was close to it. Given these values we can return to the mean values and draw our conclusions. It appears that there is no reason to conclude that publicly provided services are generally rated lower than privately provided services.

Measuring Statistical Significance

Chi Square, χ^2

known sampling distribution
A distribution in which there is a known probability for each value when samples are drawn from a population in which two variables are not related.

chi square, χ^2
A statistic that tells us whether the measured strength of a relationship is also statistically significant; used for nominal- and ordinal-level data.

The previous section described sampling distributions that fit the shape of the normal curve. Several other **known sampling distributions** have been devised and are commonly used. This phrase means that we know the probability of getting each value when samples are drawn from a population in which there is no association between two variables. Three that are commonly used are χ^2, F, and t, each of which is described on the following pages. When we find a value for any of these statistics and also know the size of the sample, we can tell how likely it is that the sample was drawn from a population where was no relationship between the variables of interest. This likelihood tells us how much confidence we can have in the relationships we are exploring.

We begin with **chi square**, or χ^2. It is designed to be used with nominal-level measures but often is used with ordinal measures as well. First we compute a measure of relationship for nominal variables using lambda or Q as described in chapter 10. Then if we find support for our hypothesized relationship, we need to ask a second question: what is the chance that the relationship could have turned up by chance if in reality there is no relationship in the population? In short, a χ^2, like all significance measures, asks whether a relationship between two variables found in a sample is strong enough that we can have confidence there is in fact a relationship in the population.

TABLE 12.3

Trust in Government, by Gender

Trust	Men	Women	N
Yes	A	C	50
No	B	D	20
N =	40	30	70

Look at the data in table 12.3 that deal with trust levels of men and women. Actually it provides only limited information since it only reports the total number of men and women and the total of those saying "yes" and "no." These are the marginal values, or row and column totals. Note that we need absolute numbers to determine chi square rather than percentages, since chi square depends on knowing the marginals, the total numbers in each row and column.

By using these marginals, we can determine how many cases would fall in each cell if there were *no* relationship between the variables. That is, if women and men are equally likely to say "yes," then we can compute the values in each cell by simply examining the total values, or the numbers in each row and column. To get these estimated numbers, we multiply the figures in the margins and divide by the total number of cases.

$$\text{Cell A} = (50 \times 40) \div 70 = 29$$

$$\text{Cell B} = (20 \times 40) \div 70 = 11$$

$$\text{Cell C} = (50 \times 30) \div 70 = 21$$

$$\text{Cell D} = (20 \times 30) \div 70 = 9$$

These figures are the expected values for each cell, assuming there is no relationship between the independent and dependent variables. That is, assuming that a person's gender has no influence on whether a person votes, twenty-nine men would say "yes," twenty-one women would say "yes," eleven men would say "no," and nine women would say "no." If there is a relationship, however, then gender will influence the numbers in the cells, and the observed values will differ from these expected values.

Chi square is a statistic that measures how much difference there is between the expected and observed values, and that tells us whether the difference is large enough to make us confident that there is a relationship in the population between gender and trust. If we can be confident, then we can say that the relationship is significant. Significance depends on two factors: size of the chi square value, and size of the sample. The larger both of these are, the more confident we can be there is a relationship between gender and voting in the population at large, or the more statistically significant the results are.

The formula for finding the chi square value is

$$\chi^2 = \Sigma \left[\frac{(O - E)^2}{E} \right]$$

where O = the observed value and E = the expected value. Remember that the sigma, Σ merely says to add these values together.

Consider an example. The data in table 12.4 report the number of women employed in state government who perceive they are being discriminated against. The data are divided by income group, and the figures in the cells indicate the number and percentage at each income level that believe there is sex discrimination. Why would this be interesting information to have? One possibility is that high-income women are probably more self-confident about their skills than are low-income women and more apt to blame a failure to be promoted on some external factor, such as discrimination, than on their own inadequacy. Note, however, that data on perceptions do not tell you how much discrimination there is in reality.

In addition to asking whether there is a relationship between income and perception, we also want to know whether the differences in this sample are large enough to make us confident that there is indeed a relationship in the population. To repeat, we are interested in whether or not women perceive they are being discriminated against. We cannot interview all female employees of state governments, so we take a sample. We are particularly interested in whether different income groups have different perceptions of discrimination. It may be that lower-income women do not feel discriminated against but that higher-income women do. Therefore, we ask whether the differences we find among the

TABLE 12.4

Perception of Employment Discrimination by Women Employed in State Government, by Income

Sex Discrimination	Income				
	To $7,999	*8,000–$9,999*	*$10,000–$14,999*	*Over $15,000*	*N*
No	89% (196)	82% (106)	68% (81)	61% (17)	400
Yes	11 (25)	18 (23)	32 (38)	39 (11)	97
	100%	100%	100%	100%	
Total *N*	221	129	119	28	497

Source: Anne Hopkins, "Perceptions of Employment Discrimination in the Public Sector," *Public Administration Review* 40, no. 2, 1980: 131–137.

income groups in the sample are large enough to justify the hypothesis that there is a difference in perceptions among the income groups in the entire population of women employed in state government.

We could select two of the columns and compute a percentage difference to see whether it is large enough to be significant. For example, we could subtract 68 percent ($10,000–$14,999 group saying "no") from 89 percent (low-income group saying "no") and ascertain if that is significant. We get a difference of 21 percentage points. The numbers in the two groups are 119 and 221. Now look back at table 12.1, in the column for 90 and the row for 150 (closest to the numbers in the groups). We see that there has to be a difference of 14 percentage points to be significant. Because we have a difference of 21, we have a good idea that the difference is significant.

Chi square however, enables us to be more precise about our level of confidence in these results. It is particularly useful because it takes into account all of the cells and not just the two we happened to select for comparison. We can compute it using the following procedure:

Cell	Expected Frequency (E)	($O - E$)	($O - E$)^2	$\dfrac{(O - E)^2}{E}$
A	$(400 \times 221) \div 497 = 178$	18	324	$324 \div 178 = 1.8$
B	$(97 \times 221) \div 497 = 43$	−18	324	$324 \div 43 = 7.5$
C	$(400 \times 129) \div 497 = 104$	2	4	$4 \div 104 = 0.04$
D	$(97 \times 129) \div 497 = 25$	−2	4	$4 \div 25 = 0.16$
E	$(400 \times 119) \div 497 = 96$	−15	225	$225 \div 96 = 2.3$
F	$(97 \times 119) \div 497 = 23$	15	225	$225 \div 23 = 9.8$
G	$(400 \times 28) \div 497 = 23$	−6	36	$36 \div 23 = 1.6$
H	$(97 \times 28) \div 497 = 5$	6	36	$36 \div 5 = \underline{7.2}$
				30.4

degrees of freedom (df)
Number of cells in a matrix in which you can freely insert a number; cells in which the entry is not determined by numbers in other cells.

The chi square value for these data is 30.4. In order to interpret that number's significance, we need one more item of information. It is the **degrees of freedom** (abbreviated as **df**). This figure equals $(r - 1)(c - 1)$, in which c is the number of columns and r is the number of rows. For instance, in a table with two rows and two columns, there are four cells. Once you put a number in any one of the four cells, the number in the other three cells follows automatically from the total in the rows and columns. Look back at table 12.2. Once you put a number in any of the four cells, the numbers in the other cells are determined. Thus, statisticians tell us we have one degree of freedom.

In the present case we have two rows and four columns, which produce eight cells. Once you have specified the number of cases within three of the cells, the number of cases in the other five will automatically be determined by the total numbers in each column and row. Thus, there are three "degrees of freedom"; after that the numbers are fixed. In this example:

$$(r - 1) = 2 - 1 = 1$$
$$(c - 1) = 4 - 1 = 3$$
$$1 \times 3 = 3$$

Recall that table 12.1 showed the percentage differences for various sample sizes. These were actually based on chi square values. Tables of chi square values tell us what value of χ^2 is significant at different degrees of freedom. In the back of any statistics text you will find such a table, giving the χ^2 values for different degrees of freedom and also for different levels of confidence, such as $p = .01$, and $p = .05$. Because we usually are interested only in significance at the .05 level, we have simplified this information in table 12.5.

Table 12.5 tells us that with three degrees of freedom we would need a chi square value of 7.82 to be certain that the result is statistically significant at the .05 level. In this example, the χ^2 value is 30.4, which is large enough to be significant. At the bottom of the table you would put:

$$\chi^2 = 30.4 \qquad p = .05$$

This notation indicates that the chi square value is 30.4 and that this statistic is large enough that we can be confident there is a relationship between income level and perception of discrimination in the population of all women employed by state governments and that we can be confident that 95 percent of the samples we would draw would indicate a relationship. We say $p = .05$ to indicate that only 5 percent of the time would we have gotten this result if in fact income made no difference.

Another way of stating the meaning of $p = .05$ in our example is to say that we can be 95 percent confident that income does have an influence on our perception of discrimination ($1.00 - .05 = .95$). (If you had access to a table with chi square values for different significance levels, you would find that a chi square value of this size is actually significant at the .001 level of significance.

Table 12.5
Chi Square Values at the .05 Level of Significance

Degrees of Freedom	Chi Square Values
1	3.84
2	5.99
3	7.82
4	9.49
10	18.31

Source: R. A. Fisher and F. Yates, Statistical Tables for Biological, Agricultural and Medical Research, 6th ed. (London: Longrnan, 1974), Table 4. (Previously published by Oliver and Boyd, Edinburgh.)

That is, there is less than one chance in a thousand that the result would have turned up if there was no such difference among the groups of women in the population.)

Chi square values are commonly used because it is possible to compute them by hand or with a calculator. They provide a readily understandable measure of the significance of a relationship we find in a sample. They are particularly useful if the number in the sample is small, because small samples are less apt to be significant than large ones.

Computing Chi Square Values

Practice Exercise 12.1

A. To test a version of the gender-gap hypothesis of voting, look at the relationship between gender and party vote in the following table. The Q measure of relationship is .30. Compute a chi square for the table and determine whether the Q is statistically significant at the .05 level of probability. (Answers to each question appear in the endnotes.[3])

	Gender	
Party Vote	*Male*	*Female*
Republican	14	12
Democratic	10	16

B. Determine the degree of association and statistical significance of the following table. Note: round off each result to a whole number.[4]

	Political Party	
Legislation	*Republican*	*Democratic*
Yes	23	9
No	11	17

C. What is the null hypothesis for the following table? Compute the appropriate statistic to test the null hypothesis and determine the statistical significance of the relationship.[5]

Political Participation	Amount of Television Viewed		
	Low	*Medium*	*High*
Low	6	3	5
Medium	7	9	6
High	4	6	4

1. Null hypothesis:
2. Measure of relationship:
3. Chi square:
4. Interpretation:

F Test and Analysis of Variance (ANOVA)

F **test**
Measure of statistical significance with a known sampling distribution.

The *F* **test** is another commonly used measure of significance because there is a known sampling distribution that tells us how much confidence we can have that a particular *F* value would have turned up if there was no relationship in the population. It is commonly used with interval-level data to examine differences of means, regression, and correlation coefficients. The computation of *F* is beyond the scope of this book. It can easily be derived by those using statistical packages, and it is commonly reported in published research studies. Computer analyses of differences of means, regression coefficients, and correlation coefficients commonly report the *F* value and its significance. Typically authors report the relationship measure, the *F* value, and whether or not it is significant and at what level. There is a different table of F values for each level of significance and for different degrees of freedom, found in statistics texts. If the value you find in your research is larger than the appropriate value in the table then you can assume it would be unlikely to get your result if there was no relation in the population. That is, based on this sample, there is a very small probability that there is no relationship in the population.

The F value measures the variance in a sample; recall from chapter 10 that variance is the spread of values around the mean. Assume you want to know if men and women differ in the extent to which they have trust in the political system. You decide to find the mean for each gender and then compute a difference of means. You draw a sample of women and of men and through a survey find that the mean value of trust for women is 40 and for men is 30. How confident can we be that this difference of 10 between the two sample means is true of women and men in the population? To answer this, you would carry out an analysis of variance (known as ANOVA) which produces an F statistic. The logic is straightforward. Is the variation *between* the two groups enough larger than the variation *within* the groups to suggest that the two sample groups represent different populations? That is, we said the mean value of trust for women was 40. How much variation was there among the women? Were most of them close to 40? And were most of the sample means close to their mean value of 30? If so, then it should be intuitively clear that the difference between the genders of 10 points in the sample is probably present in the population. Statisticians have computed the distribution of the means of the variance and what values fall within one, two and three standard errors from the mean. Once you find the F statistic you would look it up in special tables in statistics books to determine how much confidence you can have in it. Consult these tables to see how often the F value you found would have turned up if the trust levels of mean and women did not differ.

Consider a second example of applying the F value to a difference of means. A study hypothesizes that midwestern cities spend more per capita on education than western cities do. The analyst takes a sample of cities in each region and determines the mean value for expenditures on education in the two groups of cities. The study finds that midwestern cities as predicted spend an average of $100 more per capita on education than do western cities. The question is whether this difference in the sample is likely to exist in the actual population of the cities. The study reports an F value based on an analysis of the variance, and by consulting a table of F values is able to report a confidence or significance level of .05. This means that the difference of means between western and midwestern cities was significant at the level of .05. The analyst could therefore be confident that there is less than a 5 percent chance this difference could have turned up by chance unless there really was a difference between the mean expenditures in the two groups of cities.

Similarly, regression studies typically state the value of F, which in turn indicates the significance of the regression analysis. We are asking how likely it is to obtain this value of F with repeated random samples from a population if there is no relationship in the population. For example, if the results of your regression have an F value with a significance of .6, then you know you could expect to get this value for F six out of ten times from a population in which the variables are not related to each other. You would obviously not feel very secure with these results and would report them as not significant. By contrast, if the significance of the F value were reported as .01, then you would know there is less than one chance out of one hundred of getting this value for F if the variables in the population were not related to each other. In this case you could be very confident in the results.

t test

t test
A measure of statistical significance with a known sampling distribution; useful when sample size is fewer than thirty.

The *t* **test** is another commonly used measure of significance based on a different sampling distribution. The significance measure of t is commonly used when gamma or Somers d or the tau measures indicate there is a relationship. It is also used whenever the sample size is less than thirty.[6] Recall that the closeness of the sample means to the population increases with the size of the sample. Thus for smaller sizes of N the distribution differs from the normal distribution. It is still bell-shaped, but the values are spread out differently. As the sample size increases, it approximates the normal distribution. Since with smaller sizes we cannot assume that the means of all possible samples fall on a normal curve, the t statistic corrects for this limitation. The t distribution is flatter than the normal distribution. This fact means that a result can be farther from the mean and still be within one or two standard deviations of the mean as compared to a normal distribution. The t distributions also vary for different degrees of freedom.

Like F, t is used to determine the significance of a correlation measure or the difference between two mean values. Assume you compute the mean income for samples of men and women and report the mean income for the two sample means. You want to know if the difference could have turned up by chance. A t value can be computed, and you can consult tables of t distributions to determine if the value obtained is significant at an acceptable level. Again you can choose a t value according to the level of significance you want to achieve—a .01 or .05 probability that the difference between the means would not be found unless there was a difference in the population of men and women.

A few values for t are given in table 12.6 for several significance levels for one- and two-tailed tests. If you have two degrees of freedom and have a t value of 3, and you are carrying out a one-tailed test, you could have a .05 level of confidence that a sample showing a 30 percent turnout would not have turned up by chance if the real voting turnout was 20 percent. Put another way, you can be 95 confident that the actual voting percentage is higher than 20 percent. Assume however that you want to do a two-tail test, that you are asking whether student turnout was higher *or* lower than the 30 percent you found. Then you would be carrying out a two-tailed test and you could only have a .10 level of confidence that a sample with a 30 percent voter turnout would not have turned up by chance if the real turnout value was 20 percent.

The following study reports research using both F and t values. Table 12.7 gives regression coefficients, t values indicating the significance of each coefficient, the R^2, and the F value for this latter value. The research examines the influences on college entrance exam scores. It asks whether characteristics of the community, the size of the public school bureaucracy, the size of the school, or

TABLE 12.6
Distribution of *t*, Selected Values

	Level of Significance for One-Tailed Tests		
	.05	.025	.01
	Level of Significance for Two-Tailed Tests		
df	.10	.05	.02
1	6.3	12.7	31.8
2	2.9	4.3	6.9
3	2.3	3.1	4.5
4	2.1	2.7	3.7

Source: Adapted from table III of R. A. Fisher and F. Yates, *Statistical Tables for Biological, Agricultural and Medical Research*, 6th ed., published by Longman Group Ltd., London, 1974, table 4.

the role of teachers has any influence. Note that the authors chose these variables because they pointed to data they could collect fairly readily. As a measure of community characteristics, the study chose teen birth rate. As a measure of school size, it used the number of students and size of budget. For school bureaucracy, it used the number of administrators. For role of teachers, the study

TABLE 12.7
Correlations between College Entrance Exam Scores by Student Characteristics, Size of Bureaucracy, Size of School, and Role of Teachers

	Regression Coefficient	*t* Score
Student characteristics—teen birth	−.46	3.63*
School size	−.20	1.66
School bureaucracy	−.16	1.49
Teacher involvement in education decisions	.22	1.71
Teacher involvement in administrative decisions	−.32	2.86*

R^2 .69
F 9.87
$N = 49$ cases

Source: Adapted from Kevin Smith and Kenneth Meier, "Politics, Bureaucrats and Schools," *Public Administration Review* 54, no. 4 (November/December 1994): 556, table 3.

*$p < .05$

looked at the extent to which teachers made decisions about the curriculum and the extent to which they were involved in administration.

First, look at the correlation coefficients. Most of them are negative values, meaning that the more of these variables, the lower the scores. Only teacher involvement in education decisions is positively related to exam scores. Now look at the t scores. These tell you that only the data on teen birth rate and teacher involvement in administration are statistically significant. The teen birth rate has a fairly strong correlation. The fact that the others are not significant does not mean that the coefficients are inaccurate. It just means that we cannot be confident they did not turn up in the sample by chance. Now look at the multiple correlation measure, R^2 and its F value. All of these variables taken together have a correlation of .69 with exam scores. The F value of 9.87 means that the multiple correlation is significant at .05.

As this text has stressed throughout, these results have meaning only in the context of other research on these questions. Based on research reported in the literature, the authors were particularly interested in several of the findings. First they noted that while the size of the bureaucracy was related to lower scores, the relationship was smaller than many would expect and it is not significant. Second they were interested that giving teachers greater involvement in educational decisions such as curriculum design and the placement of students was positively related to scores, even though it was not significant. And finally, they noted the significant relationship between teacher involvement in administrative activities and test scores. They concluded with a warning that if school bureaucracies are reduced to the point that teachers have to pick up more administrative burdens, there could be a reduction in test scores.

Significance Levels

As suggested at the outset of the chapter, the word *significance* has a precise meaning as used here. It does not mean importance. Rather, it means that the differences or relationships we find in a sample probably also occur to roughly the same degree in the population. When the relationships we notice in a sample hold true for the entire population, we call these relationships significant, and they become important measures of how useful the sample results are to us. If we find that a relationship is not strong or prevalent enough that we can have confidence in it, or deem it significant, we report n.s. for "not significant." This designation does not mean there is no relationship but only that we cannot be confident there is a relationship in the population on the basis of this sample.

Studies often report the level of significance of a relationship in terms of chi square or other measures of statistical significance. In all such cases, the larger these measurement numbers are, the more likely the measure is significant. Table 12.8 illustrates how such measures frequently are reported in actual studies. The study from which this table was taken examined attitudes toward taxation in the United States. The authors developed a measure they called "tax ethics," which they used as an indicator of the extent to which people believe

TABLE 12.8
Variables Related to Tax Ethics, Pearson's r

Income level	.3560*
Sense of alienation	.3024*
General distrust of people	.2955*
Suspicion that others cheat	.2788*
Educational level	.2629*
Politicians waste their time	.2596*
Political efficacy	.2130*
Politicians manipulate people	.1029**
Age	.0576***

Source: Young-dahl Song and Tinsley Yarbrough, "Tax Ethics and Tax-payer Attitudes: A Survey," *Public Administration Review* 38 (September/October): 447.

* $p = .001$

** $p = .05$

*** $p = .18$

they have a duty to pay taxes. The level of respondents' commitment to tax ethics constituted the dependent variable. It was correlated with independent variables such as age, income, and attitudes toward politicians and other people in general. The figures in the table report the bivariate correlations (r values) between each of these indicators and tax ethics, and state the statistical significance of these correlations.

First, look at the measures of relationship, the Pearson's correlation measures. According to the data, income has the highest relationship to tax ethics: the wealthier one is, the more apt one is to rank high on tax ethics. Age has the weakest correlation: young and old are equally likely to rank high on tax ethics. The authors note that the impact of several attitudes may seem surprising. For example, a sense of alienation and distrust are positively correlated to tax ethics: the more alienated and the more distrustful, the more apt one is to rank high on tax ethics.

Next look at the information about statistical significance. The authors have placed an asterisk beside each figure, indicating the level of significance. Most of the relationships are highly significant at the $p = .001$ level: the probability of getting this relationship measure is less than one in a thousand if there is no relationship in the population. The relationship between age and tax ethics is much less significant; if we were requiring a significance level of .05, we would reject this result as not significant. The r value of .0576, which can be rounded to .06, could have occurred by chance 18 percent of the time even if there was no relationship in the population. Frequently, analysts will report the r value and its significance level, as in this case, and let the reader decide

TABLE 12.9
Privatization Levels Compared by Region, 1982 and 1992

Type of City	n	1982 Mean	1992 Mean	t Value	Significance
All cities	596	12.9	27.8	22.5	0
North	90	15.2	24.9	5.5	0
South	187	10.1	26.9	15.4	0
Midwest	164	12.2	28.2	11.4	0
West	155	14.8	29.9	11.4	0

Source: Jeffrey Greene, "How Much Privatization?" *Policy Studies Journal* 24, no. 4 (1996): 635.

Note: *t* values are at the 99% confidence level. Privatization scores were based on responses to surveys by the International City Management Association. They indicate the percentage of functions in which a city used private service delivery arrangements.

whether or not to accept it as significant. (As noted earlier, if a table indicates that the significance is .00, by the way, it does not mean that the result has no significance. In fact it means the reverse: there is virtually no chance that the sample statistic could have turned up unless there really was a relationship in the population.)

Consider a second example of significance measures. The author was interested in learning whether cities had increased the privatization of services. He sampled 596 cities, collecting information on the numbers of services privatized in 1982 and then in 1992. He then computed the mean number of services privatized for all cities and for each region and found the results reported in table 12.9.

First scan the results; in every region there has been a large increase in the mean percent of privatized services. What is the probability that the results based on these samples would turn up even if there was no difference in the population of cities over this decade? The *t* test tells us that there is virtually a zero chance that the author would have found these results if there had been no difference in the whole population of cities during this time. Note that a report of a significance of zero does not mean the results are not significant; indeed quite the reverse.

Where We Are

This and the two previous chapters covered a variety of statistical measures, all of them designed to help you summarize the major patterns and relationships in the data you have collected. Although these pages will not turn you into a statistician, it is possible to be an intelligent consumer of statistical terms and concepts without being an expert. Now that you have been introduced to the rudiments, practice them. When you encounter a table, decide first whether it is describing one or several single variables or whether it is showing a relationship between or among variables. Look at the bottom of the table to see whether any measures of significance levels are included. These measures should give you some aid in interpreting the tables and assessing their results.

There is one additional part of analysis that is important to emphasize, namely the way we present our analysis. The next chapter focuses on various techniques for presenting data graphically so that it is easily understandable by others. Too often presentation of information is an afterthought, but it is critical to learn how to present information effectively. Being careful and creative about the visual presentation of our findings can also clarify what we have found in our research and can assist us in making an effective narrative and drawing our written conclusions.

NOTES

1. Sidney Verba and Norman Nie, *Participation in America* (New York: Harper & Row, 1972).
2. Adapted from Theodore Poister and Gary Henry, "Citizen Ratings of Public and Private Service Quality, A Comparative Perspective," *Public Administration Review* 54, no. 2 (March/April 1994): 155–160.
3. Observed values are 14, 10, 12, 16; expected values are 12, 12, 14, 14; $\chi^2 = .33 + .33 + .29 + .29 = 1.24$. $df = 1$, and table 12.4 says that you need a value of 3.84 to be significant. Therefore the chi square value of 1.24 means that the relationship is not significant.
4. $Q = .6$ and $\chi^2 = 6.82$ if you round off all results to whole numbers. If you keep figures to two decimals, the chi square value is 6.55. There is 1 df. Since table 12.5 says you need 3.84 to be significant at the .05 level, this relationship is significant.
5. H_o = no relationship between amount of television viewed and political participation. Gamma = $(286 - 259)/(286 + 259) = .05$. $\chi^2 = 1.84$ with 2 df. This is not significant: thus, you cannot reject H_o.
6. G. David Garson, *Political Science Methods* (Boston: Holbrook, 1976), p. 203.
7. Sam Overman and Donna Loraine, "Information for Control: Another Management Proverb?" *Public Administration Review* 54, no. 2 (March/April 1994): 195.

EXERCISES

Exercise 12.1 Computing Relationships and Significance Values

Tables 12.10 and 12.11 present data on attitudes toward community control of public services. Table 12.10 is based on all residents in a community; table 12.11 comprises two bivariate tables that report the same attitudes according to race. The rationale is that neighborhood control over public services has been an important issue, especially for minority groups in big cities. One question is whether those who are dissatisfied with service delivery are more likely or less likely to want control over those services. A second question is whether whites and minorities differ in this respect.

TABLE 12.10

Relationship of Attitudes toward Community
Control and Attitudes about the Quality of
Local Services

Support for Community Control	Evaluation of Local Services	
	Low	High
Low	45%	66%
	(54)	(160)
High	55	44
	(67)	(81)
	100%	100%
Total N =	121	241

Source: Based on table 12.11.

1. State two hypotheses relevant to this information that fit the two questions in the introduction to this exercise.
2. Compute the Q value for all three tables in order to learn how the variables are related. What do they tell you about your questions?
3. Now compute the chi square values for these three tables to determine whether the relationship is statistically significant. Return to table 12.5.

TABLE 12.11

Racial Differences in Attitudes toward Community Control and the
Quality of Local Services

Support for Community Control	Evaluation of Local Services			
	Minority		White	
	Low	High	Low	High
Low	36%	53%	52%	71%
	(20)	(35)	(34)	(125)
High	64	47	48	29
	(36)	(31)	(31)	(50)
	100%	100%	100%	100%
Total N =	56	66	65	175

Source: Norman Fainstein and Susan Fainstein, "The Future of Community Control," *American Political Science Review* 70 (1976): 915.

Exercise 12.2 Interpreting Significance Measures

Exercise 4.2 described an experiment in which 101 students in groups of five participated in one of two approaches to decision making. Half the groups used an interactive style, and the other half a structured style. After the groups spent time making a decision, individuals were given a questionnaire. They could answer 1 to 5 for each question, and the mean responses of those using each style are reported here. The author computed the difference of means and used a *t* test of significance; the result and the significance level for these two questions are shown in table 12.12.

1. The numbers in the cells are means. What do they tell you?
2. You can easily compute a difference of means for each question. On the basis of these figures alone would you guess that one or the other or both differences in means is large enough so that one could be confident there was a difference in the population of students?
3. The table also reports the *t* test for these data and the statistical significance. Do they support the estimates you made in question 2? Interpret these results.

TABLE 12.12

Attitudes toward Involvement in Decision Making by Style of Decision Making

Question	Group Means			
	Interactive	*Structured*	*t*	*Significance*
1. "I feel I was able to express my ideas in the group."	4.52	3.63	4.53	.000
2. "The group took account of my inputs in discussion."	4.11	3.91	0.76	.448

Source: Julianne Mahler, "Structured Decision Making in Public Organizations," *Public Administration Review* 47 (July/August 1987): 340.

Exercise 12.3 Interpreting Significance Measures

Table 12.13 presents information about the characteristics of communities that have council-manager forms of government. The variables examined in the study are the population of the community, the size of the government, and the income of the community. A questionnaire was mailed to city managers or city clerks in all 283 Illinois cities with a population over 5,000 (except Chicago). One hundred sixty-nine communities, or 60 percent, responded. Correlations were computed to determine if population, size of government, and income level

TABLE 12.13
Correlations between Selected Community Characteristics and Type of Government

	Population 1986	Number Full-Time Employees	Municipal per Capita Income
Council-Manager Government	.20**	.16**	.24**

Source: Uday Desai and John Hamman, "Images and Reality in Local Government Personnel Practices," *Public Administration Review* 54, no. 4 (July/August 1994): 394, adapted.

** $P < .01$

were related to the tendency to have council-manager forms of government. What do the correlation measures indicate about (1) the strength of a relationship and (2) its direction—positive or negative? Interpret the statistical significance of the measures.

Exercise 12.4 Interpreting Statistical Significance

Table 12.14 reports correlation coefficients and their statistical significance. The research question is whether or not managers use information about projects to control costs and quality. It is an especially useful question as computers enable managers to collect and access increasing amounts of information. Do

TABLE 12.14
Correlation Coefficients for Value of Information in Enabling Managers to Control Projects

Nature of Information	Project Costs	Project Schedule	Project Quality
Quantity	−.082	.032	−.082
Timeliness	−.011	.134	−.041
Details	−.248	.006	−.153
R^2	.041	.035	.055
F value	.381	.324	.511
$p =$	.952	.973	.878

Source: Adapted from Sam Overman and Donna Loraine, "Information for Control: Another Management Proverb?" *Public Administration Review* 54, no. 2 (March/April 1994): 195.

they use the information to improve the project? The authors studied this question by examining a random sample of ninety-nine U.S. Air Force defense projects.

The authors come to the following conclusion based on these results. Explain the basis for their reasoning.

> The quantity, detail and timeliness and cost of information do not have a positive effect on project control. In fact these results were notable for their insignificance.[7]

CHAPTER THIRTEEN

Presenting and Analyzing Tabular and Graphic Data

One of the most important and difficult tasks which faces the practical statistician is that of communicating his findings to the decision makers (whether they are the government, the board of directors, or the general public). Failure in this task implies that all his work is wasted, no matter how excellent his experimental design and analysis, and no matter how sound his conclusions. It is not enough just to publish or circulate results; if the message still does not get through he has failed.

—**B. H. Mahon,** "Statistics and Decisions: The Importance of Communication and the Power of Graphical Presentation," *Journal of Royal Statistical Society Abstracts.*

The Power of Graphics and Tables

Perhaps you are like many readers who, when they come across a table or figure, skip to the note that explains what the table or figure means. Glossing over tables, however, forces you to accept whatever interpretation the author makes of the information in the tables. An author may summarize a table by saying, for instance, "Most respondents agree with the president's program," with "most" meaning anything from 51 percent to 99 percent. To interpret this statement, you need to be able to interpret tables and other graphic displays. In addition, to present the results of your own research, you should look for opportunities to present the information graphically, to capture in a figure or table the results and patterns you have found. Clear tables and graphics can add immeasurably to your presentations. As British statistician B. H. Mahon observed in the chapter-opening excerpt, if analysts fail to communicate their findings concisely, clearly, and memorably, then the analysis is a failure.

This chapter explores strategies for presenting material in tables and graphs. It will not only help you prepare your own tables more effectively but will also give you experience in reading and interpreting tables and graphs prepared by others. Finally, it will point out that while we usually associate tables and graphs with quantitative information, we also need to give thought to how we present qualitative findings. Most qualitative research is presented in narrative form, but its effectiveness often can be greatly enhanced by designing appropriate tables and graphics to present the research, even when numbers cannot be attached to the findings.

Tabular Data

tabular data
Presentation of numerical data in the form of tables of various types and sizes.

Thus far you have created relatively simple tables that describe a single variable or examine a relationship among two or more variables. This chapter begins by illustrating the basic principles of organizing data into tables. The table with which we will be working (table 13.1) provides information about a single variable, *expenditures of the U.S. government.* It is a fairly complex table, however, because it breaks down the information into a number of categories. Let us first examine its organization.

Most tables consist of three elements: (1) editorial material, or labels, (2) elements enclosed within what is called the box, and (3) the actual data.

Editorial Material

Editorial material, that is, the set of labels and explanatory notes that indicate what the table is designed to tell and how to go about finding that information, consists of the following.

Table number. Our table is numbered 13.1 because it is the first table in the thirteenth chapter. Numbers should be consistent throughout a study and should identify quickly and accurately where the table fits within the entire presentation.

Title. Tables should be self-contained. That is, readers should be able to make sense of the table without having to read the accompanying narrative. For this reason, titles sometimes appear long or awkward. That is all right, since the role of the title is to provide a clear signal to the reader of what is contained in the table. In table 13.1, the title tells the reader that the table contains data on "direct governmental expenditure," that it is organized by governmental "functions," and that it covers the years 1991–1992.

Headnote. If the table title might otherwise become too awkward, a headnote can be used to supply additional information. In our example, the headnote indicates that direct expenditure "excludes payments or other transfers of funds from one government to another." Is this an important item to note? Can you think of certain government programs that rely heavily on transfer of funds from one government to another? (Federal highway funds given to states and federal grants for welfare payments and community development are examples of indirect funding.)

TABLE 13.1

Direct Governmental Expenditure, by Function, 1991–1992 (Excludes Payments or Other Transfers from One Government to Another)

Item	Amount (Millions of Dollars)				Percentage				Amount Per Capita			
	All Governments	*Federal*	*State*	*Local*	*All Governments*	*Federal*	*State*	*Local*	*All Governments*	*Federal*	*State*	*Local*
Total direct expenditure	2,494,424	1,527,311	701,601	661,744	100.0	100.0	100.0	100.0	10,029.45	6,140.93	2,827.86	2,660.71
General expenditure	1,864,166	1,072,581	612,629	575,188	74.7	58.0	58.4	85.8	7,495.34	4,312.58	2,469.25	2,312.68
National defense and international relations	351,684	351,684	X	X	73.1	23.0	X	X	1,414.03	1,414.03	X	X
Postal service	44,890	44,890	X	X	93.6	2.9	X	X	180.49	180.49	X	X
Space research	13,550	13,550	X	X	28.2	.9	X	X	54.48	54.48	X	X
Education	346,788	48,597	211,316	238,929	13.9	1.4	12.3	36.0	1,394.35	196.84	851.73	960.67
Public welfare	202,875	142,482	155,420	33,072	8.1	3.1	17.9	4.4	815.71	572.88	626.43	132.97
Health	39,051	16,930	23,502	13,957	1.6	.6	3.3	2.1	157.01	77.35	94.73	56.12
Veterans' services	20,490	20,320	170	X	.8	1.3	X	X	82.39	81.70	.69	X
Highways	68,164	16,303	48,959	26,950	2.7	.1	5.8	4.1	274.07	65.55	197.33	108.05
Police protection	42,135	7,400	5,494	30,572	1.7	.4	.7	4.6	169.41	29.75	22.15	122.92
Housing and community development	32,941	31,887	2,668	15,880	1.3	1.0	.2	2.4	132.45	128.21	10.75	63.85
Judicial and legal admin.	20,879	7,337	7,501	10,169	.8	.2	.9	1.5	83.95	29.66	30.23	40.89
Interest on general debt	255,077	199,713	24,621	30,743	10.2	X	3.5	4.6	1,025.60	803.00	99.24	123.61
Utility and liquor stores expenditure	85,314	X	9,613	75,701	1.7	X	.7	5.75	343.03	X	38.75	304.37
Insurance trust expenditure	544,945	454,730	79,359	10,856	21.8	29.8	11.3	1.6	2,191.08	1,828.35	319.86	43.65

Source: U.S. Bureau of the Census. *1992 Census of Governments.* vol. 4, no. 5 (Washington, D.C.: U.S. Government Printing Office, 1997), tables 2, 3, 9.

Note: Because of rounding, details may not add up to totals. X means not applicable.

Footnote. Additional explanatory information may appear at the bottom of the table (outside the box) in the form of footnotes. In our example, there are three footnotes. The first is the footnote giving the source of the information; it is an essential feature of the table. In this case the source is the U.S. Bureau of the Census. Knowing the source enables readers to find additional information and to judge the reliability of the data. How would you judge the reliability of the data in table 13.1?

The second footnote indicates that the separate numbers may not add up to the reported totals because of rounding. The third footnote defines the mark X as meaning "not applicable." Is the *not applicable* designation important? If this note were omitted, you might think that the blank places in the table signified data that for some reason were unavailable. Why would a specific kind of governmental expenditure not be applicable to a given level of government? See, for example, that state and local governments have an X in the category *National defense and international relations*, indicating that these governmental levels do not have any responsibilities in these areas. Where are the other X marks? What do they tell you about the federal government in the United States?

The Box

The box is the part of the table located within the ruled lines that form the top and bottom of the table proper. Within the box are the following labels and guiding features.

Box heads. The box heads identify each category or subcategory into which the data are separated. The most general category or categories are at the top, and more specific, subordinate categories are below. In table 13.1 examples of box head material are the labels *Item, Amount (Millions of Dollars)*, and *Percentage*. Recall what it means to say that an amount is in millions of dollars. It tells you to add, mentally, six zeroes after the decimal in the amount listed in the table.

Column captions. Each column must be clearly labeled, usually with very short captions. In fact, one of the important principles of table organization is the compression of usable data. In table 13.1, column captions like *Federal, State*, and *Local* are sufficient because the table title already tells the reader that the entire table reports information on governmental expenditures, and thus it is unnecessary to repeat the word *government* in each caption.

Stub. The far-left portion of each table is a column that contains a list of the categories in which data are arranged in the rows of the table. In table 13.1, the stub is labeled *Item*.

Row captions. Labels for row categories are called row captions. In this example the row captions are all words or phrases, such as *Postal service* and *Education*. Notice that the same indentation should add up to the prior row that was not indented. Thus, in table 13.1 the items *General expenditure, Utility and liquor stores expenditure*, and *Insurance trust expenditure* add up to *Total direct expenditure*.

Totals. Large quantities of data are difficult for the reader to absorb, so data occasionally are summarized. One way to do this is to present totals at key places in the table, such as the bottom of each column (still within the box). In table 13.1, the totals are given at the top of each column, because most readers will care more about the totals than about the subordinate data.

Data Display

The third main element of the table is the data display itself. Data can be presented in "raw" form, as in table 13.1—the $2,494,424 million governmental expenditure is raw data. You could read this figure as 2 trillion, 494 billion, 424 million dollars. Raw data are actual dollars rather than percentages. Because it may be difficult to grasp the significance of complex data simply by inspecting a table, the author may assist by summarizing the raw data in the form of percentages, shown here in columns five through eight.

Reading data in a table differs from reading a narrative, in that tabular data contain no meaning by themselves; you must supply the meaning as you read. Look again at table 13.1. Scan the table for facts that explain the structure of governmental expenditures in the United States. A good rule of thumb is to begin by noting general patterns and then to look at specific figures. First, look at the *range of variation*, the distance between the largest and the smallest numbers in the set. General expenditures for all governments combined range from $7,337 million for judicial and legal administration to $351,684 million for national defense. Such a general statement about the data's range provides a sense of the magnitudes you are dealing with, but it may also mask some important differences among the levels of government. Because of these differences, you would also need to consider the range of variation within each governmental level. Identify the range of variation in expenditures for each level of government: federal, state, and local.

The second important feature of the table is the patterns in which the data are distributed. The patterns you look for depend to some extent on your research question. Imagine that you are interested in patterns of expenditures, by level of government: federal, state, and local. You note that two kinds of expenditures—national defense and postal service—are restricted entirely to the federal government, and others, such as education, are dominated by local governments. Complete the following statements:

Local governments spend more than the other two levels of government on:

_____

State governments spend more than the other two levels of government on:

_____

The federal government spends more than the other two levels of government on:

_____

Another pattern you might look for is trends; that is, shifts in the data over time. Table 13.1 indicates the way governmental expenditures are changing from one fiscal year to the next. You could investigate trends in expenditures by collecting additional data for previous years from the library.

There are at least four kinds of interpretive statements you can make about tabular data. The first focuses on individual entries. You might simply state, for example, that slightly more than 1 percent of the expenditures of the federal government were for education.

A second kind of interpretive statement makes comparisons within columns. For instance, the federal government spent less on veterans' services than on housing and community development (1.3 percent and 1.0 percent, respectively). Indicate some other comparisons within columns that strike you as interesting:

Finally, compare entries across columns. The federal government spends a lower percentage of its expenditures on education than do either the state or the local governments.

Presenting Tabular Data Effectively

Guidelines for making effective tabular-data presentation:[1]

Rule 1: Round to two significant digits. To understand any set of numbers, you have to compare the individual numbers. But this is difficult if the numbers contain more than two significant digits. If you read, for example, that a particular variable increased its value from 330.9 thousand to 597.9 thousand over a three-year period, you probably would have difficulty remembering it, much less calculating in your head the percentage of annual increase. On the other hand, if you rounded the two figures to 330 and 600, respectively, then it is not hard to see that the value has practically doubled in three years.

Sometimes tables are used to report a large amount of basic information, as is the case with table 13.1. The Census Bureau did decide to round the data to millions. If you now use some of this information in an analysis of changes in federal expenditure, you can communicate the changes more memorably by rounding the numbers even farther. Rounding does result in loss of data, but the lasting impression one makes by rounding may be more important than exact precision of findings.

Look back at table 13.1. If you followed this rounding guideline in using those data, you could report the information about total direct expenditures as follows:

Total Direct Expenditure	Table 13.1 Figures (millions)	Rounded to Two Significant Digits (billions)
All governments	2,494,424	2,500
Federal	1,527,311	1,500
State	701,601	700
Local	661,744	660

Note how much easier the information in the column of rounded figures is to grasp and remember.

It is also the case that many of the data used in political analysis have an artificial precision about them. Statistics in official reports are not as accurate as readers often are led to believe they are. For example, in the World Bank's *World Development Report, 1988*, we are told that Kenyans consumed a per capita average of 2,214 calories per day and that the upper 10 percent of the households in Peru earned 42.9 percent of that country's household income.[2] There is no way to know if these data are correct at this level of detail, and hence it is appropriate to round them to two significant digits (e.g., 2,200 calories and 43 percent).

Rule 2: Use row and column averages. When presented with a long column of figures, we usually need something to anchor an interpretation of the column. Including an average at the top or the bottom of the list can add immediate impact and significance and enable the reader to interpret the figures.

Rule 3: Figures are easier to compare in columns than in rows. Refer back to table 13.1. The top row of figures compares the total direct expenditures of federal, state, and local governments by placing them side by side. Compare how much easier it is to grasp the relative amounts in the following arrangement:

     1,393,121
       572,318
       581,207

Rule 1 suggested rounding figures. But if it is important to retain the raw data, placing them in columns improves their effectiveness. The reason is that one normally scans sets of data by moving the eye down a column instead of across a row. When data are in rows, the eye must travel relatively far to capture all the digits, and each digit must be read regardless of whether or not it is important. In reading columns, note how easy it is to take in just the first one or two digits in each number, and then to continue on to the next number below it.

Rule 4: Arrange the rows and columns to show the structure of the data. Do not assume that the patterns in the data are self-evident and easy for all to see. Here are some easy guidelines to follow. (1) Once you have decided on a table, stick with it throughout your presentations. If you are presenting several tables with information about the same group of cases, arrange them so that the same units are at the top in each table. (2) If possible, arrange the data in a sequence that emphasizes, rather than obscures, the patterns. Alphabetical order usually is the least effective method of presentation. For example, it may be preferable to group countries by geographical region or according to size or amount of some characteristic. (3) Where possible, list the larger numbers at the top of the table and the smaller numbers at the bottom, because it is easier to grasp this patterning of the figures.

Rule 5: Arrange the table's spacing and layout to make it easy to read. Figures meant to be compared should be placed close together. Double and triple spacing and wide gaps between columns usually are unnecessary. Further, avoid cramming too many data into one table. Table 13.1 is a useful source for basic data about the U.S. budget. It is less useful to support an analysis of the budget, simply because it contains so much information.

Rule 6: Use graphs only for certain purposes. Graphs can be particularly effective in transmitting the qualitative aspects of data patterns. Graphs permit readers to see complex trends or relationships quickly and to remember them longer. For communicating quantitative information, tables still are the best technique; and if the rules suggested here are followed, they can be very effective. Graphs and tables ideally should be used in tandem. Graphs can be used at the beginning and at the end of an analysis to make a lasting impression and to help readers see complicated patterns in the data easily.

Tables Designed to Examine Relationships

Thus far this chapter has dealt with tables that present information describing a single variable. There is a second kind of table—namely, one that examines relationships—and you have been studying and creating such tables throughout the book. A display of the two kinds of tables about relationships described in earlier chapters is below.

Bivariate tables display values for two variables, one of which is the independent variable (arranged across the top of the columns), and the other of which is the dependent variable (arranged vertically along the stub). *Multivariate tables* display values for three (or more) variables, one of which is the control variable (arranged across the top of the columns), one of which is the independent variable (**nested** beneath each value of the control variable), and the third of which is the dependent variable (arranged vertically along the stub).

The following information summarizes the information you have used throughout the book in creating tables showing relationships.

nesting
A technique used in the tabular display of multivariate data; the entire range of values for the independent variable is reproduced beneath each value of the control variable, producing a number of bivariate tables, each of which is nested beneath a value of the control.

bivariate table
A table presenting values of two variables in relation to each other.

Bivariate table

Dependent Variable	Independent Variable	
	Value 1	*Value 2*
Value 1	X	X
Value 2	X	X
Value 3	X	X
Value 4	X	X

Multivariate table

multivariate table
Table presenting information on three or more variables in a manner that shows whether they are related to each other.

	Control Variable			
	Control Value 1 Independent Variable		**Control Value 2 Independent Variable**	
Dependent Variable	*Value 1*	*Value 2*	*Value 1*	*Value 2*
Value 1	X	X	X	X
Value 2	X	X	X	X
Value 3	X	X	X	X
Value 4	X	X	X	X

1. *Title.* The title should mention both variables, with the dependent variable listed first. It can often be an abbreviated version of your hypothesis, for example, "Relationship between Voting and Gender." If there is a third variable, you add that as the third item. You can say, for instance, "Relationship between Voting (dependent variable) and Gender (independent variable), by Race (control variable)." Or you could say "Influence of Gender and Race on Voting." Remember that tables should stand on their own; do not rely on the text to explain what a table is reporting. (The converse is also true. You should fully explain the relevant points of a table in your text. Do not simply say, "see table x.")

2. *The independent variable.* The independent variable goes across the top of the table. This arrangement means that the information about the dependent variable for different amounts of the independent variable will be reported by reading down columns; as was just noted, this pattern is easy to read and absorb.

3. *Labels.* Each variable as well as the values for each row and column should be clearly specified.

4. *Order of values.* Normally you should order the values of the variables so that both are arranged in the same order, usually from low to high. Thus you would have *low*, *medium*, and *high* running across the columns and down the rows.

5. *Percentages.* Usually the numbers in the cells should be percentages rather than absolute numbers. Be sure to compute your percentages on the independent variable. That is, if your hypothesized causal variable is *income*, you want to know the percentage of low-income people who voted, compared with the percentage of high-income people who voted. When the table is set up in this way, you read down the columns to see how cases are distributed, and you compare the columns. In the interest of simplifying the table, you need to put a percentage sign only in the top cell of each column. You may feel that the actual numbers are so important that you want to call them to the reader's attention. In this case you could include them in each cell, usually in brackets beneath or next to the percentages.

6. *Totals.* Put "100%" at the bottom of each column of percentages to remind readers that the percentages are being added by column, not by row. Also put

graphic display
A method of portraying
or depicting data
by means of a picture
or drawing.

coordinates
Values on the horizontal
and vertical axes of a
graph; used to measure
and depict the observed
values of the variables
and to identify the data
points that correspond
to those observed values.

horizontal (x) axis
Base measurement
scale of a graph; used ordinarily for depicting
values of the
independent variable.

vertical (y) axis
Measurement scale
that rises along the left
side of a graph; used
ordinarily for depicting
values of the
dependent variable.

the number of cases for each column below the column. *Number* can be abbreviated. $N = 64$, for instance, indicates that information about sixty-four
cases is reported in that column.

7. *Footnotes.* Put the source of the data below the table. Also add any explanatory footnotes that you believe are important to communicate the meaning
of terms used in the table.

Graphics: Uses and Abuses

Graphic displays can be invaluable aids in understanding the point of a research study or analysis. They can highlight patterns and changes in memorable
ways. They also can be used to mislead readers.

Some Basics of Constructing Graphics

Graphics are based on two **coordinates,** the horizontal and vertical axes of the
graph. The **horizontal axis** of the graph is labeled the *x* axis, and the **vertical
axis** is referred to as the *y* axis (see the illustration). The scales for measuring
the variables are laid out along each axis. Data are located on the graph by

data point
Point on a graph where
the values of two vari-
ables—one from the *x*
axis and one from the *y*
axis—intersect.

placing a point where the values from each of the two axes intersect. This intersection is defined as the **data point.** As a general rule, each scale begins with
zero at the point where the *x* axis and *y* axis cross and proceeds either upward or
to the right in ascending order according to the chosen unit of measurement. If
you do not begin the scale along one of the axes with 0, or if you compress the
scale by removing part of it, you can identify these changes by means of slash
marks that break the axis (see illustration).

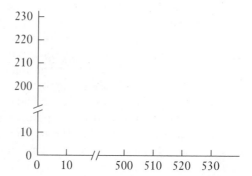

Most graphs are based on a generally accepted convention that uses the *x* axis for the independent variable and the *y* axis for the dependent variable. If the data being graphed do not link two variables in a causal fashion—if, for example, the graph depicts changes in a variable over time—the more interesting or more significant variable is placed on the *y*, or vertical, axis, and the less significant or less interesting variable is placed on the *x*, or horizontal, axis. This produces a display that shows the interesting data moving horizontally from left to right, just as we read.

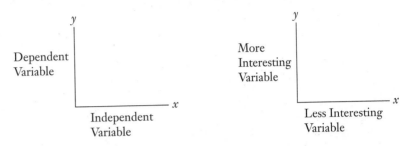

positive linear curve
A line that slopes from the lower left to the upper right, indicating that as the independent variable increases, the dependent variable also increases.

negative linear curve
A line that slopes from the upper left to the lower right, indicating that as the independent variable increases, the dependent variable decreases.

In locating a series of data points on a graph, the objective is to produce a line (or set of lines) that conveys an image of a relationship between variables. You were introduced to this skill in chapter 11's discussion of scatterplots and in the directions there on drawing regression lines. The lines on the graph suggest whether or not there seems to be a relationship between the variables and how strong it is. A straight line that moves from the lower left to the upper right is identified as a **positive linear curve** and shows that, as the independent (*x* axis) variable increases, the dependent (*y* axis) variable increases at a constant rate. A straight line that slopes from upper left to lower right is identified as a **negative linear curve** and shows that as the independent variable increases, the dependent variable decreases at a constant rate.

curvilinear line
A line that depicts a changing relationship between independent and dependent variables such that the relationship appears at times positive and at other times negative; overall effect is a line that changes direction.

S-shaped line
A line depicting two variables that change in the same direction but at varying rates during different portions of a graph.

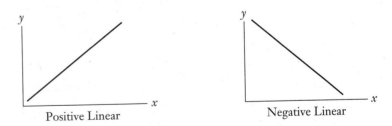

Of course, many lines seen on graphs are not straight but curved. For example, a graph may show that the relationship between the independent and dependent variables changes over time: in one portion of the graph, the relationship is positive (with both variables increasing); in another portion, the relationship may be negative (with the variables changing in opposite directions); or it may level off. Such a line would be called a **curvilinear line.** Still another kind of relationship is depicted in an **S-shaped line** in which the two variables change in the same direction but at varying rates during different portions of the graph.

exponential curve
An S-shaped curve that depicts how a variable grows by a constant percentage of the whole over time; gives dramatically greater results than simple linear growth, in which the increase is by constant raw amounts.

Probably the best-known S-shaped curves are those known as **exponential,** which depict graphically how something (say, population) grows by a constant percentage of itself over time (the same way that compound interest works in a savings account). The results of exponential growth are dramatically greater than those of linear growth, in which increases are by a constant amount instead of a constant percentage of the whole. Exponential growth curves have been used to depict how quickly we will exhaust a specific kind of natural resource, such as petroleum or uranium, even though at current usage rates it appears we have enough to last for many hundreds of years.[3]

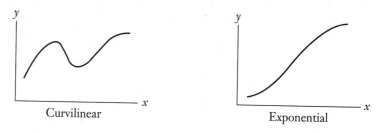

Curvilinear

Exponential

FIGURE 13.1
Pie Chart

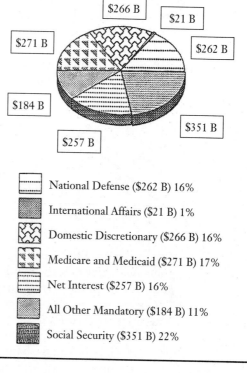

1996 Proposed Spending

$266 B $21 B
$271 B $262 B
$184 B $351 B
$257 B

National Defense ($262 B) 16%

International Affairs ($21 B) 1%

Domestic Discretionary ($266 B) 16%

Medicare and Medicaid ($271 B) 17%

Net Interest ($257 B) 16%

All Other Mandatory ($184 B) 11%

Social Security ($351 B) 22%

Pie Chart

One of the simplest graphics is the pie chart. It is useful when you want to show what portion of a whole is accounted for by different units. The portions usually are expressed as percentages of the whole. The sizes of the "pieces of pie" reflect the proportions listed for each piece. Budgets frequently are reported in pie charts. See figure 13.1.

Bar Graph

Another frequently seen graphic is the bar graph, an example of which is presented in figure 13.2. Bar graphs compare the values of several variables by means of bars that extend to various lengths along a common scale built into the graph. Bar graphs are most useful for nominal variables, because the base scale can represent the categories into which the population is divided, and the measuring scale can represent the frequency with which each category (or value) is observed.

Frequency Lines or Distribution Curves

frequency line
Line depicting the frequency of values or the shape of their distribution.

A **frequency line** depicts the general shape of the distribution of a set of values. It is used with ordinal or interval data but not with nominal-level measures. Nominal measures involve categories, and bar graphs are appropriate to depict the amount in each category. However, when there is an order in the listing of the measures, you can place them along a line. You worked with line graph

FIGURE 13.2
Bar Graph

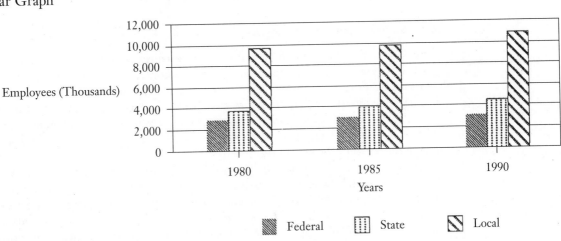

Source: *Statistical Abstract of the United States* (Washington, D.C.: U.S. Government Printing Office, 1996), Table 501.

and frequency distributions in chapter 10. The normal curve described in chapter 12 is another example of a frequency distribution.

For example, you can create a frequency line using the following voter turnout data for several U.S. presidential elections.

FIGURE 13.3
Turnout in Presidential Elections

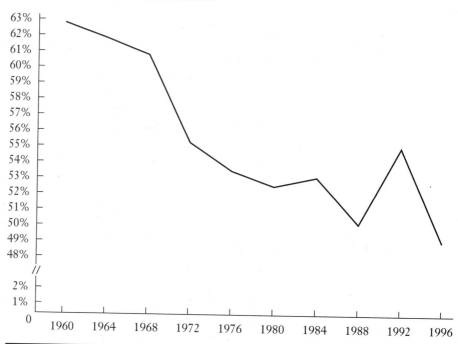

Choosing among Graphics

Several chapters have noted that different measures or ways of reporting the same information can create different impressions. Percentages, for example, can suggest a different pattern than reports of absolute amounts. People reporting data frequently use the measure that best supports the point they want to make, even if it misleads the reader. This tendency is particularly evident in presenting graphics, since writers know that readers usually focus on the visual image rather than the actual figures.

Consider different ways of describing and depicting changes in the U.S. budget, for which table 13.2 provides three sets of data: budget amounts from 1965 to 2000, GDP, and the budget as a percentage of GDP. First, create a line graph that depicts the budget amounts. Put the years along the horizontal axis at the bottom of the graph, and billions of dollars along the vertical axis, going from $100 billion to $2,000 billion.

TABLE 13.2

Federal Budget Totals, as Percentage of GNP, 1965–2000

Year	Budget Total (in billions of dollars)	GDP (in billions of dollars)	Percentage of GDP
1965	118.2	671.0	17.6
1967	157.5	793.3	19.8
1969	183.6	925.7	19.8
1971	210.2	1,050.9	20.0
1973	245.7	1,274.0	19.3
1975	332.3	1,509.8	22.0
1977	409.2	1,917.2	21.3
1979	504.0	2,429.5	20.7
1981	678.2	2,964.4	22.9
1983	808.4	3,316.5	24.4
1985	946.4	3,967.7	23.9
1987	1,003.9	4,452.4	22.5
1989	1,143.2	5,173.3	22.1
1991	1,323.4	5,676.4	23.3
1993	1,408.7	6,258.6	22.5
1995 (est.)	1,538.9	7,024.1	21.9
1997 (est.)	1,684.7	7,814.9	21.6
1999 (est.)	1,822.2	8,705.1	20.9
2000 (est.)	1,905.3	9,186.1	20.7

Source: *Historical Tables, Budget of the United States Government. Fiscal Year 1996.* (Washington, D.C.: Executive Office of the President, Office of Management and Budget, 1996), tables 1.2 (p. 15) and 1.3 (p. 17).

What impression is created? Your line graph should show a rapidly rising line, suggesting that the budget is wildly out of control.

Now create a line graph showing the changes in the budget as a percentage of GDP. Again, place the years along the horizontal axis. The vertical axis should list percentages; the scale should go from 18 percent to 25 percent, in increments of 1.

What impression is created in this graph? It shows a much flatter line, suggesting that the budget has risen much more gradually. Note that both sets of figures are accurate, but they do give different impressions, impressions that are made more vivid through graphics.

Create a third graph in which you present the same information—changes in the budget as a percentage of GDP. This time, however, change the vertical scale so the percentages listed on the left range from 10 percent to 90 percent.

What impression is created this time? The line is even flatter, suggesting that budget changes are virtually imperceptible. You would probably agree that this choice is misleading. It is included to illustrate that it is possible to create different impressions simply by presenting data in different ways and by altering the scale you use.

Checklist of Items in Preparing Graphic Data Displays

1. *Simplicity.* The graph must be simple. The only virtue (although it is a considerable one) of graphics is that they simplify data displays in order to make a more vivid, immediate, and lasting impression. Graphics must not include

all the information from a table. For that reason, they should never be used without a supporting table.

2. *Choose the graphic display according to the nature of the variable.* The graphs should fit the kinds of variables displayed or the kinds of scales used to measure them. Nominal scales should be depicted by bar graphs. They can also be depicted by pie charts when your main point is to compare how the parts contribute to the whole. Ordinal- or interval-level data should be depicted by frequency lines. If the data being depicted are changes in the value of a variable over time, use line graphs.

3. *Accuracy.* The graph should accurately reflect the data being reported. Because graphs intentionally discard data in the interest of simplification, it is easy to distort the reporting of the data. Without cluttering up the graph, make certain that readers can clearly understand the units of measurement, the scales, and any other information needed to make sense of the data. Be careful to avoid distorting the scale of the y axis to show patterns and relationships that are not true.

4. *Titles and source material.* The discussion of table construction stressed the importance of clear titles and labels. Like tables, graphs should stand on their own, and readers should be able to interpret them without relying on the discussion in the text. A full reporting of source material is as important with graphs as with tables.

Presenting Qualitative Data

As discussed in chapter 8, your research questions may lead you to collect information that is qualitative in nature, meaning that it is primarily descriptive and cannot be translated into numerical quantities. Such information may be collected to complement, qualify, or amplify quantitative findings. Typically, one presents conclusions from such research in the form of a narrative or a description, either because that is the way in which the information is collected or because that seems most fitting to this kind of information. As stressed in chapter 8 such information can often be presented more systematically in the form of tables or graphics. This strategy is particularly appropriate when you use some structure in your data gathering. Recall that chapter 8 proposed various ways to structure qualitative data through establishing a framework or codes or categories. We continue that discussion here in describing ways to present that information to make it more usable and informative to others.

In chapter 8 you were asked to plan research on citizen participation by observing a neighborhood commission meeting. Table 8.2 suggested a list of items you could prepare ahead of time to structure your observations, including the characteristics of those attending, the substance of the meeting, and the style of the meeting. Chapter 8 also introduced several graphical techniques: a matrix, a two-dimensional table that describes the intersection between two sets of variables; a checklist; and a flowchart under the heading "Analyzing and Presenting

Qualitative Data." Miles and Huberman suggest the following questions, which are here applied to a study of neighborhood organization meetings:[4]

1. *Descriptive versus explanatory intent.* Are you mainly interested in describing the meetings, or do you want to try to explain why the meetings proceed as they do? Explanation involves more organization and ordering of the information.
2. *Single-site versus multiple-site data.* As stated throughout this text, you should look for chances to carry out comparative studies, to look at citizen meetings at several sites. If you do this, then the rows or columns in your matrix will be those sites.
3. *Ordered versus nonordered.* Can you order your information in some way, such as degrees of conflict experienced in the citizen meetings? If so, then *conflict* could provide one dimension of the matrix.
4. *Time-ordered versus not time-ordered.* Are you looking at information over time? If so, then one dimension of your matrix could refer to time, such as changes over a series of three meetings.
5. *Categories of variables.* Are you looking at cases, such as individuals, groups, or sites? Or are you looking at behavior, such as actions taken at citizen meetings? Your answer to this question determines the units inside the cells of your matrix.
6. *Kinds of information.* Are you going to use direct quotes, field notes, or ratings based on the views of several observers?

There are several rules of thumb for designing useful matrices:

1. Keep the display on one sheet.
2. Try to include no more than five or six rows and columns.
3. Expect to revise the matrix several times.
4. Be willing to collapse and expand rows and columns until you get a series that helps you analyze and report the information you have collected.

Where We Are

As a researcher and student of political science studies, you need to be able to read and interpret tables that report a good deal of information, such as table 13.1, based on data on governmental expenditures collected by the Census Bureau. Tables and graphics can also contribute to your own analysis if you take care in creating them. As an analyst, you will probably be creating tables that are much simpler than table 13.1 and whose purpose is to highlight the information on which your analysis is based. Tables and graphs should both be self-contained; that is, they should provide all the information necessary to interpret them. And as noted earlier, your text should also stand on its own and should describe the important points in the table and not simply direct the reader to study or read the table. You need to take care in creating all the techniques described in this chapter, thinking carefully about the selection of titles and labels, and setting them up to accomplish your purposes. Finally, and especially with graphs, you need to be sure you are not creating misleading impressions through the scale you select or the manner in which you report the data.

NOTES

1. Based on A. S. C. Ehrenberg, "Rudiments of Numeracy," *Journal of the Royal Statistical Society Abstracts* 140, part 3 (1977): 222–297.
2. *World Development Report, 1988* (Washington, D.C.: World Bank, 1988), pp. 272, 278.
3. Gregory A. Kimble, *How to Use (and Misuse) Statistics* (Englewood Cliffs, N.J.: Prentice-Hall, 1978). See also Donella Meadows et al., *The Limits to Growth*, 2d rev. ed. (New York: Signet, 1974), p. 33.
4. Matthew B. Miles and A. Michael Huberman, *Qualitative Data Analysis: A Sourcebook of New Methods* (Beverly Hills, Calif.: Sage, 1984), pp. 211–215 and passim.

EXERCISES

Exercise 13.1 Creating Graphs

Create an appropriate graphic to portray each set of information.

A. *Unemployment rates, 1950 to 1995.* Rate refers to percent of the labor force. (You may want to review the discussion in chapter 3 on the method for measuring unemployment.) The average unemployment rate for the following years was 1950, 5.3%; 1960, 5.5%; 1970, 4.9%; 1980, 7.1%; 1990, 5.5%; 1995, 5.6%.

B. *Immigration rates.* Rate refers to rate per 1,000 U. S. population. *1900–1910*, 10.4; *1911–1920*, 5.7; *1921–1930*, 3.5; *1931–1940*, .4; *1941–1950*, .7; *1951–1960*, 1.5; *1961–1970*, 1.7; *1971–1980*, 2.1; *1981–1990*, 3.1; *1991–1993*, 4.8.

C. *Estimated population by country, 2000. The Global 2000 Report to the President*, prepared by the Council on Environmental Quality and the U.S. Department of State, estimates that in 2000 the world's population will be 6,351 million. It estimates the population by region as follows (figures in millions): China, 1,329; India, 1,021; Indonesia, 226; remainder of Asia and Oceania, 1,054; Africa, 814; temperate South America, 53; remainder of Latin America, 584; the former Soviet Union, 309; Eastern Europe, 152; Western Europe, 378; United States, 248; remainder of North America, Australia, and New Zealand, 50; Japan, 133. Would this information be more interesting displayed as percentages or absolute amounts? Indicate the reasons for your choice.

Exercise 13.2 Creating a Table

The following text presents data on governmental revenue. You are told what revenue the federal government gave to states and local governments in 1989–1990. The amounts are in millions of dollars and are taken from the same source as table 13.1. Prepare two tables showing this information. In addition to reporting the amounts, compute the percentage of general and intergovernmental revenues that came from other levels of government for each category. Write a paragraph interpreting the information. Be certain you include clear titles and labels and a reference to the source.

State governments had an aggregate total revenue of $532,172, of which $517,429 was general revenue. (*General* means that the money is not earmarked for any particular expenditure.) They received $126,329 in intergovernmental revenue. Of this amount the federal government gave $118,353. The federal government's portion to the states was divided as follows: $21,271 for education, $5,904 for health and hospitals, $59,397 for public welfare, $13,931 for highways, $1,499 for housing and community development, and $16,780 for other services. Local governments also contributed to the intergovernmental revenue of state governments in the amount of $7,976. Of this, $579 was for education, $3,028 was for public welfare, $792 was for health and hospitals, $633 was for highways, and $2,945 was not allocated or was for other purposes.

Local governments received a total of $580,193 in revenue, of which $512,322 was from general revenue sources. Of this amount, $190,723 was from intergovernmental revenue. The federal government gave $18,449, of which, $1,962 was for education, $564 was for public welfare, $429 was for health and hospitals, $437 was for highways, $8,155 was for housing and community development, and $6,902 was for other services. Local government received a total of $172,274 from states. Of this, $108,627 was for education, $19,937 was for public welfare, $5,900 was for health and hospitals, $7,559 was for highways, $14,956 was for general government support, and $15,294 was for other purposes.

TABLE 13.3
Growth of Real GDP per Capita, 1965–2000 (Average Annual Percentage Change, Unless Noted)

Group	Population 1989 (millions)	1965–1973	1973–1980	1980–1989	Projection for 1990s
Industrial countries	773	3.7	2.3	2.3	1.8–2.5
Developing countries	4,053	3.9	2.5	1.6	2.2–2.9
Sub-Saharan Africa	480	2.1	0.4	−1.2	0.3–0.5
East Asia	1,552	5.3	4.9	6.2	4.2–5.3
South Asia	1,131	1.2	1.7	3.0	2.1–2.6
Europe, Middle East, and North Africa	433	5.8	1.9	0.4	1.4–1.8
Latin America and the Caribbean	421	3.8	2.5	−0.4	1.3–2.0
Developing countries weighted by population	4,053	3.0	2.4	2.9	2.7–3.2

Source: *World Development Report 1991* (Washington, D.C.: World Bank, 1991), p. 374.

Exercise 13.3 Interpreting Tables

Examine the information in table 13.3, and do the following:

1. Given the source, do you assume the data are reliable?
2. Which figures are
   actual numbers?
   percentages?
   estimates?
3. Describe at least two individual entries that are interesting to you.
4. Compare several figures within a column and report your findings:
5. Compare several figures across columns and report your findings:
6. Are there any noteworthy trends?

Exercise 13.4 Creating a Pie Chart

The popular vote for the three major presidential candidates in 1996 was as follows:

Clinton:	47,401,185	49.24%
Dole:	39,197,469	40.71%
Perot:	8,085,294	8.40%

Source: "1996 Official Presidential General Election Results," http://www.fec.gov/96fed/geresult.htm, 19 May 1997.

Create a pie chart using these figures. Select an appropriate title, individual items, and percentages, as illustrated by figure 13.2.

Exercise 13.5 Creating a Bar Graph

Based on the following data, create a bar graph that depicts the percentage of thirteen-year-olds in selected countries who spend two or more hours a day on homework and who watch five or more hours of TV a day.

	Two or More Hours a Day Spent on Homework	Five or More Hours a Day Spent Watching TV
Hungary	58%	13%
United States	29	20
England	33	14
Spain	64	10
Canada	27	14

Source: "Table 393—Classroom, Home and Mathematics Activities of 13-Year-Olds in Educational Systems Participating in the International Assessment of Educational Progress: 1991," *Digest of Education Statistics 1995* (Washington, D.C.: U.S. Department of Education, 1995).

Exercise 13.6 Creating a Frequency Distribution

Using the following data on the turnout in off-year elections for the House of Representatives, create a graph on which you plot two lines. One line is for turnout in presidential elections, using the data from figure 13.3 in the graph on turnout in presidential elections. The second line should plot the turnout for the House elections. You will need to change the vertical scale so that it starts at 30 percent. You will need to change the horizontal scale to include the intervening years. Distinguish between the two lines in some way; for example, make the line for turnout in presidential elections solid and the other line dashes or dots.

Turnout for off-year elections, House of Representatives: 1962, 45.4; 1966, 45.4; 1970, 43.5; 1974, 35.9; 1978, 34.9; 1982, 38.0; 1986, 33.4; 1990, 33.1; 1994, 36.0.

CHAPTER FOURTEEN

Designing and Writing a Research Paper

I don't know about other people, but beginning a new paper gives me anxiety's classical physical symptoms: dizziness, a sinking feeling in the pit of the stomach, a chill, maybe even a cold sweat. The dual possibilities, one as bad as the other, that the world has no real order or that, if it does, I can't find it, now or ever, are philosophically, almost religiously, frightening. The world may be a meaningless mess, but that is not a philosophical position one can live with easily. Not being able to figure out the first sentence makes that possibility palpable.

Do I have a cure for the disease I've described? Yes and no. A lot of other activities, especially sports, provoke paralyzing fears that keep people from getting started . The advice of experts in these areas is always the same. Relax and do it!

—Howard S. Becker, *Writing for Social Scientists*

The Process of Carrying Out and Reporting On Research

The purpose of this chapter is to provide an overview of the research process, specifically how to bring together all the elements of research described throughout this book. It will also stress how to organize and write your final research report. While it resists providing a simple formula for doing research, the discussion offers guidelines that are intended to be reassuring rather than daunting. It is hoped you will appreciate the many ways in which the process of carrying out and reporting on your research provides opportunities for you to be creative and imaginative as well as clear and precise.

Recall the dilemma stated in chapter 1. On the one hand it would be helpful if the book were to conclude with a clear set of rules, rules that would reinforce the "habits of thought" discussed throughout the book and the value in being systematic, logical, and orderly in conducting your research. In support of this purpose, the book has stressed the need to formulate clear questions, to find appropriate and relevant measures and data sets, and then to analyze and present the results so that they relate back to your original question(s). At the same time the book has presented other themes. It has asked you to think laterally and consider alternative perspectives to a question, to compare several designs, to use multiple measures and data sets when possible. It has counseled you to be mindful of the tradeoffs in selecting one approach rather than another. From these perspectives the research process appears less neat and predictable, requiring you to make choices and adjustments as you proceed. Indeed as chapter 1 suggested, at times the research process can even be somewhat messy.

Why is political research inherently "messy"? Recall that chapter 1 described the characteristics of political discourse that make political concepts hard to talk about and observe. Many of the terms we are interested in, such as participation, apathy, power, relative strength, and development, are vague and abstract, and it is not always clear what evidence to use to examine them. Second, the data we need often are hard to acquire, or when available they frequently are biased or not in a form we can use. Third, there often are multiple relationships or explanations we can examine, and it is difficult to know just which one to pick or how far we need to go in asking whether there are other factors we have left out of our design. Finally, the book has confirmed that there is a variety of research strategies and indicated that they each have their uses, depending on the questions we are asking.

These are the realities of doing research about political issues and problems. Your task is not to pretend that the world of political discourse is any neater and more orderly than it is, but to acknowledge the problems and carve out a topic on which you can shed some light. It means you are unlikely to prove a relationship decisively. It means you are unlikely to demonstrate that a particular factor almost always causes a certain result. It does mean, however, that you can try to provide evidence that helps us understand a potentially interesting relationship somewhat better than we do now.

Because the political arena itself is messy and because there is no single research strategy that is always preferable, most of us have to experiment with a number of ideas, sometimes in an unsystematic way, in the process of clarifying our research. Howard Becker, quoted at the outset of the chapter, comments that faculty often do students a disservice by urging them to develop an outline for a paper, to write the paper on the basis of the outline, and then to turn it in for a grade. The problem with this approach is that often we are not clear about where we are going until we work through an argument on paper. Instead of following a predesigned outline, we may have to proceed step by step to see where our questions and data are taking us. And we may have to try several ideas at the same time, dropping one and revising the other, before we proceed. The catch is that this more realistic model of the research process will work only if we are willing to go back and rewrite our initial drafts. From this perspective, rethinking and rewriting are at the heart of the research and writing process.[1]

The point of these comments is not to make a difficult process even more difficult. Rather, it is to assure you that coming up with a clear research design is difficult. If you spend time trying out different ideas, end up following some blind leads, change your outline several times, or reject some evidence you originally thought would be useful, you are probably on the right track. You are experiencing the problems that face most researchers on political questions. You can even turn these problems to your advantage by including a section in your report in which you reflect on the problems in designing research on your particular question. Instead of just indicating how you finally decided to measure a concept, discuss some of the problems you had in coming to that decision, some of the original ideas you had and why you discarded them. Such a section would show that you had succeeded in grasping the problems and opportunities implicit in most research about political issues and perhaps help other researchers avoid taking the same tortuous path.

In spite of the foregoing disclaimers, it is possible to outline a series of steps in designing research. They fall under five headings: identify your questions, select a design or methodology, define your terms in light of available evidence, analyze the results, and present them in a well-organized narrative and where possible include a visual presentation. These steps are outlined in the following list, and then each is described more fully. The discussion not only reviews prior material but also tries to take into account the realities of actually conducting and writing about our research.

Identify Research Questions

What do you want to know more about?

What theories or studies are available to build on?

What factors are associated with the item of interest?

Consider possible associated variables and explanations.

Try to formulate the question as a proposition or hypothesis.

Why is this an interesting or important question?

Select a Research Design or Methodology

Which research design is appropriate:

Experiments?

Natural experiments?

Correlation studies?

Case studies—single, or comparison of several cases?

Identify your major variables.

Is it possible to take into account several influences?

Is it relevant to identify one or more controls?

Is it possible or appropriate to propose a causal model?

Define Terms and Plan How to Collect Data

What variables are relevant to your concepts?

What indicators will both define your variables and point to data that are feasible to collect?

What instruments can you use to measure your indicators: Surveys? Questionnaires? Interviews? Observations? Analysis of written records? Collected data?

What validity and reliability problems are present?

Which subjects or cases will you study, and how will you select them?

Having considered these issues, do you need to revisit and perhaps revise your original question?

Analyze the Results

Return to your original questions and propositions and report the results in terms of these. Do they qualify, confirm, or challenge your questions?

Present your factual results, separating these from your interpretation or analysis of the results.

Do the results lend themselves to quantitative analysis?

What descriptive measures are appropriate?

If you have data on relationships, which correlation measures might be appropriate?

If you have taken a sample, can you establish statistical significance?

How reliable are the results; that is, to which individuals, groups, or population do they apply?

Present Results in a Coherent Narrative and If Possible Add Visuals

Your narrative should be a coherent presentation. That is it should begin with a question, discuss your findings relevant to the question, and end up by describing how and to what extent you answer that question. This need for coherence is perhaps the most important, and the most frequently violated, guideline.

What graphic or tabular presentations are fitting?

If the data are qualitative, can you present them in a matrix or in some visual form?

What are the strengths and limitations of your study and conclusions? Do not be afraid of identifying its limitations. All studies have them, and it is better for you to acknowledge them than leave it to others to look for them.

Discuss the "so what?" aspects of your study. What are its implications?

What follow up or further studies are needed?

Formulate Research Questions

This step is not as obvious or easy as it may appear. For example, you may have a general interest in knowing more about the impact of the media on national politics. It is tempting to simply say you are going to investigate this topic. But you need to be more specific. What is it about the impact of the media that you want to study? Do the media contribute to the simplification of issues? Do the media play an important watchdog or investigatory role? Do they create cynicism because of an emphasis on crime and sensational stories? Do they have a liberal bias, as is often claimed? Do they contribute to an emphasis on charismatic leaders who speak only in sound bites? There are many other possibilities. Ask yourself which of these most interests you.

Review the relevant literature. Can you do a study that builds on or replicates another study in a new situation? Perhaps you find a study on the role of the media in the 1996 election. Could you carry out a similar study on a gubernatorial or off-year election? Or if that study focused on the national media, perhaps it would be interesting to do a similar study focusing on the local media. Or you could do a similar study, but instead of focusing on a campaign, ask how the media treat international issues.

Consider another example in which a researcher moves from a topic of general interest to a researchable question:

General issue—"Development in poor countries"

More defined issue—"The relationship between democracy and economic development in poor countries"

Possible question—"Do democratic governments find it difficult to make the hard choices necessary to promote economic development?"

Tentative proposition—"Countries with strong and active interest groups will emphasize policies that distribute benefits to these groups, more so than is true in countries with less active interest groups. As a result, the former set of countries will have a hard time generating the savings necessary to promote economic development."

A final point about selecting research topics. Get in the habit of asking what questions are posed by assigned readings in other courses and by stories in the media. Many studies describe an event or behavior or policy in a manner that suggests we know more about it than we do. For instance, you may read that the government has just passed a bill to provide public health insurance for catastrophic illness. That could generate a question about the variety and results of policies in regard to health insurance being tried in other countries. You learn your congressional representative was reelected. That could lead you to ask how many incumbents are reelected or to study the campaigns of a few candidates who successfully challenged an incumbent. Or it might lead you to ask about the sources of support for your representative and whether there is a relationship between these sources and the kinds of policies he or she supports. Virtually any finding can be used to generate related questions that could be interesting to pursue.

Identify a Research Design

This is the point in your report where you state your methodology. Assume for a moment that your research is going to come to a surprising or counterintuitive conclusion. Why should someone have confidence in your conclusions? They will only do so if you lay out a procedure or methods others feel is adequate and appropriate. For example, you are going to study whether democracies tend to engage in violence during times of transition. Readers will have confidence in your results only if they understand how you selected the democracies you look at and whether your design is a valid way of studying this issue. In its simplest terms, a research design should deal with a question you can answer with evidence that you can gather in the time available to you. This means you have to think of two aspects of research simultaneously—a research question as well as evidence that is both relevant to the question and feasible for you to collect—and move back and forth between them. The emphasis here is on the connection between these two steps and the fact that they have to be made in light of each other.

Thus your research design will look backward to your question and forward to the kinds of evidence you can reasonably gather. Given your interests and the available evidence, what specific research approach would be appropriate? Note: there is no single, correct research design to answer most questions. There are designs that are more or less enlightening, more or less feasible to carry out, more or less valid. You will have to make a number of trade-offs in finally selecting one.

Return to the previous section's question about development. How might you proceed to design research on this question? We can assume that you are unlikely to be able to visit developing countries and interview officials or even collect data firsthand. You know that if you are going to examine the experience of a large number of countries, you will probably have to rely on data that are already collected in a standard reference work. If you follow this strategy, you should go to these sources to see what information they provide. For instance, if you can find a source that provides evidence about the nature of a country's government and also about its economic growth rate, then you could follow a strategy that correlates data on these two variables. With this information in hand, you can then revise your specific research question so that it fits the information you can gather.

For example, consider the following questions:

Question 1: How does the economic growth rate in countries with democratic governments compare with the growth rate of countries with authoritarian governments?

This question would lead you to carry out a quantitative comparison of countries based on a few variables. It has the advantage of allowing you to use evidence from a sizeable number of countries and to work with evidence at either the ordinal or the interval level. Most likely you could find several measures of democracy and of authoritarian government, and hence could use what were referred to in chapter 3 as multiple indicators. Given your interest in the role of interest groups as indicated in the initial formulation of this problem, you could also frame a question that would lead you to examine what information was available on interest groups.

Question 2: What role did interest groups play in those countries that had higher rates of economic growth?

You could go to one of the source books that offer narrative profiles on a number of countries and see what you could learn about the role of interest groups. Is there enough information to pursue this question in more depth?

The second question would lead you to an aggregate study. It would be very useful in helping you see broad patterns, but less useful in understanding the process by which democracies and authoritarian governments encourage economic development. If this process were your real interest, you would need to consider whether there is evidence available that would allow you to look in more depth at the relationship between form of government and economic development in a single country. If you followed this strategy, you would be doing a case study and relying on historical or nominal-level data and descriptive analysis. It would lead you to a question such as the following:

Question 3: How did the policies and practices in South Korea, carried out while it was governed by an authoritarian military government, encourage a high rate of economic growth during the first half of the 1980s?

This case-study strategy would give you a greater understanding of the role that a government might play in stimulating economic growth. It would suggest a variety of conditions or variables that influence economic growth, other than an authoritarian political system. You would be using a particular case, South Korea, to enrich your understanding of a broader question. It thus illustrates how a case study can be used to pose further research questions rather than as an end in itself. You would probably want to discuss whether and how South Korea can shed light on other countries; is it only of interest to scholars of South Korea or Southeast Asia, or does it have a broader relevance?

This particular case, however, would not tell you anything about economic growth under a democracy. To pursue this interest, you could consider another research strategy, namely, to select two or three countries with different forms of government or degrees of democracy and study what steps each had taken to encourage economic development. Again you would need to explore the kinds of evidence that are available to you.

Question 4: Is a country with a more democratic form of government, such as India, better able or less able to stimulate economic growth than a more authoritarian regime, such as Pakistan?

Again you are making a trade-off. By comparing two or three countries, you are not able to go into as much depth as you would in a single case study. You also run the danger of a bias in picking your cases. Someone could fairly argue that your findings are true only for the particular countries and that they are not typical of other democracies or authoritarian systems. On the other hand, the effort to compare two countries allows you to work with ordinal-level data and to gain some insights that a single case study cannot offer.

The point of this discussion is that there usually is a variety of ways to design your research. You need to select a question appropriate for the issue you are interested in and for which you can find or create relevant evidence. In this sense you need to design your research by working back and forth between the question you are interested in and the kinds of evidence available to you.

This approach to research—exploring a variety of strategies—has much merit. It is realistic; it forces you to consider alternatives; it encourages you to be self-conscious about your methdology; and it should enable you to defend the strategy you finally select. It has one drawback, however. It may be so open-ended that, if you are a novice researcher, you may be overwhelmed by the options. You may feel you have to be exhaustive in considering alternatives and in knowing all the relevant research that has been done already. In reality you can be more pragmatic than that. You should consider several alternatives, but you do not have to be exhaustive. If you find an approach with which you are comfortable and for which there is some reasonably available evidence, pursue it. You may decide to replicate a study done by someone else. That usually is very defensible. Perhaps you will learn something by applying a well-documented theory to a new subject or in a new setting. If you can find some evidence to back up, or amplify, a finding that is accepted as common wisdom, that can be important.

You are unlikely to use a methodology that is problem-free, and you are unlikely to come to a conclusion of which you can be 100 percent certain. Discuss these reservations in your study. Note the qualifications that apply to your research approach. The lack of certainty is not necessarily a fault of your research; it is a function of the nature of the political and social arena. Thus, to note problems and qualifications underscores your sophistication rather than your shortcomings.

Define Terms and Data Sources

Be clear about your definition of concepts and terms. Remember, concepts such as *democracy*, *participation*, *economic development*, and *political interest* are not as self-evident as they may appear. You may be using a commonsense definition such as defining a democracy as a country that holds competitive elections. It is important to state this clearly and identify where you are going to find the relevant information.

It is hoped this book has convinced you a great variety of information is already available to you, in addition to the many ways in which you can collect information yourself. chapters 7, 8, and 9 described a variety of data sources: reference works, newspapers, interviews, questionnaires. As you read other studies, note the resources they rely on to broaden your familiarity with your options. The problem with data sources is generally not the lack of information, but the vast amount, an amount that is rapidly expanding and can be overwhelming.

Analyze Results in Light of Original Questions

As emphasized in this section and in the following section on presenting your analysis, it is imperative you connect your analysis to your original questions. If you find that your results do not really address the original question, either revise that, or explain why you were not able to collect the information you needed. Discuss what you did find and how it relates to the original question.

Part Four described a number of strategies for analyzing information, many of them quantitative in nature. It reviewed several statistical techniques to describe variables of particular interest, the patterns they assume, the relationships they have with other variables, and their significance. It is important to remember that these findings and statistical conclusions are meaningful only in the context of the research questions we have asked and in terms of the way we have measured our variables. Earlier chapters emphasized that the linkages we establish between our concepts and available data are particularly crucial in designing studies. The point here is that they are also crucial in interpreting the results of our analysis.

As an example, if your research found a strong relationship (say, $r = .6$) between apathy and failure to vote, it would be premature to conclude that apathy is the major reason for the failure to go to the polls. Before reporting that conclusion, you have to refer to the theory that guided your study and the reasons for the definitions you chose. You can interpret the meaning of a correlation coefficient only in light of the indicators you have selected for *apathy* and *participation*, whether you used several indicators, whether you asked about other reasons for lack of participation, and whether you considered how much difference apathy makes under different circumstances or for different groups of people. Only then can you make a meaningful interpretation of a relationship. If your research design was not able to take these additional factors into account, then your conclusions have to be stated more modestly and indicate the major questions that were not addressed.

We can make this point clearer by looking briefly at the history of voting studies. Voting studies up through the mid-1960s generally found a strong correlation between apathy and failure to vote—that nonvoters tend to be more apathetic than voters are. The studies usually explained the relationship by giving a special meaning to the concept of apathy. It was reasoned that if apathetic people do not vote, it must mean they are satisfied with the political system. During the 1960s, however, there were numerous and severe political protests in the

United States, and it became evident that many of the supposedly apathetic and satisfied people were in reality very angry. Apparently, the high correlation between apathy and failure to vote was masking some important differences among nonvoters. Studies began to compare two alternative hypotheses, namely, that failure to vote is correlated with passive satisfaction in some cases and with anger and alienation in others.

Part of the problem in this instance was that the original research designs focused on one view of apathy. Propositions, by their nature, tackle a problem from a particular perspective. In proposing a certain relationship, they inevitably ignore other possibilities. Chapters 3 and 4 described the complexity of social reality and the many factors that enter into most relationships. Yet, of necessity our research usually examines only a part of that reality. The assumptions we make about what is important always predispose us to look for certain factors and not to examine others. The studies of voting just described were looking for signs of passive satisfaction and therefore failed to observe the anger and alienation that were just below the surface. Our analysis and measures, therefore, always have to be interpreted in light of the questions we ask and the definitions we have used for our concepts.

The point is that our results are limited by our research design. The converse is also true: facts and figures have meaning *only* in terms of the questions we are asking and in the context of the theories, assumptions, and measures we are using. People who are concerned about the integrity of analysis in social affairs often refer disparagingly to "barefoot empiricism." In part they are saying that simply to collect facts and report them as such can be misleading and meaningless. The reason is that the facts and measures we find depend for their meaning on the assumptions we make about how and why people vote or behave as they do.

To clarify this point further, consider the research finding that individuals tend to vote for the political party that best represents their economic interests. How would you interpret this result? Does it mean that people are rational actors who can identify which party is in their interest? Or does it mean that people tend to vote for the candidates who approach problems from a perspective compatible with their own? The interpretation we make depends on our own assumptions about human behavior. The first possibility assumes that individuals calculate their best interest and behave accordingly. The second possibility assumes that people interact primarily with those in similar circumstances and are socialized into a particular political perspective. Both possibilities are based on well-established theories, and both conform with the finding that people vote consistently with their economic interests, and we can interpret this fact only by relating it to a particular theory or model of reality.

The close relationship between analytic measures and research design has another implication. This has to do with the idea that research is an ongoing search for understanding. Your results may lead you to qualify your original hypothesis or to understand it in more detail. In doing so, those results may suggest further research for you to carry out or may lead you to studies by others for the sake of comparison. Figure 14.1 illustrates the dynamics of the research

FIGURE 14.1
Political Analysis as an Ongoing Process

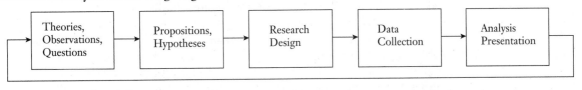

process and the idea that the results of our studies should be related to the original question we asked and to the theories and findings of others. Our analysis thus becomes part of an ongoing effort by many scholars, citizens, students, public officials, and politicians to understand better our political world and the conditions under which change is possible and desirable. The implication of figure 14.1 is that analysis is an ongoing process in which knowledge is always being clarified and revised. It is also a process that we share with others—one that we can pursue formally, as a student or professional, or informally, as a citizen and activist.

Presenting Our Analyses

As noted in chapter 13, if results are not presented effectively, our work has been wasted. Four aspects of presentation are important: organization of the study, conceptual clarifications, graphic and tabular presentations, and clarity of writing.

Organization of the study. This is a critical element in any research report. The proverbial saw is still applicable: begin by stating what you are going to say, then say it, and then conclude by telling the reader what you said. Think of your introduction and opening statements and also the subheadings as signposts to the reader. They tell the reader what you are going to do and what to look for. If you do not follow through on these signals, your study will not be clear and your failure will be held against you. Recall the statement by Becker, cited earlier in the chapter, that a central element in writing a report is revising and rewriting. If, as you work through your report, you end up at a place different from the one you expected to reach, return to the beginning and lay out a map to where you want to go.

Conceptual clarifications. Conceptual clarifications are relevant at several points in your research. Research often makes a major contribution by clarifying concepts, by considering trade-offs among different definitions, and by being clear about choice of indicators. Chapter 3 emphasized that you often have a great deal of discretion in the variables and indicators you choose and that your choice makes a major difference in your conclusions. Describe your choices and your reasoning carefully. Note any compromises you have had to make and what the likely implications of those choices are.

Graphic and tabular presentations. "A picture is worth a thousand words" in most writing and particularly in research reports. The value of the graphs and tables in chapter 13 should be apparent. Recall the several lists of rules in that chapter to make the information readily accessible and clear. A confusing list of numbers is not necessarily an improvement. And remember that tables and graphs should stand on their own. Even if you must write an awkward title, use one that tells the reader exactly what is in the table. Refer to the guidelines in chapter 13 about row and column headings, percent signs, and so forth to be as clear as possible. In addition to the visuals described in chapter 13, look for occasions to provide a simple list of questions or variables to give the reader a reference point and sense of where you are going.

Visual presentations are also important when you are working with qualitative data, for which precise summary measures usually are inappropriate. In such cases it is tempting to assume that a written paragraph of text is adequate. Chapters 8 and 13 urged you to look for ways to organize your material visually in matrices or diagrams even when you cannot attach numbers to your conclusions. Chapter 6 also described a number of ways to diagram your study, from causal chains to more precise causal modeling.

Writing a coherent and clear report. As noted in the last section, the importance of a clearly organized report cannot be stressed enough. Earlier you were counseled to revise. A common temptation in revising work is to add portions to make things clearer, but not to remove any material. Or if you begin with one question and then change it somewhat during the study, it is easy to add the change but keep the original question. Revising means adding and deleting. Remove whatever could be confusing or contradictory or could send a misleading signal to the reader.

Clarity is a final concern in presenting your studies. There is no substitute for stating clearly what your hypothesis is, the definitions of your terms, and the measuring instruments you are using. You may have gotten a comment on another study that your point was not clear. You may have been annoyed because it was not confusing to you, but it obviously was to the reader. Do not expect any reader to pore over your writing if he or she has trouble figuring out what you mean.

Clarity is also important in analyzing tables and graphs and in interpreting correlation measures. It was noted that tables need to stand on their own; the text needs to repeat your salient points in the tables that are relevant to your analysis. Several of the exercises gave you practice in interpreting tables. The usual rule is to begin by observing overall patterns. State them precisely, and then note any exceptions or additional points of interest. Consider the following data, used earlier. First, write a paragraph interpreting the information in table 14.1. Then read the two analyses in the text, A and B. Ask yourself

TABLE 14.1

Rating the Effectiveness of Government by Degree of
Trust in Government

Rating of Effectiveness	Trust		
	Little	*Some*	*A Lot*
Almost always	1%	1%	7%
Ususally	5	15	38
Somewhat	19	46	43
Very little	43	33	12
Never	32	6	1
	100%	100%	100%
	N = 540	2,366	1,717

Note: Totals may not equal 100% due to rounding.
gamma = −.61
tau$_c$ = −.39

which paragraph gives a better understanding of the data. Compare your own analysis with these two examples.

Your analysis:

_____

_____

_____

_____

_____

_____

_____

Analysis A. Only 2 percent of persons with little or some trust rated government as almost always effective. Seven percent of those with a lot of trust rated government almost always effective. Five percent of those who had little trust rated the government usually effective; 19 percent rated it somewhat effective. Forty-three percent of those with little trust rated the government as having very little effectiveness. And so forth.

Analysis B. The data show that those with a lot of trust tend to rate the government as more effective than those with little trust. For example, of those with a lot of trust, 45 percent said the government is usually or almost always effective. Of those with a little trust, only 6 percent said it is usually or almost always effective, and 75 percent rated its effectiveness as little or none. A second interesting result is that a very small percentage of respondents rated the government as almost always effective, irrespective of how much trust they had.

While the factual statements in analysis A are all supported by the data in the table, Analysis B is much clearer than analysis A because it focuses on the most interesting overall patterns. It cites a few specific examples to illustrate the patterns, and the reader does not get lost in a list of details that are hard to connect to one another. The first answer, by contrast, just lists specific entries and fails to provide a sense of the overall pattern. The reader gets lost in the details.

The two exercises that follow this chapter ask you to practice some of these skills. The first exercise asks you to identify a research topic of interest and develop three ways to design research on the topic. It leads you to review the different approaches to research design and to think through the trade-offs among them. The second exercise provides you with some data and asks you to develop hypotheses related to the data and to carry out an analysis of the information. Both exercises emphasize that you have a variety of options in designing research. They should also help you appreciate the broad range of skills you have acquired. Enjoy using them.

NOTE

1. Howard S. Becker, *Writing for Social Scientists* (Chicago: University of Chicago Press, 1986).

EXERCISES

Exercise 14.1 Designing Alternative Research Strategies

Chapter 5 described current research on "social capital" by Robert Putnam. Recall Putnam's concern with the level of trust and cooperative norms in a democracy and his claim that people are less engaged in social activities than was formerly true in our society. In a memorable phrase, he observes that there is now more "bowling alone" than there used to be. That is, whereas individuals used to join bowling leagues, now they bowl as individuals or family groups rather than as part of more inclusive social units. Obviously he is using bowling as a metaphor for a broad range of activities. Critics respond that individuals are still interacting in social groups, but that the nature of the groups has changed. For example, parents are spending more of their free time attending Little League and soccer games on weekends or working in soup kitchens. Both Putnam and his critics, however, agree that such social activities are important elements in a democracy for building norms of trust and respect for others.

Generally they all assume that social activities correlate with political interest, political trust, and social tolerance.

Your assignment is to design three research projects related to this general topic, using three different designs. Each of your designs should do the following:

1. Identify your research question, proposition, or hypothesis if appropriate.
2. List your variables and indicators.
3. Describe your research design (experiment, quasi-experiment, correlation, case study).
4. Describe your measuring instruments, data sources, or strategies for collecting relevant information. Identify level of measurement.
5. Discuss the trade-offs you had to make and the validity and reliability problems you faced. In light of these describe the strengths and weaknesses of each design.

   Conclude with a paragraph comparing the merits and problems in each of these studies.

Exercise 14.2 Interpreting Data

Examine table 14.2 and answer the questions that follow. The table reports percentages rather than absolute numbers. For each year, the percentage in each

TABLE 14.2

Voting in Presidential Elections, by Demographic Characteristics, 1988, 1992 and 1996 (in Percentages)

| | Demographic Characteristics of Voters | | | | | | | | | | |
| | *Gender* | | *Race* | | | *Religion* | | | *Education* | | |
Vote	*Men*	*Women*	*White*	*Black*	*Hispanic*	*Protestant*	*Catholic*	*Jewish*	*No High School*	*High School*	*College Graduate*
1988											
Republican	58	49	57	33	38	58	49	73	39	53	46
Democratic	40	50	41	86	61	40	50	27	60	46	39
1992											
Republican	37	36	39	11	24	45	21	10	27	36	39
Democratic	41	47	40	83	62	34	37	78	56	44	41
1996											
Republican	44	38	45	12	20	47	37	16	28	35	46
Democratic	44	54	44	84	73	43	54	78	60	52	44

Source: 1988 data, *National Journal*, 12 November 1988, p. 2855; 1992 and 1996 data, *National Journal*, 9 November 1996, p. 2407.

category voting for the Republican and Democratic candidates is close to 100 percent. The remaining percentage voted for third-party candidates.

1. State three hypotheses that you could test with these data.
2. Develop tables to test each hypothesis. Briefly interpret the results using percentage differences in your analysis.
3. What statistical measures could you use to analyze the tables? Compute any you are able to, and interpret them. Do they support your conclusions based on percentage differences?
4. Assume you are doing a study on liberalism, and for an indicator of liberalism you use the democratic vote. Write a brief analysis of some aspect of liberalism based on these results.

GLOSSARY

abstract symbols   Symbols that stand for, or in place of, things that cannot be directly observed or measured.

aggregate data   Empirical data that pertain to, or describe, the behavior of social units (e.g., political parties, cities) or collectivities (e.g., mobs, voters).

aggregate study   Study of groups of cases; usually involves studying them on only a few dimensions or according to only a few variables.

approach   Perspective we adopt in analyzing a problem; lens through which we view an event; set of assumptions.

associated   Indicates there is a relationship between two variables in which changes in one variable occur together with changes in the other.

bar graph   A graphic way of depicting changes in a variable by means of bars that rise or fall on a scale that is shown on the left (vertical) axis.

base year   Year that is assigned the value of 100 in a series of annual index calculations; year to which all other annual index measurements are compared to demonstrate trends or changes over time.

before-after   Compare a thing before and after an event or treatment to determine the effect of the treatment.

beta coefficient   ß Measure of a regression slope in terms of the standard deviation for that variable; allows us to compare the influence of several variables.

bivariate table   Table presenting information on two variables in a manner that shows whether they are related to each other.

case study   Study of a single unit, usually in some depth.

causal chain   Sequence of related events in which the effect of one variable becomes the cause of a third variable; multiple causes and effects.

causal relationship   A relationship in which changes in one variable bring about changes in another variable.

central tendency   Value around which most of the data values are clustered; center of a series of numbers or observations.

checklist   List of items relevant to a research question, used to guide and report research findings.

chi square, χ^2   A statistic that tells us whether the measured strength of a relationship is also statistically significant; used for nominal and ordinal data.

classify   To categorize cases into several groups according to some dimension of interest.

closed question   A question that asks a respondent to choose among several alternative answers.

cluster sample   A sample in which the population is divided into geographic clusters, and respondents are selected at random within each cluster.

coding   A technique for transforming information about discrete historical events into a numerical format for subsequent manipulation by statistical techniques.

comparative research   Systematic comparison of different units to understand their similarities and differences.

comparison of cases   Selection of cases by criteria that will enable us to test theory.

concept   Abstract term referring to a group of phenomena.

concept validity   When a logical or theoretical connection exists between indicators and the concepts they are measuring.

concrete symbols   Symbols that stand for, or in place of, things that can be directly observed and measured.

confidence interval   Numerical range within which an estimated value is likely to fall; tells us the extent to which the characteristics of a whole population will match those of a smaller sample of that population.

content analysis   Analysis of written and oral communications for the frequency with which selected words or themes are used; can be used to study the causes of the communication, the motivations of the author(s), or the effects of the communication on audiences.

contingency analysis   Recording of the frequency with which certain words or themes appear in a communication in conjunction with other selected words or themes.

controlling   Examining a relationship for different values of a third, or control, variable.

convergent validity   When various indicators of a concept produce consistent results.

coordinates   Values on the horizontal and vertical axes of a graph; used to measure and depict the observed values of the variables and to identify the data points that correspond to those observed values.

correlated   When a relationship exists between two variables such that changes in one variable occur together with changes in the other.

correlation coefficient   A measure of relationship.

correlational analysis   Use of nonexperimental design to see whether a correlation exists between two or more variables.

counting and coding   A technique for transforming information about discrete historical events into a numerical format for subsequent manipulation via statistical techniques.

co-vary   When a relationship exists between two variables such that changes in one variable occur together with changes in the other.

criterion validity   When each of the indicators of a variable bears the same relationship to the indicators of a second variable.

curvilinear line   A line that depicts a changing relationship between independent and dependent variables such that the relationship appears at times positive and at other times negative; overall effect is a line that changes direction.

data point   Point on a graph where the values of two variables—one from the x axis and one from the y axis—intersect.

data specifications   A set of rules that tell what to look for, what to record, what to ignore, and how to classify, rate, score, or otherwise evaluate each piece of evidence.

deduction   Practice of developing a hypothesis from theory or logic.

degrees of freedom *(df)*   Number of cells in a matrix in which you can freely insert a number; cells in which the entry is not determined by numbers in other cells.

dependent variable   Variable we wish to explain; its value is influenced by that of the independent variable.

description   Information about a single case in some depth or about patterns and trends in a number of cases.

dichotomy   A division of values into two categories.

difference of means or medians   Comparison of the appropriate central tendency in two groups.

direct data gathering   Collecting evidence firsthand through questions or observations.

dispersion   Extent to which the data are spread out from their central tendency.

empirical data   Data gathered directly from personal experience, experimentation, or observation.

event data   Data about discrete historical events, transformed into numerical terms.

experiment   A strategy to test the effect of an independent variable by applying it to one group of cases but not to a second.

explanation   Analysis designed to determine why an event occurs.

exploratory study   Collecting data in order to develop research questions and propositions.

exponential curve   An S-shaped curve that depicts how a variable grows by a constant percentage of the whole over time; gives dramatically greater results than simple linear growth, in which the increase is by constant raw amounts.

external validity   Extent to which a study applies to other cases and phenomena beyond those being studied.

***F* test**   Measure of statistical significance with a known sampling distribution.

face validity   When a logical or theoretical connection exists between indicators and the concepts they are measuring.

feasibility   When indicators point to data that are available with a reasonable expenditure of time and effort.

field research   When researchers talk to people within their own setting; takes the context of action into account.

flowchart   Visual display of events or activities over time.

framework   A set of categories in which to place observations.

frequency   Number of cases for each value of a variable.

frequency analysis   Recording of the frequency with which certain words or themes appear in a communication.

frequency line   Line graph depicting the frequency of values or the shape of their distribution.

gamma   Relationship measure for ordinal-level data; tends to be higher than other measures because it does not count cases tied on a value.

graphic display   A method portraying or depicting data by means of a picture or drawing.

horizontal (x) axis   Base measurement scale of a graph; used ordinarily for depicting values of the independent variable.

hypotheses   Propositions stated so they can be tested empirically.

independent variable   Variable we propose as the cause of the dependent variable.

index   A single number that transforms data on several different variables into a single measure that stands for the composite of the several variables taken together.

index construction   Process by which variables are weighted and combined with one another to form a summary indicator of the entire group.

indicator   Identifies the evidence used to describe a variable; part of an operational definition.

indirect data gathering   Using data collected by others, usually for purposes different from our own.

induction   Practice of developing a hypothesis on the basis of our own observations or of studies carried out by others.

instrument   Specific evidence used to measure a variable or concept.

intangible resources   Things of value that cannot be directly observed and measured.

intercept, a   Point on the y axis of a graph that indicates the value of the dependent variable when the value of the independent variable (x) is zero.

internal validity   Extent to which conclusions follow from a study.

interpretive research   Research designed to understand the meaning behind individual's actions and opinions.

interquartile range   A measure of dispersion that indicates the difference between the lowest and the highest quarters, or fourths, of the cases.

interval measure   A variable based on a common and known unit so that we can tell the interval between different amounts of the variable.

interview schedule   A list of topics to be covered in an interview.

judgmental scores   Ratings achieved by transforming narrative-format data by assigning preestablished values to decisions, events, and other types of cases.

known sampling distribution   A distribution in which there is a known probability for each value when samples are drawn from a population in which two are not related.

lambda   Relationship measure for nominal-level data.

lateral thinking   Contrasts with vertical, or logical, thinking; emphasizes speculation and imagination.

level of measurement   Amount of information an indicator provides; specifically, whether it tells the interval between cases, merely tells how they are ordered, or tells only categories into which the cases fall.

level of significance   Probability that the population parameter falls within the confidence interval we have established; hence, the likelihood that we can draw a conclusion about the population from which the sample is drawn.

line graph   A graphic depiction of change in the observed values of a single variable over time.

matrix   Two-dimensional table that describes the interaction between two sets of variables.

mean   Central tendency of interval-level data; obtained by totaling the observed values and dividing by the number of cases.

measure of reduction in error   Extent to which we can reduce possible errors in estimating the value of a case if we know its value on a second variable.

median   Midpoint in an ordered series of data values; used primarily with ordinal measures.

mode   Value that appears most frequently in a data series; used primarily with nominal measures.

multiple correlation, R, R^2   A measure that indicates how closely observations fit the regression line; R is the measure expressing this cumulative influence.

multiple regression   Regression analysis expressing the influence of more than one independent variable on a dependent variable.

multiple strategies   Conscious effort to pursue several different approaches to data collection.

multivariate analysis   Examination of relationship among three or more variables.

multivariate relationship   Relationship among more than two variables; usually examines the influence of several independent variables on a single dependent variable.

multivariate table   Table presenting information on three variables in a manner that shows whether they are related to each other.

narrative research   Descriptions of events, drawing on multiple sources of information, to understand more fully what happened.

negative association   A statement that two phenomena are related to each other, either positively—the more of one, the more of the other—or negatively—the more of one the less of the other.

negative linear curve   A line that slopes from the upper left to the lower right, indicating that as the independent variable increases, the dependent variable decreases.

nesting   A technique used in the tabular display of multivariate data; the entire range of values for the independent variable is reproduced beneath each value of the control variable producing a number of bivariate tables, each of which is nested beneath a value of the control.

nominal measure   A nonquantitative measure that can name a case only according to a category or class, such as region or race.

nonequivalent comparison group   A control group used in quasi-experiments that is similar to the treatment group in some, but not all, respects.

nonexperimental design   When observations are made on a large number of cases under varying conditions in order to approximate the control in an experiment.

normal curve   A symmetrical, bell-shaped curve in which the distribution of values bears a direct and known relationship to the size of the standard deviation: a given percentage of cases are within 1, 2, and 3 standard deviations from the mean.

normative statement   A statement that indicates a preference or a value about what ought to happen.

observation   A collection of information about an event, a person, or an activity.

open-ended question   A question that allows respondents to formulate their own answer.

operational definition   A restatement of a concept so that it can be tested empirically; a reference to the operations to be used in measuring the concept.

ordinal measure   A measure allowing us to rank observations according to their order on some dimension but without knowing the number of units in each observation.

parameter   A characteristic of the population we are studying.

partial correlation coefficient   Strength of relationship between the dependent variable and one of several independent variables when the other independent variables are controlled.

Pearson's correlation, r   A measure that indicates the strength of relationship between interval-level data.

per capita amount   Summary figure for a group or geographic unit divided by the population figure.

percentage   A figure that reports some number of units as a proportion of 100; enables us to compare numbers with different bases.

percentage difference   Difference between the percentage values of the dependent variable for different groups of the independent variable.

pie chart   A circular graphic or picture used to portray how an overall total amount of some variable is distributed, in percentage terms, among various subgroups of variables.

political analysis   Process used to discover the reasons why a given political phenomenon occurs.

political discourse   Communication of politically relevant thoughts via words.

politics   Process of deciding how resources will be distributed in a society.

polyotomy   A division of values into more than two categories.

population   Group of phenomena we are studying.

positive association   A statement that two phenomena are related to each other—the more of one, the more of the other.

positive linear curve   A line that slopes from the lower left to the upper right, indicating that as the independent variable increases, the dependent variable also increases.

predictive validity   When the predicted result of an indicator matches known evidence.

process study   An examination of the logic, dynamics, and implications of a relationship between two variables.

proposition   Statements that two or more factors are related to each other.

psychobiography   Application of psychoanalytic techniques to the lives of noted persons in order to analyze the inner dimensions of their political behavior.

psychohistory   Application of psychoanalytic techniques to the lives of noted persons in order to analyze the inner dimensions of their political behavior.

qualitative research   Data that reflect the content and meaning of an event or the perspective of an individual; often deals with subtleties and with evidence that cannot be handled quantitatively.

quantitative research   Data gathered in a form that allows the researcher to assign numbers to them.

quasi-experiment   Analysis of the results of a policy or decision in a way that approximates the control in an experiment.

r^2, variance   A measure of the extent to which variation in Y, the dependent variable, is explained by variation in X, the independent variable.

range   A measure of dispersion that indicates the difference between the lowest and the highest values.

ratio measure   An interval measure in which it is possible to have zero amount.

reactive data   Data that are influenced or altered by the process of collecting them.

reasoning by analogy   Analysis of a phenomenon by reference to another, substitute phenomenon that corresponds closely to it.

regression line, b   On a graph, a line that shows how much change occurs in the dependent variable (Y) for a given change in the independent variable (X).

relationship measures   Single numbers indicating how strongly two or more variables are related to each other; examples include Q, lambda, gamma, tau_b, and tau_c.

reliability   Degree to which a measurement gives the same result under all circumstances.

research design   Statement of research that defines terms, specifies propositions to be tested, lists data needed and how to get them, describes tests to be performed, and establishes a sequence of steps to complete project.

S-shaped line   A line depicting two variables that change in the same direction but at varying rates on different portions of a graph.

sampling error   Degree to which a sample statistic differs from the population parameter.

scatterplot A graphic used to depict bivariate data when both variables are measured on an interval or ordinal scale; each bivariate observation is represented by a data point with a horizontal value equal to the value of the first variable and a vertical value equal to the value of the second variable.

simple random sample A sample in which each member of the population has an equal chance of being selected.

Somer's *d* Relationship measure for ordinal data; useful for causal analysis.

spurious relationship A relationship in which two variables that are not causally linked appear to be so because a third variable is influencing both of them.

standard deviation A measure of dispersion for interval data; based on finding the variation around the mean.

standard error The standard deviation of the sampling distribution; it depends on the standard deviation in the sample and the size of the sample.

standardize scores Make figures comparable by converting to the same base so they can be combined into a single index number.

statistic An estimate of a parameter based on a sample.

stratified random sample A sample in which the population is divided into strata, or groups, based on known characteristics, and a random sample is selected from each stratum.

strength of relationship Extent to which changes in one variable are accompanied by changes in another variable.

structured data gathering When data are collected according to specified categories or criteria.

***t* test** A measure of statistical significance with a known sampling distribution; useful when sample size is less than thirty.

tabular data Presentation of numerical data in the form of tables of various types and sizes.

tangible resources Things of value that can be directly observed and measured.

tau$_b$, tau$_c$ Relationship measures for ordinal data, for square and rectangular tables, respectively; tends to be lower than gamma because it counts pairs in which cases have the same value on one variable.

theory A set of proposed explanations, logically or systematically related to each other, that set out to explain or predict a phenomenon.

time series analysis Use of regression analysis to examine whether there is a trend over time and to use the trend to extrapolate data for other years.

unit of analysis Smallest element we are studying and about which we wish to generalize; examples: individuals, cities, nation-states.

unstructured data gathering Data collected with no set criteria in mind; open-ended data collection.

use of multiple strategies Conscious effort to pursue several different approaches to data collection.

validity Extent to which an indicator tells you what you want to know about a concept or that points to relevant aspects of a concept.

value   Characteristic of a variable; or amount of a characteristic.

variable   A characteristic of a thing that can assume varying degrees or values. The variable "gender" includes the values male and female.

variance   A measure of dispersion for interval data; based on finding the variation around the mean.

vertical (*y*) axis   Measurement scale that rises along the left side of a graph; used ordinarily for depicting values of the dependent variable.

Yule's *Q*   Statistical measure for nominal data with only two values.

INDEX